Scotland!
Vol. II

By

Ronald Pattinson

Mini Book Series volume XXVIII: Scotland! FG

Copyright © 2017 Ronald Pattinson

The right of Ronald Pattinson to be identified as the author of his work has been asserted by him in accordance with the

COPYRIGHT, DESIGNS AND PATENTS ACT OF 1988

All rights reserved. No part of this publication may be reproduced, stored in a retrieval system, or transmitted, in any form or by any means without the prior written permission of the publisher, nor be otherwise circulated in any form other than that in which it is published and without a similar condition being imposed upon the subsequent purchaser.

First edition

Published in March 2017 by

Kilderkin
171 hs Warmondstraat, Amsterdam, Noord- Holland

ISBN 978-94-90270-30-8

Contents

Contents

Scotland! 1
Contents 3
Foreword 10
Introduction 11
1840 – 1880 From Shilling to Pale 12
   Introduction 12
   Breweries 12
   Beer production 13
      Exports 14
   Ingredients 16
      Malt 16
      Sugar 17
      Hops 17
      Yeast 18
      Water 18
   Techniques 21
      Mashing 21
      Sparging 22
      Boiling 22
      Fermentation 25
      Vatting 27
      Union sets 28
      Brewing IPA in the 1840's 28
   Styles 29
      Table Beer 29
      Pale Ale/IPA 30
      Porter and Stout 35
      Shilling Ales 38
      Mild Ales 39
      Stock Ale 41
      Lager 42
   Recipes 43
      1847 William Younger T 43

- 1868 William Younger T Table Beer 45
- 1851 William Younger X Mild Ale 46
- 1868 William Younger XXX Mild Ale 47
- 1879 William Younger XX 48
- 1847 William Younger 60/- 49
- 1847 William Younger 100/- 50
- 1851 William Younger 120/- 51
- 1851 William Younger 140/- 52
- 1868 William Younger 80/- 53
- 1879 William Younger 50/- 54
- 1879 William Younger 160/- 55
- 1851 William Younger DBS Stout 56
- 1868 William Younger DBS 57
- 1869 William Younger BS Porter 59
- 1849 William Younger Export 60
- 1851 William Younger XP 61
- 1858 William Younger Ex Pale Ale 62
- 1865 William Younger Ext 63
- 1851 William Younger XXS Stock Ale 64
- 1868 William Younger XS Export Stock Ale 65
- 1879 William Younger No. 1 66
- 1879 William Younger No. 2 68
- 1868 William Younger No. 4 Ale Export 69
- 1868 William Younger No. 3 Ale Export 70

1880 – 1914 Dropping your gravity pants 71
- Introduction 71
  - Breweries 71
  - Beer production 72
- Ingredients 75
  - Malt 75
  - Sugar 76
  - Adjuncts 76
  - Hops 76
  - Yeast 77
  - Water 77
- Techniques 78

- Mashing 78
- Boiling 80
- Fermentation 83
- Dry Hopping 85
- Cereal cooker 85
- Brewing at William Younger in the 1880's 85
- Styles 89
  - Pale Ale 89
  - Mild Ales 93
  - Stock Ales 97
  - Shilling Ales 100
  - Porter and Stout 104
  - Strong/Scotch Ale 107
  - Lager 108
- Recipes 111
  - 1909 Maclay Table Beer 28/- 111
  - 1885 Thomas Usher 100/- 112
  - 1894 Thomas Usher 60/- 113
  - 1898 William Younger 80/- 114
  - 1898 William Younger 140/- 115
  - 1912 Thomas Usher 100/- 116
  - 1913 William Younger 160/- 117
  - 1898 William Younger XX 118
  - 1909 Maclay Mild 56/- 119
  - 1885 Thomas Usher Stout 121
  - 1894 Thomas Usher Export Stout 123
  - 1899 William Younger S1 125
  - 1909 Maclay OMS 63/- 126
  - 1912 Thomas Usher 48/- Stout 127
  - 1885 Thomas Usher PA 60/- 129
  - 1885 Thomas Usher Ex PA 131
  - 1894 Thomas Usher IPA 132
  - 1909 Maclay PI 60/- 133
  - 1912 Thomas Usher IP 134
  - 1913 William Younger LAE 136
  - 1894 Thomas Usher XX 60/- 137

- 1898 William Younger XXXX 139
- 1913 William Younger No. 1 140
- 1885 William Younger No. 3 142
- 1909 Maclay Strong Ale 143
- 1881 William Younger PXX Pils 144

1914 – 1939 Pale Ale Rules 145

- Introduction 145
  - Beer production 146
  - Breweries 146
  - Foreign markets 147
  - WW I restrictions 148
- Ingredients 150
  - Malt 150
  - Sugar 150
  - Adjuncts 151
  - Hops 151
  - Water 151
- Techniques 152
  - Mashing 152
  - Boiling 157
  - Fermentation 160
  - Dry hopping 164
  - Colouring 166
- Styles 167
  - Pale Ale 167
  - Mild Ale 177
  - Shilling Ale 183
  - Brown Ale 184
  - Stout 187
  - Strong/Scotch Ale 200
  - Lager 205
- Recipes 207
  - 1914 Thomas Usher 80/- MA 207
  - 1917 Thomas Usher 100/- 208
  - 1918 Thomas Usher GA 209
  - 1920 Drybrough 60/- Mild 210

1933 William Younger XX 211
1931 Thomas Usher Brown Ale 212
1915 Drybrough XXX Stout 213
1917 Thomas Usher 54/- Stout 214
1921 William Younger MBS 216
1921 William Younger Btg DBS 218
1931 Thomas Usher Stout 30/- 219
1914 Drybrough PI 220
1917 Drybrough PI 221
1932 Lorimer & Clark XXP 6 222
1932 Lorimer & Clark XXP 7 224
1932 Lorimer & Clark XXP 8 226
1933 Drybrough P80/- 227
1933 William Younger XXPS 229
1939 Maclay PA 6d 230
1918 Thomas Usher X 60/- 231
1928 Thomas Usher OSA 232
1933 William Younger No. 1 233
1933 William Younger No. 3 234
1933 Lorimer & Clark SA 235
1933 Drybrough Burns Ale 237

1939 – 1970 Austerity to Prosperity (and oblivion) 239
  Introduction 239
    Beer production 240
    Breweries 241
  Ingredients 244
    Malt 244
    Sugar 244
    Adjuncts 244
    Hops 245
    Water 245
  Techniques 246
    Mashing 246
    Boiling 246
    Fermentation 249
    Dry hopping 251

- Parti-gyling 252
- Colouring 252
- Styles 255
  - Pale Ale 255
  - Mild Ale 260
  - Brown Ale 262
  - Shilling Ales 264
  - Stout 265
  - Strong/Scotch Ale 271
  - Lager 279
- Recipes 281
  - 1939 William Younger XX 281
  - 1939 William Younger XXX 283
  - 1949 William Younger XXX 285
  - 1970 Drybrough M Special Mild 286
  - 1949 William Younger Double Century Ale 287
  - 1958 Bernard Double Brown Ale 288
  - 1966 Drybrough MBA Brown Ale 289
  - 1949 William Younger Btlg DBS 290
  - 1957 Robert Younger SS 292
  - 1958 Bernard Export Stout 293
  - 1966 Maclay Oat Malt Stout 294
  - 1949 William Younger 200/- 295
  - 1939 William Younger LAE 296
  - 1940 William Younger P Btlg 297
  - 1939 William Younger Ext 298
  - 1949 William Younger LAE 299
  - 1949 William Younger Pale XXPS 301
  - 1954 Drybrough Export 302
  - 1957 Robert Younger 60/- 303
  - 1958 Bernard Pale 1/1 304
  - 1965 Maclay SPA 306
  - 1957 Robert Younger Old Edinburgh Ale 307
  - 1949 William Younger No. 1 308
  - 1949 William Younger No. 3 Btlg 309
  - 1954 Drybrough Burns Ale 310

- 1958 Robert Younger Strong Ale 311
- 1971 Maclay Strong Ale 312
- 1970 Drybrough Continental Lager 313

Appendix I - Let's Brew 314

William Younger 314
- 1840 - 1880 314
- 1880 - 1914 336
- 1914 - 1939 364
- 1939 – 1970 377

Thomas Usher 383
- 1880 – 1913 383
- 1914 – 1939 400

Drybrough 413
- 1914 – 1939 413
- 1939 – 1970 422

Maclay 432
- 1880 – 1913 432
- 1914 – 1939 434
- 1939 – 1970 436

Robert Younger 440
- 1939 - 1970 440

T & J Bernard 442
- 1939 – 1970 442

Appendix II – weights and measures 444
- Weight 444
- Volume 444
- Liquid 444
- Money 444
- Temperature 445

Index 446

Foreword

The book you're holding in your hand (or more likely looking at on a screen) is something I've wanted to write for years: a definitive history of Scottish beer and brewing techniques.

After a decade of research, I was finally ready to dive into the word pool and start writing. Never to hit bottom. If only I'd known when to surface. Result: a book as over-stuffed as a New York sandwich. Probably not what a publisher – or average reader - is looking for. This book isn't aimed at them.

I'm writing the book in two phases. I've reached the end of the first. After letting the chapters grow wildly, I'll need to perform some aggressive pruning to get the thing into exhibition shape. The hard bit, phase two. With a professionally-publishable book at the end.

Meanwhile, I'm self-publishing the full-geek version. With far too many tables and a ludicrous number of recipes. Not for everyone. But obviously for you.

Ron Pattinson

21st February 2017.

Introduction

Scottish beer – has there more rubbish been written on any other zythological topic? Probably not. Though IPA would be its closest rival.

The huge level of misinformation about Scottish beer and Scottish brewing is the main reason I decided to write this book. I've spent so much time and effort refuting ridiculous tales I thought it useful to have one handy reference to point people at. This is it.

The first section gives a quick overview of Scottish brewing from 1850 to 1990. There's a short description of the ingredients, techniques and beer styles for each period. Followed by detailed recipes. I can safely say it's the most detailed and accurate description of beer in Scotland that has ever been written. Basically because most of the rest has just been made up.

The second section contains a mass of less-detailed recipes.

Throughout the book I'll be comparing and contrasting Scottish beer and brewing practices with those in England. There was plenty of variation in English brewing, between urban and rural and between North and South. To simplify matters I'll be using London beers as the benchmark of English brewing.

For much of the period covered London had some of the largest breweries in England, but also the largest concentration of big breweries. Only Burton ever came close to rivalling the capital. I've also got much more information on brewing in London than elsewhere. And I'm too lazy to commit to more primary research.

Note: all the recipes are for 5 imperial gallons/6 US gallons/23 litres.

1840 – 1880 From Shilling to Pale

Introduction
Scottish brewing was transformed in the second half of the 19th century. As brewers grasped the opportunities offered by Empire. Scottish brewers had an established trade with England, but after 1840 they turned their eyes further afield.

Shilling Ales, the Scottish equivalent of Mild Ales were still brewed in large quantities. Often to stupidly high gravities.

They were able to boost their output far above what the Scottish market could ever have supported. But not all brewers profited. Only those in the right location: readily available raw materials, good quality water, access to railways or the sea. The industry was increasingly concentrated in a small number of towns in the Central Belt, most notably Edinburgh and Alloa.

Breweries
At the start of this period, Scotland still boasted an impressive number of breweries, over 500 in total. Though this looks tiny compared to those in England:

Brewers & beer retailers in 1838			
	England	Scotland	Ireland
	No.	No.	No.
Brewers of strong beer not exceeding 20 barrels	8,996	62	29
Brewers of strong beer exceeding 20 but not exceeding 50 barrels	8,520	24	1
Brewers of strong beer exceeding 50 but not exceeding 100 barrels	10,445	28	11
Brewers of strong beer exceeding 100 but not exceeding 1000 barrels	18,306	211	55
Brewers of strong beer exceeding 1000 barrels	1,597	114	145
Brewers of table beer	14	90	
Retail brewers under 5 Geo. IV. C. 54	18	20	
Total brewers	47,896	549	241
Source:			
"A Cyclopaedia of Commerce, Mercantile Law, Finance, Commercial Geography and Navigation", by William Waterston, 1863, page 79			

Even the largest Edinburgh brewers, William Younger and William McEwan, couldn't compare in scale to the giants of British brewing such as Barclay Perkins, Guinness or Bass. In the early 1840's just 195,000 barrels were brewed in Edinburgh[1].

To put that figure into context, total UK beer production was between 14 and 16.5 million barrels a year in the 1840's.[2] While the four largest London breweries made more than 1 million barrels a year in the same period[3].

---

[1] "A Dictionary, Practical, Theoretical, and Historical, of Commerce and Commercial Navigation" by John Ramsay McCulloch, 1844, page 9.
[2] "The Sessional Papers of the House of Lords in the session 1854; Reports from Select Committees of the House of Commons, and Evidence; Public Houses" "Minutes of Evidence Taken by the Select Committee on Public Houses, etc." page 145.
[3] "The British Brewing Industry, 1830-1980" T. R. Gourvish & R.G. Wilson, pages 610-611.

By 1880, publican brewers, never as widespread in Scotland as in England, almost totally disappeared. In 1888, there were just 36 remaining[4]. Brewing was dominated by a few dozen brewers, mostly within spitting distance of each other. "The London and Suburban Licensed Victuallers' Directory" of 1874 lists 130 Scottish breweries[5]. This is a breakdown by region:

Scottish breweries by region in 1874			
north	central	west coast	south
27	79	17	7

The industry was becoming very concentrated in the central lowlands and Edinburgh, with 26 breweries, was by far the biggest brewing centre[6]. Tiny Alloa boasted six breweries, not that many fewer than the ten of far larger Glasgow. Aberdeenshire, with 14, was the only other region with a decent number of breweries[7].

Beer production

In the first half of this period there was a big increase in Scottish beer production, which more than doubled between 1850 and 1865. Output was stable throughout the 1866's and hit another peak in 1873, before declining again for the rest of the decade.

Beer production (barrels) 1850 - 1880			
Year	UK	Scotland	% Scotland
1850	15,478,569	476,000	3.08%
1857	17,984,773	588,552	3.27%
1858	18,166,635	673,000	3.70%
1859	19,152,564	774,000	4.04%
1860	20,340,096	810,727	3.99%
1861	19,534,460	767,000	3.93%
1862	19,989,313	802,000	4.01%
1863	20,081,408	893,000	4.45%
1864	21,360,461	986,000	4.62%
1865	22,546,889	1,207,595	5.36%
1866	25,388,600	1,254,000	4.94%
1867	25,206,665	1,205,000	4.78%
1868	24,301,841	1,171,000	4.82%
1869	24,542,664	1,089,000	4.44%
1870		1,026,000	
1871	26,431,760	1,227,308	4.64%
1872		1,342,000	
1873		1,424,000	
1874		1,403,000	
1875	31,014,381	1,179,244	3.80%
1876		1,158,000	
1877		1,127,000	
1878		1,279,000	

---

[4] Dundee Courier - Friday, 01 March 1889, page 3.
[5] "The London and Suburban Licensed Victuallers' Directory" by H. D. Miles, 1874, page 229.
[6] "The London and Suburban Licensed Victuallers' Directory" by H. D. Miles, 1874, page 229.
[7] "The London and Suburban Licensed Victuallers' Directory" by H. D. Miles, 1874, page 229.

Beer production (barrels) 1850 - 1880			
Year	UK	Scotland	% Scotland
1879		1,003,000	
1880	30,742,649	1,142,710	3.72%
Sources: "Statistics of British commerce" by Braithwaite Poole, 1852, page 6. "Hops; their Cultivation, Commerce, and Used in Various Countries" by P.L., Simmonds, 1877, page 133. Brewers' Almanack 1928, page 109. "A History of the Brewing Industry in Scotland" by Ian Donnachie, 1998, pages 147-148.			

Between 1840 and 1880, Scotland had around 10% of the UK population. Yet it was only producing 5% of the UK's beer at most. Clearly Scottish brewing still had a lot of ground to make up on England.

Exports

One area where Scottish brewers were more successful was in exporting beer. A canny early move into Pale Ale brewing, while still keeping up their reputation for Strong Ale, left Scottish brewers with steady exports to both the Eastern and Western hemispheres.

Scottish brewers were starting to build a reasonable export trade. Between 1857 and 1867 exports almost doubled.

Scottish Exports 1857 - 1867 (barrels)			
Year	Scotland	UK	% Scotland
1857	38,248	435,334	8.79%
1863	47,415	491,631	9.64%
1866	61,723		
1867	66,909		
Sources: The industries of Scotland: their rise, progress, and present condition by David Bremner, 1869, pages 437 - 438, "Annals of British Legislation, vol. V" 1859, pages 328 and 333 Brewers' Almanack 1928, p. 115 "Sessional Papers, House of Lords, Vol. VII, Accounts and Papers", 1864, pages 20-21			

British India was the largest single market, but the Americas combined (North and South America and the Caribbean) accounted for almost 50% of Scottish exports.

Scottish beer exports in 1867 (barrels)		
Hamburg	1,370	2.05%
Mauritius	1,250	1.87%
the continental territories of British India	13,975	20.89%
Singapore	1,564	2.34%
Victoria	4,337	6.48%
New South Wales	455	0.68%
Queensland	557	0.83%
New Zealand	1,420	2.12%
British North America	1,904	2.85%
the British West Indies	8,797	13.15%
Foreign West Indies	5,161	7.71%
the United States	3,346	5.00%
Chili	956	1.43%
Brazil	2,715	4.06%
Uruguay	3,636	5.43%
Argentine Republic	5,965	8.92%
Others	9,501	14.20%
total	66,909	100.00%

Source:
The industries of Scotland: their rise, progress, and present condition by David Bremner, 1869, pages 437 - 438,

Ingredients

After 1840 the UK was beginning to struggle to feed itself. The gap between agricultural production and demand was just as big for brewing as it was for other basic foodstuffs.

Soon the UK was importing brewing materials from all over the world: hops from the USA; barley from Chile and the Middle East. As beer output expanded more quickly than UK agriculture, the need to import grew as the century progressed.

Scotland, which had long imported almost all its hops, wasn't immune to this trend. There are William Younger batches where the only Scottish ingredients were the water and yeast.

Malt

For most of this period, the rules on what could be used in beer were very strict. The 1830 Beer Act had abolished the tax on beer, instead taxing malt and hops. Meaning a brewer using anything other than malt was effectively dodging task. Consequently a sort of Reinheitsgebot applied: beer could only be brewed from water, malt, hops and yeast. Though in 1847 the rules were loosened to allow the use of sugar, as long as duty had been paid on it.

Scottish brewers were never big users of coloured malts. If they hadn't been brewing Porter and Stout, they would have used nothing but pale malt. Crystal malt, though it had been developed, was rarely used even in England before 1880. In Scotland it was never common, perhaps because the Mild Ales in which it was principally used were never as popular.

At the start of this period Scottish brewers were still using bigg, a type of primitive, tough barley which was well suited to the Scottish climate. Though the fact that it wasn't quite as good as barley was reflected in a lower tax on bigg malt. As good-quality barley – in particular from East Anglia – became more readily available bigg disappeared from Scottish brew houses.

Bigg appears in some William Younger's recipes in the late 1840's, mostly in cheaper products such as Table beer or 60/- or 80/-. But by 1850 it had disappeared[8].

Scottish brewers might have been using foreign barley, but they mostly made their own malt. This was particularly important in Edinburgh, which was famed from its very pale-coloured Ales. And later became an important centre of IPA brewing. As the quality and paleness of the malt was essential to the main styles being brewed, just as in Burton, Edinburgh brewers didn't trust third parties to make their malt for them.

That Scottish brewers performed their own malting is one of the main reasons no peat was used in kilning malt used for brewing. Scotland's brewers were concentrated in the central belt, where almost no peat but large amounts of coal. Coke, a smokeless form of coal, was the standard fuel used for malting.

In an interview before a Commons select committee, James Meiklejohn, a brewer in Alloa, revealed some interesting details about malting in Scotland. He stated that he made all his own malt, using either English or Scottish grain. However he preferred English barley because it was of better quality

---

[8] William Younger brewing record held at the Scottish Brewing Archive, document number WY/6/1/2/3.

and used more of it than Scottish. English grain performed better in the brew house, giving a greater extract than Scottish. The produced with it also tasted better.[9]

It was simple enough for Meiklejohn to bring in English grain. Alloa had a harbour and, unsurprisingly given its name, Meiklejohn's Shore Brewery was right next to it. Ease of sea transport partly why Scottish brewing came to be so concentrated in the central lowlands. Cities there such as Edinburgh, Alloa and Glasgow had good connections to the sea. After the development of the railways, cities integrated into the network – as those in central lowlands were – gained a further advantage.

Sugar

When sugar was first allowed in 1847, many brewers briefly experimented with its use, but then returned to brewing all-malt. Only in the 1870's was sugar used with any great regularity in England. Even then, Scottish brewers were slow to adopt its use.

The types of sugar available to brewers were at first quite limited: either raw cane sugar or pure sucrose. Though towards the end of this period the classic numbered invert sugars were increasingly employed.

A few William Younger beers contained a little sugar in the late 1840's. It use was mostly confined to the stronger Shilling Ales[10]. In 1849 it disappeared again. Younger only routinely employed sugar in their beers after 1880.

Hops

We all know few hops were grown in Scotland in the last couple of hundred years. But that doesn't mean Scottish brewing **used** few hops. They used plenty. They just had to import them. Initially, that was from England, but later, just as elsewhere in the UK, hops were imported from all over the world.

In the 1850's, the principal foreign source of hops was the USA, mostly New York State. Later large quantities of quality hops were sourced from Central Europe, and somewhat less good ones from France and Belgium. All make regular appearances in Scottish recipes.

Naturally, many English hops were shipped North, mostly from Kent and, in the form of Farnham hops, Surrey. Often these were used in conjunction with cheaper American hops. Though sometimes all the hops were foreign, with Saaz or Hallertau playing the role of quality English hops. These were about the only foreign hops considered good enough by British brewers to be used for aroma purposes.

William Younger's records of the 1840's and 1850's show hops from three English regions: Kent, East Kent and Farnham. The latter, located in Surrey, produced the most highly-regarded – and expensive – hops[11]. By the 1860's large quantities large quantities of foreign hops are showing up in their

---

[9] "Report from the Select Committee on Petitions Complaining of the Additional Duty on Malt in Scotland", 1821, pages 64 - 65.
[10] William Younger brewing record held at the Scottish Brewing Archive, document number WY/6/1/2/3.
[11] William Younger brewing records held at the Scottish Brewing Archive, document numbers WY/6/1/2/3 and WY/6/1/2/5.

brewing logs, mostly described as Bohemian, American or Saaz[12]. Younger seemed particularly fond of the latter, using them as a substitute for quality English hops.

Yeast

English brewers were very protective of their yeast and tried their best to keep a healthy, proprietary strain of their own. The Scots were more promiscuous, enthusiastically swapping yeast with their neighbours.

In one period in 1852, William Younger scarcely brewed with their own yeast, but used that of just about every other brewery in Edinburgh[13]. And they weren't alone. Other Edinburgh brewers regularly used rivals' yeast. Which leads me to conclude that they probably didn't really have proprietary yeast, but there was just one communal Edinburgh yeast.

Once Scottish brewers had quite a different way of pitching their yeast than the English, mixing yeast with incompletely cooled wort. Though it seems the practice had just about died out by the 1840's.

> "The mode which the Scottish brewers adopt in pitching their tuns is very similar to that in England; though, generally speaking, they do not now, as formerly, let down a small portion of the worts into the gyle-tun at a higher temperature, along with some of the store. That former practice, which appears to me very judicious, as it gives the brewer some idea of the strength of the store before he mingles it with the whole of his worts, is still employed by a few."
> "The Scottish ale-brewer and practical maltster" by William Henry Roberts, 1847, pages 114 - 115.

Water

Edinburgh had a reputation for good brewing water, even in the pre-industrial age. One of the reasons so many of the city's breweries were clumped around the Holyrood end of the Royal Mile was because of the water. Evert brewery had at least one well of its own on the brewery premises.

Edinburgh's water was relatively rich in minerals, though not quite on the same scale as Burton. While the magnesium level was quite high, it was still only half that of Burton. Similarly the SO4 content of Edinburgh water was high relative to most regions, but well below that of Burton.

---

[12] William Younger brewing record held at the Scottish Brewing Archive, document number WY/6/1/2/21.
[13] William Younger brewing record held at the Scottish Brewing Archive, document number WY/6/1/2/3.

Classification of Hard Brewing Waters (parts per 100,000)									
	Carbonate ratio	Total solids	Na	Mg	Ca	NO3	Cl	S04	C03	Geological formation
GROUP A.									
1. Burton-on-Trent	13	219.2	4.6	8.2	51.2	4.3	6.7	130.1	141	Keuper marl
2. Burton-on-Trent	25	22.6	3	6.2	26.8	3.1	3.6	65.8	141	Gravel beds
3. Burton-on-Trent	39	81.1	4.3	5.8	15.6	5	7.3	29.3	13.8	" "
4. Bedfordshire	49	78.8	6	0.9	19	4.8	3.1	30	15	Lias
GROUP B.										
5. Co. Durham	54	76.5	7.4	3.5	14.4	1.2	11.4	21.1	16.5	Magnesian Limestone
6. Dortmund	60	101.2	6.9	2.3	26	—	10.7	28.3	27	
7. Gloucestershire	60	67.8	4.5	4	13.6	0.3	3.6	23.5	18.3	Magnesian Limestone
8. Bedfordshire	66	55.5	4.6	0.8	13.9	0.6	3	17.6	15	Oolites
GROUP C.										
9. Lancashire	68	51.5	3.9	4.5	12.1	0.3	6.7	14	20	New Red Sandstone
10. Lincolnshire	69	45.8	3.4	0.4	12.2	4	3	9.6	12.2	Lower Oolite
11. Edinburgh	70	80	9.2	3.6	14	3.1	6	23.1	21	Old Red Sandstone
12. Yorkshire	77	41.2	2.3	1.7	10.5	1.8	3	6.6	15.3	New Red Sandstone
13. Lancashire	78	24.7	1.6	1.4	5.5	1.7	2.4	2.9	9.2	" "
14. Berkshire	80	30.3	0.5	0.9	10	0.5	3.6	0.6	14.2	Chalk
GROUP D.										
15. Gloucestershire	85	27.7	0.9	0.6	8.8	1	1.6	2.4	12.4	Lias
16. London M.W.B.	85	32	2.4	0.4	9	0.3	1.3	5.8	12.3	
17. Nottinghamshire	85	24.6	1.2	3.2	3.6	0.2	1.6	3.4	11.4	New Red Sandstone
18. Surrey	86	29.7	1.6	0.2	9.3	2.6	2.3	1.4	12.3	Chalk
19. Hertfordshire	92	44.6	3.8	7	11.8	3.2	3.5	4.5	17.1	"
GROUP E.										
20. Munich, Dublin	97	27.5	0.1	1.9	8.1	0.3	0.1	0.5	16.5	
21. Lancashire	100	23.9	2.7	1.4	4.4	0.9	1.7	2.7	10.1	New Red Sandstone
22. Lancashire	100	38.4	1.9	3.4	8.4	-	1.7	1.8	21.2	" "

Source:
Brewing: Science and Practice 1: by Harbert Lloyd Hind, 1940, page 458.

William Younger had five wells in the 1870's, each 180 ft. deep[14]. The water they provided wasn't just packed with useful minerals, it also lacked contamination by organic matter and the like:

> "The superiority of their ale is partly owing to the adoption of all mechanical and other improvements, and also to the chemical properties of the water, of which, by sinking to an immense depth, they get an abundant supply. Professor Dr. George Wilson and Dr. Maclagan, having made several analyses of the water, found it free from colour, taste, and odour, and after having subjected it to the most rigid chemical tests, scarcely found a single

---

[14] "Belgravia, Volume 19", 1873, pages 63 - 68.

trace of organic matter. Its most abundant properties are carbonate of lime and magnesia, sulphate of lime and soda, and chloride of sodium."
"The official illustrated guide to the Lancaster and Carlisle, Edinburgh and Glasgow and Caledonian Railways" by George S. Measom, 1859 , page 198.

As we'll soon learn, freedom from contamination was even more important that the mineral content. A brewer could add minerals easily enough to their water but removing contaminants was far more tricky.

James Aitken, a middle-sized brewery in Falkirk, had problems in securing a water supply. Founded in 1740, originally all the water they used had to be carted in. Not a very efficient method of moving the large quantity of water required by brewing[15].

In the early 19th century, Aitken went over to using the town's water supply. However , in 1861 they had to stop taking water from this source when it was polluted by mine workings. It was so serious that Aitken had to resort to carting in water again[16]. The permanent to solution was to dig their own well on the brewery premises, which they did in 1864[17].

---

[15] "The Brewers' Journal 1940" page 151.
[16] Falkirk Herald - Thursday 6 June 1861, page 3.
[17] Stirling Observer - Thursday 25 August 1864, page 6.

Techniques

Mashing

In the first half of the 19th century Scottish mashing schemes were, in general, much simpler than in England, with sparging playing big role.

In the 1840's, William Younger essentially mashed all their beers exactly the same way, except for Table Beer which was sparged somewhat cooler. This is a typical mashing scheme of Younger's:

William Younger 1847 80/- Ale mashing scheme	
strike heat	178° F
time mashed	20 minutes
time stood	2 hours
1st sparge heat	184° F
2nd sparge heat	180° F
1st tap heat	148° F
2nd tap heat	145° F
3rd tap heat	155° F
Source: William Younger brewing record held at the Scottish Brewing Archive, document number WY/6/1/2/3.	

Note that the sparging temperatures are on the high side. The strike heat varied a little depending on the time of year. The example above is from a cool month. In the summer the strike heat was a couple of degrees cooler.

Compare the above with a mashing scheme for a London Mild Ale:

Barclay Perkins 1845 X Ale mashing scheme		
Mash	strike heat	tap heat
1	165° F	
2	136° F	146.5° F
3	134° F	148° F
S	136° F	155° F
Source: Barclay Perkins brewing record held at the London Metropolitan Archives document number ACC/2305/01/551.		

Even though the mashing method is quite different, with two quite hot mashes following the initial infusion rather than a sparge, the tap heats are very similar. The tap heat being the temperature of the wort as it is drawn off from the mash tun.

Let's take a look at one of the other types of beer being brewed in Scotland at the time, Stout.

William Younger 1851 DBS Stout mashing scheme

strike heat	175° F
time mashed	25 minutes
time stood	2 hours
1st sparge heat	184° F
2nd sparge heat	184° F
1st tap heat	146° F
2nd tap heat	143° F
3rd tap heat	156° F
Source: William Younger brewing record held at the Scottish Brewing Archive, document number WY/6/1/2/3.	

Here's the scheme of a typical London Porter:

Barclay Perkins 1848 Porter mashing scheme

Mash	strike heat	tap heat
1	158° F	146.5° F
2	178° F	161.5° F
3 S	158° F	157° F
Source: Barclay Perkins brewing record held at the London Metropolitan Archives document number ACC/2305/01/540.		

You can see that the London system of mashing Porter was different for the system used for Ale, with two mashes followed by a single sparge. The sparge temperature is much cooler than for William Younger. Although the first and second worts had similar temperatures to at William Younger, the heat of the middle wort is very different.

There much less variation in the schemes employed by Younger for Ales and Stout than there was at Barclay Perkins. Younger mashed all their beers in a pretty similar way. In London, Ale and Porter brewing were handled quite separately, often even in separate brew houses.

Sparging

Scotland's biggest contribution to brewing techniques is undoubtedly sparging. Developed in the early 19th century, by the 1840's it was standard practice in Scotland.

Scottish mashing schemes, consisting of a single infusion mash followed by sparging, were far more complex than those in England. South of the border brewers many continued to employ multiple mashes throughout the century. Though in the latter decades combined with sparging.

Boiling

The usual tale is that Scottish brewers boiled their worts for several days, reducing the first wort to a gloopy syrup. There's just one slight problem with this story: there's not a scrap of evidence to back it up. And plenty to contradict it.

In the late 1840's, few of William Younger's beers were boiled for more than 75 minutes. Many weren't even boiled for an hour. This was in stark contrast to English practice, where a 90-minute boil was the absolute minimum and 2 hours or more was common, especially for later, weaker worts.

These are the boiling times at for William Younger's Shilling Ales:

\multicolumn{6}{	l	}{William Younger Shilling Ale boiling times 1848 - 1849}
Date	Year	Beer	OG	boil time (hours)	boil time (hours)
19th Apr	1848	42/-	1043	1.33	
19th Feb	1848	60/-	1074	2	
13th Mar	1848	80/-	1038	1.25	1.25
5th Oct	1848	100/-	1101	1	
18th Feb	1848	120/-	1112	1	
11th Mar	1848	140/-	1130	0.92	
4th Apr	1849	160/-	1134	1	
		Average		1.21	1.25
\multicolumn{6}{	l	}{Source: William Younger brewing record held at the Scottish Brewing Archive, document number WY/6/1/2/3.}

It's unusual that for most of the beers there was only a single wort, meaning that the worts from the mash and the sparge had been combined before boiling. London brewers always boiled each mash and sparge wort separately.

One reason for the short boil times was the type of beer being produced. Edinburgh was famous for pale, delicate Ales. A longer boil would darken the colour and tend to a harsher bitterness.

> "**Scotch Ale-** The Scotch, particularly the Edinburgh ales of the present day, made partly on the old plan, are esteemed equal, if not superior, to any in Britain; and certainly some of the best Scotch ales have a flavour extremely vinous, and approaching the nearest of any of our ales to some of the light French wines. They are particularly mild in their flavour and pale in colour, and the taste of the hop does not predominate."
> "An Encyclopædia of Domestic Economy" by Thomas Webster, William Parkes, 1855, page 598.

Thirty years later, Younger's boils had lengthened, by half an hour for the first wort and a full hour for the second:

William Younger Shilling Ale boiling times in 1879

Date	Year	Beer	OG	ABV	boil time (hours)	boil time (hours)
4th June	1879	50/-	1036	3.84	1.75	2.25
5th June	1879	S 50/-	1042	3.97	2	
5th June	1879	H 60/-	1039	3.84	2	
16th June	1879	H 60/-	1040	4.76	1.75	2.5
6th June	1879	80/-	1059	5.16	1.5	2
4th June	1879	100/-	1070	5.82	1.5	2
13th June	1879	120/-	1083	6.75	1.5	2
8th Aug	1879	140/-	1096	6.48	1.33	1.83
18th Nov	1879	160/-	1109	7.87	2.25	3
		Average			**1.73**	**2.23**

Source:
William Younger brewing record held at the Scottish Brewing Archive, document number WY/6/1/2/28.

Younger's boil times continued to grow longer after 1880, as we'll see in the next chapter.

Let's see how that compares with London practice, using Whitbread as our reference this time:

Whitbread Ale boil times in 1879

Year	Beer	Style	OG	boil time (hours)	boil time (hours)
1879	FA	Pale Ale	1052.4	1.75	
1879	KK	Stock Ale	1078.4	2	3
1879	KKK	Stock Ale	1083.9	2	2.5
1879	PA	Pale Ale	1058.2	2	
1879	X	Mild	1061.2	1.75	2.25
1879	XL	Mild	1070.4	1.75	2.25
1879	XX xpt	Mild	1075.3	2	3.17
		Average		**1.89**	**2.63**

Source:
Whitbread brewing records held at the London Metropolitan Archives, document numbers LMA/4453/D/01/044 and LMA/4453/D/01/045.

Whitbread's boiling times were, in 1879, a little longer than William Younger's, both for the first and the second boil.

Hop additions

WH Roberts confirms the short boiling times of Scottish Ales, but also reveals some useful details about hop additions, something that is rarely mentioned in brewing records.

> "Our practice of brewing, from January to March, was to allow ten pounds of hops per quarter of malt, when the wort was from 96 to 100 of specific gravity. Four pounds of hops were put into the copper when the wort was about 200º of heat, and boiled briskly for the space of twenty minutes; and the remaining six pounds were then added and allowed to boil

thirty of forty minutes, according to circumstances. If the gravity of the wort was from 85 to 90, we only made use of eight instead of ten pounds per quarter, boiling four pounds for fifteen minutes, and the remaining four pounds from forty to fifty minutes, as mentioned above. But if the gravity of the wort was only 70 to 80, seven pounds a quarter only were employed. Two pounds of these were boiled for twenty minutes, and the remaining five pounds put in and boiled for forty or fifty minutes, as before."
"Scottish Ale Brewer", by WH Roberts, Edinburgh, 1847, pages 89-90.

Here are those hop addition details in handy table form:

OG	1st addition		2nd addition	
	time	amount	time	amount
1096-1100	60 minutes	50%	40 minutes	50%
1085-90	60 minutes	50%	45 minutes	50%
1070-80	70 minutes	40%	50 minutes	60%

Note that, contrary to what you might expect, the stronger Ales had a shorter boil.

Fermentation

Several authors have rather ludicrously claimed that Scottish beer was fermented at near-Lager temperatures. Even more ridiculously claiming that the climates of Edinburgh and Munich are similar. While in reality, they aren't even in the same climate group.

If you just look at the pitching temperatures, you could be forgiven for thinking Scottish beer was fermented cooler than English. A look at full fermentation records soon put me straight. Many Scottish beers were pitched a few degrees cooler than the English norm of around 60 F.

There's a simple explanation: a higher percentage of very strong beers were made in Scotland. The higher the gravity, the lower the pitching temperature to accommodate the extra heat generated during fermentation. The maximum fermentation temperatures in England and Scotland were roughly similar.

The other claim is that primary fermentation was much longer in Scotland than in England, because of the low temperature it was carried out at. To put it bluntly, this is total bollocks. Most Scottish brewing records contain a full fermentation record making it easy to check. Scottish beer took no longer to ferment than English.

The William Younger brewing logs have columns charmingly entitled "Heats and Beats in Guile". They record the progress of the fermentation and when the wort was roused to encourage fermentation. Here's an example:

William Younger Shilling Ale fermentations in 1848

Beer	OG	day 1	day 2	day 3	day 4	day 5	day 6	day 7
		Heats and Beats in Guile						
Table	1035	59° F	60° F	62° F	64° F			
42/-	1043	59° F	61° F	63° F	66° F			
60/-	1064	58° F	59° F	62° F	65° F			
80/-	1074	58° F	59° F	62° F	64° F	66° F	67° F	
100/-	1086	57° F	58° F	60° F	63° F	66° F	68° F	68° F
120/-	1103	54° F	56° F	59° F	62° F	66° F	69° F	70° F
140/-	1115	54° F	58° F	62° F	66° F	70° F	72° F	

Source:
William Younger brewing record held at the Scottish Brewing Archive, document number WY/6/1/2/3.

Fermented almost as cold as Lager? I think not. Seven days primary fermentation for a beer with an OG of over 1100º is by no means excessive.

I'll admit that this totally contradicts what W.H. Roberts wrote about Scottish fermentation temperatures:

> ". . while the English brewers frequently set their worts as high as 75º, or, according to some practical writers, occasionally 80º, the Scottish seldom if ever exceed 58º, and, in some cases, fall so low as 44º.
> . . . it is not uncommon for Scottish brewers to have their gyles in the tun for twenty-one days, whilst in England, so long a period as even six days is considered as of rare occurrence."
> "Scottish Ale Brewer" by W.H. Roberts, 1847, page 108.

It's a contemporary account, written by someone with practical experience of brewing. But, In this case, I have to go with the William Younger's brewing records. They show temperatures well above 58º F and nothing anywhere near as low as 44º F. I've never seen a Scottish fermentation that was longer than 7 days. It's hard to reconcile with Roberts' description. Perhaps he was talking about older practices that had been superseded.

Three decades later, the fermentation profiles looked quite different.

William Younger Shilling Ale fermentations in 1879

Beer	OG	pitch heat	day 1		day 2		day 3		day 4		day 5
			AM	PM	AM	PM	AM	PM	AM	PM	AM
50/-	1036	59.5° F	61.5° F	63.5° F	66.5° F	69° F	63° F	58° F			
S 50/-	1042	61.5° F	62° F	65° F	66.5° F	65.5° F	68.5° F	64° F	68.5° F		
H 60/-	1039	62° F	63.5° F	66.5° F	69° F	69° F	71.5° F	65° F	59° F		
80/-	1059	61° F	65° F	70° F	75.5° F	70.6° F	65° F	59° F			
100/-	1070	60° F	63° F	67° F	70° F	75° F	70° F	60° F	62.5° F		
120/-	1083	59.5° F	62° F	66.5° F	72° F	75.5° F	78.5° F	72° F	64.5° F	60.5° F	
140/-	1096	56° F	58° F	59° F	61° F	64° F	68° F	71° F	62° F	69.5° F	62.5° F
160/-	1109	55° F	60° F	65° F	69.5° F	68° F	65.5° F	62.5° F	60.5° F	57.5° F	

Source:
William Younger brewing record held at the Scottish Brewing Archive, document number WY/6/1/2/28.

The shaded cell indicates when the beer was dropped from the tun to the square.

There's clear indication of the use of attemperators in the square. While in 1848 the temperature continued to rise during the fermentation, in 1879 the temperature starts to fall a short time after dropping. We'll learn about the dropping system next.

Fermentation system
In the 18870's, William Younger employed a system of fermentation similar to the dropping method common in the South of England. Most of the fermentation took place in wooden rounds, being dropped into shallower squares to help the yeast settle out and allow fermentation to complete.

This is how a visitor described the fermentation room at Younger:

> "In a spacious chamber, in which are fifty-six tuns capable of containing thirty-six imperial-gallon barrels of beer, the work of fermentation goes on. There is a fall of only two or three feet from the refrigerating to the fermenting department. As the wort enters it receives the necessary portion of barm, and is allowed there to remain in fermentation for four, five, or six days, according to the description of beer under treatment.
>
> The wort having after several days' fermentation become beer, it is run off from the vats to the 'brightening squares' on the ground floor. These are huge square wooden vessels, where the beer 'flattens' and brightens up to the extent desired—an operation which occupies generally two or three days. At length the beer is conveyed by elastic tubes from the squares to the 'stock-room vats,' which, as is usually the case, put with some dry hops into barrels and sent to the export stores for bottling, to meet demands in the British and other markets."
> "Belgravia, Volume 19", 1873, pages 68 - 69.

This method of cleansing wasn't used for all their beers. The Pale Ales were cleansed in union sets.

In the William Younger brewing log from 1879, the dropping is plain to see. At a certain point in the fermentation record it says "Sq", indicating when the beer was dropped into the square. This mostly occurred in day two of the fermentation, though for very strong beers it could be day three[18].

Vatting
William Younger must have been vatting beer because their Abbey brewery contained a dozen large vats.

> "Emerging from the cellars we enter another enormous apartment, in which we find a dozen round vats of gigantic proportions towering up to the height of three stories. Four of these, they will tell you, contain each three hundred and twelve of the thirty-six imperial-gallon barrels; and of the remainder, each contains one hundred and eighty barrels of the same size that we have seen upstairs "
> "Belgravia, Volume 19", 1873, pages 68 - 69.

---

[18] William Younger brewing record held at the Scottish Brewing Archive, document number WY/6/1/2/28.

Though large is a relative term. The big London Porter brewers had vats holding thousands, or even tens of thousands of barrels.

Union sets

Unsurprisingly, given the amount of IPA brewed in Scotland, Burton union sets were common. They were seen as an essential piece of equipment for brewing top-quality Pale Ales and any brewer who was seriously brewing the style installed them. For example, William Younger had them in their Holyrood brewery, which was mainly dedicated to the brewing of Pale Ale.

Union sets aren't fermentation vessels, but cleansing vessels, i.e. where the final phase of the fermentation takes place and most of the yeast is removed. Before being transferred to the union beer would have already undergone a conventional open fermentation.

Brewing IPA in the 1840's

One of the earliest detailed descriptions of brewing IPA is in "Scottish Ale Brewer", by W.H. Roberts, published in Edinburgh in 1847. It provides a unique insight into the brewing methods of the time and, more importantly, the reasoning behind them.

Roberts thought some brewers caused themselves problems by mashing at too high a temperature. Over-attenuated IPA's were the result. 168º to 170º F he recommended as a striking heat when the ambient temperature was 40º to 45º F. If the air temperature was 35º to 40º F, 170º to 172º F was his suggested striking heat. When the wort was tapped at the end of mashing, its temperature should be 145º to 150º F[19].

Mashing – the process of actively mixing the grains with water in the tun – needed to be as quick as possible, no more than 20 to 25 minutes if using internal mechanical rakes. At the start of mashing the temperature was checked at various points in the mash. If it was much below 145º F, hot water was added to raise it to 150º F. When mashing finished the wort was left to stand for between 100 and 120 minutes[20].

Roberts recommended kicking off sparging a few minutes before drawing off the first wort, using water between 185º and 190º F. The taps were closed as soon as the first wort had been run off. While sparge water continued to be added until the grain bed was covered again. Because, Roberts commented: "it being highly detrimental to let the surface of the goods to be dry"[21].

His suggestions for hop additions are very much based around gyle brewing, where each gyle was hopped and boiled separately. For a beer hopped at 22 lbs per quarter of malt (5 to 7 lbs per barrel, depending on the OG), 6 lbs were added to the first wort at the start of a 70 minute boil, a further 8 lbs were added 20 minutes later. The second wort received a single hop addition of 8lbs at the start of a two hour boil[22].

Rapid cooling of the wort after boiling was important:

---

[19] "Scottish Ale Brewer", WH Roberts, Edinburgh, 1847, pages 161-162.
[20] "Scottish Ale Brewer", WH Roberts, Edinburgh, 1847, pages 162-163.
[21] "Scottish Ale Brewer", WH Roberts, Edinburgh, 1847, page 163.
[22] "Scottish Ale Brewer", WH Roberts, Edinburgh, 1847, pages 164-165.

"Reducing the temperature of worts in the coolers is now generally accomplished by artificial means, and with great rapidity, it being important that they should be reduced to the pitching temperature, with as little delay as possible."
"Scottish Ale Brewer", WH Roberts, Edinburgh, 1847, pages 165-166.

By artificial, he means that the wort wasn't just left in a shallow cooler until it reached a suitable temperature for pitching yeast. But that it was also cooled by a simple heat exchanger. This consisted of a washboard of copper pipes filled with chilled brine over which the wort was run. This combined method of cooling was standard in British breweries until after WW II.

The pitching temperature Roberts recommended was 58º and 60º F, depending on the air temperature. He expected a rapid and vigorous fermentation with the temperature rising to around 70º F. After just 24 to 30 hours the beer passed on to the next phase: cleansing[23].

In this early phase of Pale Ale production cleansing still took place in puncheons, large casks holding several barrels set up vertically on stillions. Wort was ejected from the top of these vessels into a trough, from which the puncheons were refilled every two or three hours[24]. This system of cleansing was common in the big London breweries, but in Burton – and later in Scotland, too - was replaced by the more sophisticated and less labour intensive unions.

The method of dry hopping Roberts proposes is a bit odd. The hops were mixed with a little boiling strong Ale wort, which, after cooling, was added to the casks of IPA[25].

Some brewers liked to deliberately rack their beer into trade casks with dregs, arguing that it helped prevent the beer spoiling during the long trip to India. Roberts reckoned it was better to rack IPA clear[26].

Styles
The number of styles brewed in Scotland was very limited at the start of this period, amounting to little more than Table Beer, Porter/Stout, Shilling Ales, Mild Ales and Stock Ales. With the Shilling Ales making up by far the largest part of production.

Let's take a look at each of those general types in more detail.

Table Beer
Scottish brewers had quite a reputation for producing top-class Table Beer. This is reflected in the fact that it was often exported to England. While what Table Beer there was brewed in England was usually for quick, local consumption.

One of the odd characteristics of Scottish brewing is that it featured far more beers at the top and bottom end of the strength range than in England. Table Beer also hung around longer in Scotland.

---

[23] "Scottish Ale Brewer", WH Roberts, Edinburgh, 1847, pages 166-167.
[24] "Scottish Ale Brewer", WH Roberts, Edinburgh, 1847, pages 167-168.
[25] "Scottish Ale Brewer", WH Roberts, Edinburgh, 1847, page 168.
[26] "Scottish Ale Brewer", WH Roberts, Edinburgh, 1847, pages 168-169.

The last London Table Beer I've seen in the brewing records was produced in 1869. While William Younger was still brewing one in 1898.

The "beer" part of the name wasn't random. The weakest malt liquors in the 18th century were almost always beers because, with low levels of alcohol, they needed the extra protection of more hops. And you can clearly see evidence of that in William Younger's Table Beer, which was hopped at 11 to 12 pounds per quarter of malt. That's a similar hopping rate to a Stock Ale.

William Younger Table Beer 1848 - 1849							
Date	Year	Beer	OG	FG	ABV	App. Attenuation	lbs hops/ qtr	hops lb/brl
15th Apr	1848	T	1035	1010	3.31	71.43%	12.00	1.74
14th Nov	1849	T	1040	1014	3.44	65.00%	11.00	1.69
Source: William Younger brewing record held at the Scottish Brewing Archive, document number WY/6/1/2/3.							

Younger continued to brew a similar Table Beer in the succeeding decades, though the gravity fell over time, as did the hopping rate after 1868.

William Younger Table Beer 1851 - 1879						
Year	Beer	OG	FG	ABV	App. Attenuation	lbs hops/ qtr	hops lb/brl
1851	T	1037	1013	3.18	64.86%	12.00	1.69
1852	T	1037	1011	3.44	70.27%	11.11	1.32
1858	T	1035	1014	2.78	60.00%	16.43	1.44
1868	T	1031	1010	2.78	67.74%	16.25	1.37
1879	T	1030	1005	3.31	83.33%	6.67	0.89
Sources: William Younger brewings record held at the Scottish Brewing Archive, document numbers WY/6/1/2/5, WY/6/1/2/14, WY/6/1/2/21 and WY/6/1/2/28.						

There's not a huge deal to say about the grists. For the whole period they were 100% pale malt. Other than right at the start, when sometimes it was 100% pale malted bigg.

Pale Ale/IPA

Scotland, more specifically Edinburgh, was one of the first places outside Burton to take up brewing the trendy new IPA style. As early as the 1840's, Edinburgh brewers were producing IPA for both the home and the Indian markets.

Trying to split apart Pale Ale and IPA in this early period is pointless. Brewers were highly inconsistent in their use of the two terms. In general, IPA was used to describe all early Pale Ales, regardless of their characteristics. Later in the 19th century Scottish brewers generally adopted the term Pale Ale instead, though IPA was sometimes used to denote one particular beer in a range of Pale Ales. Confused? You should be. I've been trying to get my head around this for a decade and still struggle.

Here's confirmation that that early date Scotland was both exporting, and drinking, IPA:

> Large quantities of a light, pale, and highly-hopped variety of ale have been for some considerable time past exported to the East Indies, where it is in high estimation; and is now, also, rather extensively used in summer in this country."
> "A Dictionary, Practical, Theoretical, and Historical, of Commerce and Commercial Navigation" by John Ramsay McCulloch, 1844, page 9.

Despite what you may have been told to the contrary, early IPAs were not particularly strong beers, at least by the standard of the day. They were, however, extremely heavily hopped. AT levels that just look plain crazy today. Heavy hopping was very necessary for export versions, if the beer were to arrive in India in good shape.

WH Roberts provides some intriguing analyses of Scottish-brewed IPAs in the 1840's. Some are surprisingly weak, even ones genuinely exported to India:

Early 19th century IPA

Year	Beer	Price	size	package	FG	OG	ABV	App. Atten-uation
1844	90/- IPA Export, India	20.00d	gallon	bottled	1007.75	1067.6	7.60	88.54%
1844	84/- IPA Export	18.67d	gallon	draught	1005.25	1060.4	7	91.30%
1844	95/- IPA Export	21.11d	gallon	draught	1008	1069.4	7.8	88.48%
1844	90/- IPA Export, India	20.00d	gallon	draught	1008	1066.3	7.4	87.93%
1844	84/- IPA Export, India	18.67d	gallon	draught	1010	1062	6.6	83.86%
1844	81/- IPA Home	18.00d	gallon	draught	1012	1059.3	6	79.75%
1844	60/- IPA Export, India	13.33d	gallon	bottled	1006.5	1053.8	6	87.91%
1844	60/- IPA Export, India	13.33d	gallon	bottled	1005	1053.8	6.2	90.71%
1844	60/- IPA Export, India	13.33d	gallon	bottled	1013	1054.2	5.23	76.00%
1844	90/- IPA Export, India	20.00d	gallon	bottled	1012	1065.6	6.8	81.69%
1844	95/- IPA Export, India	21.11d	gallon	bottled	1007.25	1067.1	7.6	89.20%
1844	90/- IPA Export	20.00d	gallon	bottled	1007.5	1068.9	7.8	89.12%
1844	60/- IPA Home	13.33d	gallon	bottled	1005	1044.7	5.04	88.81%
1844	60/- IPA Home	13.33d	gallon	bottled	1004.25	1049.9	5.8	91.49%
1844	60/- IPA Home	13.33d	gallon	bottled	1006	1047.2	5.23	87.28%
1844	81/- IPA Export	18.00d	gallon	bottled	1003	1061.3	7.4	95.10%
1844	81/- IPA Export	18.00d	gallon	bottled	1003.25	1058.4	7	94.43%
1844	66/- IPA Export	14.67d	gallon	bottled	1004	1054.4	6.4	92.65%
1844	90/- IPA Export, India	20.00d	gallon	bottled	1010.25	1070.1	7.6	85.38%
1844	90/- IPA Export	20.00d	gallon	bottled	1009	1067.3	7.4	86.62%
1845	81/- IPA Home	18.00d	gallon	draught	1006.5	1053.8	6	87.91%
1845	81/- IPA Home	18.00d	gallon	bottled	1006	1054.8	6.2	89.06%
1845	81/- IPA Home	18.00d	gallon	bottled	1005	1058.6	6.8	91.46%
1845	81/- IPA Home	18.00d	gallon	bottled	1005	1060.1	7	91.68%
1845	81/- IPA Home	18.00d	gallon	bottled	1005.25	1058.8	6.8	91.07%
1845	90/- IPA Export	20.00d	gallon	draught	1012.25	1062.7	6.4	80.45%
1845	90/- IPA Export	20.00d	gallon	draught	1012.25	1064.2	6.6	80.93%
1845	90/- IPA Export	20.00d	gallon	draught	1012	1062.4	6.4	80.77%
1845	90/- IPA Export, India	20.00d	gallon	bottled	1010.5	1068.5	7.4	84.68%
1845	60/- IPA Export	13.33d	gallon	bottled	1004.25	1048.4	5.6	91.21%

Early 19th century IPA

Year	Beer	Price	size	package	FG	OG	ABV	App. Attenuation
1845	60/- IPA Export	13.33d	gallon	draught	1004.25	1048.4	5.6	91.21%
1845	63/- IPA Export	14.00d	gallon	draught	1005.5	1049.6	5.6	88.91%
1845	81/- IPA Export	18.00d	gallon	bottled	1003.75	1058.9	7	93.63%
1845	63/- IPA Export	14.00d	gallon	bottled	1003.25	1055.2	6.6	94.11%
1845	90/- IPA Export	20.00d	gallon	draught	1007.5	1068.9	7.8	89.12%
1845	90/- IPA Export	20.00d	gallon	draught	1007.75	1069.2	7.8	88.80%
1846	90/- IPA Export	20.00d	gallon	draught	1006	1054.8	6.2	89.06%
1846	90/- IPA Home	20.00d	gallon	draught	1006.5	1055.3	6.2	88.25%
1846	90/- IPA Export	20.00d	gallon	bottled	1005	1052.3	6	90.43%
1846	65/- IPA Export	14.44d	gallon	bottled	1005.25	1062	7.2	91.53%

Source:
"Scottish Ale Brewer", by W.H. Roberts, Edinburgh, 1847, pages 171 and 173

The weakest IPA exported to India was just over 5% ABV. That's not even a strong beer by modern standards. It's interesting that they go all the way from 60/- to 90/-. The latter is very rare as a beer designation. Though weirdly it popped up again in the 1920's to describe a low-gravity (low 1030º's) bottled Pale Ale. More recently it's been used for Strong/Scotch Ales.

The IPAs William Younger was brewing a few years later look remarkably similar to those analysed by Roberts.

William Younger Pale Ales 1851 - 1853

Year	Beer	OG	FG	ABV	App. Attenuation	lbs hops/ qtr	hops lb/brl
1851	XP	1060	1018	5.56	70.00%	20.00	5.15
1851	XXP	1072	1018	7.14	75.00%	24.00	8.18
1852	XP	1056	1018	5.03	67.86%	20.00	4.66
1852	XXP	1067	1017	6.61	74.63%	24.00	8.20
1853	XP	1056	1015	5.42	73.21%	20.00	5.14

Source:
William Younger brewing record held at the Scottish Brewing Archive, document number WY/6/1/2/5.

Younger's early Pale Ales look very similar to those in the earliest IPA records I've seen, from London brewer Reid.

Reid Pale Ale 1838 - 1839

Year	Beer	Style	OG	FG	ABV	App. Attenuation	lbs hops/ qtr	hops lb/brl
1839	IPA	IPA	1056.8	1007.0	6.59	87.67%	26.6	5.88
1839	BPA	Pale Ale	1056.0	1007.0	6.48	87.49%	22.67	5.61
1839	IPA	IPA	1056.2	1007.0	6.51	87.55%	28.62	6.53

Source:
Reid brewing record held at the Westminster City Archives, document number 789/264.

Both sets share a fairly modest gravity but an insane level of hopping. Five or six pounds per barrel is a huge amount for a beer that isn't really all that strong. These must have been incredibly bitter beers.

Looking at William Younger's Pale Ales over a longer period, one trend is obvious: a reduction in the hopping rate.

\multicolumn{7}{	l	}{William Younger Pale Ales 1853 - 1879}
Year	Beer	OG	FG	ABV	App. Atten- uation	lbs hops/ qtr	hops lb/brl
1853	XP	1055	1016	5.16	70.91%	20.00	4.76
1860	XP	1054	1013	5.42	75.93%	14.80	4.40
1858	XXP	1059	1016	5.69	72.88%	21.05	5.00
1859	EX	1063	1016	6.22	74.60%	22.86	5.45
1868	XP	1051	1013	5.03	74.51%	10.00	2.78
1869	XXP (home trade)	1053	1014	5.16	73.58%	11.67	2.39
1873	XP	1050	1013	4.89	74.00%	12.12	2.92
1879	XP	1052	1016	4.76	69.23%	11.74	2.73
1879	2XP	1046	1009	4.89	80.43%	9.00	1.94
\multicolumn{8}{	l	}{Source: William Younger brewing records held at the Scottish Brewing Archive, document numbers WY/6/1/2/5, WY/6/1/2/14, WY/6/1/2/21 and WY/6/1/2/28.}

What you can't see in the table is a change in the type of hops as well as the quantity. In the 1850's, all the hops were English: Kent, East Kent and Farnham. Good quality hops that you would expect to see in expensive beers like Pale Ales. While by 1868, their Pale Ales contained all foreign hops, either Bavarians (usually meaning Spalt), Saaz or Bohemian.

It's unusual to see exclusively foreign hops in a Pale Ale. A sure sign of the regard in which central European hops were held by British brewers. About the only ones they reckoned equal to the best English hops.

English Pale Ales 1865 - 1877

Year	Brewer	Beer	OG	FG	ABV	App. Attenuation	lbs hops/qtr	hops lb/brl
1865	Whitbread	PA	1061.8	1012.7	6.49	79.37%	14.67	4.36
1869	Whitbread	PA	1063.2	1016.3	6.19	74.12%	15.05	4.85
1873	Whitbread	FA	1052.1	1015.8	4.80	69.68%	14.36	3.67
1873	Whitbread	PA	1061.5	1022.7	5.13	63.06%	14.48	4.42
1879	Whitbread	PA	1058.2	1013.6	5.90	76.67%	14.83	4.20
1879	Whitbread	FA	1055.1	1009.1	6.08	83.42%	11.09	2.96
1877	Truman	Pale Ale	1055.7	1016.6	5.17	70.15%	17.00	3.85
1877	Truman	P2	1063.7	1018.6	5.97	70.87%	19.00	5.01
1877	Truman	P2 K	1062.3	1020.5	5.53	67.11%	19.04	4.84
1877	Truman	P1	1066.5	1022.2	5.86	66.67%	19.16	5.35
1877	Truman	P1 R	1066.5	1019.4	6.23	70.83%	19.00	5.21
1877	Truman	P1 K	1067.3	1023.5	5.79	65.02%	19.00	5.13
1877	Truman	P1 B	1069.5	1024.9	5.90	64.14%	20.00	5.86

Sources:
Whitbread brewing records held at the London Metropolitan Archives, document numbers LMA/4453/D/01/030, A/4453/D/01/035, LMA/4453/D/01/039, LMA/4453/D/01/039, LMA/4453/D/01/044 and LMA/4453/D/01/045.
Truman brewing record held at the London Metropolitan Archives, document number B/THB/BUR/35.

By the late 1860's there's a clear divergence in the hopping rates of William Younger's and English Pale Ales. Younger's Pale Ales averaged around 10lbs of hops per quarter of malt while Whitbread's averaged 14.5 lb and Truman 19 lbs. The English versions also had a higher gravity, over 1060º for the top of the range Pale Ale, while Younger's were in the low 1050's. The changes seem to have been mostly North of the border. The English versions still have more similar gravities and hopping rates to the early Pale Ales.

A decade later and Younger's hopping had changed again. Now their Pale Ales were including hops from the continent, Kent and North America:

2nd June 1879 Wm. Younger XP

hop	lbs	%
Spalt	40	17.39%
American	40	17.39%
East Kent	110	47.83%
Californian	40	17.39%
Total	*230*	

Source:
William Younger brewing record held at the Scottish Brewing Archive, document number WY/6/1/2/28.

The use of the terms "American" and "Californian" is to differentiate between hops from the East and West coasts of the USA.

An expansion in the use of foreign hops also occurred in England at the same time, with continental, particularly Bavarian and Bohemian, and American hops being the most common types.

Porter and Stout

Spurred on by their enormous popularity amongst Scottish drinkers, local brewers began to brew their own versions to rival those brewed in England. Though it never quite attained the level of popularity in England, considerable quantities were brewed in Scotland.

Initially, these Scottish versions seem to have closely mimicked the London originals, in the second half of the 19th century Scottish Porter, and more importantly Stout, began to acquire their own unique character.

While most English provincial dropped brown malt from their Porter and Stout grists early in the 19th century, Scottish brewers continued to use it, and to use it large quantities.

William Younger Porter and Stout in 1851								
Date	Beer	Style	OG	FG	ABV	App. Atten- uation	lbs hops/ qtr	hops lb/brl
3rd Nov	BS	Porter	1056	1015	5.42	73.21%	23.87	2.86
11th Oct	BS	Porter	1057	1017	5.29	70.18%	21.75	3.08
29th Nov	BS	Porter	1060	1024	4.76	60.00%	27.37	3.17
29th Oct	DBS	Stout	1078	1015	8.33	80.77%	13.40	5.63
13th Dec	DBS	Stout	1089	1025	8.47	71.91%	14.00	5.68
Source: William Younger brewing record held at the Scottish Brewing Archive, document number WY/6/1/2/5.								

By the 1870's, William Younger had discontinued their Porter and introduced a new range of Stouts, S1, S2 and S3. These were far more lightly hopped than DBS and often contained large quantities of spent hops. S3 had an unusually low gravity for the 19th century, some examples being under 3% ABV. The new Stouts, in contrast to DBS, were not dry hopped.

William Younger Porter and Stout in 1879								
Date	Beer	Style	OG	FG	ABV	App. Atten- uation	lbs hops/ qtr	hops lb/brl
19th Sep	S1	Stout	1070	1026	5.82	62.86%	6.47	2.07
6th June	S2	Stout	1060	1020	5.29	66.67%	3.33	0.87
13th June	S3	Stout	1032	1011	2.78	65.63%	all spent hops	
11th Aug	S3	Stout	1043	1010	4.37	76.74%	4.71	0.86
20th Nov	DBS	Stout	1073	1035	5.03	52.05%	12.86	5.00
Source: William Younger brewing record held at the Scottish Brewing Archive, document number WY/6/1/2/28.								

Throughout this period William Younger aged Porter and DBS in vats. S1, S2 and S3, however, were not vatted.

Here are Whitbread's Porter and Stouts for comparison purposes:

Whitbread Porter and Stout 1851 - 1879

Year	Beer	Style	OG	FG	ABV	App. Attenuation	lbs hops/qtr	hops lb/brl
1851	India Beer	Porter	1066.2	1020.2	6.08	69.46%	22.03	5.89
1851	K	Porter	1061.5	1018.8	5.64	69.37%	20.33	5.28
1851	P	Porter	1063.4	1018.3	5.97	71.18%	11.19	3.13
1851	S	Stout	1075.3	1027.1	6.38	63.97%	10.86	4.56
1851	SSS	Stout	1091.4				11.15	4.55
1869	P	Porter	1050.1	1015.2	4.62	69.61%	12.14	2.61
1869	SS	Stout	1077.6	1028.0	6.56	63.93%	13.00	4.90
1869	SSS	Stout	1098.3	1033.8	8.54	65.63%	13.00	6.22
1869	xp S	Stout	1072.3	1022.7	6.56	68.58%	17.54	5.71
1879	P	Porter	1056.5	1017.2	5.20	69.61%	7.86	2.01
1879	SS	Stout	1077.6	1028.0	6.56	63.93%	8.60	3.53
1879	SSS	Stout	1095.3	1037.7	7.62	60.47%	8.60	4.33
1879	XPS	Stout	1071.1	1019.9	6.76	71.93%	14.13	5.01

Sources:
Whitbread brewing records held at the London Metropolitan Archives, document numbers LMA/4453/D/09/045, LMA/4453/D/09/063, LMA/4453/D/09/073 and LMA/4453/D/09/074.

The hopping rates for both Younger's and Whitbread's beers fell as the century progressed, though it was somewhat greater at the former, with the exception of DBS, were it remained fairly constant. Some of Younger's cheaper Stouts increasingly used some, or even all, spent hops. This isn't a practice I've ever seen employed in London, other than for Table Beer.

There was no Younger equivalent for several of the Whitbread beers, such as Keeping Porter and the very strong SSS Stout. Far fewer Stouts were brewed in Scotland and those that were mostly fell into the lower gravity bands.

While most English provincial brewers dropped brown malt from their Porter and Stout grists early in the 19th century, Scottish brewers continued to use it, and to use it large quantities. Though there was a point in the 1860's when William Younger used amber malt rather than brown.

William Younger Porter and Stout grists 1851 - 1879

Year	Beer	pale malt	brown malt	black malt	amber malt	black sugar
1851	BS	24.65%	56.13%	19.21%		
1851	BS	42.83%	32.50%	24.67%		
1851	BS	26.00%	59.20%	14.80%		
1851	DBS	71.47%	19.72%	8.81%		
1851	DBS	72.49%	22.01%	5.50%		
1868	Bg	92.22%		7.78%		
1869	BS	45.16%		13.71%	41.13%	
1869	P	68.71%		10.43%	20.86%	
1868	DBS	82.85%		5.72%	11.43%	
1869	DBS	77.57%		5.61%	16.82%	
1869	DBS	74.78%		6.31%	18.92%	
1869	DBS	65.71%		6.23%	28.05%	

William Younger Porter and Stout grists 1851 - 1879

Year	Beer	pale malt	brown malt	black malt	amber malt	black sugar
1879	S1	69.76%	18.15%	4.54%		7.55%
1879	S2	82.18%	11.88%	5.94%		
1879	S3	56.85%	21.57%	21.57%		
1879	S3	70.72%	19.52%	9.76%		
1879	DBS	86.43%	9.05%	4.52%		

Sources:
William Younger brewing record held at the Scottish Brewing Archive, document number WY/6/1/2/5.
William Younger brewing record held at the Scottish Brewing Archive, document number WY/6/1/2/21.
William Younger brewing record held at the Scottish Brewing Archive document number WY/6/1/2/28.

The roasted malt content of some grists from 1851 is extremely high, over 50% in some cases. This could only possibly have worked if the brown malt was diastatic, even though this is a really late date for such malt.

London brewers were very faithful to a combination of three malts, pale, brown and black:

Whitbread Porter and Stout 1851 - 1879

Year	Beer	Style	OG	pale malt	brown malt	black malt	sugar
1851	India Beer	Porter	1066.2	71.0%	25.0%	4.0%	
1851	K	Porter	1061.5	71.0%	25.0%	4.0%	
1851	P	Porter	1063.4	71.0%	25.0%	4.0%	
1851	S	Stout	1075.3	71.0%	25.0%	4.0%	
1851	SSS	Stout	1091.4	71.0%	25.0%	4.0%	
1869	P	Porter	1050.1	68.2%	13.6%	6.8%	11.3%
1869	SS	Stout	1077.6	73.1%	13.7%	4.6%	8.6%
1869	SSS	Stout	1098.3	73.1%	13.7%	4.6%	8.6%
1869	xp S	Stout	1072.3	68.5%	18.3%	4.6%	8.6%
1879	P	Porter	1056.5	79.2%	13.3%	7.5%	
1879	SS	Stout	1077.6	64.3%	23.0%	4.6%	8.1%
1879	SSS	Stout	1095.3	64.3%	23.0%	4.6%	8.1%
1879	XPS	Stout	1071.1	59.3%	21.5%	6.0%	13.3%

Sources:
Whitbread brewing records held at the London Metropolitan Archives, document numbers LMA/4453/D/09/045, LMA/4453/D/09/063, LMA/4453/D/09/073 and LMA/4453/D/09/074.

Note that London brewers had already started using sugar in the 1860's. Other than the occasional experiment, William Younger only adopted sugar in the late 1870's.

Most of Younger's grists from 1879 look quite similar Whitbread's, containing around 20% brown malt and 5% black malt. This convergence wouldn't last. We'll see in the next chapter how Scottish and London Stout continued to drift apart.

Shilling Ales

These beers formed the bulk of production in Scotland until the growth of Pale Ale in the second half of the century. The name derived from the wholesale price per 54-gallon hogshead. They have no connection with the 60/-, 70/- and 80/- of post-WW II.

Though not everything with a shilling designation was what I'm calling a Shilling Ale. You also had things like 54/- Stout or 60/- Pale Ale. Shilling Ales were essentially the Scottish version of Mild Ale. Unlike English Mild Ales, however, they were mostly sold in bottled form. After racking, hogsheads or half hogsheads were sent to bottlers, who repackaged the beer and sold it.

Scotch Ales in the 1840's

Price	OG	FG	ABV
£3	1080-86	1032-35	6.625
£4	1090-95	1036-39	7
£5	1100-1108	1040-44	7.75
£6	1110-1116	1045-47	8.375
£7	1120-1125	1048-50	9.25
Source: Scottish Ale Brewer, WH Roberts, Edinburgh, 1847, page 117			

At William Younger in the late 1840's, there were seven Shilling ales, ranging in gravity from 1043º to 1134º. That's a considerable spread, but they did have several features in common, such as a poor degree of attenuation and relatively modest hopping, though this wasn't always the case at the top end of the strength range.

To put the hopping into context, English Mild Ales at this time had 8-9 lbs of hops per quarter. Looking at the hopping per quarter of malt allows the comparison of beers of different gravities. You can see in the table below that the rate was rather lower, around 4lbs per quarter, for most of William Younger's Shilling Ales.

William Younger Shilling Ales 1848 - 1849

Date	Year	Beer	OG	FG	ABV	App. Attenuation	lbs hops/qtr	hops lb/brl
19th Apr	1848	42/-	1043	1012	4.10	72.09%	15.00	2.65
19th Feb	1848	60/-	1074	1037	4.89	50.00%	3.33	1.18
13th Mar	1848	80/-	1088	1038	6.61	56.82%	4.00	1.69
5th Oct	1848	100/-	1101	1039	8.20	61.39%	4.52	2.16
18th Feb	1848	120/-	1112	1045	8.86	59.82%	4.17	2.70
11th Mar	1848	140/-	1130	1059	9.39	54.62%	7.61	4.71
4th Apr	1849	160/-	1134	1063	9.39	52.99%	12.96	7.94
Source: William Younger brewing record held at the Scottish Brewing Archive, document number WY/6/1/2/3.								

Move forward 30 years and some significant changes have taken place. The most obvious being that the gravities had fallen between 20% and 45%, with those at the weaker end taking the biggest hit.

William Younger Shilling Ales in 1879

Date	Year	Beer	OG	FG	ABV	App. Attenuation	lbs hops/ qtr	hops lb/brl
4th June	1879	50/-	1036	1007	3.84	80.56%	6.92	0.95
5th June	1879	S 50/-	1042	1012	3.97	71.43%	2.94	0.55
5th June	1879	H 60/-	1039	1010	3.84	74.36%	2.94	0.51
16th June	1879	H 60/-	1040	1004	4.76	90.00%	6.25	1.06
6th June	1879	80/-	1059	1020	5.16	66.10%	8.15	2.32
4th June	1879	100/-	1070	1026	5.82	62.86%	8.79	2.90
13th June	1879	120/-	1083	1032	6.75	61.45%	9.50	4.00
8th Aug	1879	140/-	1096	1047	6.48	51.04%	8.89	3.44
18th Nov	1879	160/-	1109	1049.5	7.87	54.59%	6.25	4.74

Source:
William Younger brewing record held at the Scottish Brewing Archive, document number WY/6/1/2/28.

The hopping rates for the stronger Shilling Ales (80/- and up) increased from around 4lbs per quarter of malt to 8 lbs. Only the very strongest, 160/-, saw a fall. Some of the weaker versions saw hopping fall to the very minimal rate of under 3lbs per quarter. It's all rather confusing.

Mild Ales

Differentiating Shilling Ales and Mild Ales is, in many, totally arbitrary. But I'm going to do it anyway. If only because Scottish brewers liberally sprinkled the X's I associate with the style around their brewing records.

Putting on my serious hat, there was one defining difference between the two beers types. Both were sold young. But Shilling Ales were shipped out to retail outlets in hogsheads for bottling while Mild Ales were filled into barrels and kilderkins for sale on draught. Though they may have been born of the same mash, the method of conditioning differentiated them. Just like Mild Ale and Brown Ale in the 20th century.

Younger Mild Ales 1851 - 1854

Year	Beer	OG	FG	ABV	App. Attenuation	lbs hops/ qtr	hops lb/brl
1851	X	1075	1036	5.16	52.00%	1.94	1.82
1851	XX	1082	1035	6.22	57.32%	9.16	2.42
1851	XXX	1095	1037	7.67	61.05%	17.94	5.50
1852	X	1071	1034	4.89	52.11%	8.00	2.73
1853	X	1070	1031	5.16	55.71%	7.73	2.83
1853	XX	1076	1030	6.09	60.53%	8.00	3.08
1853	XXX	1088	1038	6.61	56.82%	8.00	3.69
1854	X	1053	1017	4.76	67.92%	10.00	2.50

Source:
William Younger brewing record held at the Scottish Brewing Archive, document number WY/6/1/2/5.

At mostly around 8 lbs of hops per quarter of malt, the hopping rate is very similar to London Mild Ales. Whitbread's Ales of the same period look very similar to those of William Younger:

Whitbread Ales in 1851

Beer	OG	FG	ABV	App. Attenuation	lbs hops/ qtr	hops lb/brl
X	1074.8	1025.2	6.56	66.30%	9.07	3.21
XX	1088.6	1030.2	7.73	65.94%	9.07	3.81
XXX	1099.2	1041.6	7.62	58.10%	9.23	4.46

Source:
Whitbread brewing record held at the London Metropolitan Archives document number LMA/4453/D/01/16.

On average, Whitbread's Ales were a little more heavily hopped, but not by a significant amount. The big difference is in the rate of attenuation, which is very low in the Younger Milds. Poor attenuation is a fairly constant feature of Scottish brewing. And may account for why Scottish beers were often perceived as sweeter than their English counterparts.

Moving forward a couple of decades, Younger's Milds have dropped considerably in gravity:

William Younger Mild Ales in 1868

Year	Beer	OG	FG	ABV	App. Attenuation	lbs hops/ qtr	hops lb/brl
1868	X	1053	1023	3.97	56.60%	6.30	1.36
1868	XX	1057	1024	4.37	57.89%	9.58	2.25
1868	XXX	1068	1028	5.29	58.82%	8.00	2.55

Source:
William Younger brewing record held at the Scottish Brewing Archive, document number WY/6/1/2/21

X has fallen from 1075º to 1053º, XX from 1082º to 1057º and XXX from 1095º to 1068º. Though the hopping rate, averaging around 8 lbs per quarter of malt has remained pretty constant.

Similar changes had taken place at Whitbread:

Whitbread Mild Ales in 1868

Year	Beer	OG	FG	ABV	App. Attenuation	lbs hops/ qtr	hops lb/brl
1868	X	1056.8	1014.4	5.61	74.63%	7.41	1.93
1868	XL	1066.2	1019.7	6.16	70.29%	10.34	3.28
1868	XX	1080.9	1027.1	7.11	66.44%	9.61	3.54

Source:
Whitbread brewing record held at the London Metropolitan Archives, document number LMA/4453/D/01/034.

The strongest Mild, XXX had been discontinued and a new beer, XL, introduced with a gravity between X and XX. The fall in the gravity of Whitbread X, from 1075º to 1057º wasn't quite as large as at Younger, but still considerable. XX, on the other hand, only had a small reduction in gravity from 1087º to 1081.º. The hopping of the two sets, averaging around 8 lbs per quarter of malt, remained roughly similar.

Between 1851 and 1868 the strength of William Younger's Milds diverged considerably from Whitbread's. Though they continued to be hopped at a similar rate.

Stock Ale

As in England these were essentially aged versions of Mild Ale. One of the unusual features of Scottish brewing is the large number of very strong beers which were sold young. A much lower percentage of strong Scottish beers were aged.

Being expected to last for years, Stock Ales were hopped more heavily than the equivalent Shilling Ale. S and XS were the Stock equivalents of 100/- and 120/-, respectively, the main difference being that they contained double the amount of hops.

William Younger Stock Ales in 1849

Date	Year	Beer	OG	FG	ABV	App. Attenuation	lbs hops/ qtr	hops lb/brl
7th Apr	1849	S	1097	1031	8.73	68.04%	12.00	4.92
13th Nov	1849	S	1095	1028	8.86	70.53%	10.31	4.85
12th Nov	1849	XS	1108	1036	9.53	66.67%	11.50	6.73

Source: William Younger brewing record held at the Scottish Brewing Archive, document number WY/6/1/2/3.

There's some overlap between the higher value Shilling Ales and Stock Ales. Half of the batch of 1868 XXS below, for example, was packaged as 140/-. As these stronger Shilling Ales were already heavily hopped, there was no real difference with the Stock Ale recipe. Presumably the only difference was how quickly the beer was sold.

William Younger Stock Ales 1851 - 1868

Year	Beer	OG	FG	ABV	App. Attenuation	lbs hops/ qtr	hops lb/brl
1851	S	1098	1027	9.39	72.45%	12.90	6.35
1851	XS	1109	1036	9.66	66.97%	11.61	9.00
1851	XXS	1126	1052	9.79	58.73%	12.00	9.00
1858	XS	1102	1032	9.26	68.63%	10.00	6.27
1858	XXS	1113	1036	10.19	68.14%	9.76	6.25
1859	XXXS	1128	1053	9.92	58.59%	9.78	7.26
1869	XXXX	1089	1021	9.00	76.40%	11.67	5.76
1868	S	1077	1032	5.95	58.44%	6.86	2.79
1868	XS Export	1092	1033	7.81	64.13%	6.82	3.70
1868	XXS	1102	1045	7.54	55.88%	4.91	3.25
1868	XXXS	1129	1066	8.33	48.84%	7.60	6.33

Sources: William Younger brewing records held at the Scottish Brewing Archive, document numbers WY/6/1/2/5, WY/6/1/2/14 and WY/6/1/2/21.

The hopping rate declined over time, though, admittedly, it did start at a ridiculously high level. Even in 1868, with 3 lbs or more per barrel, they weren't lightly hopped beers.

Over in London, Whitbread's Stock Ales couldn't quite match Younger's for strength, but they did keep up their hopping rate.

Whitbread Stock Ales 1851 - 1868							
Year	Beer	OG	FG	ABV	App. Atten- uation	lbs hops/ qtr	hops lb/brl
1851	KXX	1082.3	1030.5	6.85	62.96%	12.52	4.55
1851	KXXX	1090.9	1028.8	8.21	68.29%	12.50	5.25
1858	KXX	1080.3	1026.3	7.15	67.24%	16.92	6.25
1858	KXXX	1088.4	1030.5	7.66	65.52%	15.60	6.82
1868	KK	1075.1	1024.7	6.67	67.16%	14.73	5.37
1867	KKK	1082.3	1030.2	6.89	63.30%	14.47	5.60
Sources: Whitbread brewing records held at the London Metropolitan Archives, document numbers LMA/4453/D/01/014, LMA/4453/D/01/022, LMA/4453/D/01/023, LMA/4453/D/01/033 and LMA/4453/D/09/034.							

The weakest Younger Stock Ale, S, was roughly similar to Whitbread's KXXX in 1851. But a divergence in the hopping meant that by 1867, Whitbread's beer was hopped at about double the rate of Younger's.

You may see a pattern starting to emerge. One where hopping rates are starting to fall in Scotland after 1850, making Scottish differ more and more from equivalent English beers whose hopping rates remained either constant or only fell slightly.

Lager

The very first British Lager was brewed in Scotland. No, not by Tennent, but by the obscure Edinburgh brewer John Muir. Anton Dreher and Gabriel Sedlmayr spent time at Muir's brewery during their grand tour of British breweries in the 1840's. Muir and Sedlmayr remained in contact after the latter's return to Munich, and bottom-fermenting yeast was dispatched to Scotland.

Though Muir's bottom-fermenting beer proved popular, he had to abandon its production. After a while he was unable to maintain the culture and, not having easy access to Lager yeast, had to revert to top-fermenting.

Recipes

1847 William Younger T

Yet another Scottish recipe. But one there's a very good reason for. Albeit purely selfish.

I'm steaming through my new Scottish book. Not totally voluntarily. The thing has to be finished – at least a reasonable first draught – by the middle of March. Which isn't that far away. If I can keep up with this week's pace (10,000 words and counting so far) that shouldn't be a problem.

I already have most of the information I need. But there is the odd gap. One pretty glaring one was the lack of any recipes from the 1840's. I'm starting to put that right today.

The beer is a particular Scottish speciality, Table Beer. Down in London, there wasn't a huge amount of Table Beer brewed after 1830. Probably because it had disappeared as a tax category. Despite it being specifically against the law, I suspect much Table Beer was brewed to be mixed with Strong Beer. The latter was taxed at 10 shillings per barrel, four times the rate of Table Beer. By blending Strong and Table you could get yourself two barrels of full-strength stuff for 12s 6d tax rather than 20s.

In Scotland, in contrast, Table Beer was a serious product. As can be seen by the fact that not only was it exported to England, it also went overseas. A Dutch newspaper advertisement from 1881[27] includes not only the Strong Scotch Ales, IPAs and Stouts that you would expect, but also Table Beer. It sold for 12.50 guilders a kilderkin, the same as the weakest Porter in the list

Now there's one wee problem in recreating this beer. It wasn't brewed from barley malt, but from bigg, a primitive type of barley that could grow in harsher conditions. This around the end of the time bigg was still used in commercial brewing. In William Younger's 1847 records it turns up occasionally, mostly in weaker beers such as 60/-, 80/- and, as here, Table Beer. I've substituted mild malt.

Goldings should be right for the hips. The log lists them as East Kent and Farnham. So definitely types of whitebine. Even knocking down the hopping rate a little to take into account the age of the hops, it still comes out with a very respectable calculated 35 IBU.

All in all, it's a nice, light drinking beer. Probably, as the name implies, perfect for accompanying your supper.

---

[27] "Het Nieuws van den Dag", 23rd May 1881.

1847 William Younger T		
mild malt	7.50 lb	100.00%
Goldings 90 min	1.25 oz	
Goldings 30 min	1.25 oz	
OG	1033	
FG	1010	
ABV	3.04	
Apparent attenuation	69.70%	
IBU	35	
SRM	4	
Mash at	150° F	
Sparge at	184° F	
Boil time	90 minutes	
pitching temp	58° F	
Yeast	WLP028 Edinburgh Ale	

1868 William Younger T Table Beer

Table Beer continued to popular in the second half of the 19th century both in Scotland and in export markets. At a time when London brewers had mostly abandoned the style.

Despite the extremely simple grist, this beer presents a major problem when trying to write a recipe. It's all to do with the hopping. Because almost two-thirds of those used were spent hops. Converting them to a quantity of fresh hops isn't just problematic, it's never likely to match 100% with the original.

My solution was to reduce the quantity of hops by about a third. Which may not be enough. If you have any hops you've just fished out of another brew, you could try 1 oz. fresh Saaz and 2 oz. of spent hops.

In this case the FG is probably about correct.

1868 William Younger T Table Beer		
pale malt	7.25 lb	100.00%
Saaz 90 min	2.00 oz	
OG	1031	
FG	1010	
ABV	2.78	
Apparent attenuation	67.74%	
IBU	27	
SRM	4	
Mash at	154° F	
Sparge at	185° F	
Boil time	120 minutes	
pitching temp	60° F	
Yeast	WLP028 Edinburgh Ale	

1851 William Younger X Mild Ale

Deciding what does and doesn't count as a Mild Ale in Scotland can be difficult. Unless the brewer was helpful enough to actually call the beer Mild.

Especially when, as at William Younger, the same brew would receive a Shilling or X designation depending on how it was packaged. One batch could magically become both 60/- and X at racking time. Anything filled into hogsheads and intended for bottling had a Shilling name, while what went into barrels for sale on draught had an X name.

There's not much to say about the recipe, it being just pale malt and Goldings. One salient point about the process should be mentioned: the short boil. Contemporary London X Ales were very similar in other respects – OG and hopping rate – but had longer boils. In the case of Whitbread, the difference was just 15 minutes, but Barclay Perkins boiled their X Ale for a whopping 3 hours.

The true level of attenuation would have been higher, 1029º being the cleansing rather than racking gravity. I'd guess that the actual FG was 1020-1025º.

1851 William Younger X Mild Ale		
pale malt	16.75 lb	100.00%
Goldings 75 min	3.50 oz	
Goldings 30 min	3.50 oz	
OG	1072	
FG	1029	
ABV	5.69	
Apparent attenuation	59.72%	
IBU	92	
SRM	6	
Mash at	153º F	
Sparge at	184º F	
Boil time	75 minutes	
pitching temp	57º F	
Yeast	WLP028 Edinburgh Ale	

1868 William Younger XXX Mild Ale

As in England, there was a downward trend in gravities during the second half of the 19th century, especially for Mild Ales.

Which explains why the 1868 version of XXX was weaker than the X of 1851. But an even bigger transformation was the source of the raw materials. All the hops and half of the malt (or at least the barley the malt was made from) came from abroad. While back in 1851 all the hops had been English and the malt Scottish.

After 1850, enormous quantities of foreign hops were imported and often accounted for 25-50% of the hops used in the UK. The USA provided the greatest quantity, but the hops themselves weren't highly rated by British brewers, who didn't like their flavour. Top-quality central European hops like Saaz, Hallertau or Spalt were much better regarded. Using Saaz as dry hops, as in this beer, tells you how high quality they were considered.

Other changes from 1851 included a much longer boil and a reduced level of hopping. Though, at over 50 IBU (calculated) it's far hoppier than you'd expect of a current Mild Ale.

Once again, the FG is a cleansing gravity. I'd estimate the true FG to be 1020-1024º.

1868 William Younger XXX Mild Ale		
pale malt	15.75 lb	100.00%
Poperinge 90 min	1.00 oz	
Saaz 90 min	1.00 oz	
Saaz 60 min	2.00 oz	
Saaz 20 min	2.00 oz	
Saaz dry hops	0.75 oz	
OG	1068	
FG	1028	
ABV	5.29	
Apparent attenuation	58.82%	
IBU	58	
SRM	6	
Mash at	154º F	
Sparge at	185º F	
Boil time	120 minutes	
pitching temp	60º F	
Yeast	WLP028 Edinburgh Ale	

1879 William Younger XX

Though it was never a huge part of their business, William Younger brewed draught Mild Ales right through the 19th century and even into the 1950's. Most Scottish brewers had abandoned the style after WW I.

By this point, Younger's Milds were weaker than the equivalent London X Ale. In 1879, Whitbread X Ale had an OG of 1062°[28] and in 1880 Barclay Perkins XX Ale was 1079.5°[29]. I've no idea why this should have happened. Though the Mild Ales of London were famous for being strong.

It's difficult to read the brewing record, but it lists two different types of pale malt. My guess is that one was from UK barley and the other imported barley. At this date it would be unusual if all the malt had been made from British barley. The UK's agriculture just couldn't keep up with the brewing industry's demand for raw materials.

British agriculture's shortcomings are revealed by the presence of American hops, some of which are referred to as "American" and others "Californian'. My guess is that the former refers to East Coast hops, probably from New York State. It's fairly well hopped for a moderate strength Mild.

1879 William Younger XX		
pale malt	12.00 lb	100.00%
Cluster 90 min	1.00 oz	
Fuggles 90 min	1.00 oz	
Goldings 60 min	1.00 oz	
Goldings 30 min	1.00 oz	
Goldings dry hops	0.75 oz	
OG	1052	
FG	1019	
ABV	4.37	
Apparent attenuation	63.46%	
IBU	62	
SRM	5	
Mash at	150° F	
Sparge at	170° F	
Boil time	90 minutes	
pitching temp	59° F	
Yeast	WLP028 Edinburgh Ale	

---

[28] Whitbread brewing record held at the London Metropolitan Archives, document number LMA/4453/D/09/045.
[29] Barclay Perkins brewing record held at the London Metropolitan Archives, document number ACC/2305/01/579.

1847 William Younger 60/-

I thought I'd treat you with another early William Younger beer. A very different type of 60/- Ale.

By different, I mean different from the post-WW II beer of the same name. As I've already told you 7 gazillion times, the 60/- and 80/- of the 19th century were essentially types of Mild Ale. While the late 20th-century versions were all Pale Ales. Though, just to make things extra confusing, by colouring 60/- with caramel, it performed a passing imitation of Dark Mild.

There's a huge difference in strength between the 60/- Ales of the two eras. After WW II, the style wasn't much over 1030º and barely 3% ABV. The version from the 1840's was about double the OG, though a pretty crappy degree of attenuation leaves the ABV at not much over 4%. Or so it seems.

While writing my new Scotland book, I've been investigating exactly how William Younger fermented. In the 1870's, they were using something like the dropping system, with the fermentation starting in rounds and then, after six or seven days, dropped into square vessels. Younger's records only record the phase. In the two or three days the beer was cleansing there would have been further fermentation. So the real FG would have been lower.

Looking at analyses I have from the 19th century of Scottish beers as sold, the degree of attenuation is higher than what I see in brewing records. Many examples from the 1870's and 1880's have apparent attenuation of over 80%. My guess is that the real degree of apparent attenuation would have been at least 65%

Before 1880, most of William Younger's beers were all malt. It containing sugar, this is quite unusual. The year is no coincidence. 1847 was the year sugar was allowed in addition to malt. Doubtless Younger was just experimenting with its use. I've seen the same in London records from 1847. Most breweries soon abandoned sugar again and its use did really pick up until the 1870's.

The hops were all English, mostly East Kent but some unspecified. I've gone for sure bet Goldings.

1847 William Younger 60/-		
pale malt	10.25 lb	83.67%
table sugar	2.00 lb	16.33%
Goldings 90 min	1.50 oz	
Goldings 30 min	1.00 oz	
OG	1061	
FG	1028	
ABV	4.37	
Apparent attenuation	54.10%	
IBU	30	
SRM	5	
Mash at	150° F	
Sparge at	184° F	
Boil time	90 minutes	
pitching temp	58° F	
Yeast	WLP028 Edinburgh Ale	

1847 William Younger 100/-

In the late 1840's Younger was brewing Table Beer, a bit of Pale and Stock Ale, and bucket-loads of Shilling Ales.

They varied hugely in strength, from 42/- at 1043º to 160/- at 1134º. The main difference between the beers at the top and bottom end. Up to 60/- was hopped at 4lbs per quarter of malt, 120/- upwards at 8-9 lbs. The two beers inbetween, 80/- and 100/-, seem to have been made in two variations. One with the higher level of hopping and one with the lower. This example is of the latter kind.

In English terms, this would be a strong Mild Ale that was a little light on the hops. 100% pale malt, as almost everything was at this point, and a few quality English hops. A London Mild of this strength would have contained about double the hops.

1847 William Younger 100/-		
pale malt	20.25 lb	100.00%
Goldings 70 min	1.75 oz	
Goldings 30 min	1.50 oz	
OG	1090	
FG	1040	
ABV	6.61	
Apparent attenuation	55.56%	
IBU	30	
SRM	8	
Mash at	151º F	
Sparge at	184º F	
Boil time	70 minutes	
pitching temp	56º F	
Yeast	WLP028 Edinburgh Ale	

1851 William Younger 120/-

In the middle of the 19th century, the higher number Shilling Ales had daunting gravities. 100/- and upwards all had gravities over 1100º. The Scots certainly like their beer strong back then.

The Shilling Ales seem to have been mostly destined for local consumption. Pale Ale, Stout, Table Beer and the occasional super-strong Ale were Scotland's main exports. The bulk of the Shilling Ales weren't going far. Probably no further South than Sunderland.

The main features of this iteration of 120/- are the short boil and fairly heavy hopping. Though, given the very high OG, it's by no means excessive. The short boil is slightly surprising, given that this was brewed single-gyle.

It's strange how many of William Younger's very strong beers were brewed that way. Normal practice would have been to brew something of that gravity in a parti-gyle with a weaker beer. In Younger's context, something like 50/- or 60/-.

It's not total clear what the source of the malt was for this brew. There were 21 quarters of "Com" and 10 quarters of "Ch". I suspect the former was malt bought in from maltsters, while the latter was malt they made themselves. Or maybe the other way around. But it does look as if, just like with the hops, that it was all sourced from the UK.

1851 William Younger 120/-		
pale malt	27.50 lb	100.00%
Goldings 75 min	4.00 oz	
Goldings 50 min	2.00 oz	
Goldings 20 min	2.00 oz	
OG	1118	
FG	1047	
ABV	9.39	
Apparent attenuation	60.17%	
IBU	72	
SRM	8	
Mash at	154° F	
Sparge at	184° F	
Boil time	75 minutes	
pitching temp	55° F	
Yeast	WLP028 Edinburgh Ale	

1851 William Younger 140/-

Finally, a beer of the type that made Scottish brewing famous: Scotch ale. And one that's really that, not some modern geek's guess at what it should be.

A characteristic of Scotch Ale (or Edinburgh Ale) that is often mentioned is its lovely pale colour. Not what people expect of a strong Scotch Ale nowadays, which would invariably be dark. But the dark colour is a much more recent development, achieved by the simple means of caramel. I don't think I've ever seen any dark malts in a real Scotch Ale, i.e. one actually brewed in Scotland.

It took me a long while to work out what Scotch Ale was. The strength distracted me. But it's now clear: most is a sort of Mild Ale. A very strong Mild Ale, but one nonetheless. Why am I so confident of that? Because of its secondary conditioning. Strong Shilling Ales were filled into hogsheads and half hogsheads and immediately delivered to customers, who after a short period bottled it and it was ready for consumption. An Ale that was sold young? That's Mild Ale in my book*.

It's not the world's most complicated recipe: pale malt and Goldings. But that's the recipe of some of my favourite recreations, like 1832 Truman XXXX. You might be surprised at the IBU level. I am, too. I'd have expected it to be higher. "Didn't Scottish brewers use very few hops?" I hear you ask. No, they didn't. The often used several imperial shitloads. And whatever you do, don't put any fucking smoked malt in this. Not unless you want me coming around your house and putting all the windows in.

That's all I have to say. Here's the recipe. And remember what I said about smoked malt . . . . .

1851 William Younger 140/-		
pale malt	30.00 lb	100.00%
Goldings 70 min	5.00 oz	
Goldings 50 min	3.00 oz	
Goldings 20 min	3.00 oz	
OG	1129	
FG	1054	
ABV	9.92	
Apparent attenuation	58.14%	
IBU	84	
SRM	9	
Mash at	155º F	
Sparge at	184º F	
Boil time	70 minutes	
pitching temp	55º F	
Yeast	WLP028 Edinburgh Ale	

Mini Book Series volume XXVIII: Scotland! FG

1868 William Younger 80/-

Don't get confused by the name. 80/- of the 1860's was a totally different style of beer to what it is today.

The lower end of the Shilling Ales were effectively sorts of Mild Ale. That is, moderately-hopped beers that were sold young. In the case of Shilling Ales, that was usually in bottled form. That's given away by the casks into which it was racked. This particular brew was packaged into 8 hogshead, 34 half hogshead and 10 quarter hogsheads. These were bottler's rather than pub casks. Draught beer was mostly packaged in barrels and kilderkins.

There are a couple of odd features of this beer. A quarter of the hops were spent hops from another brew. I've greatly reduced the hopping to account for that. On the other hand, it's very heavily dry-hopped. Which is unusual for a weaker Shilling Ale.

The original fermentation was pretty short. It was brewed on 5th September and racked on the 10th. I'm not convinced that the gravity was fully tracked in the fermentation record. My guess for the true FG would be more like 1025º.

There's an interesting note at the bottom of the page saying that the 6th September was a particularly hot day with the temperature hitting 80º F. Which demonstrates the power of attemperators, as the fermentation profiles look the same as in cooler weather.

1868 William Younger 80/-		
pale malt	15.75 lb	100.00%
Goldings 90 min	2.00 oz	
Goldings dry hops	1.25 oz	
OG	1068	
FG	1030	
ABV	5.03	
Apparent attenuation	55.88%	
IBU	29	
SRM	6	
Mash at	154º F	
Sparge at	185º F	
Boil time	120 minutes	
pitching temp	60º F	
Yeast	WLP028 Edinburgh Ale	

1879 William Younger 50/-

The Scots brewed to a much larger range of gravities than English brewers. From super strong to super watery.

You might have found beers with gravities as low as 1040º in the English countryside, but not in London. A small provincial brewery wouldn't have been brewing stuff at Imperial strength as well. Younger spanned the both. From the modestly-strengthed drinking Ales of the sticks, to the headiest beers of the capital.

At the lower end of the Shilling Ales, this would have been considered a Table Beer. More of a refreshment than an intoxicant. It's a very straightforward beer, with a reasonable bitterness for its strength.

1879 William Younger 50/-		
pale malt	8.25 lb	100.00%
Cluster 90 min	1.00 oz	
Goldings 20 min	1.00 oz	
Goldings dry hops	0.75 oz	
OG	1036	
FG	1007	
ABV	3.84	
Apparent attenuation	80.56%	
IBU	35	
SRM	4	
Mash at	154º F	
Sparge at	170º F	
Boil time	105 minutes	
pitching temp	59º F	
Yeast	WLP028 Edinburgh Ale	

1879 William Younger 160/-

Here's the top of the range Shilling Ale from William Younger, so you can compare and contrast it with their No. 1 Ale.

Obviously, this being 19th-century Scotland, the recipe isn't very complicated. Just pale malt and a load of hops. Strange how they used so many hops, despite them not growing in Scotland. (That's irony, by the way.) It's not quite as heavily hopped as No. 1. But it's still stuffed with hops.

The biggest differences I can see with No. 1 is the degree of attenuation (lower) and the dry hopping rate (much lower). It's not a massive difference. Then again, I struggle to understand why Younger brewed more than 20 different beers, many that look extremely similar to each other. They've easily the largest beer range of any brewery that I've studied. And not just part-gyled from the same worts. Most of Younger's beers were brewed single gyle.

The combination of heavy hopping and high FG must have resulted in a thick, bittersweet beer. I did brew one of the weaker Shilling Ales recently. It turned out really, really nice. I brewed it SMaSH: just pale malt and lots of Goldings. It had the wonderfully hoppiness that you get from huge quantities of Goldings.

Shilling Ales were meant to be drunk young. Which makes sense, as they are really a form of Mild Ale. Which means the FG in the log must have been pretty close to the FG when the beer hit drinkers' lips.

1879 William Younger 160/-		
pale malt	25.25 lb	100.00%
Cluster 90 min	3.50 oz	
Cluster 60 min	3.50 oz	
Cluster 30 min	1.75 oz	
Goldings 30 min	1.75 oz	
Goldings dry hops	0.18 oz	
OG	1109	
FG	1049.5	
ABV	7.87	
Apparent attenuation	54.59%	
IBU	132	
SRM	8	
Mash at	158° F	
Sparge at	161° F	
Boil time	90 minutes	
pitching temp	55° F	
Yeast	WLP028 Edinburgh Ale	

1851 William Younger DBS Stout

Like my life in general, the blog is hostage to my frantic attempts to finish the Scottish book.

I spent today extracting mashing details and boiling times. What everyone dreams of doing on their day off. Which is what today was for me. My 90% day.

Spent staring at brewing records. The most difficult bit. Exactly why the mashing stuff wasn't in my standard spreadsheet. Too difficult to neatly record. That said, today's big revelation came from doing exactly that. Lumping together information in a table. Thank you data.

As important as carving data into edible form is throwing together as many recipes as possible for the book. Noticing the early period was poorly represented, I jumped on this mid-19th-century Stout from William Younger.

The classic pale, brown, black malt combination is complimented by a shitload of hops. The attenuation is surprisingly high for something Scottish.

Have to get back to watching the TV with Dolores. Longish boil, quite warm fermentation. In my book I'll be going into ball-crushing detail about fermentation temperatures.

OK Dolores. I'm, done.

1851 William Younger DBS Stout		
pale malt	13.75 lb	71.43%
brown malt	3.75 lb	19.48%
black malt	1.75 lb	9.09%
Goldings 90 min	4.00 oz	
Goldings 60 min	4.00 oz	
Goldings 30 min	4.00 oz	
OG	1078	
FG	1015	
ABV	8.33	
Apparent attenuation	80.77%	
IBU	139	
SRM	50	
Mash at	150° F	
Sparge at	184° F	
Boil time	120 minutes	
pitching temp	64° F	
Yeast	WLP028 Edinburgh Ale	

1868 William Younger DBS

Time for another Scottish recipe. Especially as I forgot to post a recipe last week. Apologies for that. A pure oversight on my part. Though the extra Saturday recipes I threw in mean I've still averaged more than one a week so far.

Though Scottish brewers all made Porter and Stout, it was never as important a product as for many of their English colleagues. Especially those in London. William Younger had three: Porter, Bottling Porter and DBS. The first two were both pretty weak, 1041º and 1046º, respectively. All three were brewed in small quantities, far less than most of their Scottish Ales, Strong Ales and Pale Ales.

I assume this was for a combination of factors. A limited market in Scotland for Stout. But also what they could sell in export markets. Scottish brewers were famous for Strong Ales and Pale Ales and these were what they sold to England and beyond. While in these markets London and Irish brewers controlled the Stout trade.

The grist is very different to a London Stout. There's no brown malt, something that appeared in every London Porter and Stout from the 18th century to the 1970's. But there is amber malt, something you mostly only saw in the better quality London Stouts. Whereas Irish Stouts were usually just pale and black malt.

Younger DBS is also weaker than London Stouts of the period. Truman's weakest Stout, Running Stout, had an OG of 1070º. Whitbread's, SS, an OG of 1082º. Barclay Perkins BSt 1089º.

But there's one thing that makes this brew very special. It also appears in the personal brewing book of Carl Jacobsen, son of Carlsberg's founder. A couple of years later he was brewing his own beer called DBS back in Copenhagen. With an OG of 1077º, his was a bit stronger than Younger's. And the grist was a little different:

    2 pale
    9 amber
    1 patent
    3 brown

Quaint that Jacobsen still listed the grain quantity in Imperial quarters. I was more shocked to see that even in 1932 Carlsberg Porter, the successor to DBS, still contained 21% brown malt. Who would have expected that?

Nothing left but the recipe itself . . .

1868 William Younger DBS		
pale malt	12.25 lb	81.67%
amber malt	1.75 lb	11.67%
black malt	1.00 lb	6.67%
Poperinge 90 min	2.75 oz	
Goldings 60 min	2.50 oz	
Saaz 20 min	2.50 oz	
OG	1062	
FG	1014	
ABV	6.35	
Apparent attenuation	77.42%	
IBU	85	
SRM	31	
Mash at	150° F	
Sparge at	185° F	
Boil time	120 minutes	
pitching temp	62° F	
Yeast	WLP028 Edinburgh Ale	

1869 William Younger BS Porter

Porter, the big beer hit of the 18th century, didn't take long to spread from London, first to other parts of England and then north of the border into Scotland.

Initially it was all imported. A poem published in a newspaper in 1774, bemoaned the money Scots wasted importing Porter from England: "Why drain our cash be-south the Tweed?" Local brewers took heed and picked up the style.

Stout was popular in Scotland right through into the 20th century, but standard-strength Porter never took hold like it did in England. By the middle of the 19th century, little of it was brewed. Making this a rare Scottish example of the style.

Most striking is the very low gravity for the 19th century. A good bit lower than in England. For example, in 1879, Whitbread's Porter had an OG of 1050.9^{30}. The grist is odd, too. There's a surprisingly high percentage of amber malt. There's so much that I suspect it must have been diastatic. A London Porter of this period might have contained a little amber malt, but would certainly have contained brown malt.

The hopping is very tricky on this one. All of the hops were second-hand, having already been used once in another brew. I've greatly reduced the quantity to take that into account. Though whether that's really the same is open to debate. If they have them to hand, you could try using 3 oz. of spent hops instead.

1869 William Younger BS Porter		
pale malt	4.50 lb	45.00%
amber malt	4.25 lb	42.50%
black malt	1.25 lb	12.50%
Goldings 90 min	1.25 oz	
OG	1041	
FG	1017	
ABV	3.18	
Apparent attenuation	58.54%	
IBU	22	
SRM	36	
Mash at	150° F	
Sparge at	185° F	
Boil time	120 minutes	
pitching temp	61° F	
Yeast	WLP028 Edinburgh Ale	

---

[30] Whitbread brewing record held at the London Metropolitan Archives, document number LMA/4453/D/09/063.

1849 William Younger Export

It's odd how names come around again. Younger's Export was an early Scottish Pale Ale and a century later the term would again be used for a strong Pale Ale

Just for the record, Export was probably considered an IPA in the day. But I'm going to refer to it as a Pale Ale, as I can't be bothered to differentiate between the two. It saps my power, man.

Like all early Pale Ales it's just a stack of pale malt and truckloads of top-quality English hops. The short boil could be an attempt to keep the colour as pale as possible. Or just because Younger preferred short boils. Some of their beers had even shorter boils.

The dry hops are my guess. It could even have been more.

1849 William Younger Export		
pale malt	14.00 lb	100.00%
Goldings 80 min	6.00 oz	
Goldings 30 min	5.00 oz	
Goldings dry hops	0.50 oz	
OG	1062	
FG	1015	
ABV	6.22	
Apparent attenuation	75.81%	
IBU	126	
SRM	6	
Mash at	152° F	
Sparge at	184° F	
Boil time	80 minutes	
pitching temp	56° F	
Yeast	WLP028 Edinburgh Ale	

1851 William Younger XP

Edinburgh brewers jumped onto the Pale Ale train early. Something that was to serve them well in export markets.

William Younger was no exception, and one of their classic IPAs was XP, a beer that was brewed for a century. Not quite as long as its big brother XXP, but still a very decent run.

What makes this an IPA? The fact that at this early date in the IPA tale, there wasn't a separate thing called Pale Ale. The two term both related to the same thing. The classic Bass IPA, for example, was always officially called simply Pale Ale. Things only get confused later in the century when all sorts of weaker versions of Pale Ale appeared.

In the early days, Scottish Pale Ales were hopped as heavily as anywhere in England. As XP nobly demonstrates. That's a lot of hops for a beer of this strength. I've not included dry hops in the recipe because they aren't recorded in the brewing record. My guess would be 0.5-0.75 oz.

Don't feel obliged to stick to that FG. 1015º is probably more realistic for the real end gravity.

1851 William Younger XP			
pale malt	13.50 lb	100.00%	13.50 lb
Goldings 75 min	4.50 oz		
Goldings 45 min	4.50 oz		
Goldings 30 min	4.50 oz		
OG	1058		
FG	1020		
ABV	5.03		
Apparent attenuation	65.52%		
IBU	180		
SRM	5		
Mash at	153º F		
Sparge at	184º F		
Boil time	75 minutes		
pitching temp	57º F		
Yeast	WLP028 Edinburgh Ale		

1858 William Younger Ex Pale Ale

Here's something doubtless more in tune with modern tastes: a hoppy Pale Ale.

Is it a Pale Ale or an IPA? No effing idea. It's not even a sensible question for an 1850's beer. There wasn't really much of a consistent demarcation between the two. All I can say is that this looks pretty close to a beer like Bass Pale Ale, the classic English IPA.

Younger's used pretty much an identical mashing schemes for all their beers, with the exception of their Stouts which had lower mashing temperatures. Their Pale Ales were mashed just the same way as their Scottish Ales.

I'm really struggling for much to say about this beer. Other than that it was pale and hoppy. Very hoppy. Loads of Goldings in the boil and loads more as dry hops. Leaving an impressive IBU count of 142. And that's using BeerSmith's default of 5% alpha acid content. Most of the old analyses of Goldings show over 6% alpha.

This looks like a Stock Pale Ale, meaning a long secondary conditioning is appropriate. Anything from 3 to 12 months. If you're the patient sort. And the real FG would have been lower. These export beers usually had 80% plus attenuation.

Me done. Recipe. Off for a walk now . . .

1858 William Younger Ex Pale Ale		
pale malt	14.75 lb	100.00%
Goldings 90 min	4.00 oz	
Goldings 60 min	4.00 oz	
Goldings 20 min	4.00 oz	
Goldings dry hops	2.50 oz	
OG	1063	
FG	1016	
ABV	6.22	
Apparent attenuation	74.60%	
IBU	142	
SRM	5	
Mash at	154° F	
Sparge at	185° F	
Boil time	120 minutes	
pitching temp	61° F	
Yeast	WLP028 Edinburgh Ale	

1865 William Younger Ext

Here's a special treat. A beer from the William Younger brewing record I hadn't really looked at.

Younger had two breweries pretty much door to door to each other. Their original Abbey Brewery and the newer Holyrood Brewery. Each had its own brewing book. I've mostly stuck to the Abbey Brewery's records, but do have photos of two Holyrood logs.

There's a logic behind my decision. Holyrood was mostly a Pale Ale brewery. There are pages and pages of XP and XXP, with the occasional other beer. But it doesn't look like they brewed anything close to the full set there. While at Abbey they brewed XP and XXP alongside their Shilling Ales, Stouts and Strong Ales. In other words, the full set. Or so I thought.

Giving the 1865 Holyrood book the once over, I spotted a beer that wasn't in the Abbey records from that period: Ext. Which I'm pretty sure stands for Export. A Strong Pale Ale that they were still brewing in 1949, almost 100 years later.

Do you know what this beer looks like to me? A classic Burton Pale Ale. An OG in the mid-1060's and lots and lots of hops. And a pretty high degree of attenuation for Younger. They mostly struggled to hit 65%, but this is over 75%.

The recipe is just pale malt and hops. A combination of US, Bavarian and Kent hops. With a huge amount of dry hops. There are some 20th-century Younger recipes that use fewer kettle hops than this beer has in dry hops. What a wacky place the 19th century was.

It wouldn't surprise me if this beer was aged for months before sale. The hopping – especially all those dry hops – indicates to me a beer that wasn't going to be drunk quickly. Meaning the FG, when drunk, would have been lower and the ABV higher, possibly by as much as 1-1.5%.

1865 William Younger Ext		
pale malt	14.75 lb	100.00%
Cluster 90 min	2.75 oz	
Goldings 60 min	3.00 oz	
Goldings 30 min	2.00 oz	
Spalt 30 min	1.50 oz	
Goldings dry hops	2.00 oz	
OG	1064	
FG	1015	
ABV	6.48	
Apparent attenuation	76.56%	
IBU	132	
SRM	5	
Mash at	152° F	
Sparge at	185° F	
Boil time	90 minutes	
pitching temp	59° F	
Yeast	WLP028 Edinburgh Ale	

1851 William Younger XXS Stock Ale

In the early part of the 19th century, William Younger brewed a crazy number of crazily strong beers. They had half a dozen beers with gravities over 1100º in their range. That XXS was neither the strongest nor the most heavily hopped of the set tells you a lot.

One unusual feature of William Younger's brewing methods is that they didn't much go in for parti-gyling. While this isn't so odd in the case of standard-strength beers like Pale Ale or the weaker Milds, it's very unusual to brew super high-gravity beers like this single gyle. For a simple reason: it wasn't very economical.

The method most breweries employed to produce very strong beers was to parti-gyle them with something much weaker. The strong beer would get all first wort and the weaker beer a blend of first and later worts. When brewing something strong single-gyle, either you'd need to boil the buggery out of the later worts to make them stronger, or you'd waste some extract.

Given this beer had a very short boil, the first of those wasn't an option. Which begs the question: where did the weaker worts go? I don't believe for a minute that they'd just throw away extract. Perhaps they used them as return worst. That is, they'd use the wort to mash another brew.

Not only is this beer very high gravity, it's also hopped like mad.

This being a Stock Ale, it would have undergone an extensive maturation, probably in vats. Whether it took place in vats or in trade casks, one thing would have remained the same: the action of Brettanomyces. The secondary fermentation the beer underwent while ageing would have been accomplished by Brettanomyces slowly eating away less fermentable sugars, drying the beer out and producing the highly-valued, vinous aged character.

I'd recommend ageing this at least six months with Brettanomyces. By which time the FG should be down in the 1020's.

1851 William Younger XXS Stock Ale		
pale malt	24.25 lb	100.00%
Goldings 70 min	6.00 oz	
Goldings 50 min	6.00 oz	
Goldings 20 min	6.00 oz	
OG	1125	
FG	1050	
ABV	9.92	
Apparent attenuation	60.00%	
IBU	137	
SRM	9	
Mash at	154° F	
Sparge at	184° F	
Boil time	70 minutes	
pitching temp	55° F	
Yeast	WLPC28 Edinburgh Ale	

1868 William Younger XS Export Stock Ale

A couple of decades later and Younger's Stock Ales were still powerful beasts, capable of taking down the strongest man or woman.

In line with general trends, there are now foreign hops in addition to those from England. The ones given in the recipe as Strisselspalt are from the Alsace, which at the time was part of France. A couple of years later it was annexed by the new German state. The change in ownership doesn't appear to have troubled British brewers, who continued to buy hops from the region.

The rate of hopping for all Younger's Stock Ales had fallen quite a bit since the early 1850's, unlike the gravities, which had remained the same. The hopping rate per quarter of malt, which was 14-18 lbs in 1851, was down to 6-9lbs in 1868.

As with all Stock Ales, you really need to age it with Brettanomyces for at least six months. Longer, if you're the patient type. The FG looks about correct for the end of primary fermentation. After proper ageing, it should end up at around 1020º.

1868 William Younger XS Export Stock Ale		
pale malt	21.50 lb	100.00%
Strisselspalt 90 min	1.25 oz	
Goldings 60 min	2.50 oz	
Goldings 40 min	2.50 oz	
Saaz 20 min	1.75 oz	
Goldings dry hops	0.75 oz	
OG	1092	
FG	1033	
ABV	7.81	
Apparent attenuation	64.13%	
IBU	73	
SRM	8	
Mash at	154º F	
Sparge at	185º F	
Boil time	90 minutes	
pitching temp	56º F	
Yeast	WLP028 Edinburgh Ale	

1879 William Younger No. 1

Someone commented the other day that they were disappointed Scotland! contained no recipes. He has a point. One which I've been addressing.

You may have noticed the odd Scottish recipe appearing in amongst those for Mild or from the 1950's. That's because I've been working on three books simultaneously: the new edition of Mild!, Victory! and Scotland! vol. II.

So far I've written 60 new Scottish recipes. Nothing nearly like enough. I'm aiming for at least 200. I hope that they'l open people's eyes to the real nature of Scottish beer. No long boils, normal fermentation temperatures and roast barley nowhere to be seen. And plenty of hops.

Younger's No. 1 is a good example. With its three imperial shitloads of hops and ridiculously low degree of attenuation, it's typical of strong Scottish beers of the 19th century. William Younger brewed a crazy number of crazily high-gravity beers. They had two parallel ranges of Strong Ales, one with shilling designations, the other numbered. The numbered range seem to have been inspired by the Strong Ales of Burton-on-Trent.

These are the two sets:

| William Youngers Strong Ales in 1879 ||
beer	OG
100/-	1070
120/-	1083
140/-	1096
160/-	1109
1	1098
2	1084
3	1074
Source: William Younger's brewing record held at the Scottish Brewing Archive, document number WY/6/1/2/28.	

I love the simplicity of Younger's recipes from this period: pale malt and loads of hops. The majority from the US, but some Kent hops, too. Not much more I can say, really.

I imagine the biggest challenge for you will be getting an FG that high. Though in the case of the numbered beers, the FG in the log may not be the real FG. In the case of the Shilling Ales, which were shipped in hogsheads for immediate bottling and rapid consumption, the FG probably is about right. While the numbered Ales might have been aged before sale. I simply don't know.

1879 William Younger No. 1		
pale malt	22.75 lb	100.00%
Cluster 90 min	3.75 oz	
Cluster 60 min	3.75 oz	
Goldings 30 min	2.50 oz	
Goldings dry hops	1.50 oz	
OG	1098	
FG	1040	
ABV	7.67	
Apparent attenuation	59.18%	
IBU	136	
SRM	7	
Mash at	156° F	
Sparge at	165° F	
Boil time	90 minutes	
pitching temp	57° F	
Yeast	WLP028 Edinburgh Ale	

1879 William Younger No. 2

Of Younger's four numbered ales, No. 1 and No. 3 had the most legs, stretching past WW II. No.2 didn't quite manage such a long run, being discontinued during WW I.

It's another very simple recipe. It includes two types of pale malt. That's about all I can say about the malt, as the description is an unreadable squiggle. If you were to hold a gun to my head, I'd guess that some was from foreign barley.

The hops are listed as Spalt, American, Californian and Kent. The quantity of Spalt, however, is so small that I've combined it with the Goldings. As in the recipe below, the bulk of the hops were from the USA.

Lasting 8 days, the fermentation was longer than most at Younger. Fairly warm, too, as most of it was in the high 60's F.

The finished beer looks to be very pale and very bitter. It probably tastes like a modern DIPA.

1879 William Younger No. 2		
pale malt	19.50 lb	100.00%
Cluster 90 min	3.50 oz	
Cluster 60 min	3.50 oz	
Goldings 30 min	1.75 oz	
Goldings dry hops	1.50 oz	
OG	1084	
FG	1035	
ABV	6.48	
Apparent attenuation	58.33%	
IBU	135	
SRM	6	
Mash at	156° F	
Sparge at	165° F	
Boil time	90 minutes	
pitching temp	55° F	
Yeast	WLP023 Edinburgh Ale	

1868 William Younger No. 4 Ale Export

When William Younger first introduced their numbered Ales, they went from No. 1, the strongest, to No. 4. The baby of the bunch didn't last that long. A decade after this beer was brewed, it had disappeared.

A feature of some Younger beers of this period is the complete absence of local ingredients, other than water and yeast. The malt is simply listed as "foreign", while the hops are described as "Bohemian" and "Saaz".

No. 4 is very heavily hopped with good quality, low alpha hops. Something which can have a magical effect. There's also extremely heavy dry hopping. All those factors taken together imply that this beer might well have been allowed to age for a while before sale. I'd go for 3 to 6 months. Not too long, as it doesn't really have the gravity to spend years maturing.

1868 William Younger No. 4 Ale Export		
pale malt	15.75 lb	100.00%
Saaz 90 min	3.00 oz	
Saaz 60 min	3.50 oz	
Saaz 20 min	3.00 oz	
Saaz dry hops	2.50 oz	
OG	1068	
FG	1022	
ABV	6.09	
Apparent attenuation	67.65%	
IBU	84	
SRM	6	
Mash at	154° F	
Sparge at	185° F	
Boil time	120 minutes	
pitching temp	59° F	
Yeast	WLP028 Edinburgh Ale	

1868 William Younger No. 3 Ale Export

Of all William Younger's numbered Strong Ales, No. 3 has proved the most resilient. It's the only one to make it into the 21st century.

This new set of Strong Ales was presumably inspired by those from Burton. Several Burton brewers produced a range of numbered beers. Exactly why Younger suddenly introduced them is a bit of a mystery as they already had high-gravity Shilling Ales and Stock Ales. It's hard to work out exactly what the differences were between all these beers.

For once, there's reasonably decent attenuation. Though, as this is an export beer, it probably underwent some ageing before sale. Not just during whatever journey it undertook, but before leaving the brewery, too. The heavy dry hopping is presumably to help it survive on its travels. The large quantity of copper hops, too.

20th-century versions of No. 3 would look very different.

1868 William Younger No. 3 Ale Export		
pale malt	18.00 lb	100.00%
Strisselspalt 90 min	5.00 oz	
Goldings 30 min	5.00 oz	
Saaz 20 min	1.00 oz	
Goldings dry hops	2.75 oz	
OG	1077	
FG	1022	
ABV	7.28	
Apparent attenuation	71.43%	
IBU	108	
SRM	6	
Mash at	154° F	
Sparge at	185° F	
Boil time	105 minutes	
pitching temp	58° F	
Yeast	WLP028 Edinburgh Ale	

1880 – 1914 Dropping your gravity pants

Introduction

Looking through brewing records for this period left me with one question: why was Scottish beer getting weaker than English beer?

I keep finding beer with gravities which would have been unthinkable in London: 1037º, 1031º. Really watery stuff, back then. The difference is reflected in the statistic. The average OG in Scotland was lower than in England. But you need to remember that a large amount of strong beer was being brewed for export in Scotland. The stuff being drunk locally was probably even weaker than the average OG.

| UK OG by country 1900 - 1914 ||||
Year	England	Scotland	Ireland	UK
1900	-	-	-	1054.93
1905	1052.54	1049.6	1063.49	1053.23
1910	1052.3	1048.48	1064.78	1053.2
1911	1052.03	1048.18	1065.22	1053.02
1912	1051.76	1048.11	1065.43	1052.72
1913	1051.52	1047.85	1065.73	1052.64
1914	1051.69	1047.67	1065.93	1052.80
Sources:				
Brewers' Journal 1920, page 345.				
Brewers' Journal 1921, page 246.				
Brewers' Almanack 1928, page 110.				

But why is that? Go back a couple of decades, and there's no difference in strength between London and Edinburgh beers. Could the new tax system have focused the minds of Scottish brewers?

By the outbreak of WW I, the difference in average OG between England and Scotland had grown to four points. That's equivalent to a difference of about 0.4% ABV. Which is significant. There was still a small difference in gravity between England and Scotland but by the 1930's that had completely disappeared.

Breweries

The 1890's were boom years for brewing in the UK. The large profits which were being made prompted many brewing businesses to bring in outside capital by becoming limited companies. Most had been partnerships until this point, though some, like William McEwan, had been held in sole ownership. McEwan, by the way, made a fortune from going public.

The great difference with England, where there was also a wave of breweries turning into limited companies, was how the money raised was used. In England, breweries used the cash to secure outlets by buying pubs. This didn't happen in Scotland. Breweries had far smaller tied estates than in England and most of the trade was, at least nominally, free. In practice, most pubs were tied to a brewery through loans.

There were huge profits to be made in the 1890's. As William McEwan showed. These were the dividends paid on the ordinary shares, which were all owned by directors of the company:

McEwan profits 1892 - 1896		
year	% dividend and bonus	amount
1892	15	£75,000
1894	20	£100,000
1895	25	£125,000
1896	30	£150,000
total		**£450,000**
Sources: Dundee Courier - Tuesday 2 August 1892, page 2. Aberdeen Journal - Thursday 2 August 1894, page 3. Manchester Evening News - Saturday 3 August 1895, page 3. Sheffield Daily Telegraph - Saturday 1 August 1896, page 8		

When McEwan went public in 1889, 50,000 £10 preference shares were sold to the public, while the 50,000 £10 ordinary shares were retained by the board. 43,000 of those ordinary shares were kept by William McEwan himself[31]. In addition to the half million pounds raised from the public, the board had made almost another half million in dividends in just four years. William McEwan must have been a very wealthy man.

He'd also earned huge sums in the years leading up to the floatation.

William McEwan profits 1885 - 1889	
Year ending 30th June 1885	£89,090 11 1
Year ending 30th June 1886	£83,419 15 2
Year ending 30th June 1887	£95,440 1 8
Year ending 30th June 1888	£100,854 17 1
Year ending 30th June 1889	£93,372 7 9
	£462,177 15 9
Average annual profit	£92,435 11 1
Source: Glasgow Herald - Thursday 25 July 1889, page 1.	

Despite the industry being very profitable, the number of breweries was in decline. Between 1880 and 1899 the number fell from 216 to 139[32]. By the time war broke out in 1914, that was down to just 75[33].

Beer production

In 1880, Scottish brewing was in a bit of a slump. The 1870's had been a decade of economic depression in the UK and this was reflected in beer production figures. As the economy started to

---

[31] Dundee Courier - Wednesday 15 January 1890, page 4.
[32] Aberdeen Journal - Saturday 20 May 1899, page 7.
[33] "A History of the Brewing Industry in Scotland" by Ian Donnachie, 1998, page 234.

pick up in the 1880's, so did the brewing trade. Between 1885 and the pre-war peak in 1899, Scottish beer output increased by 76%.

Beer production (standard barrels) 1882 - 1914			
Year	UK	Scotland	% Scotland
1882	27,870,526	1,088,000	3.90%
1883	27,140,891	1,122,360	4.14%
1884	27,750,091	1,216,319	4.38%
1885	27,986,493	1,237,323	4.42%
1886		1,236,000	
1887		1,322,000	
1888		1,392,000	
1889		1,485,000	
1890	30,808,315	1,666,897	5.41%
1891	30,868,315	1,767,000	5.72%
1892		1,736,000	
1893		1,700,000	
1894		1,744,000	
1895	31,678,486	1,758,879	5.55%
1896	33,826,354	1,970,000	5.82%
1897	34,203,049	2,000,000	5.85%
1898	35,632,629	2,055,000	5.77%
1899	36,498,390	2,179,000	5.97%
1900	37,091,123	2,136,992	5.76%
1901	36,394,827	2,137,000	5.87%
1902		2,075,000	
1903		1,939,000	
1904		1,877,000	
1905	34,404,287	2,021,374	5.88%
1906		1,825,000	
1907		1,811,000	
1908		1,811,000	
1909		1,720,000	
1910	32,947,252	1,758,879	5.34%
1911		1,769,000	
1912		1,886,000	
1913	34,805,291	1,837,000	5.28%
1914	36,057,913	1,977,000	5.48%
Sources: Brewers' Almanack 1928, page 109. "A History of the Brewing Industry in Scotland" by Ian Donnachie, 1998, pages 147-148.			

In addition to increasing in absolute terms, Scotland's share of UK production also increased, from under 4% in 1882 to almost 5.5% in 1914. The good times weren't to last. WW I severely dented beer output and pre-WW I levels weren't matched until the 1970's[34].

"THE SCOTCH BREWING TRADE.

---

[34] "The Brewers' Society Statistical Handbook 1988" page 7.

The gradual extinction of the small brewer in Scotland (writes a London correspondent) appears to have almost ceased. Only three have been absorbed or have disappeared in the past twelve months, and the total number of all kinds brewing for sale is only 139 (when the beer duty was introduced in 1880 there were 216 brewers), although there are 11,335 persons licensed to sell beer in Scotland. The average number to each brewery is therefore 82 licensed houses. It is a little singular that brewing for private purposes is confined to Ballater, Peterhead, and Inverness districts. In no other part of Scotland was a licence obtained for this purpose during the year. The number of this class, by the way, has decreased by one-third in two years. In Glasgow there are ten breweries to 2189 beer sellers. It seems strange that notwithstanding the increased consumption of beer there is not a much greater increase in the quantity of malt and prepared grain used than the returns for the brewing year show. Last year 31,000 quarters were worked up, against 30,000 two years earlier. One explanation is no doubt that in the interval an addition of 90 tons has been made to the quantity of sugar used. In the Edinburgh district, where 34 breweries are at work, while in the same period an additional 14,000 quarters of malt have been added to the consumption of the year, the use of sugar has increased to the extent of 650 tons, which is almost twice as much as was used in the whole of Scotland in the last year of the duty on malt. Then the total was 355 tons, now it is twelve times that quantity. Raw grain is only used in Edinburgh.

In Ireland there has been a slight increase in the number of brewers during the past few years, but the total for that country, 41, is small. In Dublin they number 8 to 1580 retailers of beer, and these eight between them used 530,000 qrs. of malt and 13 cwt. of sugar; this is an increase of 20,000 qr. and 5 cwt. of sugar in two years. In Belfast and Londonderry the trade has decreased materially, but all other centres show an increase.

In England the homebrewed houses have been bought up in hundreds, and amalgamation has reduced the number of large factories very considerably. Even in London there has been a reduction of 18 per cent. in two years. Altogether 1288 breweries, 102 of which were large, have been shut up since 1896, and the total number in existence is now 7000, against 23,000 when the duty on beer was reimposed. With one exception there has been a reduction in the number of all classes up to that which includes those brewers who pay between £15,000 and £30,000 a year duty; the exception is the class which pays from £6000 to £9000 annually. Until last year Guinness and Bass, with a united output of 3.5 millions of barrels, had a class to themselves, but the amalgamation of three of the largest breweries in London has caused another to be added to the class, and these three manufactured five millions of barrels and paid a duty of over 1.5 millions between them. This is more than one-eighth of the duty paid in the United Kingdom."

Aberdeen Journal - Saturday 20 May 1899, page 7.

Ingredients

The year 1880 was a year of huge change in British brewing, with the system of taxing beer changing completely. Instead of taxing malt, excise duty was now calculated based on the OG of the beer. At the same time the rules on ingredients were also overhauled. Before using any ingredient other than malt was effectively tax dodging. Now tax was no longer levied just on malt, it opened up the possibility to allow other ingredients, which is what happened. Brewers could use anything they liked in their beer, as long as it was fit for human consumption. The name of the legislation says it all: the Free Mash Tun Act.

Almost immediately Scottish brewers began to move away from all-malt beers. Most started to use unmalted adjuncts of one sort or another.

Malt

The inability of the UK to grow enough malting barley to satisfy the demands of the brewing industry meant that large quantities of grain had to be imported. Barley was imported from all over the world and then malted in the UK.

Scottish brewers had long been bringing in grain from England to malt – pretty much every brewery of any size had its own maltings – but barley continued to be grown in Scotland. Though judging by some brewing records, in woefully inadequate quantities to feed the industry.

A glance at Thomas Usher's brewing records from 1912 shows how diverse the origin of their barley was. There's malt described as Hungarian, Danish, Calcutta, Smyrna (Turkey), Ouchak (also Turkey), Polish, Karachi, Danubian, Roumanian, Tunis, Californian, Oregon, Bulgarian, Spanish, Canadian and finally, three pages in, the first mention of Scotch[35]. (Remember that this is the source of the barley, not where the malt was made. The malting would have been performed mostly in Scotland, perhaps some in England.) Malt from locally-grown barley was always less than 50% of the grist.

The situation was the same at other Scottish brewers, such as Drybrough and William Younger. Each brew had at least three different types of pale malt and sometimes as many as six[36]. Using multiple kinds of pale malt in a beer was standard practice across the UK. It helped to iron out differences between individual batches of malt. But there was one constant factor: malt from Scottish barley was a minority of the grist.

Scottish brewers used very little coloured malt at this time. Stouts usually contained black malt and sometimes brown and crystal malt as well. In the 1890's William Younger included amber malt in their Stout grists and just before WW I chocolate malt.

Most other styles had nothing but pale malt in the grist. Though Thomas Usher did use some crystal malt in their Shilling Ales. In general, very little crystal appears in grists.

---

[35] Thomas Usher brewing record held at the Scottish Brewing Archive, document number TU/6/1/5.
[36] Drybrough brewing record held at the Scottish Brewing Archive, document number D/6/1/1/1.
William Younger brewing records held at the Scottish Brewing Archive, document numbers WY/6/1/2/31, WY/6/1/2/34, WY/6/1/2/45 and WY/6/1/2/58.

Sugar

Sugar had beer allowed since 1847 but, after an initial period of experimentation with this new ingredient, most breweries dropped it again and returned to brewing all-malt. After 1880, the vast majority of breweries in England embraced sugar and it usually made up 10-15% of the grist, depending on the style of beer being brewed.

The Scots were more reluctant to adopt sugar. William Younger, for example, only used it in around half of their beers in the 1830's[37]. In the same period, some of Thomas Usher's Mild Ales contained sugar, but none of their Pale Ales or Stock Ales[38] It's odd that they didn't use it in Pale Ales as in England even the classiest Pale Ales often had grists with 20% sugar. The reason was simple: sugar helped keep the body and colour light.

Adjuncts

Brewers both sided of the border immediately began to experiment with unmalted grains. In England, flaked rice was initially popular, but soon replaced by cheaper flaked maize. In Scotland maize was the most popular adjunct, but, in contrast to English practice it was mostly used in the form of grits.

While flaked maize can just be thrown into the mash tun with the malt, grits require an extra step to gelatinise them To brew with grits breweries needed to install an extra piece of equipment, a cereal cooker, in which this gelatinsation was performed.

Some breweries, Drybrough for example, used rice either instead of or in addition to, maize[39]. This was always in form of flakes which could be added directly to the mash tun. The practice gradually petered out, presumably on cost grounds.

Hops

Huge quantities of foreign hops were imported into the UK in the three decades before WW I. The USA and Central Europe supplied the most, though hops from just about country that produced them were brought into the country. How they were used depended very much on their origin.

Top-quality hops like Saaz and Hallertau were highly valued and used in much the same way as the best Kent hops. That is in the form of late aroma additions and dry hops. While cheaper hops from the USA, whose flavour wasn't greatly liked, were usually early bittering hop additions. The same was true of other less fashionable ones like Poperinge hops from Belgium.

Hops from the USA were given a variety of descriptions. Originally they were just called American, but later in the century, as the US hop growing centres began to move from the East to the West Coast, terms like Pacific, Oregon or California were used as well. Presumably to help differentiate between hops from the East and West.

On the eve of WW I, William Younger was using mostly Pacific hops, the rest coming from Kent. For example, in December 1913, of the total 11,970 lbs of hops they used, 9,110 lbs (slightly more than

---

[37] William Younger brewing records held at the Scottish Brewing Archive, document numbers WY/6/1/2/31 and WY/6/1/2/34.
[38] Thomas Usher brewing record held at the Scottish Brewing Archive, document number TU/6/1/1.
[39] Drybrough brewing record held at the Scottish Brewing Archive, document number D/6/1/1/1.

75%) were Pacific.[40] Unusually, Drybrough were using all English hops in 1906, though by 1914 there were also some Californian and continental hops in their beers as well[41].

Yeast

Pasteur, grandfather of yeast study, dropped by William Younger's brewery and gave their yeast the once over under his microscope:

> "He informed us that during past years many distinguished persons had visited the Abbey and Holyrood Breweries—notably Mons. L. Pasteur, who was the guest of Mr. H. J. Younger during his visit to the Scottish capital at the tercentenary celebrations of the Edinburgh University. In honour of his visit a brass tablet was put up on the wall of the head brewer's room, where M. Pasteur was greatly interested in the microscopic examination of the yeast in use at the time in the Abbey and Holyrood Breweries, which he pronounced to be pure, active specimens, and he was much pleased to find that his researches had been practically applied and taken advantage of."
> "Noted Breweries of Great Britain and Ireland vol. II", by Alfred Barnard 1889, page 26.

Water

The availability of water suitable for brewing was one of the main factors determining the location of breweries in Edinburgh. Until the late 19th century these had been clustered around the Royal Mile at the Holyrood end of town. Then several breweries decided to relocate to the tiny hamlet of Duddingston, just outside the city. Two factors favoured Duddingston: good quality well water and excellent access to the rail network.

There was an extra incentive for brewers to leave the centre of Edinburgh: pollution of their wells by the city's other industries. In 1905, James Muir & Son of the Calton Hill Brewery sued the Edinburgh and Leith Gas Commissioners for fouling their well. When the gas company was dismantling its New Street plant a large quantity of tarry residue, a by-product of gas production, was discharged into the ground, polluting the brewery's well. The pollution was so serious, it was estimated that the well would be unusable for at least ten years. Muir claimed £10,000 damages, but were awarded just £3,730 by the judge. Still a substantial sum back then.[42]

By the late 19th century treatment of brewing water was standard practice. Few breweries had the perfect water without some sort of chemical adjustment. London brewer Barclay Perkins had several different water treatments for different types of beer. One for Pale Ales, one for Mild Ales, one for Burton Ales and one for Porter and Stout.

Things seem to have been much simpler in Scotland, probably because they weren't brewing as many different styles. Drybrough, for example, had a single water treatment in 1906 for all its beers, consisting of 16 quarts of sulphate of lime, 6 quarts of magnesium, 6 pints of calcium chloride and 3

---

[40] William Younger brewing record held at the Scottish Brewing Archive, document number WY/6/1/2/58.
[41] Drybrough brewing records held at the Scottish Brewing Archive, document numbers D/6/1/1/1 and D/6/1/1/2.
[42] Edinburgh Evening News - Thursday 29 June 1905, page 4.

gallons of bisulphate of lime[43]. It looks to me like they were attempting to get a Burton-like profile. Not surprising, as the bulk of what they brewed was Pale Ale.

At Maclay in 1909, the water adjustments were slightly more complicated. Their Strong Ale and Pale Ales received 40 lbs gypsum, 6 lbs calcium chloride and 6 lbs magnesium. While their Mild Ales and Stouts got 30 lbs salt and 8 lbs calcium chloride[44].

Techniques

Mashing

Scottish brewers continued to mash somewhat differently from their English counterparts. South of the border mashing schemes remained more complicated than the preferred Scottish method of a single infusion followed by multiple sparges.

Thomas Usher used two different mashing schemes This was how they mashed their Pale Ales:

Thomas Usher IP and PA mashing scheme 1894			
	Strike heat	mash tun	underback
mash	156° F	151° F	150° F
sparge 1	180° F	156° F	155° F
sparge 2	165° F	159° F	155° F
sparge 3	155° F	153° F	152° F
Source: Thomas Usher brewing record held at the Scottish Brewing Archive, document number TU/6/1/2.			

While all their other beers were mashed cooler:

Thomas Usher 80/- and 100/- mashing scheme 1894			
	Strike heat	mash tun	underback
mash	154° F	144° F	144° F
sparge 1	170° F	154° F	153° F
sparge 2	160° F	160° F	159° F
sparge 3	155° F	156° F	155° F
Source: Thomas Usher brewing record held at the Scottish Brewing Archive, document number TU/6/1/2.			

Something similar was going on at William Younger, where there was one mashing scheme for the Pale Ales and Shilling Ales:

---

[43] Drybrough brewing record held at the Scottish Brewing Archive, document number D/6/1/1/1.
[44] Maclay brewing record held at the Scottish Brewing Archive, document number M/6/1/1/2.

William Younger 1898 XPSc Ale mashing scheme	
strike heat	164° F
time mashed	14 minutes
time stood	2.25 hours
mash temperature	149° F
1st sparge heat	160° F
2nd sparge heat	160° F
1st tap heat	148° F
2nd tap heat	150° F
3rd tap heat	152° F
Source: William Younger brewing record held at the Scottish Brewing Archive, document number WY/6/1/2/45.	

And another, warmer, one for the numbered Strong Ales and Milds:

William Younger 1898 No. 3 Ale mashing scheme	
strike heat	167° F
time mashed	16 minutes
time stood	2.25 hours
mash temperature	153° F
1st sparge heat	160° F
2nd sparge heat	160° F
1st tap heat	150° F
2nd tap heat	153° F
3rd tap heat	155° F
Source: William Younger brewing record held at the Scottish Brewing Archive, document number WY/6/1/2/45.	

The initial and tap heats for Younger's Pale Ales are a couple of degrees cooler than Usher's.

Compare the simplicity of the Scottish mashes with this example from Barclay Perkins:

Barclay Perkins 1899 X Ale mashing scheme		
	strike heat	tap heat
mash 1	156° F	
underlet	170° F	150° F
mash 2	168° F	156° F
sparge 1	165° F	152° F
sparge 1	160° F	152° F
Source: Barclay Perkins brewing record held at the London Metropolitan Archives document number ACC/2305/1/593/1.		

In summary, there isn't a huge difference between the mashing temperatures at William Younger and Barclay Perkins, but Thomas Usher mashed significantly warmer. It's easier to see in this overview:

Tap heat overview 1890's

	tap heat 1	tap heat 2	tap heat 3	tap heat 4
Usher IP and PA	155° F	155° F	152° F	
Usher 80/- and 100/-	153° F	159° F	155° F	
William Younger XPSc	148° F	150° F	152° F	
William Younger No. 3	150° F	153° F	155° F	
Barclay Perkins X	150° F	156° F	152° F	152° F

Boiling

This is where things start getting confusing. Boiling times were on the increase at the start of the period, but then began to fall again. If I'm honest, 've no idea why this occurred.

William Younger's boil times were, on average, around an hour longer in 1898 than they were in 1885. This was across the board and not limited to one particular style.

William Younger numbered Strong Ales 1885 - 1914

Year	Beer	OG	ABV	boil time (hours)	boil time (hours)
1885	1	1103	9.00	2	2.5
1885	2	1091	8.86	2	2.5
1885	3 pale	1076	6.75	2	2.5
	Average			*2*	*2.5*
1898	1	1104	9.79	3	3.5
1898	3	1074	7.28	3	3.5
	Average			*3*	*3.5*
1913	1	1097	7.94	2.5	3
1914	2 Sc	1076	6.75	2.5	
1913	3	1065	5.75	2	2.5
1913	3a	1072	6.22	2.25	
	Average			*2.39*	*2.89*
Source: William Younger brewing records held at the Scottish Brewing Archive, document numbers WY/6/1/2/31, WY/6/1/2/45 and WY/6/1/2/58.					

Unsurprisingly, as they also included low-gravity beers, the boil times for Shilling Ales were shorter than for the Strong Ales. But the same pattern of an increase of around an hour in the middle of the period before falling back to the original value is repeated.

Year	Beer	OG	ABV	boil time (hours)	boil time (hours)
William Younger Shilling Ales 1885 - 1914					
1885	50/-	1036	3.31	2	2.5
1885	S 50/-	1042	3.18	2	
1885	B 50/-	1044	3.70	2.5	
1885	H 60/-	1041	3.97	2	2.5
1885	60/-	1052	3.84	2	2.5
1885	80/-	1064	4.89	2.5	
1885	100/-	1074	5.82	2	2.5
1885	120/-	1086	6.09	2	2.5
1885	140/-	1099	7.41	2.5	
1885	160/-	1115	8.60	2	
	Average			**2.15**	**2.50**
1898	H 60/-	1044	4.23	2.75	3.5
1899	60/-	1050	3.57	3.25	3.5
1898	80/-	1061	4.50	3.25	
1899	100/-	1073	4.89	2.75	
1898	120/-	1086	6.35	3.5	
1898	140/-	1100	8.07	3	
1898	160/-	1111	9.13	3	
	Average			**3.07**	**3.50**
1913	H 60/-	1044	4.10	2	2.5
1913	60/-	1047	3.18	1.75	
1913	80/-	1056	3.84	1.75	
1913	100/-	1066	4.50	2.25	
1913	160/-	1097	7.81	2.25	
	Average			**2.00**	**2.50**

Source:
William Younger brewing records held at the Scottish Brewing Archive, document numbers WY/6/1/2/31, WY/6/1/2/45 and WY/6/1/2/58.

Looking at the picture longer term, it's even more confusing, with changes both up and down over a period of 70 years:

Boil times of William Younger Shilling Ales 1848 - 1913		
Year	1st wort	2nd wort
1848	1.21	1.25
1879	1.73	2.23
1885	2.15	2.5
1898	3.07	3.5
1913	2	2.5

Source:
William Younger brewing records held at the Scottish Brewing Archive, document numbers WY/6/1/2/3, WY/6/1/2/28, WY/6/1/2/31, WY/6/1/2/45 and WY/6/1/2/58.

At Whitbread, the boiling times varies much less over the same period:

Boil times of Whitbread Ales 1848 - 1913

Year	1st wort	2nd wort	3rd wort
1848	1.5	2	2
1879	1.87	2.36	
1885	1.6	2.06	
1898	1.69	1.9	
1913	1.64	1.81	

Sources:
Whitbread brewing records held at the London Metropolitan Archives document numbers LMA/4453/D/01/044, LMA/4453/D/01/045, LMA/4453/D/01/050, LMA/4453/D/01/051, LMA/4453/D/01/063, LMA/4453/D/01/064 and LMA/4453/D/01/078.

To summarise, William Younger had shorter boil than Whitbread in 1848, about the same length in 1879, A little longer in 1885, much longer in 1898 and a little more again in 1913.

At Thomas Usher the lengthening of boil times wasn't as great and the subsequent fall was to below the starting level.

Thomas Usher Pale Ales 1885 - 1912

Year	Beer	OG	ABV	boil time (hours)	boil time (hours)	boil time (hours)
1885	IP	1047	4.50	1.5	2	
1885	PA	1054	4.89	1.5	2	
1885	Ex PA	1060	5.95	2.5	2.5	
1885	KPA	1060	5.95	2.25	2.25	
1885	PA 60/-	1060	5.69	1.5	2	
	Average			1.85	2.15	
1888	IP	1046	4.37	1.5	2	
1888	PA	1050	4.76	2	2	
1888	Expt	1054	5.56	3		
	Average			2.17	2	
1894	IP	1044	3.97	1.5	2	
1894	PA	1049	4.63	1.5	2	
1894	PA 60/-	1055	5.29			
	Average			1.50	2	
1912	IP	1042	3.57	1.5	2.5	
1912	PA	1048	4.37	1.5	2	2.5
1912	PA 60/-	1054	5.03	1.5	2	2.5
	Average			1.50	2.17	2.5

Source:
Thomas Usher brewing records held at the Scottish Brewing Archive, document numbers TU/6/1/1 and TU/6/1/2.

Whitbread's Pale Ales were boiled rather less than Usher's in 1885.

| Whitbread Pale Ale boil times 1885 - 1912 ||||||
Year	Beer	OG	ABV	boil time (hours)	boil time (hours)
1885	PA	1060.1	5.97	1.33	1.75
1885	FA	1052.1	5.46	1.5	1.75
	Average			*1.42*	*1.75*
1895	FA	1051.0	4.76	1.67	1.75
1895	PA	1059.3	5.86	1.5	1.75
1895	2PA	1052.9	5.41	1	2.17
1895	FA	1049.6	4.97	1.5	2
	Average			*1.42*	*1.92*
1912	PA	1061.0	5.82	1.83	1.92
1912	2PA	1053.6	5.37	1.83	1.92
1912	FA (Butts & casks)	1047.4	4.94	1.5	1.92
1912	IPA	1048.2	4.79	1.83	1.75
1912	FA	1047.6	5.11	1.5	1.75
	Average			*1.70*	*1.85*
Source: Whitbread brewing records held at the London Metropolitan Archives, document numbers LMA/4453/D/01/051, LMA/4453/D/01/060, LMA/4453/D/01/061, LMA/4453/D/01/061, LMA/4453/D/01/061 and LMA/4453/D/01/077.					

But, by 1912, the first wort was boiled for longer than Usher's and the second wort for a shorter period. Not much of a pattern there.

Fermentation

The profile of William Younger's fermentations had changed by the 1880's. Back in 1848, Younger pitched their beers quite cool, 54º - 59º F and let the temperature rise throughout the fermentation. The highest temperature, in the high 60's or low 70's F, was attain on the last day of fermentation.

In 1885, the pitching temperatures were similar, but the maximum temperature, still in the high 60's or low 70's F, was reached on the first or second day, after which it fell back to around 55º F. The fermentations were also quicker, none matching the six or seven days of the 1840's.

William Younger fermentation temperatures in 1885

er	OG	pitching heat	1st day AM	1st day PM	2nd day AM	2nd day PM	3rd day AM	3rd day PM	4th day AM	4th day PM	5th day AM	5th day PM
	1047	60.0° F	65.0° F	70.0° F	69.0° F	65.0° F	65.0° F	57.0° F	55.5° F			
-	1053	59.0° F	60.0° F	63.0° F	66.0° F	68.0° F	65.0° F	58.0° F				
-	1064	59.0° F	61.0° F	64.0° F	70.0° F	70.0° F	63.0° F	57.0° F				
/-	1074	57.5° F	62.0° F	66.5° F	70.0° F	65.0° F	60.0° F	56.0° F				
/-	1086	56.5° F	59.5° F	62.0° F	67.5° F	71.0° F	69.5° F	61.0° F				
/-	1087	59.0° F	64.0° F	69.0° F	68.0° F	65.0° F	64.5° F	58.0° F	53.0° F			
/-	1101	56.0° F	59.0° F	65.5° F	72.5° F	70.0° F	67.0° F	64.0° F	60.0° F	30.0° F	48.0° F	
/-	1115	55.5° F	59.0° F	63.0° F	73.5° F	73.0° F	67.5° F	65.0° F	65.0° F	32.0° F	59.0° F	
	1048	61.0° F	63.0° F	66.0° F	64.0° F	61.0° F	56.0° F	52.0° F	52.0° F			
	1054	60.5° F	68.0° F	69.0° F	59.0° F	56.5° F	54.0° F	52.0° F	54.0° F			
X	1065	58.0° F	61.5° F	66.0° F	67.5° F	64.5° F	56.0° F	56.0° F	53.0° F			
3 Pale	1076	56.0° F	58.0° F	61.0° F	67.0° F	67.5° F	64.0° F	62.0° F	60.0° F			
3	1081	57.5° F	63.0° F	68.0° F	71.0° F	69.0° F	66.5° F	62.0° F	58.0° F			
2	1091	55.0° F	57.0° F	59.5° F	65.5° F	71.5° F	71.0° F	64.0° F	60.0° F	55.0° F		
1	1102	55.5° F	57.5° F	60.0° F	67.5° F	71.0° F	70.0° F	65.0° F	65.0° F	61.0° F	58.0° F	55.0° F
	1073	57.75° F	60.0° F	63.5° F		69.0° F	63.0° F	57.0° F				
S	1073	56.5° F	62.0° F	65.0° F	72.0° F	70.5° F	58.0° F	56.5° F	55.0° F	54.0° F		
	1047	60.5° F	67.0° F	70.5° F	64.0° F	63.0° F	58.0° F	57.0° F	55.0° F			
	1053	59.0° F	68.0° F	68.0° F	63.0° F	60.0° F	57.0° F	55.0° F				

Source:
William Younger brewing record held at the Scottish Brewing Archive, document number WY/6/1/2/31.

I've been scratching my head as to what the difference was between Shilling Ales and X Ales. On paper, they look very similar: same OG, same level of hopping. Now I can see that the fermentation profiles were different:

William Younger Shilling Ale and X Ale fermentations in 1885

beer	OG	pitching heat	1st day morning	1st day evening	2nd day morning	2nd day evening	3rd day morning	3rd day evening	4th day morning
60/-	1053	59.0° F	60.0° F	63.0° F	66.0° F	68.0° F	65.0° F	58.0° F	
XX	1054	60.5° F	68.0° F	69.0° F	59.0° F	56.5° F	54.0° F	52.0° F	54.0° F
80/-	1064	59.0° F	61.0° F	64.0° F	70.0° F	70.0° F	63.0° F	57.0° F	
XXX	1065	58.0° F	61.5° F	66.0° F	67.5° F	64.5° F	56.0° F	56.0° F	53.0° F

Source:
William Younger brewing record held at the Scottish Brewing Archive, document number WY/6/1/2/31.

The X Ales were achieving the maximum temperature about a day earlier, after which they were cooled quite quickly. Their final temperatures were 4º F cooler than the equivalent Shilling Ale.

Here's what they did at Fullers by way of comparison:

Fuller fermentation temperatures in 1902										
		Pitching heat	1st day	2nd day		3rd day		4th day		5th day
Beer	OG		evening	morning	evening	morning	evening	morning	evening	morning
X	1051	59.5° F	65° F	70° F	72° F	63.0° F	62° F	61° F	60.0° F	
AK	1046.3	58.5° F	66° F	67.5° F	71° F	69.5° F	67.5° F	64.5° F	60.0° F	59°
BO	1074.2	60° F		70° F	74° F	74.5° F	66.5° F	62° F	60° F	60°
IPA	1054	59° F	65° F	73° F	67° F	65.5° F	61.5° F	59.5° F	57° F	57.5°
Porter	1050.7	59.5° F	66.5° F	71° F	66.5° F	59.5° F	55.5° F	58° F		
BS	1070.6	58° F	74° F	66° F	63.5° F	64° F	63.5° F			59°
Source: Fullers brewing record held at the brewery.										

Dry Hopping

One annoying feature of brewing records is that they often fail to record dry hopping details. Fortunately, William Younger did note it down. Their brewing log from 1885 even has a guide to the amount of dry hops to be used in each different beer.

William Younger dry hopping in 1885			
Beer	Style	OG	oz. hops per barrel
50/-	Mild Ale	1036	4
H60/-	Mild Ale	1041	6
X	Mild Ale	1048	3
XX	Mild Ale	1056	4
XXX	Mild Ale	1065	5
XXXX	Stock Ale	1079	12
1	Strong Ale	1103	16
2	Strong Ale	1091	12
3	Strong Ale	1076	10
P	Pale Ale	1047	8
XP	Pale Ale	1054	10
Source: William Younger brewing records held at the Scottish Brewing Archive, document numbers WY/6/1/2/31.			

Some of the weaker Mild Ales contain surprisingly large quantities of dry hops, not that much less than the lowest OG Pale Ale.

Cereal cooker

The use of grits, a form of maize that needs to gelatinised before it can be thrown into the mash tun required an additional piece of equipment: a cereal cooker. Grits were heated up in it with a small amount of malt and the resulting mush added to the mash tun.

Brewing at William Younger in the 1880's

Alfred Barnard. What a great bloke. I'd like to shake his hand. For the service he did to history grubbers like me by recording so many classic breweries of the late 19th century. He might have been vague on the beers. I can fill that information in from brewing records. Barnard noted the nuts and bolts of breweries. The mash tuns, coolers, coppers, fermenters and cleansers.

Luckily for us, Barnard dropped by William Younger on his travels. After a couple of chapters on Younger's extensive maltings, he gets onto the useful stuff, the Abbey Brewery. Kicking off with the mashing stage.

> "At one corner of the place a pair of mill rollers were actively at work crushing the malt as it fell from a receptacle above, and we saw the grist " Jacobed " as they call it here—i.e., lifted by an elevator to an immense hopper fixed in the centre of the house, to be ready for the first process. From the apex of this hopper protrudes a large-size Steel's mashing machine, which serves two mash tuns, each of which holds forty quarters. They are both constructed of wood, lined with copper, and possess gun-metal draining plates."
> "Noted Breweries of Great Britain and Ireland vol. II", by Alfred Barnard 1889, pages 18 - 19.

A Steel's masher is a large screw in which water and malt are mixed on their way into the mash tun. Invented by a Mr. Steel in the 1850's, it proved immensely useful and popular. Older British breweries like Fullers and Harveys still use them. It's a very simple and effective way of getting a mash with a good consistency from the minute it enters the tun.

A tun of forty quarters could mash enough wort for around 160 barrels of 1056º beer. However, looking at Younger's records for 1888, they weren't mashing at full capacity every time. Or even any time. Mostly it was just 20-odd quarters per brew. The largest I can find was just 35 quarters.

The wort would have flown from the mash tun to the underback.

> "The next object that attracted our attention was the underback, also a copper vessel of some ten barrels capacity, which is placed in the basement of the building, and from which the wort is pumped direct into the coppers."
> "Noted Breweries of Great Britain and Ireland vol. II", by Alfred Barnard 1889, page 19.

A ten barrel underback seems very small to contain wort from a 40-quarter mash tun. That's enough to produce around 160 barrels of beer at 1055º and 80 barrels even at a gravity of 1100º.

> "Returning to the mashing floor we were shown the two coppers, wherein the wort is boiled with the hops. These are of cylindrical form, and rise from the floor of the house to a great height. They are also constructed of copper, and their tops are reached by means of a gangway protruding from the second stage. We noticed in close proximity another vessel called the heating tank, which supplies the hot water to the mash tuns, etc. The hot wort is conveyed from the coppers in pipes, stretching across the western corner of the building to the hop-back, which is placed on a long gallery overhead. From this vessel the strained liquor runs by gravitation to the coolers placed on the floor of the next building."
> "Noted Breweries of Great Britain and Ireland vol. II", by Alfred Barnard 1889, page 19.

Cooling was performed the classic late 19th-century way, with a combination of large, open, shallow coolers and heat-exchanging refrigerators:

> "Pursuing our investigations, we next ascended a stair to the first stage, and by a doorway entered the cooling or cooler room. It is a large apartment, with latticed sides, measuring 90 feet by 40 feet, and contains two open coolers of large dimensions, and two of Morton's refrigerators."
> "Noted Breweries of Great Britain and Ireland vol. II", by Alfred Barnard 1889, page 19.

The initial stage in the coolers wasn't just for cooling purposes. These shallow vessels were also perfect for dropping out a lot of the gunk in the wort.

A Morton's refrigerator is like a washboard of copper pipes through which brine is circulated. The wort runs over these pipes, cooling quickly. And presumably oxidising nicely at the same time.

> "Leaving this place, we passed down some steps into another building, devoted to the fermenting operations, and first entered the square room, which measures 140 feet by 50 feet, and contains twenty-eight fermenting squares. It was here that we saw the beer in active, or as the brewer designated it lively, fermentation, and were treated to a sniff of carbonic acid gas, much to the amusement of our guide. Crossing this floor we found ourselves in another and much larger room, which covers an area of 6,000 square feet. The floor is laid with asphalte, and it contains 160 union casks. Descending a stair, we passed through the rooms below this and the adjoining buildings, all of which are used as racking floors and store cellars. In one of them there are twenty cleansing squares or settling backs, each of an average content of 120 barrels."
> "Noted Breweries of Great Britain and Ireland vol. II", by Alfred Barnard 1889, page 19.

Next Barnard visited Younger's newer brewery, Holyrood, which had been specifically built to brew Pale Ale.

> "Here there are three mash-tuns, each capable of mashing forty quarters of grist at one time, over which are the hoppers referred to, and each vessel contains gun-metal stirring gear and draining plates, manufactured by Messrs. Stewardson & Hodgson of Edinburgh."
> "Noted Breweries of Great Britain and Ireland vol. II", by Alfred Barnard 1889, page 27.

The mash tuns remained of a modest size in the new brew house. A big London brewery had much larger mash tuns. Barclay Perkins had ones capable of holding 130 quarters[45]. Even after the introduction of the Steel's masher, mash tuns still often had internal rakes. Rakes were useful for preventing a stuck mash and, for brewers adding extra, hotter water to their mash, a way of mixing it through the grain.

This is an interesting remark about the way wort was boiled.

> "In the old brewhouse, at the back of the tuns, there are two other wort coppers of 120 barrels content. The ale wort is kept boiling, with the hops in the coppers for about two hours, and the great object of the operator now is to preserve the delicate aroma of the

---

[45] Barclay Perkins brewing record held at the London Metropolitan Archives, document number ACC/2305/1/544.

hops. The flavour of the ale partly depends upon a careful attention to the process at this stage, as, if kept too long boiling, the fine aroma, which now so pleasantly greeted us as we approached the coppers, being evanescent, flies off with the vapour, if not carefully watched."
"Noted Breweries of Great Britain and Ireland vol. II", by Alfred Barnard 1889, page 28.

Scottish brewers seemed very keen on retaining delicate hop aroma. Presumably another reason why their boils were so short earlier in the century.

Styles

In many ways Scotland led the way in terms of style evolution in the UK. The move from Mild to Pale Ale, then Pale Ale to Lager both occurred much earlier than in England.

Pale Ale

The further the 19th century progressed, the greater the popularity of Pale Ales and they more they started to diverge from English versions. In hopping and gravity, if not in ingredients.

Gravity and hopping

William Younger Pale Ales 1885 - 1914							
Year	Beer	OG	FG	ABV	App. Attenuation	lbs hops/qtr	hops lb/brl
1885	P	1047	1007	5.29	85.11%	8.82	1.79
1885	XP	1054	1013	5.42	75.93%	11.50	2.84
1885	XP Scotch	1055	1016	5.16	70.91%	11.00	2.72
1898	SLE	1054	1015	5.16	72.22%	13.10	2.97
1898	XPSc	1053	1013	5.29	75.47%	8.97	2.05
1898	SE	1067	1018	6.48	73.13%	14.40	4.34
1898	LAE	1051	1014	4.89	72.55%	11.43	2.58
1898	SLE	1054	1013	5.42	75.93%	13.10	2.99
1899	B XPSc	1053	1014	5.16	73.58%	10.38	2.33
1913	LAE	1045	1013	4.23	71.11%	10.00	1.77
1914	SLE	1055	1014	5.42	74.55%	10.36	2.20
1914	MM	1048	1015	4.37	68.75%	3.91	0.70
Source: William Younger brewing records held at the Scottish Brewing Archive, document numbers WY/6/1/2/31, WY/6/1/2/45 and WY/6/1/2/58.							

Thomas Usher Pale Ales 1885 - 1912							
Year	Beer	OG	FG	ABV	App. Attenuation	lbs hops/qtr	hops lb/brl
1885	IP	1047	1013	4.50	72.34%	8.00	1.61
1885	PA	1054	1017	4.89	68.52%	9.00	2.16
1885	Ex PA	1060	1015	5.95	75.00%	16.00	4.17
1885	KPA	1060	1015	5.95	75.00%	16.00	4.23
1885	PA 60/-	1060	1017	5.69	71.67%	8.00	2.05
1888	IP	1046	1013	4.37	71.74%	8.00	1.88
1888	PA	1050	1014	4.76	72.00%	9.00	2.30
1888	Expt	1054	1012	5.56	77.78%	15.00	4.16
1894	IP	1044	1014	3.97	68.18%	8.00	1.83
1894	PA	1049	1014	4.63	71.43%	8.00	1.89
1894	PA 60/-	1055	1015	5.29	72.73%	8.00	2.12
1912	IP	1042	1015	3.57	64.29%	6.50	1.13
1912	PA	1048	1015	4.37	68.75%	6.75	1.37
1912	PA 60/-	1054	1016	5.03	70.37%	6.75	1.54
Source: Thomas Usher brewing records held at the Scottish Brewing Archive, document numbers TU/6/1/1 and TU/6/1/2.							

There's a clear drop in the hopping rate of Usher's Pale Ales after 1900. From 8 or 9 lbs per quarter of malt to 6.5 to 6.75 lbs. Also observable is a decline in FG. IP from 1047º to 1042º; PA 1054º to 1048º, PA 60/- from 1060º to 1054º.

Starting at a slightly lower level than at Whitbread, Usher's hopping rates declined even more, leaving their Pale Ales significantly more lightly hopped. Though as you'll soon see, they weren't the most extreme example.

Whitbread Pale Ales 1885 - 1912

Year	Beer	OG	FG	ABV	App. Atten-uation	lbs hops/ qtr	hops lb/brl
1885	PA	1060.1	1015.0	5.97	75.12%	14.03	4.10
1885	FA	1052.1	1010.8	5.46	79.26%	10.47	3.18
1895	FA	1051.0	1015.0	4.76	70.57%	10.87	2.47
1895	PA	1059.3	1015.0	5.86	74.70%	12.00	3.15
1895	2PA	1052.9	1012.0	5.41	77.32%	11.94	2.82
1895	FA	1049.6	1012.0	4.97	75.80%	10.99	2.52
1912	PA	1061.0	1017.0	5.82	72.14%	8.91	2.41
1912	2PA	1053.6	1013.0	5.37	75.73%	8.91	2.12
1912	FA (Butts & Casks)	1047.4	1010.0	4.94	78.89%	9.01	1.90
1912	IPA	1048.2	1012.0	4.79	75.10%	10.01	2.15
1912	FA	1047.6	1009.0	5.11	81.11%	10.01	2.10

Source:
Whitbread brewing records held at the London Metropolitan Archives, document numbers LMA/4453/D/01/051, LMA/4453/D/01/060, LMA/4453/D/01/061, LMA/4453/D/01/061, LMA/4453/D/01/061 and LMA/4453/D/01/077.

The situation with gravity was more complicated at Whitbread. There was no change for PA, but FA fell from 1052º to 1048º.

Drybrough Pale Ale in 1914

Year	Beer	OG	FG	ABV	App. Atten-uation	lbs hops/ qtr	hops lb/brl
1914	Pl 48/-	1040.0	1014.0	3.44	65.00%	5.07	0.83
1914	Pl	1044.0	1015.0	3.84	65.91%	4.97	0.91
1914	Pl 60/-	1054.0	1018.0	4.76	66.67%	5.07	1.12

Source:
Drybrough brewing record held at the Scottish Brewing Archive, document number D/6/1/1.3.

The hopping rates Drybrough's Pale Ales look very low compare to London brewers. Whitbread's were hopped at 9 to 10 lbs per quarter, around double the rate at Drybrough. The same was also true of Barclay Perkins, where the hopping rate was 8.5 to 122 lbs per quarter. Drybrough Pl 48/- has about the same quantity of hops per barrel as Whitbread's 1923 MA, a cheap Mild with a gravity of just 1027º[46].

---

[46] Whitbread brewing record held at the London Metropolitan Archives, document number LMA/4453/D/01/088.

It's clear that Drybrough's Pale Ales were very low in bitterness just before WW I.

Barclay Perkins Pale Ales 1886 - 1908

Year	Beer	OG	FG	ABV	App. Attenuation	lbs hops/ qtr	hops lb/brl
1886	PA	1059.0	1016.1	5.68	72.77%	16.00	3.88
1892	PA	1063.0	1021.1	5.55	66.58%	12.46	3.03
1900	PA	1060.0	1017.0	5.69	71.67%	11.38	4.00
1900	XLK	1052.5	1012.0	5.36	77.14%	11.38	2.17
1907	PA Ex	1058.0	1012.0	6.09	79.31%	10.00	2.53
1908	PA	1060.4	1011.5	6.47	80.96%	12.00	3.00
1906	XLK	1050.0	1010.0	5.30	80.06%	8.50	1.81

Sources:
Barclay Perkins brewing records held at the London Metropolitan Archives, document numbers ACC/2305/1/584, ACC/2305/1/588, ACC/2305/1/593, ACC/2305/1/605 and ACC/2305/1/599.

Grists

Before 1880, when there was a virtual Reinheisgebot in the UK, there wasn't much scope for diversity in Pale Ale grists. Pale malt and perhaps sugar. That was it. With the Free Mash Tun Act in 1880, a new world of possibilities was opened up to brewers.

Thomas Usher Pale Ales 1885 - 1912

Year	Beer	OG	pale malt	high dried malt	flaked maize	no. 1 sugar	other sugar	hops
1885	IP	1047	100.00%					Bavarian, Californian, Alsace
1885	PA	1054	95.00%	5.00%				Bavarian, Californian, Alsace
1885	Ex PA	1060	100.00%					Hallertau, Alsace
1885	KPA	1060	100.00%					Hallertau, Alsace
1885	PA 60/-	1060	100.00%					Bavarian, Californian
1888	IP	1046	89.47%				10.53%	Kent, Hallertau
1888	PA	1050	89.01%			10.99%		
1888	Expt	1054	100.00%					Kent, Hallertau
1894	IP	1044	85.71%				14.29%	Worcester, Kent
1894	PA	1049	75.00%				25.00%	Kent, Sussex
1894	PA 60/-	1055	85.71%				14.29%	Kent, Sussex
1912	IP	1042	78.00%		12.00%		10.00%	
1912	PA	1048	78.18%		10.91%	10.91%		
1912	PA 60/-	1054	78.18%		10.91%	10.91%		

Source:
Thomas Usher brewing records held at the Scottish Brewing Archive, document numbers TU/6/1/1 and TU/6/1/2.

After 1885, the percentage of pale malt fell, first sugar and then a combination of sugar and flaked maize replacing it. The hops came from a variety of sources. In the early 1880's they were all foreign, then a combination of English and foreign, then mostly English.

Let's look at how that compares with London Pale Ale grists.

Whitbread Pale Ale grists 1885 - 1912

Year	Beer	OG	pale malt	PA malt	no. 1 sugar	other sugar	hops
1885	PA	1060.1	78.57%			21.43%	English
1885	FA	1052.1	85.11%			14.89%	English
1895	FA	1051.0	50.00%	32.00%		18.00%	English
1895	PA	1059.3	64.38%	13.70%		21.92%	English
1895	2PA	1052.9	64.38%	13.70%		21.92%	English
1895	FA	1049.6	78.08%			21.92%	Wurtemberg, English
1912	PA	1061.0	20.22%	60.00%	19.78%		EK
1912	2PA	1053.6	20.22%	60.00%	19.78%		EK
1912	FA (Butts & casks)	1047.4	20.74%	60.83%	18.43%		EK
1912	IPA	1048.2	20.56%	46.90%	32.55%		EK
1912	FA	1047.6	20.74%	60.83%	18.43%		EK

Source:
Whitbread brewing records held at the London Metropolitan Archives, document numbers LMA/4453/D/01/051, LMA/4453/D/01/060, LMA/4453/D/01/061, LMA/4453/D/01/061, LMA/4453/D/01/061 and LMA/4453/D/01/077.

Whitbread were quicker to adopt sugar, with it averaging about 20% of the grist right through this period. Most London brewers would also have included an adjunct, usually flaked maize.

Speaking of which, see the contrast with fellow London brewer Barclay Perkins:

Barclay Perkins Pale Ale grists 1886 - 1908

Year	Beer	OG	pale malt	flaked maize	flaked rice	no. 1 sugar	no. 2 sugar	other sugar	hops
1886	PA	1059.0	75.00%	9.38%		15.63%			EK, Worcester
1892	PA	1063.0	77.14%	11.43%		11.43%			EK, Worcester
1900	PA	1060.0	73.58%	7.55%				18.87%	EK
1900	XLK	1052.5	73.58%	7.55%				18.87%	EK
1907	PA Ex	1058.0	85.71%			14.29%			EK, Worcester
1908	PA	1060.4	88.24%				11.76%		EK
1906	XLK	1050.0	71.68%	10.62%				17.70%	MK, EK, Worcester, Alsace

Sources:
Barclay Perkins brewing records held at the London Metropolitan Archives, document numbers ACC/2305/1/584, ACC/2305/1/588, ACC/2305/1/593, ACC/2305/1/605 and ACC/2305/1/599.

Most of Barclay Perkins' Pale Ales did contain about 10% adjuncts, either rice or maize in flaked form. The beers from 1907 and 1908 which contain none were brewed on their small plant. That might explain the lack of adjuncts.

Those two excepted, Barclay Perkins Pale Ales had a slightly lower malt percentage than either Usher or Whitbread. Though the combination of pale malt, sugar and adjuncts looks very similar to Usher's

1912 grists. Whitbread's only really differ in their eschewing of adjuncts. But they were funny about that and quite atypical of English brewers.

Like Whitbread, Barclay Perkins mostly stuck to English hops. Both much more so than Usher. But it does make sense. London was the trading centre for English hops. Most of the buying and selling took place in Southwark, just a stone's throw from Barclay Perkins brewery. Many London brewers Whitbread, for example, owned hop gardens in Kent. Further from where hops were grown and traded, Scottish brewers were more easily seduced by imports.

Mild Ales

This period is quite confusing with regard to Mild Ale. Brewers continuing to produce Shilling Ales – which were mostly the equivalent of English Mild Ales – but also made beers which were specifically called Mild Ale or designated by X's as Mild Ales were in England.

William Younger further muddied the waters by giving the same beer an X designation when intended to be sold on draught and a shilling designation when destined for bottling. It's taken me several years of study to get my head around and I still sometimes get confused.

William Younger Mild Ales 1885 - 1913

Year	Beer	Style	OG	FG	ABV	App. Attenuation	lbs hops/qtr	hops lb/brl
1885	X	Mild	1048	1009	5.16	81.25%	5.29	0.99
1885	XX	Mild	1056	1012	5.82	78.57%	6.19	1.53
1885	XXX	Mild	1065	1021	5.82	67.69%	6.67	1.86
1898	XX	Mild	1061	1016	5.95	73.77%	5.45	1.50
1898	XXX	Mild	1074	1018	7.41	75.68%	8.81	2.74
1913	XX - X	Mild	1055	1017	5.03	69.09%	4.07	0.88
1913	XX	Mild	1055	1018	4.89	67.27%	4.07	0.87
1913	XXK	Mild	1056	1016	5.29	71.43%	4.07	0.81
1913	XXX	Mild	1065	1021.5	5.75	66.92%	4.55	1.15

Source:
William Younger brewing records held at the Scottish Brewing Archive, document numbers WY/6/1/2/31, WY/6/1/2/45 and WY/6/1/2/58.

For comparison purposes, here are some London Milds from the end of the 19th century and early 20th century:

London Mild Ales 1885 - 1912

Year	Brewer	Beer	OG	FG	ABV	App. Attenuation	lbs hops/qtr	hops lb/brl
1885	Truman	X Ale	1059.0				7.3	1.87
1885	Whitbread	X	1059.6	1015.0	5.90	74.88%	7.49	1.90
1886	Barclay Perkins	X	1055.0	1010.0	5.96	81.87%	6.42	1.61
1886	Barclay Perkins	XX	1076.0	1022.7	7.05	70.11%	12.00	3.86
1887	Fuller	X	1050.7	1013.6	4.91	73.22%	6.64	1.41
1887	Fuller	XX	1064.8	1023.3	5.50	64.10%	6.64	1.93
1891	Barclay Perkins	X	1058.0	1015.0	5.69	74.21%	8.32	2.07
1894	Truman	X Ale	1056.5				9.0	2.19
1894	Whitbread	X	1058.4	1016.0	5.62	72.62%	8.23	2.09
1897	Fuller	X	1049.6	1012.2	4.95	75.42%	6.58	1.44
1909	Barclay Perkins	X	1053.6	1013.9	5.26	74.16%	7.49	1.62
1909	Truman	X Ale	1056.8				5.8	1.41
1910	Fuller	X	1052.6	1014.7	5.01	72.08%	5.2	1.21
1912	Whitbread	X	1054.0	1012.0	5.56	77.78%	4.49	1.05

Sources:
Barclay Perkins brewing records held at the London Metropolitan Archives, document numbers ACC/2305/1/584, ACC/2305/1/587 and ACC/2305/1/601
Whitbread brewing records held at the London Metropolitan Archives, document numbers LMA/4453/D/01/051, LMA/4453/D/01/060 and LMA/4453/D/01/077.
Truman brewing record held at the London Metropolitan Archives, document number B/THB/C/166, B/THB/C/175 and B/THB/C/190.
Fullers brewing records held at the brewery.

General trends seem to be William Younger's Mild Ales becoming less heavily hopped and lower gravity than equivalent London beers. A similar trend of a fall in hopping rate can also be seen in London. Whitbread and Truman's hopping declined from over 7 lbs per quarter in 1885 to around 5 lbs, while Fuller's fell from 6.5 lbs to 5 lbs. Only Barclay Perkins had a pretty much unchanged hopping.

Note that the stronger Milds had all disappeared in London by 1914. X Ale reigned supreme in the capital.

Usher's hopping rates by the eve of WW I were quite similar to those in London:

Thomas Usher Mild Ales 1885 - 1914

Year	Beer	OG	FG	ABV	App. Attenuation	lbs hops/ qtr	hops lb/brl
1885	54/- M	1062	1023	5.16	62.90%	5.00	1.42
1885	68/- M	1080	1025	7.28	68.75%	10.00	3.44
1914	44/- MA	1032	1012.5	2.58	60.94%	5.00	0.69
1914	50/- MA	1035	1013	2.91	62.86%	5.00	0.75
1914	60/- MA	1038	1015	3.04	60.53%	5.00	1.07
1914	80/- MA	1046	1016.5	3.90	64.13%	5.00	1.29
1914	100/- MA	1065	1027	5.03	58.46%	5.00	1.40

Sources:
Thomas Usher brewing records held at the Scottish Brewing Archive, document numbers TU/6/1/1, TU/6/1/2 and TU/6/1/5.

Usher's three weakest Mild Ales in 1914, 44/-, 50/- and 60/-, were far weaker than anything brewed in London.

Younger's grists underwent quite some transformation between 1885 and 1913:

William Younger Mild Ale grists 1885 - 1913

Year	Beer	Style	OG	pale malt	grits	sugar
1885	X	Mild	1048	100.00%		
1885	XX	Mild	1056	100.00%		
1885	XXX	Mild	1065	100.00%		
1898	XX	Mild	1061	69.23%	13.19%	17.58%
1898	XXX	Mild	1074	90.00%		10.00%
1913	XX - X	Mild	1055	54.38%	43.13%	2.50%
1913	XX	Mild	1055	54.38%	43.13%	2.50%
1913	XXK	Mild	1056	54.38%	43.13%	2.50%
1913	XXX	Mild	1065	55.10%	42.86%	2.04%

Source:
William Younger brewing records held at the Scottish Brewing Archive, document numbers WY/6/1/2/31, WY/6/1/2/45 and WY/6/1/2/58.

Initially 100% pale malt, by 1913 the grists contained a little sugar and a huge proportion of maize grits. It doesn't look great. That much maize must have had a considerable effect on the flavour of the finished beer.

Usher's Mild grists started simple, just pale malt and occasionally sugar, but became more complicated as WW I approached.

Mini Book Series volume XXVIII: Scotland! FG

Thomas Usher Mild Ale grists 1885 - 1914

Year	Beer	OG	pale malt	crystal malt	flaked maize	sugar
1885	54/- M	1062	87.10%			12.90%
1885	68/- M	1080	100.00%			
1914	44/- MA	1032	67.35%	6.12%	6.12%	20.41%
1914	50/- MA	1035	67.35%	6.12%	6.12%	20.41%
1914	60/- MA	1038	75.00%	5.36%	5.36%	14.29%
1914	80/- MA	1046	67.35%	6.12%	6.12%	20.41%
1914	100/- MA	1065	67.35%	6.12%	6.12%	20.41%

Sources:
Thomas Usher brewing records held at the Scottish Brewing Archive, document numbers TU/6/1/1, TU/6/1/2 and TU/6/1/5.

First flaked maize and then crystal malt were introduced just before WW I. The 20% sugar content in 1914 is quite high. Usually around 15% was the maximum.

London Mild grists were more diverse

London Mild Ale grists 1885 - 1912

Year	Brewer	Beer	OG	pale malt	brown malt	black malt	amber malt	crystal malt	flaked maize	flaked rice	sugar
1885	Truman	X Ale	1059.0	88.3%		0.2%					11.5%
1885	Whitbread	X	1059.6	92.4%							7.6%
1886	Barclay Perkins	X	1055.0	81.8%							18.2%
1886	Barclay Perkins	XX	1076.0	100.0%							
1887	Fuller	X	1050.7	44.4%			24.2%	10.1%			21.2%
1887	Fuller	XX	1064.8	0.0%			78.7%				21.3%
1891	Barclay Perkins	X	1058.0	45.6%	24.0%			2.4%		12.0%	16.0%
1894	Truman	X Ale	1056.5	91.7%							8.3%
1894	Whitbread	X	1058.4	93.8%							6.3%
1897	Fuller	X	1049.6	73.2%	1.1%						25.8%
1909	Barclay Perkins	X	1053.6	60.8%			10.8%		10.2%		18.2%
1909	Truman	X Ale	1056.8	74.3%				4.0%	9.3%		12.4%
1910	Fuller	X	1052.6	74.0%					6.6%		19.4%
1912	Whitbread	X	1054.0	85.1%							14.9%

Sources:
Barclay Perkins brewing records held at the London Metropolitan Archives, document numbers ACC/2305/1/584, ACC/2305/1/587 and ACC/2305/1/601
Whitbread brewing records held at the London Metropolitan Archives, document numbers LMA/4453/D/01/051, LMA/4453/D/01/060 and LMA/4453/D/01/077.
Truman brewing record held at the London Metropolitan Archives, document number B/THB/C/166, B/THB/C/175 and B/THB/C/190.
Fullers brewing records held at the brewery.

Fuller's grists were the most eccentric, with as much as 25% sugar and one beer with a base of amber rather than pale malt. By around 1910 all the London breweries listed except Whitbread had adopted flaked maize. Whitbread were a bit odd in their refusal to use unmalted adjuncts. The vast majority of English breweries did employ adjuncts, usually in the form of flaked maize.

Stock Ales

At the upper end of the gravity scale William Younger had beers with an X designation which were brewed as Stock Ales, that is beers not meant for immediate sale. These were hopped a little less than London Stock Ales. In the late 1880's Whitbread's KK and KKK Stock Ales contained 13-14 lbs of hops per quarter, which is a pretty massive amount. Younger's versions weren't lightly hopped by any means, just not as crazily hopped as London beers.

William Younger Stock Ales 1885 - 1913

Year	Beer	Style	OG	FG	ABV	App. Attenuation	lbs hops/ qtr	hops lb/brl
1885	XXXX	Stock Ale	1079	1020	7.81	74.68%	7.42	2.97
1898	XXXX	Stock Ale	1076	1020	7.41	73.68%	10.70	3.62
1913	XXXX	Stock Ale	1070	1024	6.09	65.71%	9.72	2.71

Source:
William Younger brewing records held at the Scottish Brewing Archive, document numbers WY/6/1/2/31, WY/6/1/2/45 and WY/6/1/2/58.

Younger's Stock Ales had very heavy dry hopping – between 8 oz. and 16 oz. per barrel.

Though lower in gravity than Younger's, Usher's Stock Ales had a similar level of hopping in the 19th century. Though by WW I that had fallen somewhat.

Thomas Usher Stock Ales 1885 - 1914

Year	Beer	OG	FG	ABV	App. Attenuation	lbs hops/ qtr	hops lb/brl
1885	X	1050	1013	4.89	74.00%	9.00	2.00
1888	XXX	1054	1011	5.69	79.63%	11.00	3.58
1888	X	1050	1012	5.03	76.00%	11.00	2.75
1888	XX	1054	1012	5.56	77.78%	12.00	3.24
1894	XX 60/-	1055	1015	5.29	72.73%	10.00	2.77
1912	X 60/-	1052	1016	4.76	69.23%	6.75	1.49
1912	X	1045	1014.5	4.03	67.78%	6.50	1.21

Sources:
Thomas Usher brewing records held at the Scottish Brewing Archive, document numbers TU/6/1/1, TU/6/1/2 and TU/6/1/5.

Here are a few London Stock Ales for comparison purposes:

London Stock Ales 1885 - 1912

Year	Brewer	Beer	OG	FG	ABV	App. Atten- uation	lbs hops/ qtr	hops lb/brl
1885	Whitbread	KK	1070.1	1024.9	5.97	64.43%	15.03	4.62
1885	Whitbread	KKK	1083.7	1030.7	7.00	63.25%	15.05	5.61
1887	Barclay Perkins	KKK	1088.0	1028.0	7.94	68.21%	17.69	6.64
1891	Barclay Perkins	KKK	1085.0	1023.8	8.09	71.97%	14.09	5.37
1891	Barclay Perkins	KK	1074.0	1018.8	7.30	74.55%	14.23	4.51
1894	Whitbread	KK	1077.6	1033.0	5.89	57.45%	14.09	4.88
1894	Whitbread	2KKK	1081.4	1035.0	6.14	57.02%	14.04	5.12
1894	Whitbread	KKK	1088.6	1037.0	6.83	58.26%	14.07	5.67
1909	Barclay Perkins	KK	1073.0	1021.1	6.87	71.16%	14.00	4.25
1910	Barclay Perkins	KKK	1087.3	1026.3	8.07	69.86%	14.00	5.33
1912	Whitbread	KK	1071.2	1022.0	6.51	69.10%	11.96	3.75
1912	Whitbread	2KKK	1077.4	1026.0	6.80	66.39%	11.96	4.07
1912	Whitbread	KKK	1081.5	1029.0	6.94	64.40%	11.96	4.29

Sources:
Barclay Perkins brewing records held at the London Metropolitan Archives, document numbers ACC/2305/1/583, ACC/2305/1/587 and ACC/2305/1/601
Whitbread brewing records held at the London Metropolitan Archives, document numbers LMA/4453/D/01/051, LMA/4453/D/01/059 and LMA/4453/D/01/077.

The hopping rate was falling in London, too. But at 12 and 14 lbs per quarter of malt, Barclay Perkins and Whitbread's Stock Ales remained heavily hopped. This is one of the few examples where Scottish versions of a style have a higher degree of attenuation than the English ones.

Younger's Stock Ale grists could hardly have been simpler:

William Younger Stock Ale grists 1885 - 1913

Year	Beer	Style	OG	pale malt	sugar
1885	XXXX	Stock Ale	1079	100.00%	
1898	XXXX	Stock Ale	1076	91.07%	8.93%
1913	XXXX	Stock Ale	1070	93.60%	6.40%

Source:
William Younger brewing records held at the Scottish Brewing Archive, document numbers WY/6/1/2/31, WY/6/1/2/45 and WY/6/1/2/58.

They consisted of nothing but pale malt and sometimes a little sugar. In contrast to Younger's later Mild Ales, their Stock Ales contained no maize grits.

Things were a little more complicated at Usher:

Thomas Usher Stock Ale grists 1885 - 1914

Year	Beer	OG	pale malt	black malt	flaked maize	sugar
1885	X	1050	99.35%	0.65%		
1888	XXX	1054	90.24%			9.76%
1888	X	1050	100.00%			
1888	XX	1054	100.00%			
1894	XX 60/-	1055	94.03%			5.97%
1912	X 60/-	1052	80.47%		9.62%	9.91%
1912	X	1045	78.00%		12.00%	10.00%

Sources:
Thomas Usher brewing records held at the Scottish Brewing Archive, document numbers TU/6/1/1, TU/6/1/2 and TU/6/1/5.

Usher used a similar percentage of sugar to Younger, but after 1900 they also used flaked maize in their Stock Ales.

Usher's Stock Ales had a much higher malt percentage than their Mild Ales, mostly because of the lower sugar content. The Mild Ales mostly included 20% after 1900, about double the amount of the Stock Ales.

The Stock Ales brewed in London, meanwhile, had much more complicated grists:

London Stock Ale grists 1885 - 1912

Year	Brewer	Beer	OG	pale malt	brown malt	crystal malt	SA malt	flaked maize	flaked rice	sugar
1885	Whitbread	KK	1070.1	85.86%						14.14%
1885	Whitbread	KKK	1083.7	86.96%						13.04%
1887	Barclay Perkins	KKK	1088.0	74.40%					9.60%	16.00%
1891	Barclay Perkins	KKK	1085.0	70.39%		3.35%			11.73%	14.53%
1891	Barclay Perkins	KK	1074.0	69.12%		4.56%			12.28%	14.04%
1894	Whitbread	KK	1077.6	14.00%	2.00%		70.67%			13.33%
1894	Whitbread	2KKK	1081.4	11.17%	2.23%		75.42%			11.17%
1894	Whitbread	KKK	1088.6	11.83%	1.78%		72.19%			14.20%
1909	Barclay Perkins	KK	1073.0	52.08%		3.47%	19.44%	9.72%		15.28%
1910	Barclay Perkins	KKK	1087.3	69.62%		4.10%		9.22%		17.06%
1912	Whitbread	KK	1071.2	28.97%	2.07%		55.17%			13.79%
1912	Whitbread	2KKK	1077.4	28.97%	2.07%		55.17%			13.79%
1912	Whitbread	KKK	1081.5	28.97%	2.07%		55.17%			13.79%

Sources:
Barclay Perkins brewing records held at the London Metropolitan Archives, document numbers ACC/2305/1/583, ACC/2305/1/587 and ACC/2305/1/601
Whitbread brewing records held at the London Metropolitan Archives, document numbers LMA/4453/D/01/051, LMA/4453/D/01/059 and LMA/4453/D/01/077.

Whitbread, quite unusually, had brown malt and SA in their Stock Ales. SA was a malt specifically designed for Stock Ales. It produced a less easily fermentable wort, the assumption being that the final phase of the fermentation would be performed by Brettanomyces, which could chew its way through those less fermentable sugars.

While over at Barclay Perkins, crystal malt and unmalted adjuncts, either rice of maize. And sometimes SA malt. The sugar content for both breweries was quite similar at 13-17%. Which is around double what the Scots were using.

Note that the Scots had no coloured malts in their Stock Ale grists. This is typical of Scottish brewing: very little coloured malt in anything other than Stout.

Shilling Ales

For Shilling Ales, this period was their last hurrah. WW I pretty well killed them off. Though it did open up the possibility of using the shilling names for other types of beer, which is exactly what happened between the wars.

In the 1880's, Shilling Ales were still fairly popular and William Younger produced a very large variety of them, with gravities ranging from 1036º to 1115º. In the following decades the range was gradually whittled down, from ten in 1885 to seven in 1898 and just five in 1913. It's clear that this type of beer was on the way out. WW I only hastened its inevitable demise.

The weaker Shilling Ales were mostly lightly hopped, with no more than 5 lbs of hops per quarter. By means of comparison Whitbread, a big London brewers, hopped its ordinary Mild, X Ale, at 8lbs per quarter. While their Stock and Pale Ales contained 10-14 lbs per quarter[47].

Stronger versions, 120/- and up, had rather more generous hopping at 6-8 lbs per quarter. This may only be at about the level of London Mild Ale, but because of the high OG of these beers it meant they could contain 4-5 lbs per barrel, a significant amount.

William Younger Shilling Ales 1885 - 1914							
Year	Beer	OG	FG	ABV	App. Atten- uation	lbs hops/ qtr	hops lb/brl
1885	50/-	1036	1011	3.31	69.44%	5.45	0.81
1885	S 50/-	1042	1018	3.18	57.14%	3.85	0.45
1885	B 50/-	1044	1016	3.70	63.64%	3.85	0.85
1885	H 60/-	1041	1011	3.97	73.17%	6.67	1.12
1885	60/-	1052	1023	3.84	55.77%	5.00	1.06
1885	80/-	1064	1027	4.89	57.81%	5.00	1.35
1885	100/-	1074	1030	5.82	59.46%	5.00	1.71
1885	120/-	1086	1040	6.09	53.49%	5.67	2.46
1885	140/-	1099	1043	7.41	56.57%	6.23	3.04
1885	160/-	1115	1050	8.60	56.52%	8.54	5.25
1898	H 60/-	1044	1012	4.23	72.73%	6.52	1.21
1899	60/-	1050	1023	3.57	54.00%	5.19	1.12
1898	80/-	1061	1027	4.50	55.74%	5.36	1.36

---

[47] Whitbread brewing record held at the London Metropolitan Archives, document number LMA/4453/D/01/054.

William Younger Shilling Ales 1885 - 1914

Year	Beer	OG	FG	ABV	App. Attenuation	lbs hops/ qtr	hops lb/brl
1899	100/-	1073	1036	4.89	50.68%	5.76	1.88
1898	120/-	1086	1038	6.35	55.81%	7.14	3.07
1898	140/-	1100	1039	8.07	61.00%	7.14	3.57
1898	160/-	1111	1042	9.13	62.16%	8.48	4.59
1913	H 60/-	1044	1013	4.10	70.45%	4.00	0.67
1913	60/-	1047	1023	3.18	51.06%	3.04	0.28
1913	80/-	1056	1027	3.84	51.79%	3.60	0.75
1913	100/-	1066	1032	4.50	51.52%	3.60	0.89
1913	160/-	1097	1038	7.81	60.82%	5.33	2.83

Source:
William Younger brewing records held at the Scottish Brewing Archive, document numbers WY/6/1/2/31, WY/6/1/2/45 and WY/6/1/2/58.

After 1880, Younger's grists became more complicated. Not necessarily for the better.

William Younger Shilling Ales 1885 - 1914

Year	Beer	OG	pale malt	grits	sugar	colour
1885	50/-	1036	100.00%			
1885	S 50/-	1042	100.00%			
1885	B 50/-	1044	95.12%		4.88%	
1885	H 60/-	1041	100.00%			
1885	60/-	1052	100.00%			
1885	80/-	1064	100.00%			
1885	100/-	1074	100.00%			
1885	120/-	1086	100.00%			
1885	140/-	1099	91.89%		8.11%	
1885	160/-	1115	88.10%		11.90%	
1898	H 60/-	1044	100.00%			
1899	60/-	1050	100.00%			
1898	80/-	1061	100.00%			
1899	100/-	1073	91.58%		8.42%	
1898	120/-	1086	91.74%		8.26%	
1898	140/-	1100	91.74%		8.26%	
1898	160/-	1111	92.48%		7.52%	
1913	H 60/-	1044	55.00%	45.00%		
1913	60/-	1047	52.94%	44.12%	2.94%	
1913	80/-	1056	51.37%	43.15%	5.48%	4 galls
1913	100/-	1066	47.26%	47.26%	5.48%	4 galls
1913	160/-	1097	51.67%	41.67%	6.67%	

Source:
William Younger brewing records held at the Scottish Brewing Archive, document numbers WY/6/1/2/31, WY/6/1/2/45 and WY/6/1/2/58.

Up until 1900 or so, Younger's Shilling Ales were all malt, or mostly malt with a touch of sugar. Then just before WW I, like all Younger's other beers, they contain ridiculous amounts of maize grits. It has me wondering just how Younger managed to have a good name for their beers in the first half of the 20th century. The grists look like total crap.

Before we continue with Thomas Usher's Shilling Ales, I must mention something. These could just ne Mild Ales. The differentiation between Shilling Ales and Mild ales isn't always clear. And, after all, Shilling Ales were really a type of Mild Ale, anyway.

Thomas Usher Shilling Ales 1885 - 1913							
Year	Beer	OG	FG	ABV	App Atten- uation	lbs hops/ qtr	hops lb/brl
1885	80/-	1058	1023	4.63	60.34%	5.00	1.28
1885	100/-	1078	1033	5.95	57.39%	5.00	1.72
1888	80/-	1054	1020	4.50	62.96%	5.00	1.29
1888	100/-	1074	1027	6.22	63.51%	5.00	1.77
1894	60/-	1040	1018	2.91	55.00%	5.00	0.86
1894	80/-	1053	1020	4.37	62.26%	5.00	1.15
1894	100/-	1068	1030	5.03	55.38%	5.00	1.47
1913	40/-	1029	1010	2.51	65.52%	5.75	0.69
1912	44/-	1034	1013	2.78	61.76%	5.00	0.71
1912	60/-	1039	1015	3.18	61.54%	5.00	0.81
1912	80/-	1049	1018	4.10	63.27%	5.00	1.02
1912	100/-	1064	1029	4.63	54.69%	5.00	1.34
Sources: Thomas Usher brewing records held at the Scottish Brewing Archive, document numbers TU/6/1/1 and TU/6/1/2.							

Some of the examples from just before WW I were shockingly weak. 40/- and 44/- look like wartime beers. 1040º was considered piss weak in London. Sub-1030º beers were unheard of in England. Even Harvest Beers were stronger.

Just for a change, I'm throwing in a non-London comparison. Partly to show that what went on in the capital wasn't necessarily the same as what went on in the sticks. Like, say, in Suffolk.

Adnams Mild Ales 1879 - 1913							
Year	Beer	OG	FG	ABV	App. Atten- uation	lbs hops/ qtr	hops lb/brl
1879	X	1037.4				14.67	2.58
1879	XX	1052.6					
1879	XXXX	1067.9				12.50	4.44
1890	XX	1043.8				10.00	1.80
1890	XXXX	1059.8				9.29	2.39
1913	X	1033.0	1005.5	3.64	83.33%	3.73	0.54
1913	XX	1039.0	1008.0	4.10	79.49%	3.83	0.65
Source: Adnams brewing records held at the brewery.							

Unlike in London, there were sub-1040º Milds out in the countryside. In the weird pre-WW I world, the large industrial breweries didn't beat the tiddlers on price. There were very standard prices across the country and time. The big boys sold stronger beer for the same price. It seems very odd. Especially as beer strengths weren't public knowledge.

Usher's grists were quite different from Younger's:

Thomas Usher Shilling Ales 1885 - 1913						
Year	Beer	OG	pale malt	crystal malt	flaked maize	sugar
1885	80/-	1058	88.64%			11.36%
1885	100/-	1078	88.64%			11.36%
1888	80/-	1054	88.64%			11.36%
1888	100/-	1074	88.64%			11.36%
1894	60/-	1040	75.00%			25.00%
1894	80/-	1053	75.00%			25.00%
1894	100/-	1068	75.00%			25.00%
1913	40/-	1029	80.23%			9.30%
1912	44/-	1034	62.43%	5.20%	6.94%	25.43%
1912	60/-	1039	62.43%	5.20%	6.94%	25.43%
1912	80/-	1049	62.43%	5.20%	6.94%	25.43%
1912	100/-	1064	62.43%	5.20%	6.94%	25.43%
Sources: Thomas Usher brewing records held at the Scottish Brewing Archive, document numbers TU/6/1/1 and TU/6/1/2.						

Both breweries introduced adjuncts after 1900, but the percentage was hugely different: just 7% at Usher, over 40% at Younger. To compensate, Usher used a large proportion of sugar, 25% from 1894 onwards. And crystal malt. An ingredient that was becoming standard in Mild Ales in England.

Adnam's Mild Ales contained pretty crazy amounts of sugar – while not matching quite the insane grits content of William Younger's beers.

Adnams Mild Ale grists 1879 - 1913							
Year	Beer	OG	pale malt	crystal malt	MA malt	flaked maize	sugar
1879	X	1037.4	67.74%				32.26%
1879	XX	1052.6	75.00%				25.00%
1879	XXXX	1067.9	71.43%				28.57%
1890	XX	1043.8	69.23%				30.77%
1890	XXXX	1059.8	72.97%				27.03%
1913	X	1033.0			83.17%		16.83%
1913	XX	1039.0		6.53%	68.56%	6.53%	18.38%
Source: Adnams brewing records held at the brewery.							

A common factor in Scottish Mild/Shilling Ales and English Mild Ales is the increasing presence of crystal malt after 1900.

It's odd that brewing in the metropolitan Scottish capital should in some ways resemble rural English brewing more than that of London.

But the truth is that British brewing was very diverse before 1914. A diversity that isn't always fully reflected in the brewing records. Yeast strains, fermentation systems and other regional differences would have played a part as well.

Porter and Stout

Standard-strength Porter, which had never been hugely popular in Scotland, gradually dwindled away towards the end of the 19th century. Though some brewers weren't that precise in their use of the terms. In the 1860's William Younger had a beer they sometimes called P (Porter) and others BS (Brown Stout)[48]. Lower in gravity than standard London Porter, it wouldn't have been considered a Stout in England.

Towards the end of the 1800's a new type of Stout began to evolve in Scotland. One completely different from anything brewed in England. Its defining features were an – even for Scotland – very poor degree of attenuation and an extremely low level of hopping. Very often spent hops – that is hops which had already y been boiled in another brew – were used. The resulting beer must have been very malty and sweet

William Younger

William Younger, however, continued to brew a more traditional type of Stout, DBS, as well as one that sat between the two other types of Stout, MBS.

William Younger Stout 1885 - 1913

Year	Beer	OG	FG	ABV	App. Atten- uation	lbs hops/ qtr	hops lb/brl
1885	S1	1073	1033	5.29	54.79%	1.43	0.43
1885	S2	1064	1030	4.50	53.13%	2.50	0.66
1885	DBS	1073	1025	6.35	65.75%	15.86	5.51
1899	S1	1069	1035	4.50	49.28%	2.31	0.32
1898	S2	1059	1029	3.97	50.85%	3.49	0.30
1899	SS1	1068	1029	5.16	57.35%	1.47	0.42
1899	SS2	1058	1023	4.63	60.34%	1.47	0.36
1898	DBS	1069	1023	6.09	66.67%	7.50	2.26
1898	MBS	1065	1025	5.29	61.54%	3.68	1.10
1913	S1	1065	1031	4.50	52.31%	1.88	0.50
1913	S2	1059	1029	3.97	50.85%	1.88	0.45
1913	DBS	1065	1022	5.69	66.15%	10.65	2.63
1913	MBS	1065	1020	5.95	69.23%	3.50	0.74

Source:
William Younger brewing records held at the Scottish Brewing Archive, document numbers WY/6/1/2/31, WY/6/1/2/45 and WY/6/1/2/58.

While there were few changes in the general specifications of Younger's Stouts, there were big modifications to the grist. In 1885, their grists looked very much like classic London Stout ones: a simple combination of pale, brown and black malts:

---

[48] William Younger brewing record held at the Scottish Brewing Archive, document number WY/6/1/2/21.

William Younger Stout grists in 1885

Beer	OG	pale malt	brown malt	black malt
S1	1073	71.43%	21.43%	7.14%
S2	1064	70.83%	20.83%	8.33%
DBS	1073	65.52%	27.59%	6.90%

Source:
William Younger brewing record held at the Scottish Brewing Archive, document number WY/6/1/2/31.

A decade and a bit later, gone was the brown malt, replaced by amber malt, grits and sugar:

William Younger Stout grists in 1898

Beer	OG	pale malt	black malt	amber malt	grits	sugar
S1	1069	61.61%	13.39%	5.36%	10.71%	8.93%
S2	1059	57.00%	15.00%	6.00%	12.00%	10.00%
DBS	1069	64.66%	12.93%	5.17%	10.34%	6.90%
MBS	1065	60.55%	13.76%	5.50%	11.01%	9.17%

Source:
William Younger brewing record held at the Scottish Brewing Archive, document number WY/6/1/2/45.

One the eve of WW I, the black malt percentage had been halved, amber malt replaced by chocolate malt, the grits content massively increased and caramel added, presumably to make up for the loos of colour from black malt:

William Younger Stout grists in 1913

Beer	OG	pale malt	black malt	choc. Malt	grits	caramel	sugar
S2	1059	42.86%	6.59%	6.59%	32.97%	3.30%	7.69%
DBS	1065	42.42%	6.06%	6.06%	33.33%	4.04%	8.08%
MBS	1065	49.09%	5.45%	5.45%	32.73%	3.64%	3.64%

Source:
William Younger brewing record held at the Scottish Brewing Archive, document number WY/6/1/2/58.

These big changes in ingredients must have had a considerable impact on the character of Younger's Stouts.

Thomas Usher

Let's take a look at another Edinburgh brewer's Stouts and see how they match up with London Stouts. You'll see that there are some significant differences.

Thomas Usher vs London Porter and Stout 1909 - 1912

Year	Brewer	Beer	Style	OG	FG	ABV	App. Atter-uation	lbs hops/qtr	hcps lb/brl
1912	Whitbread	P	Porter	1054.3	1013.0	5.47	76.03%	4.92	1.16
1912	Whitbread	LS	Stout	1055.3	1013.0	5.60	76.50%	4.92	1.18
1912	Whitbread	Exp S	Stout	1068.4	1020.0	6.41	70.77%	13.05	4.24
1912	Whitbread	SS	Stout	1079.9	1030.0	6.60	62.43%	8.48	3.12
1912	Whitbread	SSS	Stout	1095.8	1039.0	7.51	59.23%	8.48	3.74
1910	Barclay Perkins	OMS	Stout	1053.2	1016.5	4.86	68.93%	7.50	1.82
1910	Barclay Perkins	BS Ex	Stout	1076.0	1022.5	7.08	70.39%	12.00	4.12
1910	Barclay Perkins	E P Ex	Porter	1063.5	1020.0	5.75	68.50%	12.00	3.40
1911	Barclay Perkins	RDP	Porter	1068.2	1023.5	5.91	65.54%	8.00	2.52
1909	Truman	Imperial Stout	Stout	1094.2				5.6	2.72
1909	Truman	SS	Stout	1072.0				5.6	2.08
1909	Truman	Runner L & C	Porter	1054.3				6.1	1.38
1909	Truman	Country Runner	Porter	1058.2				7.5	2.01
1909	Truman	Bottling	Porter	1052.6				7.5	1.82
1909	Truman	Export Stout	Stout	1069.3				9.9	3.35
1909	Truman	Runner	Porter	1058.2				8.2	2.31
1909	Truman	Keeping Stout	Stout	1069.3				9.5	3.29
1912	Thomas Usher	48/-	Stout	1046	1023	3.04	50.00%	6.50	1.36
1912	Thomas Usher	54/-	Stout	1054	1026	3.70	51.85%	6.50	1.60
1912	Thomas Usher	Stt	Stout	1070	1029	5.42	58.57%	6.50	2.07

Sources:
Barclay Perkins brewing record held at the London Metropolitan Archives, document number ACC/2305/1/602
Whitbread brewing record held at the London Metropolitan Archives, document number LMA/4453/D/09/106
Truman brewing record held at the London Metropolitan Archives, document number B/THB/C/112
Thomas Usher brewing record held at the Scottish Brewing Archive, document number TU/6/1/5.

Usher's Stouts were far lower in gravity than those from London. The middle-strength Stout was only about the same strength as a standard porter from the capital. There's nothing even vaguely approaching the gravity of Whitbread SS or Truman Imperial Stout. The market for Stout was much smaller in Scotland meaning brewers north of the border were unlikely to brew to such a wide range of strengths.

Usher's grists were quite different from William Younger's, including brown, chocclate and crystal malt:

Thomas Usher Stout gists in 1912

Beer	OG	pale malt	brown malt	chocolate Malt	crystal malt	sugar
48/-	1046	66.39%	4.92%	6.15%	6.15%	16.39%
54/-	1054	66.39%	4.92%	6.15%	6.15%	16.39%
Stt	1070	66.39%	4.92%	6.15%	6.15%	16.39%

Source:
Thomas Usher brewing record held at the Scottish Brewing Archive, document number TU/6/1/5.

Maclay

Tiny Maclay holds an important place in the history of Stout as the first brewery to produce an Oatmeal Stout.

Maclay came up with the idea of an Oat Malt Stout in the 1890's. So keen were they on the idea that they patented it. Not that it stopped other breweries imitating them. Their rivals simply called their beers Oatmeal Stout instead.

Maclay claimed all sorts of wonderful properties for their new invention. This is from an early advertisement:

> And one of many Unsolicited Testimonials received states that - "Its tonic properties are fully demonstrated in the marvellous results produced by its use in convalescent and in chronic wasting diseases, where its nourishing and stimulating effects are admirable. Its delicate flavour renders it palatable to even the most sensitive palates."
> J. STUART-ARCHIBALD,
> B.M., CM., Edinburgh University.
> Falkirk Herald - Saturday 23 January 1897, page 2.

It sounds lovely.

The percentage of oats in Maclay's beer was very high at around 30%. Other brewers were more stingy with oats. London brewers Whitbread and Barclay Perkins used token amounts in their Oatmeal Stouts, never more than 3% and often less than 1%.

In addition to oat malt and pale malt, Maclay's Stouts also contained amber malt and sugar:

Maclay Stout grists in 1909						
Beer	OG	pale malt	black malt	amber malt	oat malt	sugar
OMS 63/-	1062	47.62%	9.52%	3.17%	28.57%	11.11%
DBS 54/-	1044	50.28%	10.06%	3.35%	30.17%	6.15%
Source: Maclay brewing record held at the Scottish Brewing Archive, document number M/6/1/1/2.						

Strong/Scotch Ale

Scotland – and Edinburgh in particular – was well known for its Strong Ales, or Scotch Ales as they were called in England. These formed a large part of Scottish exports, particularly to the West Indies.

Earlier in the century Strong Ales had been the upper echelons of Shilling Ales. Beers like 100/-, 120/- 140/- and even 160/-. These were higher-gravity versions of the weaker Shilling Ales, which generally filled the slot occupied by X Ale and XX Ale in England. Though these stronger versions were much more heavily hopped, sometimes containing over five pounds per 36-gallon barrel.

Around 1860 William Younger had introduced another range of Strong Ales, referred to by a number rather than shillings. The strongest being No. 1 and the weakest No. 4. The naming convention was possibly adopted in imitation of Burton practice. Brewers there such as Bass and Evershed used the system. The latter is particularly significant as at least one member of the Younger family had an apprenticeship there.

No. 1 and No.3 were longer-lived than the strong Shilling Ales that preceded them. No. 1 survived until well after WW II and No 3 is still around today albeit with a couple of interrupts in production.

You can see in the table that gravities began to be eroded after 1900, especially for No. 2 and No. 3. This process continued – and was even more dramatic – later in the 20th century.

William Younger numbered Strong Ales 1885 - 1914							
Year	Beer	OG	FG	ABV	App. Attenuation	lbs hops/qtr	hops lb/brl
1885	1	1103	1035	9.00	66.02%	12.44	6.26
1885	2	1091	1024	8.86	73.63%	9.76	4.80
1885	3 pale	1076	1025	6.75	67.11%	10.33	3.56
1898	1	1104	1030	9.79	71.15%	16.90	8.35
1898	3	1074	1019	7.28	74.32%	8.81	2.97
1913	1	1097	1037	7.94	61.86%	10.28	7.40
1914	2 Sc	1076	1025	6.75	67.11%	9.35	2.36
1913	3	1065	1021.5	5.75	66.92%	4.55	1.15
1913	3a	1072	1025	6.22	65.28%	5.48	1.22
Source: William Younger brewing records held at the Scottish Brewing Archive, document numbers WY/6/1/2/31, WY/6/1/2/45 and WY/6/1/2/58.							

There weren't really equivalent beers in London. Instead, I'm using beers from Truman's Burton brewery, which did produce beers of a similar type.

Truman (Burton) numbered Ales 1883 - 1887							
Year	Beer	OG	FG	ABV	App. Attenuation	lbs hops/qtr	hops lb/brl
1883	S4	1075.9	1026.6	6.52	64.96%	9.60	3 15
1887	S3	1092.8	1027.7	8.61	70.15%	11.33	5 00
1887	R4	1078.7	1024.9	7.11	68.31%	7.00	2 58
1887	S5	1074.5	1020.5	7.15	72.49%	10.19	3 44
Sources: Truman brewing records held at the London Metropolitan Archives, document numbers B/THB/BUR/35 and B/THB/BUR/11.							

Lager

After 1880 Lager began to be brewed on an industrial scale for the first time in Scotland. We've already learned that the small Edinburgh brewery owned by John Muir was the first to experiment with bottom-fermentation. The second Scottish brewer to try their hand at Lager brewing probably wasn't who you would have expected. It wasn't Tennent, but William Younger, who first had a go at a Pilsner in 1880.

This shouldn't really come as a surprise. Because there were personal links between William Younger and that pioneer of Lager brewing, Carlsberg. Karl Jacobsen, son of the brewery's founder, served an apprenticeship in Britain, spending time at Evershed in Burton and William Younger in Edinburgh.

There was a reason why Scottish brewers became interested in Lager brewing towards the end of the 1800's. They had a large export trade to Asia, mostly British colonies. But around this time continental Lager brewers began nibbling away their business there. Brewing Lager themselves was a way to combat this threat. It wasn't just Scottish brewers, Allsopp, one of the big Burton brewers, installed a Lager plant (purchased in the USA) around 1900.

William Younger Pilsner in 1881							
Year	Beer	OG	FG	ABV	App. Attenuation	lbs hops/ qtr	hops lb/brl
1881	PX	1058	1017	5.42	70.69%	2.92	1.51
1881	PXX	1068	1020	6.35	70.59%	3.17	2.04
1881	PXX	1064.5	1023	5.49	64.34%	3.85	1.92
Source: William Younger brewing record held at the Scottish Brewing Archive, document number WY/6/1/3/9.							

The experiment at Younger didn't last long. After a few brews they abandoned their Pilsner. Lager brewing firmly established itself in Scotland only in 1889 when Tennent built, at great expense, a dedicated plant, designed and constructed by German engineers[49]. Though they had been brewing Lager since 1885[50].

Sadly, Tennent's Lager brewing records haven't survived. However another document which lists a few basic details, allows a glimpse of Tennent's early Lager.

Tennent's Lager Beer in 1888						
Date	Year	Beer	OG	lbs hops/ qtr	hops lb/brl	barrels
31st Oct	1888	Lager Beer	1053.0	4.62	1.25	48
7th Nov	1888	Lager Beer	1054.0	4.62	1.18	102
14th Nov	1888	Lager Beer	1057.0	4.50	1.20	100
21st Nov	1888	Lager Beer	1060.0	4.50	1.20	100
28th Nov	1888	Lager Beer	1058.0	4.50	1.13	106
5th Dec	1888	Lager Beer	1057.0	4.50	1.12	107
12th Dec	1888	Lager Beer	1055.0	4.50	1.07	112
Source: Tennent record held at the Scottish Brewing Archive, document number T/6/1/1/5.						

---

[49] Scottish Brewing Archive Journal Vol. 1 1998, page 5.
[50] Amber, Gold and Black" by Martyn Cornell, 2008, page 216.

The level of hopping is very low, only about the same as for the weakest Shilling Ales.

Recipes

1909 Maclay Table Beer 28/-

Table Beer was a bit of a Scottish speciality in the 19th century. When this low-gravity beer was shipped to England and beyond.

English brewers – in the big cities, at least – had kicked Table Beer into touch early in the 19th century. The Scots not only persisted with it, but earned good money from it. But towards the end of the 1800's, it peters out in Scotland, too. The last William Younger example I have is from 1898. Making this the latest one I know.

Parti-gyled with 56/- Mild, you might have expected it to have the gravity. In reality, 28/- only had just over a third of the 56/- gravity of 1061º. For a pre-WW I beer, 28/- is laughably weak. Though at least in those days you paid the tax proportionate to gravity, even below 1027º.

The grist is pretty interesting for a Scottish beer, with a full three different types of malt. Yahoo! Not a huge amount of bitterness, but what would you expect in a sub-2% ABV beer?

The two mashing temperatures are after the initial infusion and after the underlet.

1909 Maclay Table Beer 28/-		
pale malt	3.00 lb	63.16%
amber malt	0.125 lb	2.63%
black malt	0.125 lb	2.63%
grits	1.00 lb	21.05%
No. 2 invert sugar	0.50 lb	10.53%
Cluster 120 min	0.25 oz	
Hallertau 60 min	0.25 oz	
Fuggles 30 min	0.50 oz	
OG	1022	
FG	1007	
ABV	1.98	
Apparent attenuation	68.18%	
IBU	16	
SRM	8	
Mash at	146/154º F	
Sparge at	170º F	
Boil time	90 minutes	
pitching temp	63º F	
Yeast	WLP028 Edinburgh Ale	

1885 Thomas Usher 100/-

Yet more Scottish brewing fun. It's almost as if I'm writing a book on Scottish brewing.

Shilling Ales, which formed the backbone of Scottish brewing in the first half of the 19th century, were gradually eclipsed in the second half by styles more similar to those from south of the border. In particular Pale Ales. Shilling Ales soldiered on until WW I, which put them out of their misery. Post war, most Scottish breweries produced a range of Pale Ales, a Stout, a Strong Ale and perhaps a Mild Ale.

It was a huge transformation, the war having an even greater impact on the styles brewed than in England. But it did help brewers rationalise their brewing. By parti-gyling they could cut back to just two recipes, one for the Stout and the other for everything else. Some even managed to parti-gyle their Stout with their Pale Ales and so needed only once recipe.

The Scots weren't ones for overcomplicated recipes. 100% pale malt up until 1880 Free Mash Tun Act, pale malt and some sort of adjunct after it. In the case of Usher, than meant sugar. With 12% sugar in this recipe, I'm amazed at how high the FG is. Though if you've been reading carefully you'll realise low levels of attenuation were pretty standard for Shilling Ales.

A word on the hopping. In the brewing record the hops are listed as California and Alsace, which I've interpreted as Cluster and Strisselspalt. Though I'm not sure if Strisselspalt was already around in the 1880's. If it wasn't, I've no idea what variety they might be.

1885 Thomas Usher 100/-		
pale malt	14.75 lb	83.06%
cane sugar	2.00 lb	11.94%
Cluster 90 min	1.50 oz	
Cluster 60 min	1.50 oz	
Strisselspalt 30 min	0.75 oz	
OG	1078	
FG	1033	
ABV	5.95	
Apparent attenuation	57.69%	
IBU	59	
SRM	5	
Mash at	155° F	
Sparge at	175° F	
Boil time	120 minutes	
pitching temp	57° F	
Yeast	WLP028 Edinburgh Ale	

1894 Thomas Usher 60/-

60/- is such a fascinating beer. Because there have been so many different types of beer called 60/- in Scotland. Most with absolutely no connection with the modern beer.

This is a beer of the most old-fashioned type of 60/-. That is, a Scottish Ale of what I call a Shilling Ale. Basically the Scottish equivalent of Mild Ale, but often sold bottled rather than on draught. Though I've never seen a 19th-century English Mild as weak as this beer. Down in London, they didn't brew anything much under 1050º.

As usual, the hop varieties are a guess. The brewing record just lists them as Kent and Sussex. Feel free to change them around, as long as you stick with English ones.

I'm not going to bore you with too much chatter. It's a simple beer, containing just pale malt and sugar. Which makes it typical of Scottish beer of this period. As does the crappy degree of attenuation.

1894 Thomas Usher 60/-		
pale malt	5.75 lb	74.19%
No. 2 invert sugar	2.00 lb	25.81%
Fuggles 90 min	0.50 oz	
Fuggles 60 min	0.50 oz	
Goldings 30 min	0.50 oz	
OG	1040	
FG	1018	
ABV	2.91	
Apparent attenuation	55.00%	
IBU	20	
SRM	8	
Mash at	146º F	
Sparge at	170º F	
Boil time	120 minutes	
pitching temp	60º F	
Yeast	WLP028 Edinburgh Ale	

1898 William Younger 80/-

You might think that you know what 80/- is. You don't. Or at least you don't know what 19th-century 80/- was. Because it has no connection with the modern style, other than originating in Scotland.

The modern style is just the Scottish version of Best Bitter and only emerged between the wars. The Scots did brew Pale Ales in the 19th century and they did often have shilling designations. But they were usually 54/- or 60/-. Don't think I've ever seen an 80/- Pale Ale from before WW I.

In the 19th century 80/- was usually an Ale. More specifically, a type of Mild Ale. William Younger's set in 1898 went from 60/- to 160/- in increments of 20/- with gravities from 1051º to 1111º. You might be surprised to see Mild Ales with such high gravities, but it wasn't that unusual back then. And as they were sold young, Mild Ales is what they were.

Younger brewed two parallel sets of Mild Ales. Ones with a shilling designation and one with X's, like in England. 80/- was basically the same as XX, but with a couple of significant differences. 80/- was intended for bottling. It was racked into hogsheads, half hogsheads and quarter hogsheads which were immediately dispatched to grocers and publicans, who would bottle the beer. XX was filled into hogsheads, barrels and half barrels and was sold on draught.

The recipes were very similar, but 80/- wasn't dry-hopped, but XX was. And while 80/- was all malt, XX contained grits and sugar. But the biggest difference was the level of attenuation. 74% for XX and just 56% for 80/-. I think I know the reason for that. XX needed to be ready for immediate consumption while 80/- would have needed some fermentables for bottle conditioning.

It's another very simple recipe, not quite SMaSH, but pretty close. In this period Younger only used English and American hops, about a third of the former to two thirds of the latter. Interestingly two types are listed: American and Pacific. Presumably that's East and West Coast respectively.

Here's the recipe

1898 William Younger 80/-		
pale malt	14.25 lb	100.00%
Cluster 90 min	2.25 oz	
Fuggles 30 min	0.75 oz	
OG	1061	
FG	1027	
ABV	4.50	
Apparent attenuation	55.74%	
IBU	54	
SRM	5	
Mash at	151º F	
Sparge at	160º F	
Boil time	90 minutes	
pitching temp	59.5º F	
Yeast	WLP028 Edinburgh Ale	

1898 William Younger 140/-

At the end of the 19th century William Younger was still producing some very powerful Shilling Ales, though not in the same quantities as 50 years earlier.

After 1880, William Younger moved away from 100% malt beers. Not that far, in this case. There's a little glucose, too. Not exactly a complicated recipe. Though slightly more than it might appear. There was only pale malt, but five different types of it. The descriptions are in tiny writing, most of which I can't read, but I can definitely make out two as being Californian and one as Scottish. You can pick just about any barley-growing country in the world as possibilities for the other three.

The hops are described as Kent, American and Pacific. The latter two meaning East Coast and West Coast USA respectively. This typical of 1890's William Younger. A couple of decades earlier they'd been big fans of Central European hops like Saaz and Hallertau. Later in the century their preference shifted to North America. Though they almost always used Kent hops in addition to foreign ones.

The hops were mostly pretty fresh. The beer was brewed in November 1898, and some of the Kent hops were from that year. The remainder of the hops were from the 1897 season. All those relatively fresh American hops leave the beer with quite a high level of bitterness. Though there's plenty of malty sweetness to balance that out.

1898 William Younger 140/-		
pale malt	20.75 lb	92.22%
glucose	1.75 lb	7.78%
Cluster 90 min	5.50 oz	
Fuggles 30 min	2.25 oz	
OG	1100	
FG	1039	
ABV	8.07	
Apparent attenuation	61.00%	
IBU	103	
SRM	7	
Mash at	151° F	
Sparge at	160° F	
Boil time	90 minutes	
pitching temp	58° F	
Yeast	WLP028 Edinburgh Ale	

1912 Thomas Usher 100/-

What shouts end of year more than a Strong Scottish beer? Or someone who's been drinking it.

Strongish, really, for the date. Or for the OG. In terms of ABV. it's not strong at all. By any standards, other than 1918.

As usual, I struggled to find an apt style in BeerSmith. So I just added one. It's called "Scottish Shilling Ale medium strong". Even with my own definition of the style, I couldn't hit all the parameters. Because BeerSmith expects better attenuation than the Scots went for. Not a dig at BeerSmith. I probably just haven't found the right parameter to tweak.

I really like that you can customise BeerSmith. I should have started earlier. Maybe I should put together an historic styles add-on and flog it. That should earn me enough to retire early, shouldn't it? No, I don't think so. If only.

On with the recipe. Onwards to oblivion and back. I finished that bastard jigsaw. Incidentally. Rather, me and the kids did. Infernal effing thing. One of the pieces was totally white, other than one short black line.

Excuse the flim-flam. Need some padding, as this is more of the same, just at a different strength. Which is pretty much what 20th-century Scottish brewing was about. Pale malt, sugar and shit, plus a decent amount of hops.

1912 Thomas Usher 100/-		
pale malt	8.00 lb	65.31%
crystal malt	0.50 lb	4.08%
flaked maize	0.75 lb	6.12%
No. 2 invert sugar	0.75 lb	6.12%
cane sugar	2.25 lb	18.37%
Fuggles 120 min	1.00 oz	
Fuggles 60 min	1.00 oz	
Fuggles 30 min	1.00 oz	
OG	1064	
FG	1029	
ABV	4.63	
Apparent attenuation	54.69%	
IBU	33	
SRM	8	
Mash at	148° F	
Sparge at	170° F	
Boil time	120 minutes	
pitching temp	60° F	
Yeast	WLP028 Edinburgh Ale	

1913 William Younger 160/-

WW I was about to devastate and transform Scottish beer, but on its eve William Younger still brewed the odd super-strong Shilling Ale.

160/- was the top of their range, though the gravity had been whittled down a little over the previous 70 years:

Year	OG
1848	1134
1868	1116
1879	1109
1885	1115
1898	1111
1913	1099

Not that this version is in any way watery. As with all Younger's beers of this period there are several types of pale malt, presumably made from UK and foreign barley. There's also a huge percentage of grits in the recipe. For most of the 20th-century up until WW II, most Younger's recipes had ludicrous amounts of grits in them.

There must have been a cereal mash, but there are no details about it in the brewing record, other than an indication of the malt that went into the cooker.

The decline of the East Coast hop industry is reflected in this beer's recipe. Fifteen years earlier, Younger were using hops described as American and Pacific. Here only Pacific hops were used, along with some from Kent.

1913 William Younger 160/-		
pale malt	11.50 lb	52.27%
No.2 invert sugar	0.50 lb	2.27%
No.3 invert sugar	0.50 lb	2.27%
grits	9.50 lb	43.18%
Cluster 90 min	2.00 oz	
Cluster 60 min	2.00 oz	
Fuggles 30 min	2.00 oz	
Goldings dry hops	0.50 oz	
OG	1099	
FG	1038	
ABV	8.07	
Apparent attenuation	61.62%	
IBU	76	
SRM	10	
Mash at	151° F	
Sparge at	160° F	
Boil time	135 minutes	
pitching temp	58° F	
Yeast	WLP028 Edinburgh Ale	

1898 William Younger XX

As I've given you the recipe for the bottled version, 80/-, I thought I may as well provide draught XX, too.

There are similarities between the beers, but also some differences. The OG is identical at 1061. The FG, on the other hand varies considerably. For XX it's 1016º, 80/- 1027º. Amongst all Younger's beers with crappy levels of attenuation, this one stands out because it looks so normal.

Younger was an enthusiastic dry hopper of their draught beers and XX is no exception, despite being a Mild. It's frustrating that many brewers didn't bother to include dry hops in their brewing records. Meaning in lots of cases I've no idea if beers were dry-hopped or not. Barclay Perkins thankfully did include the information in their 20th –century logs and I know they didn't dry hop Milds. Though they did add loads of priming at racking time.

The big difference between the grists is the inclusion of grits and invert sugar in XX. My guess is that was intended to make the wort more fermentable. Sadly, the type of invert isn't specified. Which would have a big impact on the colour of the beer. No. 3 invert would darken the colour quite a bit. I'll leave the selection of invert up to you. At this late point in the 19th century, it could have been a dark invert that they used.

1898 William Younger XX		
pale malt	8.50 lb	69.39%
grits	1.50 lb	12.24%
invert sugar	2.25 lb	18.37%
Cluster 90 min	2.00 oz	
Fuggles 30 min	1.00 oz	
Goldings dry hops	0.50 oz	
OG	1061	
FG	1016	
ABV	5.95	
Apparent attenuation	73.77%	
IBU	51	
SRM	4	
Mash at	154º F	
Sparge at	160º F	
Boil time	90 minutes	
pitching temp	58.5º F	
Yeast	WLP028 Edinburgh Ale	

1909 Maclay Mild 56/-

As I slowly assemble recipes for my new Scottish book, I realise how small a percentage of the brewing records I own I've ever turned into recipes.

The Mild Ales from Maclay are a case in point. Before WW I, like most Scottish breweries, Maclay still brewed genuine Mild Ales. At least things that were called Mild Ale in the brewery. I'm inclined to believe that they were for one good reason: their grists differ from Maclay's Pale Ales. After WW I, the Scots mostly abandoned Mild Ale. The few that were still produced I suspect were destined for the English market.

Talking of grists, the one from this beer tells a story. The tale of the gradual darkening of Mild Ale around 1900. It's a process that I've observed in England, too. I've no real evidence as to what drove this change, only wild guesses. Which I won't bore you with here. We may never know the real reason.

Neither of the two Milds Maclay brewed, 56/- and 42/-, was equivalent to London AX Ale. 56/- had a gravity around 10 points higher, while 42/-, at just 1035º, was far weaker than anything brewed in the capital. Around 1900 Scottish gravities began to diverge from those in England, with beers being brewed that were far weaker than anything seen in England until the latter phase of WW I. In 1914 the average OG in England was 1051.69º, but four points lower in Scotland at 1047.67º[51].

Maclay's Pale Ale grists also contain amber malt, though a smaller percentage at just 1.5% of the grist. Only their Milds included black malt. The purpose of the black malt was surely to darken the wort. I suspect that Maclay were already colour-correcting with caramel because there's a section in the brewing records with the title "colourings". Unfortunately, I haven't found an example where this was filled in.

As most of Maclay's beers of this period, there's a fair dose of grits, around 20% of the grist. The only exception were the Stouts, which instead contained 30% oats.

I'm not sure exactly what the sugar was. In the record it's described as "inversion". It's obviously some sort of invert sugar. Possible one that Maclay had made themselves. No. 2 is me just playing it safe. It could also have been more like another invert, for example No. 1 or No. 3. Feel free to use one of those if it suits you.

Maclay used the same combination of hops in all their beers: Hallertau of three different ages (1905, 1906 and 1907 harvests), Californian hops from 1907 and two sets of English hops from 1905 and 1908. Because of the age of some of the hops I've reduced the hopping.

---

[51] Brewers' Journal 1921, page 246.

1909 Maclay Mild 56/-		
pale malt	8.75 lb	66.67%
amber malt	0.50 lb	3.81%
black malt	0.125 lb	0.95%
grits	2.50 lb	19.05%
No. 2 invert sugar	1.25 lb	9.52%
Cluster 120 min	0.75 oz	
Hallertau 60 min	0.75 oz	
Fuggles 30 min	1.50 oz	
OG	1061	
FG	1025	
ABV	4.76	
Apparent attenuation	59.02%	
IBU	36	
SRM	12	
Mash at	146/154° F	
Sparge at	170° F	
Boil time	120 minutes	
pitching temp	61° F	
Yeast	WLP028 Edinburgh Ale	

1885 Thomas Usher Stout

Englische Woche. It's the German phrase for playing two competitive football games in a week. I've always thought of myself as a Premier League-class player. So I'm going English Week with recipes.

As you've surely twigged, it's a clever ruse to pad the blog with other crap I have hanging around. A bit like Little Dave. Hanging around, I mean. He did lots of that. I remember the one time I tried ignoring him calling around. First he rang the bell. Then banged on the front door. Then climbed up outside my room and banged on the window. I manage to ignore the banging for 36 minutes, then gave in. "Bit tired today, Dave."

Moving back on topic, I've a Scottish Stout for you. For no particular reason, other than that I had the recipe hanging around and I've a long trip coming up. Have to bash out the posts this week. If all goes well, I'll be relaxing in an Albany bar, laughing with my chums over my current level of paranoia.

Been checking my sales. Heartened to see that Decoction! is one of my self-publish best-sellers, pushing into double figures like a tentative England number 10. Yeah!

You've clocked me. I'm just trying to distract you from the normality of the recipe. Which I've just realised is my point. This is an ordinary beer. Nothing special. Something brewed without pretension and drunk without fuss. The sort of beer I love.

Did I mention the best town for beer ever? The one that pulled down the kecks and leathered the arse of other cities like my pervy music teacher with his slipper? Better than Portland, San Diego, Munich, Edinburgh and Swindon. No? You'll have to wait until next time then.

Scottish Stout, not that strong, heavy on the amber malt, all foreign hops, not stupidly under-attenuated or sweet. But surprisingly bitter.

Recipe . . .

1885 Thomas Usher Stout		
pale malt	6.50 lb	54.17%
black malt	1.00 lb	8.33%
amber malt	4.50 lb	37.50%
Cluster 90 min	1.00 oz	
Strisselspalt 60 min	0.75 oz	
Spalt 30 min	2.25 oz	
OG	1050	
FG	1015	
ABV	4.63	
Apparent attenuation	70.00%	
IBU	62	
SRM	32	
Mash at	154° F	
Sparge at	165° F	
Boil time	90 minutes	
pitching temp	60° F	
Yeast	WLP028 Edinburgh Ale	

1894 Thomas Usher Export Stout

Stout never seems to have enjoyed the same popularity in Scotland as it did South of the border. Consequently there are far fewer recipes for the style than there are for various strengths of Pale Ales.

I'm sure the reason is historical. Scotland never experienced a Porter boom the same way London did, where it was totally dominant for nigh on 100 years. Porter and Stout were popular in Scotland, but never pre-eminent. And the appeal of Brown Beer started to fade after 1850.

Usher's Export Stout is a funny beer. It doesn't look like an Export Stout to me. Not even a Stout, really. At just 5% ABV this would have been considered a Porter in London. And it has a classic mid-19th-century London Porter grist: a combination of pale, brown and black malt. Though a London Porter would have contained more pale malt and less brown. One of the weird things is that while Scottish brewers rarely used dark malts in other styles, their percentage was often very high in Stouts.

Here's a London Porter for comparison purposes:

1894 Whitbread P	
pale malt	83.33%
brown malt	7.58%
black malt	9.09%
OG	1056.8
FG	1018
ABV	5.13
Apparent attenuation	68.31%
Source: Whitbread brewing record held at the London Metropolitan Archives, document number LMA/4453/D/09/089.	

The boil is quite long at 3.5 hours. Long boils weren't unusual for London Porters in the early part of the 19th century. Especially for the later, weaker worts. But by the end of the century shorter boils were the order of the day – 1.5 to 2 hours – except for the strongest Stouts. I would wonder if the long boil here was designed to add colour, but with 30% dark malts in the grist, I don't think that would have been necessary.

It looks like a very pleasant drinking Porter to me. A beer I'd rather like to try.

1894 Thomas Usher Export Stout		
pale malt	9.50 lb	70.37%
brown malt	2.25 lb	16.67%
black malt	1.75 lb	12.96%
Cluster 210 min	1.25 oz	
Cluster 120 min	1.25 oz	
Cluster 90 min	1.25 oz	
Cluster 30 min	1.25 oz	
OG	1055	
FG	1016	
ABV	5.16	
Apparent attenuation	70.91%	
IBU	98	
SRM	46	
Mash at	148° F	
Sparge at	170° F	
Boil time	210 minutes	
pitching temp	58° F	
Yeast	WLP028 Edinburgh Ale	

1899 William Younger S1

Let me take you back to a simpler time. One before William Younger had discovered they could brew pretty much from corn grits. And when they produced a bewildering array of Stouts.

One of the main differences amongst their Stouts was the degree of attenuation. Ones they'd brewed for a while, like DBS, tended to have a more normal attenuation. While some of the ones introduced towards the end of the 1900's, er, didn't. These ones seem to be the ancestors of 20th-century Scottish Sweet Stout, a style with incredibly low attenuation and minimal alcohol.

This one still manages to come out at 4.5% ABV, but that's only because it has quite a high OG. With that FG and getting on for 20% roasted malt, this must have been a pretty thick and gloopy beer. I wonder who the drinkers were of this stuff? Was it invalids looking to restore their vitality? Or just people with a sweet tooth?

For William Younger, the recipe is just packed with different ingredients. A whole three different types of malt, plus glucose and the inevitable grits.

The trickiest aspect of this range of Stouts is the hopping. Which was minimal. Apart from the large quantities of spent hops also used. What do spent hops bring to the party? A Watneys Seven? I've no idea, if I'm honest. I've been assuming 10% of their value fresh. But that could be wildly wrong.

To add to the fun, some examples of S1 – not this one – included 3 or 4 gallons of ullage beer barrel. That's 10-12.5% returned beer. Must have added a lovely extra tang.

1899 William Younger S1		
pale malt	10.00 lb	62.50%
black malt	2.00 lb	12.50%
amber malt	0.75 lb	4.69%
grits	1.75 lb	10.94%
glucose	1.50 lb	9.38%
Cluster 120 min (spent)	0.50 oz	
Cluster 90 min	0.75 oz	
OG	1069	
FG	1035	
ABV	4.50	
Apparent attenuation	49.28%	
IBU	25	
SRM	46	
Mash at	155° F	
Sparge at	160° F	
Boil time	180 minutes	
pitching temp	59.5° F	
Yeast	WLP028 Edinburgh Ale	

1909 Maclay OMS 63/-

There's no way I could have left this recipe out. It being for the original Oat Stout.

Oat Malt Stout was invented, and patented, by Maclay in the late 19th century. Not that the patent did them much good. Other brewers just produced Oatmeal Stouts instead. Cheeky bastards.

The Maclay version differed from most of its rivals in two respects: it used malted rather than flaked oats; it used a far larger proportion of oats. London Oatmeal Stout rarely contained much more than 1% oats. Then there's the liquorice and linseed. I've seen liquorice in Stout before, but never linseed.

The grist is pretty complicated, with two coloured malts as well as the malted oats. Unlike their other beers, there are no grits in the recip. Perhaps they were worried about having insufficient enzymes to convert it.

With hops from the USA, Germany and Kent, it's typical of beers in the lead up to WW I. The UK at the time consumed a considerable percentage of all the hops produced in the world. And a large percentage of the hops used in the UK were foreign. The war would change that.

1909 Maclay OMS 63/-		
pale malt	7.50 lb	53.10%
black malt	1.50 lb	10.62%
amber malt	0.50 lb	3.54%
malted oats	3.00 lb	21.24%
caramel	0.38 lb	2.65%
No. 2 invert sugar	1.25 lb	8.85%
linseed	0.50 oz	
liquorice	0.25 oz	
Cluster 120 min	1.00 oz	
Hallertau 60 min	1.00 oz	
Goldings 30 min	2.00 oz	
OG	1062	
FG	1024	
ABV	5.03	
Apparent attenuation	61.29%	
IBU	52	
SRM	60	
Mash at	144/154° F	
Sparge at	170° F	
Boil time	120 minutes	
pitching temp	60.75° F	
Yeast	WLP028 Edinburgh Ale	

1912 Thomas Usher 48/- Stout

It's fascinating to see how Scottish Stout gradually diverged from English versions. In particular, from London Stouts which were, after all, the originals.

By the eve of WW I, English and Scottish had split wide apart. As the 20th century progressed, that gap became even wider.

Thomas Usher vs London Porter and Stout 1909 - 1912

Year	Brewer	Beer	Style	OG	FG	ABV	App. Atten-uation	lbs hops/ qtr	hops lb/brl
1912	Whitbread	P	Porter	1054.3	1013.0	5.47	76.08%	4.92	1.16
1912	Whitbread	LS	Stout	1055.3	1013.0	5.60	76.50%	4.92	1.18
1912	Whitbread	Exp S	Stout	1068.4	1020.0	6.41	70.77%	13.05	4.24
1912	Whitbread	SS	Stout	1079.9	1030.0	6.60	62.43%	8.48	3.12
1912	Whitbread	SSS	Stout	1095.8	1039.0	7.51	59.28%	8.48	3.74
1910	Barclay Perkins	OMS	Stout	1053.2	1016.5	4.86	68.98%	7.50	1.82
1910	Barclay Perkins	BS Ex	Stout	1076.0	1022.5	7.08	70.39%	12.00	4.12
1910	Barclay Perkins	EIP Ex	Porter	1063.5	1020.0	5.75	68.50%	12.00	3.40
1911	Barclay Perkins	RDP	Porter	1068.2	1023.5	5.91	65.54%	8.00	2.52
1909	Truman	Imperial Stout	Stout	1094.2				5.6	2.72
1909	Truman	SS?	Stout	1072.0				5.6	2.08
1909	Truman	Runner L & C	Porter	1054.3				6.1	1.38
1909	Truman	Country Runner	Porter	1058.2				7.5	2.01
1909	Truman	Bottling	Porter	1052.6				7.5	1.82
1909	Truman	Export Stout	Stout	1069.3				9.9	3.35
1909	Truman	Runner	Porter	1058.2				8.2	2.31
1909	Truman	Keeping Stout	Stout	1069.3				9.5	3.29
1912	Thomas Usher	48/-	Stout	1046	1023	3.04	50.00%	6.50	1.36
1912	Thomas Usher	54/-	Stout	1054	1026	3.70	51.85%	6.50	1.60
1912	Thomas Usher	Stt	Stout	1070	1029	5.42	58.57%	6.50	2.07

Sources:
Barclay Perkins brewing record held at the London Metropolitan Archives, document number ACC/2305/1/602
Whitbread brewing record held at the London Metropolitan Archives, document number LMA/4453/D/09/106
Truman brewing record held at the London Metropolitan Archives, document number B/THB/C/112
Thomas Usher brewing record held at the Scottish Brewing Archive, document number TU/6/1/5.

What were those differences? Scottish Stouts generally had lower gravities and a poorer degree of attenuation. Not even London Porter had a gravity under 1050º. 1046º is very low for a pre-WW I Stout. Usher's strongest Stout, Stt, is only about the same strength as the weakest London Stouts.

Note that the degree of attenuation increases with the OG. Leaving the FGs of the three Stouts very similar. This is a trick I've seen before in Scottish beers. Maclay did something similar with their three Pale Ales. I guess the point is to have a similar level of body and sweetness in all three.

Interestingly, one area where there is no real difference is the level of hopping. Contrary to what some would tell you about Scottish beers. Usher's Stouts have similar levels of hopping as London beers of a similar gravity. The only exceptions being the London Export Stouts which naturally would have been more heavily hopped.

The biggest change in the grist compared to their 19th-century Stouts is the absence of black malt, which has been replaced by chocolate malt. Before WW I, London brewers stuck with black malt, but Whitbread also swapped over to chocolate malt in 1922.

The original recipe contains six types of sugar: 4 cwt. CDA, 1 cwt. Maltosan, 2 cwt. oatine, 3 cwt. DL, 10 cwt Penang. I assume oatine contained oats in some form, so feel free to throw in some flaked oats if you fancy. CDA is some sort of proprietary dark sugar. No idea what Maltosar and DL are, but Penang will be some type of cane sugar. I've simplified it to just No. 3 invert.

The very long boil is probably because 48/- was parti-gyled with the stronger Stout. Or maybe they wanted to darken the wort. I won't get angry if you stick to a more conventional, shorter boil.

1912 Thomas Usher 48/- Stout		
pale malt	6.75 lb	69.23%
brown malt	0.50 lb	5.13%
chocolate Malt	0.50 lb	5.13%
crystal malt 60L	0.50 lb	5.13%
No. 3 invert	1.50 lb	15.38%
Fuggles 90 min	1.00 oz	
Fuggles 60 min	1.00 oz	
Fuggles 30 min	1.00 oz	
OG	1046	
FG	1023	
ABV	3.04	
Apparent attenuation	50.00%	
IBU	37	
SRM	24	
Mash at	148° F	
Sparge at	170° F	
Boil time	240 minutes	
pitching temp	60° F	
Yeast	WLP028 Edinburgh Ale	

1885 Thomas Usher PA 60/-

This is so much fun. Banging out another recipe that's already in the vaults. And a banging the drum opportunity about styles.

60/- Ale. If you aren't over 50, Scottish, or weirdly obsessed, you've no fucking idea what it is or was. Sorry to be so blunt, but them's just the facts. That said, this recipe is nothing like the sort of 60 bob I (very occasionally) drank in the blurry days some call my youth. Pre middle age is my preferred term. Or pre gut.

Having started off aggressively asserting this beer has no connection with the more modern 60/-, I'm going to completely turn around and say how it does. Because 60/-, despite its clever masquerade as Mild, was really just a type of Scottish Pale Ale. Eventually a pretty weak one, coloured up with caramel and filling the Mild Ale slot in Scotland.

60/- in those oldie Victorian times, designated a beer a bit over standard strength. 54/- was the baseline beer, the equivalent of an English Light Bitter. 60 bob was one step up. But still a beer for the masses.

Wars, taxes and other bollocks bolloxed up British beer categorisations. Pre-WW I classifications, cemented in an unchanging retail price for beer, became meaningless. Between the wars, shilling classifications were used with a random disregard for consistency. Which has not a grillocks' grallocks to do with the recipe below.

Usher's 60/- looks much like the Pale Ales brewed by the likes of Whitbread in London. Though if they really sold the Usher's for 3 quid a hogshead, it was a bargain compared to London Pale Ales.

The recipe? Note all foreign hops. And the exciting malt bill.

Detail time, I suppose . . . .

1885 Thomas Usher IPA

pale malt	10.75 lb	100.00%
Cluster 90 min	1.75 oz	
Spalt 30 min	1.75 oz	
OG	1046	
FG	1015	
ABV	4.10	
Apparent attenuation	67.39%	
IBU	64	
SRM	2	
Mash at	156° F	
Sparge at	175° F	
Boil time	90 minutes	
pitching temp	58° F	
Yeast	WLP028 Edinburgh Ale	

1885 Thomas Usher Ex PA

Now here's a treat for you. A recipe that isn't from William Younger. It is Scottish, though.

I know hoppy beers are popular nowadays. No idea why, give me a Dark Mild of a Milk Stout any day of the week.

Usher was another brewery with a huge range of beers. At least in the 19th century. They trimmed it down a lot in the 20th. They had four Pale Ales in total: PA, PA 60/-, IP and this beer, Ex PA. Which I assume stands for Export PA. It's the strongest and the most heavily hopped of the set.

Based on the level of hopping – double that of their other Pale Ales –I'll go out on a limb and say that this was a Stock Pale Ale. Meaning that it would have been aged before sale. Probably at least 3 to 6 months. Usher don't specify dry hopping in their logs, but there's no way a beer like this wouldn't have been dry hopped. Half an ounce is the minimum it would have contained. It could well have been as much as an ounce.

I've concentrated on the hopping because there's really nothing to say about the grist. It's just pale malt. Can't get simpler than that.

The FG when sold would have been lower. After a few months maturing, it would be down at least 4-5 points. Though the rate of attenuation is already higher than for their other beers. Their Shilling Ales and Mild Ales were only a little over 60%.

1885 Thomas Usher Ex PA		
pale malt	14.00 lb	100.00%
Strisselspalt 90 min	3.00 oz	
Strisselspalt 60 min	3.00 oz	
Hallertau 30 min	3.00 oz	
Goldings dry hops	0.50 oz	
OG	1060	
FG	1015	
ABV	5.95	
Apparent attenuation	75.00%	
IBU	95	
SRM	5	
Mash at	155° F	
Sparge at	175° F	
Boil time	150 minutes	
pitching temp	57.5° F	
Yeast	WLP028 Edinburgh Ale	

1894 Thomas Usher IPA

What makes a beer an IPA? More specifically, what makes a beer an IPA rather than a Pale Ale? It's a question to which I've yet to find a satisfactory answer.

It doesn't help that British brewers were extremely inconsistent in their use of the terms. Modern dogma would insist that, if a brewery makes both a Pale Ale and an IPA, the latter should be the stronger of the two. But I've dozens of examples of British brewers where it was the other way around. Whitbread and Barclay Perkins in London. And Usher in Edinburgh.

In the 1890's. Thomas Usher brewed three Pale Ales: IPA at 1044º, PA at 1049º and PA 60/- at 1055º. Compared to the Pale Ales of a London brewery, they look on the weak side. 1050º was about the weakest anything got in the capital. Whitbread's three Pale Ales in the same year were: FA at 1051.8º, 2PA at 1052.4º and PA at 1058.4º.

The recipe, as with most 19th-ccentury Scottish ores, is very simple, just pale malt and sugar. Not sure exactly what sort of sugar as I couldn't read the brewer's scribble. No. 1 or No. 2 invert are the obvious choices. Take your pick. I've gone for No. 2 for no particular reason.

The rate of attenuation is quite low, which is typical for Scottish beers, even Pale Ales. Leaving the ABV at just under 4%, a very low figure for a 19th-century Pale Ale of any kind. A English AK would have had a similar OG, but the higher rate of attenuation would have left it at 4.5% ABV.

1894 Thomas Usher IPA		
pale malt	8.00 lb	86.49%
No. 2 invert sugar	1.25 lb	13.51%
Fuggles 90 min	1.25 oz	
Goldings 60 min	1.25 oz	
Goldings 30 min	1.25 oz	
Goldings dry hops	0.25 oz	
OG	1044	
FG	1014	
ABV	3.97	
Apparent attenuation	68.18%	
IBU	49	
SRM	7	
Mash at	150° F	
Sparge at	180° F	
Boil time	90 minutes	
pitching temp	58° F	
Yeast	WLP028 Edinburgh Ale	

1909 Maclay Pl 60/-

Beers called 60/- Pale Ale were around for a long time, from the late 19th century until, sort of, today. Though the beer behind the name varied greatly over time.

In 1909, Pl 60/- was Maclay's top-of-the-range Pale Ale. Which, given its fairly modest gravity, might surprise. Down in England, a top-class Pale Ale would have had a much higher gravity, 1060-1065º. For whatever reason, Pale Ale strengths in Scotland had fallen from their initial level in the 1850's. Whereas in England they had stayed much the same. Perhaps the greater popularity of Pale Ale in Scotland was the reason. The best English Pale Ales remained an exclusive, expensive drink.

The percentage of grits is quite high, though not as crazy as at William Younger. More surprising is the presence of amber malt. Anything other than pale malt was pretty much unknown in Scotland before WW I. Pale malt, maize and sugar. That was it.

The combination of American, German and Kent hops was the same in all their beers in 1909. Brewers in the past tended to use mostly the same ingredients in all their beers. They might change the hopping a little for Pale Ales, but mostly the same things went into most beers. Not like today, where every beer might have its own specific hops. They didn't have time for that sort of pissing around in the old days.

The bitterness is already starting to get quite low compared to 19th-century or English Pale Ales. It would get much worse after WW II.

The two temperatures are for the initial infusion and after the underlet.

1909 Maclay Pl 60/-		
pale malt	7.00 lb	63.64%
amber malt	0.25 lb	2.27%
grits	2.50 lb	22.73%
No. 2 invert sugar	1.25 lb	11.36%
Cluster 120 min	0.75 oz	
Hallertau 60 min	0.75 oz	
Fuggles 30 min	1.50 oz	
Goldings dry hops	0.50 oz	
OG	1051	
FG	1016	
ABV	4.63	
Apparent attenuation	68.63%	
IBU	38	
SRM	7	
Mash at	147/153° F	
Sparge at	170° F	
Boil time	120 minutes	
pitching temp	63.5° F	
Yeast	WLP028 Edinburgh Ale	

1912 Thomas Usher IP

I just can't resist another watery IPA recipe. You might get the idea that I'm trying to prove a point with these recipe. As if I'd ever do something as tacky as that.

I hope you aren't getting bored of all these Scottish recipes. I see it a documentary duty to get at least a few dozen genuine Scottish recipes out there. One wee widdle into a hurricane, given the number of made up ones out there. But at least I'm trying. I have increased the number of fact-based recipes by several hundred percent this year. Looking at it positively.

It's always a good laugh looking at how a beer like this scores on the style characteristics in BeerSmith. Way wrong on every single one. The only one even vaguely close, the ABV, is wrong because it assumes a much better rate of attenuation than the original achieved.

Here's how it scored:

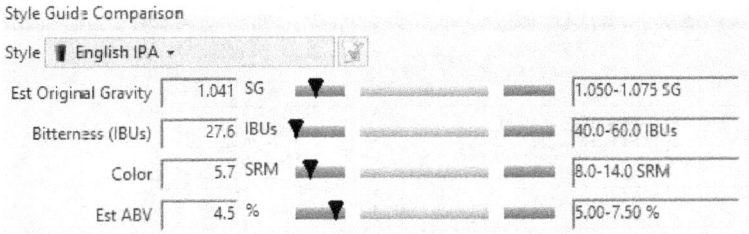

This isn't a dig at BeerSmith. It just uses the "official" BJCP styles. Hang on. BeerSmith lets me define my own style.

I've just added this one:

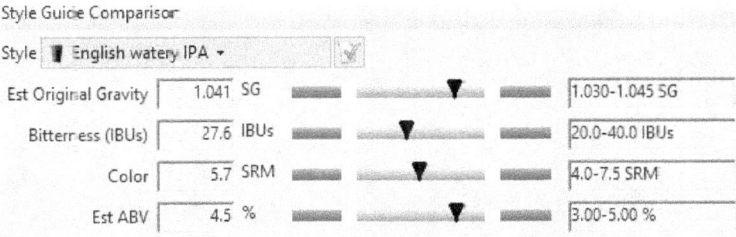

That looks way better, doesn't it? When do you reckon the BJCP will add English Watery IPA to their style guidelines? When they start gritting the roads in Hades? Even though I've done all the work for them. I can even think of at least two current examples: Greene King IPA and Harvey's IPA. Which is about as many "Southern English Brown Ales" I can think of.

I need to take this further. Add more real old styles, old and new. Entering as many recipes to BeerSmith as I am, I should be able to refine the definitions as I go on. What a fascinating project.

Almost forgot about the recipe. It's more pale malt, flaked maize and sugar. Incidentally, they're the ingredients listed in my official style definition of English Watery IPA. Do you think I should trademark the term? Wouldn't want some bastard nicking it.

What else? All English hops, which is a bit odd pre-WW I. You'd usually expect some American ones in there.

It was parti-gyled with a couple of even weaker beers, 50/- Br and 60/- Br, at 1034º and 1031º. Really, really watery for back then. I'm still wondering what the hell "Br" means. First records I have that mention it are from 1894. Could it mean "Bright" or "Brilliant", i.e. a chilled and filtered bottled beer? The 1890's is when that type of beer was appearing. None of the beers with the designation is over 1037º.

Right. Recipe time. (And tea-time for me.)

1912 Thomas Usher IP		
pale malt	7.25 lb	80.56%
flaked maize	1.00 lb	11.11%
No. 2 invert sugar	0.75 lb	8.33%
Fuggles 90 min	0.75 oz	
Fuggles 60 min	0.75 oz	
Fuggles 30 min	0.75 oz	
OG	1042	
FG	1014	
ABV	3.70	
Apparent attenuation	66.67%	
IBU	28	
SRM	6	
Mash at	150º F	
Sparge at	170º F	
Boil time	90 minutes	
pitching temp	60º F	
Yeast	WLP028 Edinburgh Ale	

1913 William Younger LAE

Time for another weird William Younger beer. Though all their beers in the run up to WW I were weird, containing huge quantities of grits.

I'm not sure exactly what LAE was sold as. It looks like some sort of Light Pale Ale. They had a rather confusing range of beers of this ilk: LDA, LAE, SLE and MM. Other than LDA (Light Dinner Ale) I've no idea what any of the initials stand for.

It's remarkable how few ingredients William Younger used at this time. Pale malt, grits, the odd bit of sugar, Pacific and Kent hops. The only place they used any dark malts was in their Stouts. Which were also a weird bunch, but we'll return to that later.

You'll not that the boil is quite long. Younger was always swapping around its boil times. In the 1850's, they were very short, often barely over an hour. By the 1860's it was 1.5 to 2 hours, in the 1880's 2 to 2.5 hours, in the 1890's around 3 hours and on the eve of WW I back to 2 to 2.5 hours. In the 1930's it was down to 1.75 hours. It's much more complicated than "Scots brewers boiled their worts for 3 days".

There's not really much else I can say about such a simple beer. Except that they were still brewing it after WW II.

1913 William Younger LAE		
pale malt	5.75 lb	56.10%
grits	4.50 lb	43.90%
Cluster 60 min	1.50 oz	
Cluster 60 min	1.50 oz	
Fuggles 30 min	1.00 oz	
Goldings dry hops	1.00 oz	
OG	1045	
FG	1013	
ABV	4.23	
Apparent attenuation	71.11%	
IBU	78	
SRM	3	
Mash at	155° F	
Sparge at	160° F	
Boil time	150 minutes	
pitching temp	60° F	
Yeast	WLP028 Edinburgh Ale	

1894 Thomas Usher XX 60/-

Here's a type of beer that was already becoming a rarity in the 1890's – a genuine Scottish Mild Ale.

I should probably be more specific. It was draught Scottish Mild that was a rarity. There were still plenty of Shilling Ales, the bottled form of Mild that was specific to Scotland. Though the popularity of these beers was on the wane, as increasing amounts of Pale Ale were brewed. The situation south of the border was very different. Mild was the favourite style and becoming ever more popular, mostly at the expense of Porter.

Like most Scottish beers of this period, it had a very simple grist, just pale malt and sugar. It's not clear exactly what sort of sugar it was. I've guessed at No. 1 invert.

To put this beer into its historical context, I've put it in a table together with the X Ale from three London breweries:

Mild Ales of the 1890's									
Date	Year	Brewer	Beer	OG	FG	ABV	App. Attenuation	lbs hops/qtr	hops lb/brl
6th Aug	1891	Barclay Perkins	X	1058.0	1015.0	5.69	74.21%	8.32	2.07
13th Jul	1894	Whitbread	X	1058.4	1016.0	5.62	72.62%	8.23	2.09
7th Jul	1894	Truman	X Ale	1056.5				9.0	2.19
28th Jul	1897	Fuller	X	1049.6	1012.2	4.95	75.42%	6.58	1.44
13th Apr	1894	Thomas Usher	XX 60/-	1055	1015	5.29	72.73%	10.00	2.77
Sources: Barclay Perkins brewing record held at the London Metropolitan Archives, document number ACC/2305/1/587 Whitbread brewing record held at the London Metropolitan Archives, document number LMA/4453/D/01/060 Truman brewing record held at the London Metropolitan Archives, document number B/THB/C/175 Thomas Usher brewing record held at the Scottish Brewing Archive, document number TU/6/1/2 Fullers brewing record held at the brewery.									

Usher's beer is surprisingly similar to the London ones, though a little more heavily hopped. Isn't that a shock? Didn't the Scots use almost no hops? Oh, I remember. That story is total bollocks. The hops themselves are just listed as Kent and Columbia in the brewing record. Cluster and Fuggles seem fair enough guesses for the varieties.

1894 Thomas Usher XX 60/-		
pale malt	11.50 lb	93.88%
No. 2 invert sugar	0.75 lb	6.12%
Cluster 105 min	1.25 oz	
Fuggles 90 min	1.50 oz	
Fuggles 60 min	1.50 oz	
Fuggles 30 min	1.50 oz	
OG	1055	
FG	1015	
ABV	5.29	
Apparent attenuation	72.73%	
IBU	78	
SRM	7	
Mash at	150° F	
Sparge at	170° F	
Boil time	105 minutes	
pitching temp	58° F	
Yeast	WLP028 Edinburgh Ale	

1898 William Younger XXXX

Scottish X Ales can be problematic. Problematic in terms of placing them in a style box.

In England, it's generally pretty easy. X's usually indicate a Mild Ale. But it's not always so clear cut in Scotland. Quite often X's are used not for Mild Ale, but for Stock Ale. Younger XXXX is a case in point. The weaker X Ales of that year to look like Mild Ales. But, with a hopping rate of almost 11 lbs per quarter of malt, this looks more like a Stock Ale. That's what I'm calling it, anyway.

The grist is typical for Younger's beers of this period: pale malt, grits and sugar. Several different types of pale malt, of course. And two types of sugar, one described as "D", the other "G". Presumably dextrose and glucose. I've simplified it to just glucose. If you want to go for more authenticity, use 1 lb. of dextrose and 0.5 lb. of glucose.

The hops – listed as Pacific, American and Kent – were half from the 1898 and half from the 1897 season. And in sufficient quantities to leave the calculated bitterness at over 100 IBU.

1898 William Younger XXXX		
pale malt	14.00 lb	82.35%
grits	1.50 lb	8.82%
glucose	1.50 lb	8.82%
Cluster 90 min	5.75 oz	
Fuggles 30 min	2.25 oz	
Goldings dry hops	2.00 oz	
OG	1076	
FG	1020	
ABV	7.41	
Apparent attenuation	73.68%	
IBU	126	
SRM	5	
Mash at	155° F	
Sparge at	160° F	
Boil time	90 minutes	
pitching temp	57° F	
Yeast	WLP028 Edinburgh Ale	

1913 William Younger No. 1

William Younger was an odd brewery. Even for Scotland.

In 1913 they brewed around 30 different beers. Just at the Abbey Brewery. And that's not including Pale Ales, which were brewed at their Holyrood brewery. It's a bewildering range. One that has me scratching my head as to what the difference is between many of them.

Then there's their love of grits. Quite a few Scottish breweries used them in preference to the flaked maize popular in England. It seems an odd choice, as grits are more trouble. They require a preliminary cereal mash, unlike flakes which can just be dumped in the mash tun with the malt.

What's unusual about Younger is the quantity of grits that they used. As much as 45%, in some cases. This has the least of any of their 1913 beers, just 40%. It does leave me wondering what these beers tasted like. That's an awful lot of grits. Though, now I think about it, the 1939 Younger's No. 1 I brewed with Pretty Things had quite a lot of grits in it and that tasted OK.

Just has a quick look at some RateBeer reviews of that.

> "Really one of the best Scotch Ale caramelized malt flavors I've ever experienced. The downfall is that the finish is marred by too much roasted grain husk, as though there's an unfortunately high percentage of dark chocolate malt";
> "Taste is sweet, chococaramel, light peat.";
> "a finish that lingers with cocoa and roasted malt";
> "Flavor is malty with light caramel, hints of nuts, light toffee, and light peat.";
> "Caramel, up front, with the herbal, peat and earthy elements arriving in the middle"

Amazing how expectations can colour our experiences. The darkest malt in the recipe was crystal. The colour all came from sugar, the wort wasn't caramelised and there certainly wasn't any peat in it. And it contains lactose, which not one reviewer spotted. It's one of the reasons I don't guess ingredients in my beer ~~reviews~~ sketches.

Back to the 1913 version. What can I say about the recipe? A shitload of grits, two and a half shitloads of US hops, a little bit of sugar. Complex t isn't. But t is an authentic Strong Scotch Ale.

1913 William Younger No. 1		
pale malt	12.00 lb	55.17%
grits	8.75 lb	40.23%
No. 3 invert	0.50 lb	2.30%
Glucose	0.50 lb	2.30%
Cluster 90 min	6.00 oz	
Cluster 60 min	6.00 oz	
Fuggles 30 min	4.00 oz	
Goldings dry hops	1.75 oz	
OG	1097	
FG	1037	
ABV	7.94	
Apparent attenuation	61.86%	
IBU	216	
SRM	8	
Mash at	155° F	
Sparge at	160° F	
Boil time	150 minutes	
pitching temp	57° F	
Yeast	WLP028 Edinburgh Ale	

1885 William Younger No. 3

No. 3 is one of the beers I'm slightly obsessed with. For a couple of reasons.

One is that a clone of it was one of the first beers me and my brother brewed way back in the early 1970's. Another is that I got to drink Scottish & Newcastle's version when they reintroduced it in the late 1970's.

I was never sure what style it was. I seem to remember someone calling it a dark Bitter. Which wasn't really what it was. Now I realise it was a Scotch Ale. Or a Strong Ale, depending on which side of the Scottish border you were. Why didn't I wonder where Nos. 1 and 2 were? I should have.

Back in the 1880's, William Younger was still brewing both No. 1 and No. 2. No. 1 made it to at least the 1950's before being dropped. That was more like the classic Strong Scotch Ale, the type that mostly only exists in Belgium today. That was an exclusively bottled beer, while No. 3 came in both bottled and draught form. When on draught, it filled the same evolutionary niche as Burton Ale.

Just as well I to d you all that as there's not a huge amount else to say. Especially about the recipe. Which is just pale malt and hops. Quite a lot of hops. At this time William Younger mainly used four types of hops: Kent, American, Spalt and Württemberg. Though occasionally they used Bohemian hops instead of the German ones. In the recipe below, I've combined the Spalt and Württemberg hops together as just Spalt.

Younger was particularly fond of dry-hopping their stronger Ales. And dry-hopping them pretty heavily. I'm intrigued as to what effect that would have. With the low rate of attenuation and heavy hopping, the resulting beer must have been bittersweet.

1885 William Younger No. 3		
pale malt	17.25 lb	100.00%
Cluster 90 min	3.50 oz	
Spalt 60 min	2.50 oz	
Fuggles 30 min	1.75 oz	
Goldings dry hops	2.25 oz	
OG	1076	
FG	1025	
ABV	6.75	
Apparent attenuation	67.11%	
IBU	108	
SRM	6	
Mash at	256° F	
Sparge at	163° F	
Boil time	90 minutes	
pitching temp	56° F	
Yeast	WLP028 Edinburgh Ale	

1909 Maclay Strong Ale

After WW I, many Scottish breweries only really had one recipe. For a Pale Ale. When they did brew a Strong Ale, it was just a high-gravity version of their Pale Ale recipe. That hadn't usually been the case before the war.

Maclay's from 1909 is an early example of that type of Strong Ale, parti-gyled, as it was, with a 54/- Pale Ale. Though the two were hopped separately. It shares the same grist as all Maclay's Pale Ales: pale and amber malt, grits and sugar.

It looks very much like the beers sold in Belgium as Scotch Ale, other than the colour. It was probably darker than given below. The brewing record under the heading "colourings" says 1.5 pints. Whatever that means. Other than that the original beer would have been darker than what just the malt would have achieved.

Quite a lot of grits in there, but also 13 lbs of malt. Should be enough to stop it tasting thin. Plus a decent amount of bitterness. Looks like a classic Scotch Ale.

1909 Maclay Strong Ale		
pale malt	13.00 lb	64.20%
amber malt	0.50 lb	2.47%
grits	4.25 lb	20.99%
No. 2 invert sugar	2.50 lb	12.35%
Cluster 120 min	2.00 oz	
Hallertau 60 min	2.00 oz	
Goldings 30 min	4.00 oz	
Goldings dry hops	1.50 oz	
OG	1096	
FG	1031	
ABV	8.60	
Apparent attenuation	67.71%	
IBU	79	
SRM	12	
Mash at	146/152° F	
Sparge at	170° F	
Boil time	90 minutes	
pitching temp	60° F	
Yeast	WLP028 Edinburgh Ale	

1881 William Younger PXX Pils

Scotland was one of the first regions in the UK to fully embrace Lager. And there's a long (comparatively) history of brewing bottom-fermenting beers.

John Muir had a try in the 1840's but the next brewery to take on the styles was several decades later, when William Younger started making one at their Holyrood Brewery. The plant was mainly dedicated to the production of Pale Ales, for which it had been specifically built.

Younger in fact brewed two Pilsners, PX at 1058º and PXX at 1068º. Which are quite high compared to the gravities of Czech Pale Lagers of the time, which were typically 1048-1050º.

I can't help wondering if the Carlsberg connection had anything to do with Younger experimenting with Lager. Karl Jacobsen, son of Carlsberg's founder, had served an apprenticeship at William Younger in 1868. He brewed some British-style top-fermenting beers on his return to Copenhagen. Perhaps Younger was returning the favour.

They seem to have tried to brew it as authentically as possible. The hops were mostly German, a genuine bottom-fermenting yeast used, as well as a decoction mash and a very low fermentation temperature.

The most unusual feature of this beer is the dry-hopping. Not just the quantity – which is pretty high – but also the type of hops used. Nothing odd about the Goldings, but American hops were very seldom used for dry hopping. For the simple reason that British brewers didn't like the flavour of them.

1881 William Younger PXX Pils		
pale malt	11.75 lb	83.93%
No. 1 invert sugar	2.25 lb	16.07%
Hallertau 90 min	1.50 oz	
Hallertau 60 min	1.50 oz	
Hallertau 30 min	1.50 oz	
Golding dry hops	1.25 oz	
Cluster dry hops	1.25 oz	
OG	1068	
FG	1020	
ABV	6.35	
Apparent attenuation	70.59%	
IBU	45	
SRM	5	
Mash rest 1	100° F	
Mash rest 2	131° F	
Mash rest 3	142° F	
Mash rest 4	163° F	
Sparge at	164° F	
Boil time	135 minutes	
pitching temp	54° F	
fermentation temp	42° F	
Yeast	WLP800 Pilsner Lager	

1914 – 1939 Pale Ale Rules

Introduction

WW I, while horribly cruel to British beer, was surprisingly good for UK breweries. They were able to put behind them the hard years from immediately before the war, where most struggled to make a profit and some went bust. Despite making far less beer, breweries were making a decent profit on what they did brew. Most ended the war in far better financial health than they started it

Another mystery of style trajectory is the sudden disappearance of Mild Ale – or the original Shilling Ales – around the time of WW I. By the 1920's, most Scottish brewers were just brewing different strengths of one Pale Ale recipe. Maybe still brewing a Stout separately. Or maybe just making it in a bizarre parti-gyle.

That's the rule. And then there's William Younger, who mashed their own particular tun. They brewed a crazy number of different beers, mostly single-gyle, unlike everyone else. Had a couple of different Strong Ales. But had a crazy percentage of corn grits in their grists.

Without the eccentricity of William Younger, Scottish brewing would have been pretty boring after WW I. With brewers using one basic recipe for all their beers for years, if no decades on end.

Beer production

Beer output in the UK and Scotland 1914 – 1936 (bulk barrels)		
Year	UK	Scotland	% Scotland
1914	37,558,767	2,288,981	6.09%
1915	34,765,780	2,042,477	5.87%
1916	32,110,608	1,917,148	5.97%
1917	30,163,988	1,816,003	6.02%
1918	19,085,043	1,141,114	5.98%
1919	23,264,533	1,325,439	5.70%
1920	35,047,947	2,186,604	6.24%
1921	34,504,570	2,096,080	6.07%
1922	30,178,731	1,770,175	5.87%
1923	23,948,651	1,598,339	6.67%
1924	25,425,017	1,800,687	7.08%
1925	26,734,825	1,895,535	7.09%
1926	26,765,610	1,884,933	7.04%
1927	25,100,461	1,673,576	6.67%
1928	25,435,145	1,365,000	5.37%
1929	24,608,000	1,419,000	5.77%
1930	25,061,956	1,346,000	5.37%
1931	23,900,000	1,121,000	4.69%
1932	20,790,812	918,000	4.42%
1933	17,950,303	1,002,000	5.58%
1934	20,182,308	1,089,000	5.40%
1935	20,864,814	1,179,000	5.65%
1936	21,969,763	1,236,000	5.63%
Sources: Brewers' Almanack 1928, p. 110; Brewers' Almanack 1955, p. 50; Brewers' Journal 1934, page 11.			

Scotland's share of beer production rose a little from 5.48% in 1914 to 6% at war's end. That percentage continued to rise until the middle of the 1920's, after which it slipped back to about its pre-war level.

The crisis in brewing caused by the emergency budget of 1931 is clear to see in the figures. In reaction to a government deficit caused by the Wall Street Crash, there was a huge bump in the tax on beer. There was a predictable slump in beer output in response.

The tax increase seems to have hit Scotland particularly hard. Between 1930 and 1932, UK beer production fell by 17%, but in Scotland the fall was 32%. This could be a result of the accompanying industrial slump, which had a massive impact on Scotland's heavy industry.

Breweries

The interwar years were hard on Scottish brewing. Almost 50% of the country's breweries closed between 1914 and 1939.

| Number of Scottish breweries and average output 1914 - 1939 ||||
Year	Output standard barrels	Number of Brewers	average output per brewery
1914	1,858,000	75	24,773
1915	1,549,000	71	21,817
1916	1,484,000	70	21,200
1917	894,000	67	13,343
1918	717,000	66	10,864
1919	1,360,000	64	21,250
1920	1,652,000	63	26,222
1921	1,438,000	60	23,967
1922	1,203,000	59	20,390
1923	1,294,000	58	22,310
1924	1,431,000	57	25,105
1925	1,425,000	56	25,446
1926	1,300,000	54	24,074
1927	1,365,000	51	26,765
1928	1,365,000	49	27,857
1929	1,419,000	49	28,959
1930	1,346,000	46	29,261
1931	1,121,000	45	24,911
1932	918,000	45	20,400
1933	1,002,000	43	23,302
1934	1,089,000	44	24,750
1935	1,179,000	42	28,071
1936	1,236,000	43	28,744
1939		40	0

Sources:
"A History of the Brewing Industry in Scotland" by Ian Donnachie, 1998, page 234.
Brewer's Almanack 1971, page 80.

Foreign markets

Scottish brewers were responsible for around 15% of UK beer exports in the late 19th century, despite Scotland having only about 10% of the population of England. After WW I that rose to over 50% of exports.

The simple truth is that without exports to both England and abroad the Scottish brewing industry would never have been nearly so large. The local market just wasn't big enough.

Before WW I their export markets had mostly been parts of the British Empire. Large quantities of beer were shipped both to the West Indies and to Australia. But the latter market mostly disappeared when the new nation of Australia introduced import tariffs to encourage local industry. Instead the Scots turned attention to a rather closer market: Belgium.

What they shipped to Belgium was pretty much their West Indies favourite: strong, dark Scotch Ales. Sometimes similar to a Strong Ale sold in Scotland, others a beer specially brewed.

Beer Exported on Drawback and Free of Duty					
	England and Wales	Scotland	Ireland	United Kingdom	UK exports
1916	581,947	174,595	46,371	802,913	
1917	314,333	73,896	30,095	418,324	
1918	174,408	30,379	16,185	220,972	
1919	470,794	195,995	33,821	700,610	
1920	312,868	146,726	16,698	485,292	390,248
1921	215,719	92,193	12,648	320,560	
1922	207,882	117,978	10,239	336,099	260,914
1923	176,913	108,544	2,270	287,727	257,454
1924	158,373	132,889	753	292,015	264,003
1925	180,731	145,603	415	326,749	290,824
1926	178,155	168,609	305	347,069	283,033
1927	156,258	179,242	232	338,732	287,445
1928	170,728	193,255		363,983	328,029
1929	176,381	223,638		400,019	352,942
1930	173,988	204,345		378,333	328,524
1931	159,278	147,527		306,805	289,516
1932	136,231	133,240		269,471	244,525
1933	117,363	126,254		243,617	217,981
Sources: Brewers' Journal 1919, page 65, Brewers' Journal 1922, page 71. Brewers' Journal 1925, page 83. Brewers' Journal 1928, page 87. Brewers' Journal 1928, page 87. Brewers' Journal 1934, page 162. Brewers' Almanack 1928, p. 115 Brewers' Almanack 1955, p. 57						

WW I restrictions

The war brought about an unprecedented level of government interference in the brewing trade. Pub hours were slashed and afternoon closing, the bane of my life as a young adult, introduced.

This is a summary of wartime rules and restrictions[52]:

1914 : Output 36,165,000 standard barrels. Duty raised from 7s. 9d. to 23s. per standard barrel.

1916 : Output 30,292,977 standard barrels. Duty raised to 24s.

March 31 1917 : Annual output reduced to rate of 26,626,039 standard barrels by the Output of Beer (Restriction) Act, 1916.

April 1 1917: Annual output reduced rate of 11,470,000 standard barrels a year. Duty raised to 25s. per barrel.

---

[52] "The Brewers' Almanack 1928" pages 100 - 101.

July 1 1917: Annual output increased to rate of 15,043,000 standard barrels. half the beer to be of a gravity not exceeding 1036º.

April 1918: Annual output reduced to rate of 12,590,000 standard barrels. The average gravity of all beer brewed not to exceed 1030º for Great Britain and 1045º for Ireland; no beer to be brewed below 1010º. Duty increased to 50s.

Jan. 1 1919 : Annual output increased to rate of 13,260,000 standard barrels. Average gravities raised to 1032º in Great Britain and 1047º Ireland.

April 1 1919 : Annual output increased to rate of 19,890,000 standard barrels. Beer duty raised to 70s. Average gravity raised to 1040º in Great Britain.

May 23 1919 : Annual output increased to rate of 25,000,000 standard barrels a Year.

July 1 1919: All restrictions on volume of beer produced removed. Average gravity increased in Great Britain to 1044º, and in Ireland to 1051º.

April 20 1920: Duty raised to 100s.

June 30 1921: All restrictions on gravities ended.

Aug. 31 1921: All control of prices abolished.

Price controls were first introduced in 1917. Initially they only covered beers at the bottom end of the gravity scale. Eventually, they covered all beer. These were the prices fixed for a pint draught beer in the public bar.

Price control 1917-1921					
Price	Oct 1917	Apr 1918	Feb 1919	Jul 1919	Apr 1920
2d				<1019	
3d			<1022	1020-1026	<1019
4d	<1036	<1030	1023-1028	1027-1032	1020-1026
5d	1036-1042	1030-1034	1029-1034	1033-1038	1027-1032
6d			1035-1041	1039-1045	1033-1038
7d			1042-1049	1045-1053	1039-1045
8d			>1050	>1054	1045-1053
9d					>1054
Sources: The Brewers' Almanack 1928 pages 100 - 101. "The British Brewing Industry 1830-1980'					

The final lot of restrictions effectively set the strengths and prices of British beer for the interwar period.

Ingredients

WW I was a turning point in British brewing in terms of ingredients. After decades of dependency on foreign barley and hops, the UK became much more self-sufficient. This was partly caused by falling gravities.

After the end of the war, imports of raw materials resumed, but never on quite the same scale as before 1914.

Malt

WW I caused many headaches for British brewers. One of which was the lack of foreign-grown 6-row barley.

Before the war 15%-20% of foreign 6-row was fairly standard in British grists. Malt made from such barley served two functions in the Brewhouse. It contained more enzymes than malt from British-grown barley – important when grists routinely contained 15% unmalted adjuncts – and with its coarser husk provided better drainage of the grain bed, helping to avoid stuck mashes.

As soon as international trade returned to normal in the 1920's, brewers started using foreign 6-row again. Though it's worth noting that this was always imported as raw grain and malted in the UK. Malt was never imported. With good reason, British maltsters generally producing a better-quality malt than their foreign counterparts.

In the 1920's the use of crystal malt in Scotland started to pick up, but only in certain styles of beer, principally Stout, though also in some of the few true Mild Ales brewed in Scotland.

Sugar

Before WW I most sugar had been in a fairly simple form: either pure cane, glucose or invert sugar. After the war proprietary sugars, usually a blend of invert, caramel and other sugars, came increasingly to the fore. These sugars were often tailored for a specific type of beer, such as Mild Ale or Oatmeal Stout. Brewers publications of the period were full of advertisements singing the praises of these products.

Scottish brewers were slower to adopt the use of sugar than their English counterparts. After WW I it's use increased, though not every brewer was as keen. William Younger, for example, used it very sparingly. Maclay, on the other hand, included No. 2 invert sugar in all their beers in the 1930's. Though, as they did only have one recipe from which they parti-gyled everything, it had to be all or nothing.

Drybrough included sugar in all their grists, usually several different types of proprietary and invert sugars.

The use of caramel for colour corrections was increasingly important. This was often added at racking time to colour the same beer to multiple shades for different markets. The same beer could be anything from straw-coloured to near black, all achieved simply with caramel.

Lactose was used rather more liberally than in England. William Younger didn't, as English brewers did, reserve it for Milk Stout. They also used some in other styles, such as Mild Ale and Strong Scotch Ale.

Adjuncts

While in England maize was almost always used in the form of flakes, in Scotland grits were popular. At William Younger, ridiculously popular. Most of their grists in the 1930's were over 40% grits. It's the highest percentage of adjuncts I've seen in British beer. Thankfully, other Scottish brewers were more restrained in their use.

During WW I, when imports of raw materials were limited due to German U-boat activity in the North Atlantic, maize disappeared entirely from British beer. At the time maize wasn't grown in the UK and importing wasn't seen as a high priority, especially for brewing.

Hops

WW I cause a massive shift in the hops used in British brewing. On the one had hostilities prevented foreign imports. On the other, the dramatic fall in beer gravities after 1916 caused the demand for hops to plummet. Only by government intervention in the form of buying up the entire crop kept English hop farmers from bankruptcy. The net result was the UK became self-sufficient in hops for the first time in 70 years.

After the war, hop imports did resume, but in much smaller quantities than before. What imports there were tended to be of high-quality central European hops.

Water

With brewers north of the border increasingly brewing little but Pale Ales, treating their water remained vital.

By the end of WW I in 1918 nothing had changed in Drybrough's water treatment. Just as in 1906 for all its beers received the same additions: 16 quarts of sulphate of lime, 6 quarts of magnesium, 6 pints of calcium chloride and 3 gallons of bisulphate of lime[53]. It still looks like Burtonisation to me.

That Drybrough needed to add so many minerals is clear proof that Edinburgh water wasn't almost identical to Burton's, as I've seen some writers claim.

William Younger was so proud of its brewing water that it was mentioned in the company's newspaper advertisements:

> "For hundreds of years - since the monks of Holyrood first brewed - Edinburgh has been famous for her Ales and THE Edinburgh Ale of to-day is that wonderful Malt Liquor Wm. YOUNGER'S SCOTCH ALE. Pure Hops and Malt - brewed with the famous Edinburgh Water."[54]

---

[53] Drybrough brewing record held at the Scottish Brewing Archive, document number D/6/1/1/3.
[54] Nottingham Evening Post - Thursday 24 January 1924

Techniques

At the start of this period changes in techniques were mostly dictated by wartime problems and shortages. Methods had to be adapted to cope with shortages of materials and fuel. The 1920's were more relaxed, and some brewers resorted to pre-war practices. The hard years of the 1930's, when beer production fell as a result of the slump in the world economy. It prompted some brewers to attempt to cut costs once more.

Mashing

WW I

Scottish mashing schemes remained simpler than those in London. A single infusion and a couple of sparges. There wasn't much variation in the method used for different beers. Sometimes a degree or two.

Thomas Usher's mashing system for a couple of their Mild Ales was typical straightforward:

Thomas Usher 1914 80/- and 100/- mashing scheme			
	Strike heat	mash tun	underback
mash	155° F	147° F	146° F
sparge 1	170° F	160° F	161° F
sparge 2	160° F	158° F	157° F
Source: Thomas Usher brewing record held at the Scottish Brewing Archive, document number TU/6/1/5.			

There wasn't much difference in the way they mashed their Pale Ales. A touch warmer, surprisingly.

Thomas Usher 1914 PA 60/- and IP mashing scheme			
	Strike heat	mash tun	underback
mash	157° F	150.5° F	149° F
sparge 1	170° F	155° F	159° F
sparge 2	160° F	160° F	153° F
sparge 3	155° F	154° F	149° F
Source: Thomas Usher brewing record held at the Scottish Brewing Archive, document number TU/6/1/5.			

William Younger did things slightly differently:

William Younger 1914 100/- Ale mashing scheme

strike heat	158° F
time mashed	10 minutes
time stood	2 hours
mash temperature	152° F
1st sparge heat	160° F
2nd sparge heat	160° F
1st tap heat	148° F
2nd tap heat	149° F
3rd tap heat	152° F
Source: William Younger brewing record held at the Scottish Brewing Archive, document number WY/6/1/2/58.	

Younger had a higher initial mash temperature than Usher, then had a cooler first sparge. Resulting in cooler runoff heats for the later worts.

Their No. 3 Strong Ale was mashed almost identically:

William Younger 1914 No. 3 mashing scheme

strike heat	160° F
time mashed	10 minutes
time stood	2 hours
mash temperature	152° F
1st sparge heat	160° F
2nd sparge heat	160° F
1st tap heat	149° F
2nd tap heat	150° F
3rd tap heat	152° F
Source: William Younger brewing record held at the Scottish Brewing Archive, document number WY/6/1/2/58.	

Large London brewer Barclay Perkins had a far more complicated way of mashing. This is their Mild Ale:

Barclay Perkins 1914 X Ale mashing scheme

	strike heat	mash heat	stood hours	tap heat
mash 1	160° F	148° F	2.25	
underlet mash 1	180° F	153° F	0.75	152° F
sparge 1	170° F			
underlet mash 2	168° F		0.5	156° F
sparge 2	160° F			152° F
Source: Barclay Perkins brewing record held at the London Metropolitan Archives document number ACC/2305/1/603.				

After the initial infusion, the mash stood for two hours, then more hot water was added via the underlet and it was left another 45 minutes. After a sparge there was another underlet mash of 30 minutes and a final sparge. With the extra mashes and longer initial stand, the Barclay Perkins method takes about 90 minutes longer than the Scottish one.

Barclay Perkins Bitter, XLK, was mashed ever so slightly warmer:

Barclay Perkins 1914 XLK Ale mashing scheme				
	strike heat	mash heat	stood hours	tap heat
mash 1	162° F	149.5° F	2.25	
underlet 1	180° F	155° F	0.75	151° F
sparge 1	170° F			
underlet 2	168° F		0.5	156° F
sparge 2	166° F			152° F
Source: Barclay Perkins brewing record held at the London Metropolitan Archives document number ACC/2305/1/603.				

Directly comparing the Scottish and English systems, the results look contradictory:

Mash and tap heats overview 1914						
	mash heat	underlet heat	tap heat 1	tap heat 2	tap heat 3	tap heat 4
Usher IP and PA	150.5° F		149° F	159° F	153° F	149° F
Usher 80/- and 100/-	147° F		146° F	161° F	157° F	
William Younger 100/-	152° F		148° F	149° F	152° F	
William Younger No. 3	152° F		149° F	150° F	152° F	
Barclay Perkins X	148° F	153° F	152° F	156° F	152° F	
Barclay Perkins XLK	149.5° F	155° F	151° F	156° F	152° F	
Whitbread X			143° F	151° F		
Whitbread IPA			149° F	155° F		
Sources: Barclay Perkins brewing record held at the London Metropolitan Archives document number ACC/2305/1/603. William Younger brewing record held at the Scottish Brewing Archive, document number WY/6/1/2/58. Thomas Usher brewing record held at the Scottish Brewing Archive, document number TU/6/1/5. Whitbread brewing record held at the London Metropolitan Archives, document number LMA/4453/D/01/080.						

Barclay Perkins initial heat is cooler, but first tap heat warmer than in Scotland. That's the result of the underlet mash which raised the initial temperature. Whitbread's first tap heat is quite similar to the Scottish ones, despite also having an underlet mash.

1921-1939

Not much had changed at Thomas Usher. In the late 1920's, they mashed their Pale Ales much as they had in 1914:

Thomas Usher 1928 PA 60/- mashing scheme

	Strike heat	mash tun	underback
mash	159° F	151° F	148° F
sparge 1	170° F	156° F	160° F
sparge 2	165° F	160° F	152° F
sparge 3	155° F	152° F	147° F

Source:
Thomas Usher brewing record held at the Scottish Brewing Archive, document number TU/6/1/6.

Obviously they had a way of working that they liked, so they stuck with it.

The same held true for William Younger. Their XXP has a near-identical method to the No. 3 from 1914:

William Younger 1933 XXP mashing scheme

strike heat	160° F
time mashed	7 minutes
time stood	2 hours
mash temperature	152° F
1st sparge heat	160° F
2nd sparge heat	160° F
1st tap heat	150° F
2nd tap heat	153° F
3rd tap heat	155° F

Source:
William Younger brewing record held at the Scottish Brewing Archive, document number WY/6/1/2/70.

Once you've simplified your mash down to a mash and two sparges, there really isn't much left to simplify. Unless you go over to a mash filter.

Underlet mashing wasn't solely confined to big London breweries. Small country outfits like Adnam employed it, too.

Adnam 1930 PA mashing scheme

	strike heat	tap heat
mash 1	158.5° F	
underlet 1	180° F	145.5° F
sparge 1	168° F	149° F
sparge 2	163° F	156° F
sparge 3	160° F	155° F

Source:
Adnam brewing record held at the brewery.

Unlike Barclay Perkins, Adnam only did one underlet. Despite the fairly similar strike heats, Adnam's initial tap heats were cooler.

Barclay Perkins remained true to underletting:

Fullers 1931 OBE, XX and X mashing scheme

	strike heat	mash heat	tap heat	stood hours
mash 1	157° F	147° F		1.42
underlet	175° F	151° F	148° F	2
sparge 1	168° F		147° F	
sparge 2	165° F		147° F	

Source:
Fullers brewing record held at the brewery.

Looking a little further, I realised underlet mashing wasn't limited to London. Lorimer & Clark were at it in Edinburgh, too:

Lorimer & Clark 1932 XXP7 mashing scheme

	strike heat	mash heat	stood hours
mash	160° F	148° F	0.33
underlet	195° F	153° F	1.5

Source:
Lorimer & Clark brewing record held at the Caledonian Brewery.

On first sight, it looks as if the Scots mashed a little warmer:

Mash and tap heats overview 1922 - 1934

Beer	mash heat	underlet heat	tap heat 1	tap heat 2	tap heat 3	tap heat 4
1928 Usher PA 60/-	151° F		148° F	160° F	152° F	147° F
1933 William Younger XXP	152° F		150° F	153° F	155° F	
1933 Drybrough P 60/-	152° F		148° F	160° F		
1932 Lorimer & Clark XX=7	148° F	153° F				
1930 Adnam PA			145.5° F	149° F	156° F	155° F
1930 Barclay Perkins XLK	148° F		155° F	153° F	157° F	153° F
1931 Fullers OBE, XX, X	147° F	151° F	148° F	147° F	147° F	
1930 Courage KKK, MC, X	146° F	149° F				
1922 Camden PA	149° F	155° F	154.5° F	157.8° F		
1934 Tetley X1	147° F	152° F	155° F	153° F	147° F	

Sources:
William Younger brewing record held at the Scottish Brewing Archive, document number WY/6/1/2/70.
Adnam brewing record held at the brewery.
Barclay Perkins brewing record held at the London Metropolitan Archives document number ACC/2305/1/616.
Fullers brewing record held at the brewery.
Camden Brewery brewing record held at the London Metropolitan Archives, document number ACC/2305/9/5.
Drybrough brewing record held at the Scottish Brewing Archive, document number D/6/1/1/4.
Tetley brewing record held at the West Yorkshire Archives, document number WYL756/ACC3349/552.
Lorimer & Clark brewing record held at the Caledonian Brewery.

However, on closer inspection, it's not that simple. True, the initial mash temperature was hotter in Scotland. But the underlet employed in England raised the temperature part of the way through the mash to a temperature similar to in Scotland. It was more a difference in technique than of temperature. In Scotland they went straight to the final mashing temperature, in England they got there in two steps.

Boiling

The war affected all aspects of brewing. Boiling practices were adapted to help conserve coal, which was in short supply later in the war. But there was also an indirect reason for shorter boiling times: very strong beers which required a long boil to hit their target gravity were no longer brewed.

At Drybrough, boiling times were reduced in 1918:

Drybrough Pale Ale boil times 1915 - 1939			
Year	1st	2nd	3rd
1915	2	2	2.17
1916	2	2	2.17
1917	2	2	2.17
1918	1.33	1.25	1.25
1919	1.5	1.25	1.25
1920	1.75	1.5	1.5
1933	2		
1939	2.25		
Sources: Drybrough brewing records held at the Scottish Brewing Archive, document numbers D/6/1/1/3 and D/6/1/1/4.			

After the war ended, Drybrough boiling times increased again and by the time WW II broke out they were boiling for longer than in 1915.

There was a similar pattern with Drybrough's Stouts:

Drybrough Stout boil times 1915 - 1920			
Year	1st	2nd	3rd
1915	2	2	2.17
1916	2	2	2.17
1917	2	2	
1918	1.33	1.33	
1919	1.5	1.25	1.25
1920	2	1.5	
Source: Drybrough brewing record held at the Scottish Brewing Archive, document number D/6/1/1/3.			

Thomas Usher also reduced their boiling times during the war:

Thomas Usher Pale Ale boil times 1914 - 1931

Year	1st	2nd	3rd	4th
1914	1.75	2.25	2.75	
1916	1.5	2	2.5	
1917	1.75	2.75		
1918	1.5	2	2.5	
1919	1.5	1.75	2.25	
1928	1.75	2	2.25	2.5
1931	1.75	2	2.5	

Sources:
Thomas Usher brewing records held at the Scottish Brewing Archive, document numbers TU/6/1,5 and TU/6/1/6.

Though here boiling times never quite went back to their pre-war level.

What was happening in London during the same period? Fuller should give us some answers:

Fuller's Pale Ale boil times 1914 - 1939

Year	1st	2nd
1914	1.5	1.75
1915	1.5	1.75
1916	1.5	1.75
1917	1.5	1.75
1918	1.5	1.75
1919	1.5	1.5
1920	1.5	1.5
1925	1.5	1.75
1931	1.5	1.75
1935	1.5	1
1939	1.5	1.75

Source:
Fullers brewing records held at the brewery.

The first thing to note is that Fuller's Pale Ale boils were shorter than either Drybrough's or Usher's. At the start of the war, the Fuller's first wort was boiled for 15 minutes less than Usher's and 30 minutes less than Drybrough's. And the Scottish breweries' boiling times remained higher in the interwar period.

Fuller's boiling times shortened a little – for the second wort only – in 1919 and 1920, then returned to their pre-war level. The effect was less than in Scotland, but Fuller's boiling times were already quite short.

To prove that Fullers weren't a freak, here are the details for Whitbread's weaker Pale Ales:

Whitbread Pale Ale boil times 1914 - 1939		
Year	1st	2nd
1914	1.5	1.75
1916	1.5	1.75
1917	1.5	1.75
1918	1.5	1.75
1919	1.17	1.42
1921	1.5	1.92
1925	1.5	1.92
1931	1.67	1.75
1935	1.5	1.5
1939	1.5	1.75
Sources: Whitbread brewing records held at the London Metropolitan Archives, document numbers LMA/4453/D/01/079, LMA/4453/D/01/081, LMA/4453/D/01/082, LMA/4453/D/01/083, LMA/4453/D/01/084, LMA/4453/D/01/086, LMA/4453/D/01/090, LMA/4453/D/01/097, LMA/4453/D/01/101 and LMA/4453/D/01/107.		

It's near identical to what was happening at Fuller's. Though the strongest Pale Ale, PA, was handled a bit differently. That was boiled at longer at the start of the war and rather less after it.

Over at the Whitbread Stout Brewhouse, things were rather different:

Whitbread Stout boil times 1914 - 1939		
Year	1st	2nd
1914	1.75	1.75
1915	1.75	1.75
1916	1.75	1.75
1917	1.5	1.67
1918	1.5	1.5
1919	1.5	1.58
1921	1.5	2.00
1925	1.75	2.00
1931	1.33	1.5
1936	1.25	1.33
1939	1.25	1.42
Sources: Whitbread brewing records held at the London Metropolitan Archives, document numbers LMA/4453/D/09/108, LMA/4453/D/09/109, LMA/4453/D/09/110, LMA/4453/D/09/112, LMA/4453/D/09/113, LMA/4453/D/09/114, LMA/4453/D/09/118, LMA/4453/D/09/123, LMA/4453/D/09/125 and LMA/4453/D/09/126.		

After bouncing back to pre-war levels in the 1920's, the boiling times fell again in the 1930's.

Whitbread's Stouts were boiled for about 15 minutes less than Drybrough's at the start of the war. The difference had increased to 30 minutes at the start of the 1920's.

Fermentation

One thing Scottish brewers were good at recording was the fermentation. Most breweries kept a detailed account of temperatures and gravities. Sadly the practice wasn't as common in England, limiting the amount of comparative material.

WW I

This is how Drybrough fermented their Pale Ales on the eve of WW I:

Drybrough Pale Ale fermentations in 1914

	Pitching gravity	heat	grv.	heat	grv.	heat	grv.	heat	grv.	heat	grv.
Pl	1044	62° F	1027.5	64° F	1033	68° F	1026	67° F	1020	67° F	1015
Pl 48/-	1040	62° F	1036	65° F	1030	66° F	1025	68° F	1019	67° F	1014
Pl 60/-	1055	62° F	1051	65° F	1040	66° F	1032	70° F	1024	69.5° F	1018
Source: Drybrough brewing record held at the Scottish Brewing Archive, document number D/6/1/1/3.											

The pitching heat isn't in the brewing record, unfortunately. Based on the temperature little way into the fermentation, I'd guess it was pitch at around 60º F. It's a fairly simple temperature profile. Rising slowly for the first couple of days before levelling out at around 70º F.

At William Younger, the fermentation profile was slightly different:

William Younger fermentations in 1914

Beer	MM	No. 3
Pitching heat	59.5° F	59° F
Pitching gravity	1047	1062
heat	61° F	63° F
gravity	1042	1056
heat	63.5° F	65° F
gravity	1038	1049
heat	69° F	67.5° F
gravity	1025	1036
heat	71° F	66° F
gravity	1019	1029
heat	69° F	62° F
gravity	1013	1022
heat	59° F	57° F
gravity	1012	1020
heat	58° F	56° F
gravity	1012	1019
Source: William Younger brewing record held at the Scottish Brewing Archive document number WY'6/1/2/58.		

The temperature rose rather more quickly than at Drybrough, but dropped back below the starting point towards the end of the fermentation.

The fermentations down at Barclay Perkins in London were quite similar to at Drybrough, though the temperature rose more quickly in the beginning:

Barclay Perkins 1914 X Ale fermentation

		OG	heat
day 1	PM	1051.3	61° F
day 2	AM	1045	63° F
	PM	1037.5	65° F
day 3	AM	1023	71.5° F
	PM	1021	73° F
day 4	AM	1005	69° F

Source:
Barclay Perkins brewing record held at the London Metropolitan Archives document number ACC/2305/1/603.

Barclay Perkins 1914 XLK Ale fermentation

		OG	heat
day 1	PM	1049.9	60.5° F
day 2	AM	1047	61° F
	PM	1039	63.5° F
day 3	AM	1020	69.5° F
	PM	1017	70.5° F
day 4	AM	1004	68° F

Source:
Barclay Perkins brewing record held at the London Metropolitan Archives document number ACC/2305/1/603.

Gradual rise at the beginning, a plateau, then finally a small drop.

Smaller London brewer Fullers had their own particular scheme:

Fullers 1914 X Ale fermentation

		OG	heat
day 1	AM	1049.6	60° F
	PM	1040.0	64° F
day 2	AM	1029.5	67° F
	PM	1018.1	67° F
day 3	AM	1013.9	67° F
	PM	1011.4	67° F
day 4	AM	1010.6	67° F
	PM	1011.1	59° F

Source:
Fullers brewing record held at the brewery.

Like at William Younger, the temperature was dropped down at the end of fermentation.

It's easier to make a comparison with all the details in a single table:

English and Scottish fermentations in 1914								
Beer	Pitching heat							
Wm. Younger MM	59.5° F	61° F	63.5° F	69° F	71° F	69° F	59° F	58° F
Wm. Younger No. 3	59° F	63° F	65° F	67.5° F	66° F	62° F	57° F	56° F
Drybrough PI		62° F	64° F	68° F	67° F	67° F		
Drybrough PI 48/-		62° F	65° F	66° F	68° F	67° F		
Drybrough PI 60/-		62° F	65° F	66° F	70° F	69.5° F		
Barclay Perkins X Ale	61° F	63° F	65° F	71.5° F	73° F	69° F		
Barclay Perkins XLK	60.5° F	61° F	63.5° F	69.5° F	70.5° F	68° F		
Fullers X	60° F	64° F	67° F	67° F	67° F	67° F	67° F	59° F
Sources:								
Barclay Perkins brewing record held at the London Metropolitan Archives document number ACC/2305/1/603. Drybrough brewing record held at the Scottish Brewing Archive, document number D/6/1/1/3. William Younger brewing record held at the Scottish Brewing Archive, document number WY/6/1/2/58. Fullers brewing record held at the brewery.								

I can't see any huge difference between the English and Scottish fermentations. The profile of Fullers X and William Younger No. 3 look pretty similar, other than Younger starting to cool the wort a little earlier.

1921 - 1939

In the years immediately after WW I William Younger did weird things to some worts after fermentation. They'd brew the beer to something like a pre-war gravity and then water it down to a weaker strength. Truman's Burton brewery did something similar. They would produce and ferment worts the same way, then blend the beers produced after fermentation. I suspect that it's to do with yeast health.

Here's an example of a fermentation from Drybrough:

	Drybrough Pale Ale fermentations in 1933										
	Pitch heat	gravity	heat	gravity	heat	grv.	heat	grv.	heat	grv.	heat	grv.
54/-	58.5° F	1030	61° F	1027.5	63° F	1023	64° F	1015	68° F	1012	59° F	1010
60/-	58.5° F	1036	61° F	1033	64° F	1027	67.5° F	1018	69.5° F	1013	58° F	1011.5
80/-	58° F	1049	60.5° F	1045	64.5° F	1036	68° F	1023	70° F	1018	56° F	1015
Source:											
Drybrough brewing record held at the Scottish Brewing Archive, document number D/6/1/1/4.											

It's a pretty simple profile. The temperature rises gradually during fermentation before being dropped back, presumably through the use of attemperators, to drop it back to around the starting point.

William Younger were still dropping the temperature at the end of their fermentation. Sometimes to quite low levels:

William Younger fermentations in 1933

Beer			XP	No. 1
		Pitching heat	61° F	57° F
		Pitching gravity	1043	1085
day 1	AM	heat	66° F	60° F
		gravity	1029	1078
	PM	heat	68° F	63° F
		gravity	1024	1070
day 2	AM	heat	68° F	69° F
		gravity	1015	1050
	PM	heat	68° F	70° F
		gravity	1013	1040
day 3	AM	heat	61° F	66.5° F
		gravity	1013	1035
	PM	heat	58° F	59° F
		gravity	1013	1034
day 4	AM	heat		58° F
		gravity		1034
	PM	heat		55° F
		gravity		1034

Source:
William Younger brewing record held at the Scottish Brewing Archive, document number WY/6/1/2/70.

Pale Ale fermentations at Shepherd Neame in Kent look much like Drybrough's:

Shepherd Neame Pale Ale fermentations in 1938

			day 1		day 2		day 3		day 4	
Beer	OG	Pitch temp	AM	PM	AM	PM	AM	PM	AM	PM
LDA	1031.3	62.5° F	62.75° F	64° F	67.25° F	68.75° F	68.75° F	68.5° F	68° F	66.5° F
BB	1039.3	62.5° F	63.75° F	65.75° F	68° F	68° F	67.75° F	67.75° F	67.75° F	66.75° F
PA	1049.0	62.75° F	65° F	67.25° F	72° F	72° F	72° F	71.75° F	71° F	70° F

Source:
Shepherd Neame brewing records held at the brewery.

Again the temperature slowly rises during the fermentation and peaks just before its end. Though the starting temperatures are a little higher, the maximum temperatures are very similar for Shepherd Neame and Drybrough.

Fullers continued to have a fermentation profile pretty close to William Younger's:

Fullers 1933 XX Ale fermentation			
		OG	heat
day 1	PM	1042.5	62° F
day 2	AM	1031.1	68.5° F
	PM	1025.6	67.5° F
day 3	AM	1018.6	67.5° F
	PM	1010.6	67° F
day 4	AM	1010.3	66.5° F
	PM	1010.0	66.5° F
day 5	AM	1010.3	60° F
Source: Fullers brewing record held at the brewery.			

The wort has clearly been cooled with attemperators at the end of the fermentation. The bulk of the gravity drop was quite early in the process, in the first two days.

Comparing the fermentations directly, we can see that Shepherd Neame fermented the warmest and Fullers the coolest:

English and Scottish fermentations 1933 - 1938

Beer	Pitching heat								
1933 Wm. Younger XP	61° F	66° F	68° F	68° F	68° F	61° F	58° F		
1933 Drybrough P 54/-	58.5° F	61° F	63° F	64° F	68° F	59° F			
1933 Drybrough P 60/-	58.5° F	61° F	64° F	67.5° F	69.5° F	58° F			
1933 Drybrough P 80/-	58° F	60.5° F	64.5° F	68° F	70° F	56° F			
1938 Shepherd Neame LDA	62.5° F	62.75° F	64° F	67.25° F	68.75° F	68.75° F	68.5° F	68° F	66.5° F
1938 Shepherd Neame BB	62.5° F	63.75° F	65.75° F	68° F	68° F	67.75° F	67.75° F	67.75° F	66.75° F
1938 Shepherd Neame PA	62.75° F	65° F	67.25° F	72° F	72° F	72° F	71.75° F	71° F	70° F
1935 Fullers X	62° F	68.5° F	67.5° F	67.5° F	67° F	66.5° F	66.5° F	60° F	

Sources:
Shepherd Neame brewing records held at the brewery.
Fullers brewing record held at the brewery.
William Younger brewing record held at the Scottish Brewing Archive, document number WY/6/1/2/70.
Drybrough brewing record held at the Scottish Brewing Archive, document number D/6/1/1/4.

I can see no evidence there that the Scots were fermenting significantly cooler than the English.

Dry hopping

It's difficult to fully track dry hopping in the UK for a very simple reason. It isn't always recorded in brewing logs. The information available is patchy.

Luckily, several Scottish brewers did note down their dry hopping regimes. Including William Younger, who dry hopped a wide range of beers:

William Younger dry hopping 1921 - 1939 (oz. per barrel)							
Year	1	3 Pale	XXX	DBS Btlg	Pale XXPS	Ext	XXP Btlg	LAE
1921	3.89	3.83	2.42	7.65	3.8			7.04
1933	2.01	2.06	1.98	6.10	2.02	6.52	1.82	4.85
1939	2.25	2.08	2.05	3.05	2.92	2.09	2.02	4.16
Source: William Younger brewing records held at the Scottish Brewing Archive, document numbers WY/6/1/2/63, WY/6/1/2/70 and WY/6/1/2/76.								

1 and 3 are Strong Ales, XXX Mild Ale, DBS Btlg Stout and the others Pale Ales. Quite a range of styles there that they were dry hopping. It was usual for Pale and Strong Ales, but unusual for things like Mild.

Down in London, Barclay Perkins dry hopped a different subset of beers:

Barclay Perkins dry hopping 1921 - 1939 (oz. per barrel)							
Year	BS Ex	IBS	XLK (bottling)	XLK (trade)	PA	KK	KK (for bottling)
1921	8	2	0	3	4	3	8
1933	8		0	3	3	3	8
1939		0	3	3	6	3	
Sources: Barclay Perkins brewing records held at the London Metropolitan Archives, document numbers ACC/2305/01/608, ACC/2305/01/609, ACC/2305/01/617, ACC/2305/01/618 and ACC/2305/01/623.							

BS Ex and IBS are Stouts, XLK and PA are Pale Ales, KK is Burton Ale. Barclay Perkins hopping was quite standard throughout the interwar period, unlike William Younger's. Strong beers like BS Ex and KK (for bottling) received a hefty dose of dry hops, a full half pound per barrel.

The 1921 KK (for bottling) had this wonderful note on the dry hopping process[55]:

> 4 oz. Saaz 1920 after 4 or 5 days rolling
> 4 oz. Champion 1920 after further week. Casks bunged down meanwhile

Note that Barclay Perkins were dry hopping with Saaz. A sure sign that it was considered a top-quality hop.

Drybrough were also very consistent in their dry hopping, using the same amount in all their Pale Ales, no matter what the strength.

---

[55] Barclay Perkins brewing record held at the London Metropolitan Archives, document number ACC/2305/01/608.

Drybrough dry hopping 1915 - 1920 (oz. per barrel)						
Year	Pl 48/-	Pl	Pl 60/-	8d PA	60/- Mild
1915	4	4	4			
1920	4	4	4	4		1
Source: Drybrough brewing record held at the Scottish Brewing Archive, document number D/6/1/1/3.					

Unusually, Drybrough also added a small amount of dry hops to their Mild.

Colouring

The Scots were never very enthusiastic about the use of dark malts. When some styles began to darken around 1900, rather than change their grists Scottish brewers instead colour-corrected their beers with caramel at racking time.

The usual story of the colour in Scottish beers coming from a super-long boil and roasted barley is total bollocks. There's no evidence of either in the brewing records. I sometimes wonder where this rubbish comes from and why it's been repeated so often.

Styles

The constraints of WW I made a good job of rooting the weak in British beers styles, and Scotland was no exception. Obviously, when government was telling you how much you could brew, you were going to keep the most popular beers and drop the less popular ones. In Scotland, that meant discarding pretty much everything other than Pale Ale.

Pale Ale

On the up for the second half of the 1880's, Pale Ale came to almost totally dominate Scottish brewing between the wars. Many Scottish firms brewed little – or even nothing – else. Though to modern eyes these beers don't look much like Pale Ales.

For a start, the Scottish enthusiasm for colouring up beer meant many weren't pale. They could be anything from straw-coloured to dark brown, depending on the market they were intended for. And while the original Scottish Pale Ales had been as heavily hopped as their English counterparts, a gradual reduction in hopping levels left them considerably sweeter. This process of falling hop rates accelerated during WW I, leaving Scottish examples very different from those brewed South of the border.

WW I

The war had a massive impact on British beer, mostly through a big drop in gravity. Scottish Pale Ales weren't immune to the trend. In some ways, the Scots were better prepared than English brewers, as they were already brewing relatively low-gravity Pale Ales.

For example, Drybrough's Pl 48/-, their weakest Pale Ale was just 1040º. No London beer had a gravity as low. The war was to make any beer over 1030º look strong. As you can see from this overview of Drybrough's Pale Ales across the war years:

Drybrough Pale Ales 1915 - 1920								
Date	Year	Beer	OG	FG	ABV	App. Atten-uation	lbs hops/qtr	hops lb/brl
8th Jan	1915	Pl 48/-	1040.0	1016.0	3.18	60.00%	4.59	0.76
8th Jan	1915	Pl	1044.0	1014.0	3.97	68.18%	4.59	0.84
8th Jan	1915	Pl 60/-	1052.0	1018.0	4.50	65.38%	4.59	0.99
7th Jan	1916	Pl 48/-	1038.0	1013.0	3.31	65.79%	5.02	0.79
4th Jan	1916	Pl	1044.0	1013.0	4.10	70.45%	4.93	0.90
4th Jan	1916	Pl 60/-	1053.0	1017.0	4.76	67.92%	4.93	1.08
16th Jan	1917	Pl 48/-	1037.0	1011.0	3.44	70.27%	3.95	0.61
16th Jan	1917	Pl	1041.0	1012.0	3.84	70.73%	3.95	0.68
16th Jan	1917	Pl 60/-	1048.0	1016.0	4.23	66.67%	3.95	0.80
20th Aug	1917	Pl 48/-	1027.0	1010.0	2.25	62.96%	4.04	0.46
21st Aug	1917	Pl	1033.0	1010.0	3.04	69.70%	4.04	0.56
24th Aug	1917	Pl	1035.0	1010.0	3.31	71.43%	4.04	0.54
15th Jan	1918	Pl 48/-	1023.4	1007.6	2.09	67.52%	4.91	0.48
22nd Jan	1918	Pl	1037.0	1011.0	3.44	70.27%	5.05	0.78
30th Jul	1918	Pl 48/-	1024.0	1007.0	2.25	70.83%	4.93	0.51
30th Jul	1918	Pl	1030.0	1009.0	2.78	70.00%	4.93	0.64
1st Nov	1918	Pl 48/-	1020.0	1009.0	1.46	55.00%	4.93	0.41
1st Nov	1918	Pl	1031.0	1009.0	2.91	70.97%	4.93	0.64

Drybrough Pale Ales 1915 - 1920

Date	Year	Beer	OG	FG	ABV	App. Attenuation	lbs hops/qtr	hops lb/brl
1st Nov	1918	Pl X	1040.0	1009.0	4.10	77.50%	4.93	0.82
25th Feb	1919	Pl 48/-	1023.0	1007.0	2.12	69.57%	5.00	0.50
25th Feb	1919	Pl	1030.0	1009.0	2.78	70.00%	5.00	0.65
10th Jul	1919	Pl	1030.0	1009.0	2.78	70.00%	4.93	0.61
10th Jul	1919	Pl 60/-	1036.0	1009.0	3.57	75.00%	4.93	0.73
17th Oct	1919	Pl 60/-	1039.0	1012.0	3.57	69.23%	4.99	0.82
17th Oct	1919	Pl 60/- X	1046.0	1015.0	4.10	67.39%	4.99	0.96
22nd Oct	1919	Pl 54/-	1033.0	1010.0	3.04	69.70%	5.06	0.71
7th Jan	1920	Pl 60/-	1039.0	1012.0	3.57	69.23%	6.07	1.07
7th Jan	1920	3d PA	1055.0	1019.0	4.76	65.45%	6.07	1.51
9th Jan	1920	Pl 54/-	1035.0	1010.0	3.31	71.43%	5.85	0.88
22nd Jan	1920	Pl 48/-	1027.0	1008.0	2.51	70.37%	4.95	0.59

Sources:
Drybrough brewing record held at the Scottish Brewing Archive, document number D/6/1/1/3.

Pl's gravity fell from 1044º in 1914 to 1030º in 1918 and 1919. Pl 48/- fared even worse, dropping from 1040º to just 1020º in November 1918. This is fairly typical of what happened in the UK as a whole. With the cheaper and more popular beers becoming non-intoxicating.

There was a financial incentive for brewers to continue to make some higher gravity beers. Ones over a certain gravity were exempt from price controls and could earn a brewer a tidy profit. As brewers were set a limit on the average gravity of all the beer they brewed, they needed to brew a lot of beer below the average to be able to brew a small quantity of strong beer.

Something similar could be observed at Thomas Usher. Though their 40/- PA looks like it belongs in 1919, not 1914. That's extraordinarily weak for before WW I.

Thomas Usher Pale Ales 1914 - 1919

Date	Year	Beer	OG	FG	ABV	App. Attenuation	lbs hops/qtr	hops lb/brl
24th Aug	1914	40/- PA	1029	1009	2.65	68.97%	7.25	0.87
24th Aug	1914	PA	1048	1014	4.50	70.83%	7.25	1.44
20th Aug	1914	PA 60/-	1053	1014.5	5.09	72.64%	7.25	1.58
14th Mar	1916	IP	1040	1013.5	3.51	66.25%	5.50	0.97
24th Feb	1916	PA	1048	1015	4.37	68.75%	6.00	1.15
24th Feb	1916	PA 60/-	1055	1017	5.03	69.09%	6.00	1.32
7th Jun	1917	IP	1035	1013	2.91	62.86%	7.25	0.83
4th Jun	1917	PA	1040	1013	3.57	67.50%	7.00	0.93
7th Jun	1917	PA 60/-	1048	1014	4.50	70.83%	7.25	1.14
7th Feb	1918	PA	1038	1014	3.18	63.16%	7.00	1.02
7th Feb	1918	PA 60/-	1047	1015	4.23	68.09%	7.00	1.27
15th Nov	1918	PA	1031	1012.5	2.45	59.68%	8.00	1.52
15th Nov	1918	PA 60/-	1049	1015	4.50	69.39%	8.00	0.96
11th Jul	1919	PA	1036	1012.5	3.11	65.28%	8.00	1.24
24th Jul	1919	PA 60/-	1041	1013.5	3.64	67.07%	7.50	1.54

Sources:
Thomas Usher brewing record held at the Scottish Brewing Archive, document number TU/6/1/5.

I'm slightly surprised that Usher managed to keep their PA 60/- at only a few gravity points below its pre-war gravity as late as November 1918. Their weaker PA also didn't fare too badly, hitting a low of 1031º in 1918.

The war years also had a big impact on the beers brewed in London.

Fuller's Pale Ales 1914 - 1920

Date	Year	Beer	OG	FG	ABV	App. Attenuation	lbs hops/qtr	hops lb/brl
20th Nov	1914	AK	1044.3	1009.1	4.65	79.38%	7.3	1.34
2nd Jul	1915	AK	1044.5	1009.7	4.61	78.22%	7.8	1.42
26th Oct	1916	AK	1041.0	1006.6	4.54	83.78%	8.4	1.43
20th Jun	1917	AK	1038.6	1006.4	4.27	83.51%	8.5	1.45
2nd Jan	1918	AK	1035.5	1007.5	3.70	78.92%	9.7	2.24
20th Jun	1918	AK	1026.2	1005.5	2.73	78.84%	9.7	1.11
15th Apr	1919	AK	1026.0	1004.4	2.86	82.98%	9.0	1.08
19th Jun	1919	AK	1028.2	1004.7	3.10	83.28%	9.7	1.14
27th Aug	1919	AK	1030.5	1006.9	3.12	77.31%	10.0	1.28
11th Feb	1920	AK	1030.6	1007.5	3.06	75.59%	9.8	1.21
17th Nov	1914	PA	1054.2	1012.2	5.56	77.52%	8.1	1.98
1st Jan	1915	PA	1053.7	1012.2	5.49	77.28%	8.9	1.97
31st Oct	1916	PA	1051.8	1009.7	5.57	81.29%	8.6	1.99
20th Jun	1917	PA	1050.6	1011.1	5.23	78.09%	8.5	1.90
2nd Jan	1918	PA	1051.1	1013.3	4.99	73.96%	9.7	6.54

Fuller's Pale Ales 1914 - 1920

Date	Year	Beer	OG	FG	ABV	App. Atten-uation	lbs hops/ qtr	hops lb/brl
20th Jun	1918	PA	1039.3	1009.4	3.96	76.06%	9.7	1.67
16th Apr	1919	PA	1041.6	1009.7	4.21	76.67%	10.0	2.50
19th Jun	1919	PA	1050.6	1012.2	5.09	75.93%	9.7	2.05
27th Aug	1919	PA	1054.2	1013.3	5.41	75.47%	10.0	2.28
11th Feb	1920	PA	1055.0	1015.2	5.26	72.31%	9.8	2.17
15th Apr	1919	XK	1028.3	1005.5	3.00	80.39%	9.0	1.17
19th Jun	1919	XK	1030.2	1005.5	3.27	81.67%	9.7	1.22
27th Aug	1919	XK	1033.8	1010.2	3.11	69.67%	10.0	1.42
11th Feb	1920	XK	1034.0	1008.6	3.36	74.74%	9.8	1.34

Source:
Fullers brewing record held at the brewery.

The gravity of AK was very badly hit by the war, falling from 1044º to just 1026º in April 1919. That's much more typical of what happened to popular beers. It seems that Fuller managed to keep PA at a reasonable gravity by brewing it in far smaller quantities than before the war. And by 1920 it had returned to its 1914 gravity.

Fuller's Pale Ales were consistently hopped at 9-10lbs per quarter of malt throughout the war. More than the 7-8 lbs at Usher and considerably more than the 5-6 lbs at Drybrough. Whose hopping looks light even for a Mild Ale.

An overview might make all those number a little more comprehensible:

Moderate-strength Pale Ales 1914 - 1919

Brewery	Beer		1914	1915	1916	1917	1918 early	1918 late	1919 early	1919 late
Fuller	AK	OG	1044.3	1044.5	1041	1038.6	1035.5	1026.2	1026	1028.2
		ABV	4.65	4.61	4.54	4.27	3.70	2.73	2.86	3.10
Usher	PA	OG	1048		1048	1040	1038	1031		1036
		ABV	4.50		4.37	3.57	3.18	2.45		3.11
Drybrough	PI	OG		1044	1044	1033	1037	1030	1030	1030
		ABV		3.97	4.10	3.04	3.44	2.78	2.78	2.78

Sources:
Fuller brewing records held at the brewery.
Thomas Usher brewing record held at the Scottish Brewing Archive, document number TU/6/1/6.
Drybrough brewing record held at the Scottish Brewing Archive, document number D/6/1/1/3.

From very similar starting points the three beers ended up with very different gravities by the end of 1919.

Now it's the turn of the grists. Scottish brewers stuck to pretty simple grists for their Pale Ales. Usually just pale malt, flaked maize and sugar. Though the war, through limits on imports had an effect on the use of ingredients.

Thomas Usher Pale Ale grists 1914 - 1919

Date	Year	Beer	OG	pale malt	flaked maize	glucose	Greenock	DL
24th Aug	1914	40/- PA	1029	80.00%	9.09%		10.91%	
24th Aug	1914	PA	1048	80.00%	9.09%		10.91%	
20th Aug	1914	PA 60/-	1053	84.43%	7.19%		8.38%	
14th Mar	1916	IP	1040	72.53%	13.19%		9.34%	
24th Feb	1916	PA	1048	77.30%	12.88%		9.82%	
24th Feb	1916	PA 60/-	1055	77.30%	12.88%		9.82%	
7th Jun	1917	IP	1035	80.00%	6.67%		13.33%	
4th Jun	1917	PA	1040	78.57%	7.14%		14.29%	
7th Jun	1917	PA 60/-	1048	80.00%	6.67%		13.33%	
7th Feb	1918	PA	1038	94.06%			5.94%	
7th Feb	1918	PA 60/-	1047	94.06%			5.94%	
15th Nov	1918	PA	1031	83.94%		7.77%	8.29%	
15th Nov	1918	PA 60/-	1049	83.94%		7.77%	8.29%	
11th Jul	1919	PA	1036	84.51%	2.11%		7.39%	5.99%
24th Jul	1919	PA 60/-	1041	84.51%	2.11%		7.39%	5.99%

Sources:
Thomas Usher brewing record held at the Scottish Brewing Archive, document number TU/6/1/5.

I assume the reason flaked maize disappeared in 1918 was due to its unavailability. The sugar content, though the exact type varied, was fairly constant at 10-15%, apart from in early 1918. Again, the change was probably prompted by shortages. Some sugar, which had plenty of uses other than for making beer, was diverted into food production during the war.

To help contextualise the Usher's grists, here are Fuller's grist for comparison:

Fuller's Pale Ales 1914 - 1920

Date	Year	Beer	OG	pale malt	flaked maize	no. 2 sugar	glucose	primings
17th Nov	1914	PA	1054.2	77.28%	2.49%	6.65%	6.65%	6.94%
20th Nov	1914	AK	1044.3	79.03%	5.85%	5.85%	5.85%	3.41%
1st Jan	1915	PA	1053.7	91.43%	3.27%		4.35%	0.95%
2nd Jul	1915	AK	1044.5	78.96%	6.27%	6.68%	6.68%	1.40%
26th Oct	1916	AK	1041.0	80.05%	4.85%	6.47%	8.09%	0.55%
31st Oct	1916	PA	1051.8	80.91%	4.95%	4.40%	6.61%	3.13%
20th Jun	1917	PA	1050.6	86.64%		3.85%	5.78%	3.74%
20th Jun	1917	AK	1038.6	86.64%		3.85%	5.78%	3.74%
2nd Jan	1918	PA	1051.1	92.25%		5.95%		1.80%
2nd Jan	1918	AK	1035.5	92.25%		5.95%		1.80%
20th Jun	1918	PA	1039.3	74.72%		19.16%	3.83%	2.29%
20th Jun	1918	AK	1026.2	74.72%		19.16%	3.83%	2.29%
15th Apr	1919	XK	1028.3	74.40%	4.56%	6.07%	8.10%	6.87%
15th Apr	1919	AK	1026.0	74.40%	4.56%	6.07%	8.10%	6.87%
16th Apr	1919	PA	1041.6	81.56%	4.69%	6.25%	7.50%	
19th Jun	1919	PA	1050.6	77.83%	6.77%	6.77%	6.77%	1.87%

Fuller's Pale Ales 1914 - 1920

Date	Year	Beer	OG	pale malt	flaked maize	no. 2 sugar	glucose	primings
19th Jun	1919	XK	1030.2	77.83%	6.77%	6.77%	6.77%	1.87%
19th Jun	1919	AK	1028.2	77.83%	6.77%	6.77%	6.77%	1.87%
27th Aug	1919	XK	1033.8	74.14%	8.08%	8.81%	8.81%	0.16%
27th Aug	1919	AK	1030.5	74.14%	8.08%	8.81%	8.81%	0.16%
27th Aug	1919	PA	1054.2	74.14%	8.08%	8.81%	8.81%	0.16%
11th Feb	1920	XK	1034.0	78.94%	13.36%	3.24%	3.24%	1.22%
11th Feb	1920	AK	1030.6	78.94%	13.36%	3.24%	3.24%	1.22%
11th Feb	1920	PA	1055.0	78.94%	13.36%	3.24%	3.24%	1.22%

Source:
Fullers brewing record held at the brewery.

The grists aren't a mile away from Usher's. Fuller used the same combination of pale malt, flaked maize and sugar. At 12-15% most of the time, the sugar content is pretty similar to at Usher. Though Fuller wasn't using any proprietary sugars at this point, unlike Usher.

The malt content of around 75% in the later war years was a little less than at Usher. And flaked maize disappeared from the Fuller's recipes at around the same time as at Usher. That can't be a coincidence and it coincides with the period (1917 and 1918) when the German U boat campaign was at its peak.

1921 - 1939

After 1921, brewing started to get back to normal. Gravities bounced back – though to significantly lower than in 1914. Though the enormous increase in beer tax during the war – from 7s 9d per standard barrel in 1914 to 100s in 1921. At the same time, the price of a pint of standard-strength Mild increased from 2d to 6d. Wages had increased during the war, but not enough to compensate. Which inevitably led to a decrease in the consumption of beer.

William Younger Pale Ales 1921 - 1939

Year	Beer	OG	FG	ABV	App. Attenuation	lbs hops/qtr	hops lb/brl
1921	XXPS	1046.1	1011.7	4.55	74.58%	4.55	0.93
1922	LE	1042	1011	4.10	73.81%	9.52	1.50
1922	SLE	1052	1015	4.89	71.15%	9.60	1.94
1922	SE	1057	1015	5.56	73.68%	9.23	2.00
1929	XXPS	1045.8	1010.7	4.64	76.67%	4.55	0.81
1929	IPA Pale	1055.1	1014.7	5.35	73.33%	5.00	0.00
1929	XXPS Pale	1040.0	1010.7	3.88	73.33%	5.00	0.00
1933	Expt	1054.0	1016.0	5.03	70.37%	4.76	1.85
1933	LAE	1046.0	1013.0	4.37	71.74%	8.26	1.44
1933	MXP E	1046.0	1012.5	4.43	72.83%	6.09	1.06
1933	P Btlg	1032.0	1011.0	2.78	65.63%	6.11	0.71
1933	XP Btlg	1039.0	1012.0	3.57	69.23%	6.11	0.87
1933	XXP	1043.0	1012.0	4.10	72.09%	5.24	0.86
1933	XXP Btlg	1043.0	1013.0	3.97	69.77%	6.11	0.95
1933	XXPS	1049.0	1013.0	4.76	73.47%	5.22	0.96

William Younger Pale Ales 1921 - 1939

Year	Beer	OG	FG	ABV	App. Attenuation	lbs hops/qtr	hops lb/brl
1933	XXPSm	1048.0	1013.0	4.63	72.92%	5.22	0.95
1939	XXPS	1046.0	1015.0	4.10	67.39%	3.04	0.51
1939	Pale XXPS	1046.0	1015.0	4.10	67.39%	4.13	0.72
1939	Ext	1054.0	1015.0	5.16	72.22%	5.40	1.10
1939	LAE	1046.0	1013.0	4.37	71.74%	4.78	0.89
1939	XXP Btlg	1040.0	1013.0	3.57	67.50%	4.21	0.63

Sources:
William Younger brewing records held at the Scottish Brewing Archive, document numbers WY/6/1/2/63, WY/6/1/2/68 and WY/6/1/2/70.

Usher settled down to brewing four different strengths of Pale Ale after the end of WW I. Later introducing a fifth, at a lower gravity than the others, rather confusingly called IPA. You may have noticed the rather inconsistent way the term was used in the UK. Sometimes for strong Pale Ales, at others for weak ones.

Thomas Usher Pale Ales 1928 - 1931

Year	Beer	OG	FG	ABV	App. Attenuation	lbs hops/qtr	hops lb/brl
1928	PA	1035	1013	2.91	62.86%	7.00	0.98
1928	PA 60/-	1041	1014	3.57	65.85%	7.00	1.15
1928	PA 70/-	1048	1014.5	4.43	69.79%	7.00	1.36
1928	PA 80/-	1055	1015	5.29	72.73%	7.00	1.53
1931	IPA	1032	1011	2.78	65.63%	5.98	0.78
1931	PA	1034	1012	2.91	64.71%	5.98	0.83
1931	PA 60/-	1040	1012.5	3.64	68.75%	6.02	0.97
1931	PA 70/-	1047	1013.5	4.43	71.28%	5.98	1.43
1931	PA 80/-	1055	1012.5	5.62	77.27%	6.02	1.35

Source:
Thomas Usher brewing record held at the Scottish Brewing Archive, document number TU/6/1/6.

This is an early use of 60/-, 70/- and 80/- to describe three different strength Pale Ales.

The quantities brewed of each beer varied enormously. Only tiny amounts of PA 80/- were made. Over 90% was the three weakest Pale Ales with PA 60/- accounting for almost two thirds of production.

Usher output by type 1st Oct - 20th Nov 1931		
Beer	barrels brewed	%
IPA	1,067.5	19.32%
PA	573	10.37%
PA 6/-	3442.5	62.32%
PA 7/-	240.25	4.35%
PA 8/-	38.5	0.70%
MA	92.5	1.67%
Stout 80/-	34.75	0.63%
Brown Ale	35	0.63%
Total	5,524	
Source: Thomas Usher brewing record held at the Scottish Brewing Archive, document number TU/3/1/6.		

Another Edinburgh brewery, Lorimer & Clark, had a similar selection of Pale Ales:

Lorimer & Clark pale Ales in 1932							
Year	Beer	OG	FG	ABV	App. Atten-uation	lbs hops/ qtr	hops lb/brl
1932	XXP5	1027.0	1007.0	2.65	74.07%	4.80	0.55
1932	XXP6	1031.0	1008.0	3.04	74.19%	4.80	0.64
1932	XXP7	1037.0	1010.0	3.57	72.97%	4.81	0.75
1932	XXP8	1045.0	1011.0	4.50	75.56%	4.80	0.92
Source: Brewing record held at the Caledonian Brewery.							

Lorimer & Clark, which was bought by Vaux of Sunderland, is now known as the Caledonian Brewery. It's the only one of the old Edinburgh breweries that's still open.

Their set of Pale Ales lacks a beer at the greatest strength, usually around 1055º and which was starting to go under the name of Export. The 5, 6, 7 and 8 after XXP refer to the price per pint. The Scots had this odd thing about naming beers by how much they cost. The prices are the same as in England for beers of similar gravities.

Whitbread prices in 1934		
	OG	retail price pint d
Porter	1027	6
Stout	1043	8
Light Ale	1026	5
X Ale	1031	6
Pale Ale	1046	8
XXX Ale	1045	8
Source: Whitbread brewing records held at the London Metropolitan Archives, document numbers LMA/4453/D/09/124, LMA/4453/D/01/098 and LMA/4453/D/09/124.		

1932 was an odd year. There was a huge tax increase in 1931 that prompted brewers to cut gravities. In the years before and after 1931 – 1933, XXP5 had the same OG as the XXP6 in the table.

Another Edinburgh brewer, Drybrough produced a similar range of Pale Ales:

Drybrough Pale Ales 1933 - 1939

Date	Year	Beer	OG	FG	ABV	App. Attenuation	lbs hops/ qtr	hops lb/brl
7th Jul	1933	P 54/-	1030	1010	2.65	66.67%	7.00	0.84
4th Jul	1933	P 60/-	1036	1011.5	3.24	68.06%	6.71	1.01
5th Oct	1933	P 80/-	1049	1015	4.50	69.39%	5.71	1.18
30th Jan	1939	P 54/-	1032	1012	2.65	62.50%	4.86	0.64
13th Feb	1939	Bottling	1034	1013	2.78	61.76%	4.83	0.68
26th Jan	1939	P 60/-	1038	1014	3.18	63.16%	4.93	0.78
26th Jan	1939	P 80/-	1050	1013	4.89	74.00%	4.93	1.02

Source: Drybrough brewing record held at the Scottish Brewing Archive, document number D/6/1/1/4.

Yet again there was a downward trend in the hopping over time, dropping from around 7 lbs per quarter in 1933 to 5 lbs in 1939.

Let's see how Fuller's Pale Ales compare with those from Scotland:

Fuller's Pale Ales 1925 - 1939

Year	Beer	OG	FG	ABV	App. Attenuation	lbs hops/ qtr	hops lb/brl
1925	AK	1032.2	1006.9	3.35	78.52%	10.46	1.20
1925	XK	1040.5	1010.8	3.93	73.34%	10.46	1.51
1925	PA	1054.3	1015.0	5.21	72.46%	10.46	2.03
1931	AK	1032.3	1006.1	3.46	81.12%	9.85	1.27
1931	XK	1040.4	1009.4	4.10	76.68%	9.85	1.58
1931	PA	1052.3	1011.6	5.38	77.74%	9.85	2.05
1935	AK	1033.4	1006.4	3.58	80.93%	9.15	1.44
1935	XK	1039.4	1008.6	4.08	78.22%	9.15	1.70
1935	PA	1053.5	1011.6	5.54	78.25%	9.15	2.31
1939	AK	1033.4	1006.6	3.53	80.07%	9.19	1.25
1939	XK	1039.3	1009.1	3.99	76.76%	9.19	1.47
1939	PA	1051.1	1013.0	5.04	74.53%	9.19	1.91

Source: Fullers brewing record held at the brewery.

Fuller's three Pale Ales correspond quite closely, in terms of gravity, to Usher's IPA, PA 60/- and PA 80/-. However, it was Fuller's strongest, PA, which was their biggest seller. In 1931 Fullers brewed about twice as much PA as XK. AK was brewed in miniscule amounts, just two to five barrels per batch. A parti-gyle in 6th May 1931 produced: AK 4 barrels, XK 92 barrels and PA 170 barrels.

The pattern was similar at other Scottish breweries. All brewed a range of Pale Ales with gravities ranging from around 1030º to 1050º. The beers at the bottom end were produced in quite small quantities and the ones at the top end in tiny quantities. By far the biggest seller was the mid-range beer, often called 60/-, which had a gravity of 1037º – 1040º.

There's a significant difference in the level of hopping, the Fuller's beers receiving about 50% more than Usher's. The hopping level declined at both breweries in the 1930's, but that ratio remained the same. Usher's Pale Ales must have been significantly less bitter than Fuller's.

Fuller's Pale Ale grists 1925 - 1939							
Year	Beer	OG	pale malt	flaked maize	no. 2 sugar	glucose	primings
1925	AK	1032.2	86.81%	8.10%	2.31%	1.54%	1.23%
1925	XK	1040.5	86.81%	8.10%	2.31%	1.54%	1.23%
1925	PA	1054.3	86.81%	8.10%	2.31%	1.54%	1.23%
1931	AK	1032.3	81.31%	14.64%	2.17%	1.08%	0.80%
1931	XK	1040.4	81.31%	14.64%	2.17%	1.08%	0.80%
1931	PA	1052.3	81.31%	14.64%	2.17%	1.08%	0.80%
1935	AK	1033.4	79.86%	14.20%	2.37%	1.18%	2.40%
1935	XK	1039.4	79.86%	14.20%	2.37%	1.18%	2.40%
1935	PA	1053.5	79.86%	14.20%	2.37%	1.18%	2.40%
1939	AK	1033.4	79.87%	14.52%	2.42%	1.21%	1.98%
1939	XK	1039.3	79.87%	14.52%	2.42%	1.21%	1.98%
1939	PA	1051.1	79.87%	14.52%	2.42%	1.21%	1.98%
Source: Fullers brewing record held at the brewery.							

Fuller's grists remained basically the same as during the war, at least in terms of the ingredients used. Pale malt, flaked maize, No. 2 invert sugar, glucose and primings. Though the proportions had changed. The pale malt content had increased from 75% to around 80%. The sugar content, both No. 2 and glucose had been dramatically reduced, leaving the total sugar content between 5% and 6%. Less than half the average level in the war years. In the 1930's there was increase in flaked maize at the expense of pale malt. That looks like a cost cutting measure to me.

Scottish brewers used less base malt and more sugar and adjuncts the Fullers:

Scottish Pale Ale grists 1921 - 1939

Year	Brewer	Beer	pale malt	black malt	enzymic malt	flaked maize	grits	malt extract	sugar
1928	Thomas Usher	PA	76.79%			12.50%			10.71%
1931	Thomas Usher	PA 80/-	78.69%			11.48%			9.84%
1933	Drybrough	P 54/-	72.36%	0.84%		16.08%		0.67%	10.05%
1939	Drybrough	P 54/-	71.02%	0.76%	1.82%	16.39%		0.91%	9.10%
1932	Lorimer & Clark	XXP5	76.06%			12.68%		5.63%	5.63%
1921	Younger, Wm.	XXPS	60.71%				39.29%		
1933	Younger, Wm.	Expt	57.14%				42.86%		
1939	Younger, Wm.	Ext	80.00%				20.00%		

Source:
Thomas Usher brewing record held at the Scottish Brewing Archive, document number TU/6/1/6.
Brewing record held at the Caledonian Brewery.
Drybrough brewing record held at the Scottish Brewing Archive, document number D/6/1/1/4.
William Younger brewing records held at the Scottish Brewing Archive, document numbers WY/6/1/2/63, WY/6/1/2/68 and WY/6/1/2/70.

The Scots were using around double the percentage of sugar as Fullers, 10% rather than 5%. Except for contrarians William Younger, who used none at all. In the 1920's Fullers used rather less maize than Scottish brewers, but in the 1930's just about the same. Once again William Younger stands out with its massive use of grits. Even when the proportion was halved in 1939, grist still made up 20% of the grist

Mild Ale

There were odd Scottish beers marketed as Mild Ale, but in reality the style was pretty much dead after WW I. Which is a huge contrast with England, where Mild was far and away the biggest seller and accounted for more than 50% of production.

Mild's place on the bar was taken by the lowest strength Pale Ales, which had gravities in the low 1030's. Though odd examples of true Mild Ales were brewed.

WW I

The war had a huge impact on Mild Ale, just as it did on all beer styles. At its start there were still quite strong Milds being brewed in Scotland. Not in any great quantities, but they still existed. The war drastically reduced the variety of Mild Ales, knocking most breweries back to just one, or even none.

Thomas Usher started WW I with an impressive array of Mild Ales, ranging in gravity from 1032º to 1065º

Thomas Usher Mild Ales 1914 - 1919

Date	Year	Beer	OG	FG	ABV	App. Attenuation	lbs hops/ qtr	hops lb/brl
26th Aug	1914	44/- MA	1032	1012.5	2.58	60.94%	5.00	0.69
26th Aug	1914	50/- MA	1035	1013	2.91	62.86%	5.00	0.75
19th Aug	1914	60/- MA	1038	1015	3.04	60.53%	5.00	0.79
26th Aug	1914	80/- MA	1046	1017	3.84	63.04%	5.00	0.99
26th Aug	1914	100/- MA	1065	1027	5.03	58.46%	5.00	1.40
14th Mar	1916	50/- MA	1033	1014	2.51	57.58%	5.00	0.32
29th Feb	1916	60/- MA	1039	1016	3.04	58.97%	5.00	0.78
14th Mar	1916	80/- MA	1047	1014	4.37	70.21%	5.00	0.51
29th Feb	1916	100/- MA	1065	1027	5.03	58.46%	5.00	1.29
3rd Jul	1917	50/-	1031	1014	2.25	54.84%	5.00	0.50
3rd Jul	1917	60/-	1038	1015	3.04	60.53%	5.00	0.61
3rd Jul	1917	100/-	1056	1025	4.10	55.36%	5.00	0.90
13th Feb	1918	50/-	1031	1015	2.12	51.61%	5.00	0.65
6th Feb	1918	MA	1032	1013	2.51	59.38%	6.00	0.67
13th Feb	1918	60/-	1038	1017	2.78	55.26%	5.00	0.79
13th Feb	1918	100/-	1055	1026	3.84	52.73%	5.00	1.15
9th Apr	1918	MA	1031	1012	2.51	61.29%	5.50	0.73
13th Nov	1918	GA	1025	1010	1.98	60.00%	7.50	0.60
7th Jan	1919	GA	1025	1010	1.98	60.00%	7.50	0.75

Source:
Thomas Usher brewing record held at the Scottish Brewing Archive, document number TU/6/1/5.

You'd have struggled to find an English Mild at the top and or bottom of Usher's range in 1914. In London they only really brewed one type of Mild at the outbreak of WW I: X Ale. That was around 1050º, though in the provinces you did find weaker Milds.

At the start of the war, Drybrough also brewed several different strength Milds, 42/-, 48/-, 60/- and 80/-. Unfortunately, these were assembled from other gyles in a way that isn't explained in the brewing log. So I've no idea even what the OG was. The 100/- was 1060º that's all I know for certain. The rest could only be guessed.

Thankfully, their records become less opaque later in the war. Unfortunately, most of the Mild Ales had been discontinued by then.

Drybrough Mild Ales 1915 - 1920

Date	Year	Beer	OG	FG	ABV	App. Atten-uation	lbs hops/qtr	hops lb/brl
8th Jan	1915	100/- m	1060.0	1020.0	5.29	66.67%	4.59	1.14
25th Jan	1915	100/- m	1060.0	1018.0	5.56	70.00%	4.65	1.09
16th Nov	1917	60/- m	1029.0	1010.0	2.51	65.52%	3.98	0.41
16th Nov	1917	80/- m	1040.0	1014.0	3.44	65.00%	3.98	0.56
9th Jan	1920	60/- Mild	1040.0	1013.0	3.57	67.50%	5.85	1.00
Source: Drybrough brewing record held at the Scottish Brewing Archive, document number D/6/1/1/3.									

Based on the gravity of 100/- and the similar beers from Thomas Usher, 42/-, 48/- and 60/- probably ranged from around 1030º to 1040º.

Just like Thomas Usher, Drybrough ended the war with a single Mild Ale. Though it wouldn't last much longer.

Down in London, Mild was still immensely popular and Whitbread brewed huge quantities of it. In 1914 they churned out 274,247 barrels of X Ale, accounting for 30% of their production. The only other beer that came even close was London Stout, of which they made 208,733 barrels that year[56].

Whitbread Mild Ale 1914 - 1920

Date	Year	Beer	OG	FG	ABV	App. Atten-uation	lbs hops/qtr	hops lb/brl
30th May	1914	X	1052.1	1010	5.57	80.80%	6.04	1.29
29th Jan	1916	X	1051	1010	5.42	80.38%	4.98	1.07
3rd Jul	1916	X	1047.9	1008	5.28	83.31%	5.95	1.26
1st Feb	1917	X	1046.5	1007	5.23	84.96%	4.83	0.98
5th Jul	1917	X	1044.3	1008	4.80	81.95%	6.52	1.25
19th Jul	1917	GA	1033.5	1005	3.77	85.08%	8.48	1.21
13th Oct	1917	GA	1041.3	1008	4.40	80.62%	7.03	1.24
7th Jun	1918	MA (weak)	1011.4	1002	1.24	82.39%	10.95	0.55
7th Jun	1918	MA (straight)	1023.7	1003	2.74	87.36%	10.95	1.16
7th Jun	1918	MA (strong)	1038.1	1005	4.37	86.86%	10.95	1.85
7th Feb	1919	MA (weak)	1010.3	1003	0.97	70.89%	10.90	0.48
6th Feb	1919	MA (straight)	1023.5	1006	2.31	74.43%	10.93	1.18
7th Feb	1919	MA (strong)	1039	1009	3.97	76.91%	10.90	1.82
10th Mar	1920	MA	1027.8	1005	3.01	81.99%	6.68	0.76
10th Mar	1920	X	1043	1009	4.49	79.05%	6.68	1.17
Sources: Whitbread brewing records held at the London Metropolitan Archives, document numbers LMA/4453/D/01/079, LMA/4453/D/01/081, LMA/4453/D/01/082, LMA/4453/D/01/083, LMA/4453/D/01/084 and LMA/4453/D/01/085.									

---

[56] Whitbread brewing record held at the London Metropolitan Archives, document number LMA/4453/D/01/079.

The popularity of Mild in London put in under particular pressure during the war. It was the obvious place to shave off spare gravity points when brewers were obliged to keep the average gravity of all the beer they brewed below a certain level. 1º off a beer you sold 200,000 barrels of would save you far more than 10º off a beer like PA (their strongest Pale Ale) which you only shifted 6,000 barrels of[57].

This probably explains why Whitbread brewed their Mild at three strengths in the later years of the war. The strongest was at a reasonable strength, the middle one not really alcoholic and the weakest a total joke. But brewing that near-water allowed Whitbread to make some Mild at a decent strength. Which they could also sell for a higher price.

I haven't seen any Scottish beer with anywhere near as low a gravity as 1011º. The low 1020's is about the limit. The government wasn't impressed with extremely weak beers. After the way the method of calculating duty, which was based on a nominal 36-gallon barrel with an OG of 1055º. The minimum duty was set for an OG of 1027º. You could brew a beer weaker than that if you wanted, but you'd pay the same tax.

At between 5 and 6 lbs per quarter of malt, Whitbread started the war with a hopping rate around the same as Drybrough and Usher. While Drybrough's hopping rate fell a little during the war, both its and Usher's remained higher after war's end.

Whitbread's hopping went up immensely at the end of the war. Probably to hide how watery some of their beer was. Ending, too, above its starting level.

1921 - 1939
Mild Ale had a very tough time of it after WW I. Many brewers simply abandoned the style. At breweries where it did survive, mostly just a single type was brewed occasionally and in quite small quantities.

Thomas Usher had one Mild, at a gravity similar to standard English Mild of the period, as we'll see later.

Thomas Usher Mild Ales 1928 - 1931							
Year	Beer	OG	FG	ABV	App. Attenuation	lbs hops/ qtr	hops lb/brl
1928	MA	1040	1015.5	3.24	61.25%	7.00	1.13
1931	MA	1040	1015.5	3.24	61.25%	3.75	0.62
Source: Thomas Usher brewing record held at the Scottish Brewing Archive, document number TU/6/1/6.							

There was a big drop in the hopping between 1928, with the rate almost halving.

As usual, William Younger were an exception, continuing to brew three Milds in the interwar years.

---

[57] Whitbread brewing record held at the London Metropolitan Archives, document number LMA/4453/D/01/079.

William Younger Mild Ales 1921 - 1939

Year	Beer	OG	FG	ABV	App. Atten-uation	lbs hops/qtr	hops lb/brl
1921	XX	1035.3	1009.6	3.39	72.73%	4.55	0.57
1921	XXX	1041.9	1011.4	4.03	72.73%	4.55	0.65
1922	XX	1036.0	1009.8	3.46	72.73%	4.55	0.53
1929	XXX	1040.1	1013.7	3.50	65.91%	4.55	0.61
1933	XX	1037.0	1012.0	3.31	67.57%	4.71	0.63
1933	XXX	1042.0	1014.0	3.70	66.67%	4.74	0.71
1933	XX Sc	1050.0	1025.0	3.31	50.00%	2.75	0.86
1939	X	1029.0	1012.0	2.25	58.62%	2.50	0.28
1939	XX	1032.0	1011.5	2.71	64.06%	2.50	0.31
1939	XXX	1037.0	1014.0	3.04	62.16%	2.50	0.36

Sources:
William Younger brewing records held at the Scottish Brewing Archive, document numbers WY/6/1/2/63, WY/6/1/2/68, WY/6/1/2/70 and WY/6/1/2/76.

Younger's sticking with Mild might well have a very simple explanation. They did a lot of trade in England, where Mild was a must-have for pubs.

Over the course of the interwar years the hopping of Younger's Milds went from light to near invisible. The 1939 iterations are extremely lightly hopped. When the recipes are run through brewing software, the bitterness comes out to just 11 IBU.

In London, the war had spawned a new type of Mild. 4d Ale, or Light Ale (LA) a successor to the watery Government Ale was a cheap and probably not very cheerful beer, brewed in small quantities.

Whitbread Mild Ale 1921 - 1939

Year	Beer	OG	FG	ABV	App. Atten-uation	lbs hops/qtr	hops lb/brl
1921	MA	1027.1	1005.0	2.93	81.58%	8.91	0.95
1921	X	1039.1	1007.0	4.25	82.10%	8.91	1.36
1925	LA	1027.3	1004.0	3.08	85.32%	5.91	6.75
1925	X	1042.2	1010.0	4.26	76.30%	5.91	1.14
1930	LA	1027.2	1010.0	2.28	63.27%	8.56	1.00
1930	X	1042.1	1006.5	4.71	84.55%	8.56	1.55
1935	LA	1028.4	1007.0	2.83	75.35%	7.44	0.90
1935	X	1035.4	1010.5	3.29	70.34%	7.44	1.12
1939	LA	1028.4	1009.0	2.57	68.31%	8.27	0.93
1939	X	1033.6	1010.0	3.12	70.24%	8.27	1.10

Sources:
Whitbread brewing records held at the London Metropolitan Archives, document numbers LMA/4453/D/01/086, LMA/4453/D/01/090, LMA/4453/D/01/096, LMA/4453/D/01/101 and LMA/4453/D/01/107.

Whitbread's take on the cheapo Mild style, LA, lingered around the magic minimum of 1027º in the interwar years. Though its sales were always on the slide, from 22,000 barrels in 1924 to 8,000 barrels in 1929[58].

Unlike at William Younger, where the hopping rate collapsed in the 1930's, it ended pretty high at Whitbread. After a fair bit of floating about.

Barclay Perkins had a single strength Mild, X Ale, in 1914. 1920's saw them with two, Ale and X. By the late 1930's three:

Barclay Perkins Mild Ales 1921 - 1939							
Year	Beer	OG	FG	ABV	App. Atten-uation	lbs hops/ qtr	hops lb/brl
1921	Ale	1028.4	1007.0	2.83	75.35%	7.53	0.85
1921	X	1040.3	1009.0	4.14	77.67%	7.53	1.23
1924	X	1043.5	1011.0	4.30	74.71%	6.00	1.07
1929	A	1028.7	1007.5	2.80	73.83%	6.50	0.70
1929	X	1042.6	1012.5	3.98	70.65%	6.50	1.10
1939	A	1030.8	1007.5	3.08	75.65%	7.00	0.84
1939	X	1034.8	1010.0	3.28	71.26%	7.00	0.95
1939	XX	1042.7	1015.0	3.66	64.87%	7.00	1.14
Sources: Barclay Perkins brewing records held at the London Metropolitan Archives, document numbers ACC/2305/01/609 ACC/2305/01/611, ACC/2305/01/614 and ACC/2305/01/623.							

The reality was even more complicated. In a quite Scottish way, Barclay Perkins created darker versions of all three Milds with caramel colour adjustments and coloured primings.

Barclay Perkins hopping, at 6 to 7 lbs per quarter of malt, was much higher than for Scottish Milds. Higher than for most Scottish Pale Ales.

Mild Ale in Scotland

Other Scottish brewers were making beers marketed as Mild. At least I've been able to find analyses for some.

---

[58] Whitbread brewing records held at the London Metropolitan Archives, document numbers LMA/4453/D/01/089 and LMA/4453/D/01/095.

Scottish Mild Ales 1920 - 1929

Year	Brewer	Beer	OG	FG	ABV	App. Attenuation	colour
1920	Usher	Mild Ale 90/-	1048	1016.5	4.07	65.63%	
1920	Usher	Mild Ale 80/-	1041	1013.5	3.56	67.07%	
1922	Younger, Geo.	Mild	1034.5	1005.9	3.73	83.04%	95
1923	Mackay	Mild	1033	1008	3.24	75.76%	
1923	Murray	Mild	1037	1006	4.03	83.78%	
1926	Mackay	60/- MA	1041	1017	3.09	58.54%	
1929	Devanha	XX	1029	1011	2.32	62.07%	
1929	Read	Mild Ale	1048	1008	5.22	83.33%	
1929	Usher	90/- Mild Ale (carbonated)	1042.5	1012	3.95	71.76%	14

Sources:
Thomas Usher Gravity Book document TU/6/11 held at the Scottish Brewing Archive.
Younger, Wm. & Co Gravity Book document WY/6/1/1/19 held at the Scottish Brewing Archive.

Usher's 80/- Mild Ale looks very much like the MA in their brewing records, which was definitely brewed as a separate beer.

The beers in the table mostly fall into the three different Mild Ale clots in London: 1029-1033º 4d, 1034-1038º 5d, 1039-1043º 6d. Though the two at 1048º are outliers. 1048º was very strong for a Mild Ale in the 1920's

Shilling Ale
This style had been in decline since the middle of the 19th century, as Pale Ales increased in popularity at its expense. WW I finally put it out of its misery. Just about. William Younger brewed a few examples in the early 1920's but within a few years they had disappeared completely.

You can see that the names had changed slightly, inflation having kicked in.

William Younger Shilling Ales 1921 -1922

Year	Beer	OG	FG	ABV	App. Attenuation	lbs hops/ qtr	hops lb/brl
1921	120/-	1082	1028	7.14	65.85%	6.58	2.49
1921	160/- B	1082	1023	7.81	71.95%	6.58	2.49
1921	160/- B	1082	1029	7.01	64.63%	7.89	
1921	200/- B	1092	1030	8.20	67.39%	7.89	
1922	200/- B	1092	1032	7.94	65.22%	9.14	3.30
1922	160/- B	1082	1029	7.01	64.63%	7.37	2.35

Source:
William Younger brewing record held at the Scottish Brewing Archive, document number WY/6/1/2/63.

They remained both strong and heavily hopped. In all their characteristics they closely resemble Younger's 160/- from 1913. They contained more hops per barrel than any of the brewery's beers in the 1920's.

Brown Ale

Brown Ale is an odd beer style. Common in the 18th century, it disappeared around 1800 when brewers went over to using pale malt as a base for all their beers. After a century in the underworld, the style, at least in name, was revived around 1900 by up and coming London Ale brewer Mann.

Few others picked up the style until the 1920's, when Brown Ale suddenly became all the rage. That its popularity wasn't limited just to England, is obvious from advertisements, vintage labels and analyses in various gravity books. Yet it rarely shows up in brewing books.

In London, two phases of Brown Ale brewing are clear. In the early 1920's both Barclay Perkins and Whitbread introduced a Brown Ale. Unlike their other beers, these were always brewed single-gyle, meaning they had different recipes to all their other beers. Coincidentally, both beers were called DB.

Whitbread later added another beer in the style, Forest Brown, the name acquired through takeover of the Forest hill Brewery. This weaker interpretation eventually elbowed out elder brother Double Brown. Unlike its predecessor, the new Brown Ale wasn't a beer in its own right but Whitbread's Brown Ale slightly tweaked.

This method of producing Brown Ale – taking Mild and maybe priming it differently – was very widespread. Yet beers specifically called Brown Ale appear rarely in brewing records. Even though every brewery had one in their portfolio.

Here's the only Scottish beer that I've found in brewing records specifically called Brown Ale, from Thomas Usher:

Thomas Usher Brown Ale in 1931							
Year	Beer	OG	FG	ABV	App. Atten-uation	lbs hops/ qtr	hops lb/brl
1931	Brown Ale	1055	1016.5	5.09	70.00%	4 26	1.89
Source: Thomas Usher brewing record held at the Scottish Brewing Archive, document number TU/6/1/6.							

It's an example of the less common, stronger type of Brown Ale. While there were similar beers brewed In London, most Brown Ales brewed in the capital were of the weaker type. These, with gravities in the low 1040's were about average strength for the day.

Here are examples of both London types:

London Brown Ales 1929 - 1932

Year	Brewer	Beer	OG	FG	ABV	App. Attenuation	lbs hops/ qtr	hops lb/brl
1929	Barclay Perkins	DB	1040.6	1009.0	4.18	77.82%	7.50	1.20
1932	Whitbread	DB	1057.8	1014.0	5.79	75.78%	9.96	2.23

Sources:
Barclay Perkins brewing record held at the London Metropolitan Archives, document number ACC/2305/01/614.
Whitbread brewing record held at the London Metropolitan Archives, document number LMA/4453/D/01/098.

Usher's and Whitbread's versions are roughly similar in terms of gravity, though the London beer is more heavily hopped.

The grist of Usher's Brown Ale was unlike that of the majority of their output, which was different strength Pale Ales.

Thomas Usher Brown Ale grist 1931

Year	Beer	OG	pale malt	crystal malt	Invert sugar	Barbados	CDM	Caramax	other sugar
1931	Brown Ale	1055	77.65%	3.53%	4.71%	4.71%	2.35%	2.35%	4.71%

Source:
Thomas Usher brewing record held at the Scottish Brewing Archive, document number TU/6/1/6.

Unsurprisingly, Usher parti-gyled their Brown Ale with their Mild Ale. They weren't brewing huge quantities of either. The big differences from their bread and butter Pale Ales lay in the use of crystal malt and a big variety of sugars. Barbados is cane sugar, CDM and Caramax some type of proprietary dark sugar. Unlike all Usher's other beers, their Brown Ale and Mild contained no flaked maize.

London Brown similarly consisted mostly of pale malt, crystal malt and sugar:

London Brown Ales 1929 - 1932

Year	Brewer	OG	pale malt	crystal malt	flaked maize	no. 3 sugar	caramel	BS	SI
1929	Barclay Perkins	1040.6	61.43%	10.65%	13.11%		1.71%	13.11%	
1932	Whitbread	1057.8	77.70%	2.18%		19.36%			0.76%

Sources:
Barclay Perkins brewing record held at the London Metropolitan Archives, document number ACC/2305/01/614.
Whitbread brewing record held at the London Metropolitan Archives, document number LMA/4453/D/01/098.

Barclay Perkins grist is the outlier, with just 61% pale malt and almost 11% crystal. And flaked maize, too. They put it in everything, even their legendary Imperial Stout.

Brown Ale in Scotland

These Scottish Brown Ales from the 1930's are an intriguing bunch:

Scottish Brown Ales 1931 - 1938

Year	Brewer	Beer	OG	FG	ABV	App. Attenuation	colour
1931	Aitchison	Brown Ale	1047.9	1015.9	4.14	66.81%	
1931	Bernard	Brown Ale	1031	1008	2.98	74.19%	
1931	EUB	Brown Ale	1055	1015	5.20	72.73%	92
1931	EUB	Brown Ale	1056	1014	5.46	75.00%	65
1931	EUB	Brown Ale	1055	1015	5.20	72.73%	75
1931	McEwan	Brown Ale	1048	1010	4.95	79.17%	110
1931	Usher	Brown Ale	1050	1013	4.81	74.00%	54
1933	Aitchison	Brown Ale	1045.5	1015.5	3.88	65.93%	
1934	Aitken	Falkirk Brown Ale	1053	1011	5.47	79.25%	
1938	Calder	Nut Brown Ale	1039.4	1013.4	3.36	65.99%	80

Sources:
Whitbread Gravity book held at the London Metropolitan Archives, document number LMA/4453/D/02/001
Thomas Usher Gravity Book document TU/6/11 held at the Scottish Brewing Archive.
Younger, Wm. & Co Gravity Book document WY/6/1/1/19 held at the Scottish Brewing Archive

Most of these breweries weren't brewing a Mild Ale at the time. The gravities – the majority above 1050º - are far too high for 1930's Mild. Only the Bernard and Calder examples could possibly be a version of Mild.

The stronger versions, with gravities in the mid-1050's, look like Whitbread's DB in terms of strength. That beer, contrary to later expectations of Brown Ale, was quite heavily hopped. I'd guess that the stronger examples above are the brewery's Export coloured up with caramel or primings. Probably caramel, as that's what Scottish brewers preferred.

London Brown Ales, on the other hand, mostly looked more similar:

London Brown Ales 1929 - 1931

Year	Brewer	Beer	OG	FG	ABV	App. Attenuation
1929	Truman	Trubrown	1044	1007.4	4.77	83.18%
1929	Watney	Combes Brown Ale	1043.5	1011	4.22	74.71%
1930	Barclay Perkins	Doctor Brown	1046	1016	3.88	65.22%
1930	Cannon Brewery	Brown Ale	1030	1010.8	2.48	64.00%
1930	Charrington	Brown Ale	1043	1010.6	4.21	75.35%
1930	Hammerton	Nut Brown Ale	1038	1007.2	4.00	81.05%
1930	Hammerton	Nut Brown Ale	1041	1008.3	4.25	79.76%
1930	Hoare	Nut Brown Ale	1036	1011.2	3.21	68.89%
1930	Meux	Nut Brown Ale	1043	1009.4	4.37	78.14%
1930	Taylor Walker	Brown Ale	1042	1012.6	3.81	70.00%
1931	Courage	Brown Ale	1043.7	1007.8	4.68	82.15%

Sources:
Whitbread Gravity book held at the London Metropolitan Archives, document number LMA/4453/D/02/001

With the odd weaker exception, most London versions of Brown Ale were in the low-1040's. The apparent attenuation averaged slightly more in London, 75%, than the 73% of the Scottish examples.

Whitbread Double brown was a very atypical London Brown Ale. It was more like versions brewed in the Northeast of England:

Northeast Brown Ales 1929 - 1931						
Year	Brewer	Beer	OG	FG	ABV	App. Attenuation
1929	Newcastle Breweries	Newcastle Brown Ale	1062.75	1014.3	6.32	77.21%
1929	Vaux	Maxim Ale	1040	1010	3.89	75.00%
1930	Vaux	Dark Brown Ale	1058.7	1012.7	6.00	78.36%
1931	Newcastle Breweries	Newcastle Brown Ale	1059.5	1014	5.93	76.47%
Sources: Thomas Usher Gravity Book document held at the Scottish Brewing Archive, document number TU/6/11. Whitbread Gravity book held at the London Metropolitan Archives, document number LMA/4453/D/02/001.						

It's possible that this explains the stronger versions brewed in Scotland. Many Scottish breweries had extensive trade in the Northeast of England and it would have been natural for them to brew beers to suit the taste and expectations of the region.

Stout

By WW I Porter had completely disappeared from Scotland. As it had from much of England, other than London and the Southeast. Stout, however, continued to be brewed, though it started to diverge even more from what was sold under the same name in England.

WW I

By the time WW I broke out, Stout was very much a niche drink in Scotland, unlike other parts of the United Kingdom. In Ireland, Stout ruled supreme, but in parts of England, London, for example, it was also still extremely popular. Even Porter, Stout's poorer cousin, retained a strong following in the capital.

Thomas Usher Stout 1914 - 1919

Date	Year	Beer	OG	FG	ABV	App. Attenuation	lbs hops/ qtr	hops lb/brl
25th Aug	1914	48/-	1046	1021	3.31	54.35%	5.00	1.04
25th Aug	1914	54/-	1056	1025	4.10	55.36%	5.00	1.27
25th Feb	1916	48/-	1046	1023	3.04	50.00%	5.00	0.96
25th Feb	1916	XP	1058	1025	3.97	54.55%	5.00	1.21
25th Feb	1916	54/-	1055	1026	3.84	52.73%	5.00	1.15
13th Jun	1917	54/- St	1048	1024.5	3.11	48.96%	5.00	0.71
29th Jan	1918	54/- St	1046	1025	2.78	45.65%	5.00	0.74
13th May	1919	Stout	1049	1025	3.18	48.98%	5.50	1.21
24th Jun	1919	St 60/-	1047	1023	3.18	51.06%	6.00	1.38
30th Jul	1919	Stout	1049	1024.5	3.24	50.00%	6.00	1.32

Source
Thomas Usher brewing record held at the Scottish Brewing Archive, document number TU/6/1/5.

Usher brewed three different strength Stouts as the start of the war. After 1916, that was reduced to just one, 54/- Stout and later just Stout. WW I wreaked havoc on the system of indicating strength by shillings. The wholesale price of beer rocketed and gravities plummeted, leaving the old designations mostly meaningless. After the war, shilling designations, when used, were mostly limited to Pale Ale.

The strength of Usher's Stout remained pretty decent throughout the war. Probably because it was brewed in quite small amounts. It was popular beers that bore the bulk of gravity cuts.

The most striking feature of Usher's Stout is totally crappy degree of attenuation. You've probably noticed that attenuation wasn't Scottish brewers' strong point. But the Stouts are particularly bad. The WW I set just about averages 50% apparent attenuation. Couple that with modest hopping and the final beer must have been quite sweet.

Drybrough, another Edinburgh brewery, started the war with a stronger Stout, XXX, than Usher. With a gravity well over 1080º, it was similar to a strong London Stout.

Drybrough Stout 1915 - 1920

Date	Year	Beer	OG	FG	ABV	App. Attenuation	lbs hops/qtr	hops lb/brl
9th Jul	1915	XXX	1087.0	1030.0	7.54	65.52%	4.68	
11th Jan	1916	XXX	1086.0	1030.0	7.41	65.12%	4.50	
21st Jul	1916	XXX	1057.0	1027.0	3.97	52.63%	4.17	1.00
21st Jul	1916	XX	1055.0	1026.0	3.84	52.73%	4.17	0.96
19th Jan	1917	XXX	1064.4	1029.0	4.68	54.97%	4.00	0.94
19th Jan	1917	XX	1054.2	1023.0	4.13	57.56%	4.00	0.79
8th Feb	1918	XX	1045.0	1020.0	3.31	55.56%	5.00	1.35
8th Mar	1918	XX	1045.0	1021.0	3.18	53.33%	5.00	1.03
13th Aug	1918	XX	1039.0	1018.0	2.78	53.85%	5.02	0.87
29th Oct	1918	XX	1040.0	1020.0	2.65	50.00%	5.02	0.82
7th Feb	1919	XX	1040.0	1020.0	2.65	50.00%	5.00	0.96
8th Jul	1919	XX	1042.0	1019.0	3.04	54.76%	5.11	0.96
21st Oct	1919	XX	1070.0	1023.0	6.22	67.14%	5.33	1.71
16th Jan	1920	XXX	1075.0	1020.0	7.28	73.33%	5.00	1.61
16th Jan	1920	XX	1045.0	1014.0	4.10	68.89%	5.00	0.97
22nd Jul	1920	BS XXX	1074.0	1019.0	7.28	74.32%	5.65	1.76
21st Oct	1920	BS	1074.0	1025.0	6.48	66.22%	3.82	1.16

Source:
Drybrough brewing record held at the Scottish Brewing Archive, document number D/6/1/1/3.

XXX's gravity had dropped by over 20 gravity points by the start of 1917, before being replaced by the weaker XX. With a gravity in the mid-1050's, it was similar to Usher's 54/- Stout. The attenuation turned to crap in 1916. I think I can see what was going on. It looks like they were deliberately keeping the FG close to what it was when the OG was much higher, presumably to leave body in the beer.

At 4 to 5 lbs of hops per quarter, the hopping is similar to Usher's.

Whitbread Porter and Stout 1914 - 1920

Date	Year	Beer	OG	FG	ABV	App. Attenuation	lbs hops/qtr	hops lb/brl
17th Jul	1914	ES	1066.8	1020.0	6.19	70.04%	7.46	2.17
30th Dec	1919	ES	1055.0	1019.0	4.76	65.46%	7.69	1.95
8th Jun	1920	ES	1055.3	1017.0	5.07	69.27%	9.57	2.44
10th Aug	1914	Exp S	1065.4	1012.0	7.06	81.64%	13.01	3.94
2nd Aug	1917	Imp.	1077.6	1030.0	6.29	61.32%	7.32	2.54
11th Jan	1918	Imp.	1074.4	1026.0	6.40	65.04%	7.25	2.42
9th Jul	1914	LS	1055.7	1016.0	5.25	71.28%	5.43	1.28
6th May	1915	LS	1054.7	1012.0	5.65	78.08%	4.92	1.19
26th Jan	1916	LS	1051.2	1012.0	5.19	76.58%	5.36	1.23
21st Oct	1918	LS	1042.8	1012.0	4.07	71.94%	7.45	1.22
24th Feb	1919	LS	1042.9	1012.0	4.09	72.05%	7.60	1.45
19th Dec	1919	LS	1049.6	1015.0	4.58	69.75%	6.82	1.46
7th Jun	1920	LS	1047.7	1012.0	4.73	74.86%	7.21	1.57
19th Dec	1919	OS	1049.6	1015.0	4.58	69.75%	6.82	1.46
7th Jun	1920	OS	1047.7	1012.0	4.73	74.86%	7.21	1.57
9th Jul	1914	P	1051.0	1015.0	4.76	70.57%	5.43	1.17
6th May	1915	P	1051.8	1012.0	5.27	76.85%	4.92	1.13
26th Jan	1916	P	1049.3	1011.0	5.06	77.67%	5.36	1.19
2nd Aug	1917	P	1049.0	1012.0	4.90	75.52%	7.32	1.60
11th Jan	1918	P	1050.7	1014.0	4.85	72.38%	7.25	1.65
21st Oct	1918	P	1037.6	1010.0	3.65	73.38%	7.45	1.07
24th Feb	1919	P	1042.9	1012.0	4.09	72.05%	7.60	1.45
19th Dec	1919	P	1044.8	1013.0	4.21	70.99%	6.82	1.32
7th Jun	1920	P	1041.4	1010.0	4.16	75.85%	7.21	1.36
30th Dec	1919	S	1059.4	1021.0	5.07	64.62%	7.69	2.10
8th Jun	1920	S	1061.0	1019.0	5.56	68.85%	9.57	2.69
19th Aug	1914	SS	1081.7	1027.0	7.24	66.96%	8.45	2.99
19th May	1915	SS	1075.0	1018.0	7.54	75.99%	7.12	2.42
26th Jan	1916	SS	1075.1	1028.0	6.23	62.70%	7.07	2.48
21st Mar	1917	SS	1075.6	1027.0	6.43	64.30%	6.99	2.42
14th Mar	1917	SS	1076.0	1024.0	6.87	68.40%	7.07	2.48
19th Aug	1914	SSS	1096.1	1035.0	8.09	63.59%	8.45	3.52
19th May	1915	SSS	1094.5	1029.0	8.66	69.30%	7.12	3.05
26th Jan	1916	SSS	1091.5	1040.0	6.82	56.31%	7.07	3.02
14th Mar	1917	SSS	1092.2	1035.0	7.57	62.04%	7.07	3.01

Source:
Whitbread brewing record held at the London Metropolitan Archives, document number LMA/4453/D/09/109, LMA/4453/D/09/110, LMA/4453/D/09/111, LMA/4453/D/09/112 and LMA/4453/D/09/113.

The Whitbread table is considerably larger for two reasons: they started the war with a wider range and changed the range around during the war, both dropping and introducing beers. Only one was brewed throughout the whole war: P (Porter). Even their basic draught Stout, LOS, was dropped for a while in 1917. Their two strongest Stouts, SS and SSS, were replaced by Imperial in 1917, which itself disappeared after 1818. Whitbread would never brew a strong Stout again.

The apparently healthy recovery in the gravity of Porter after the end of the war was illusory. In 1921 the gravity dropped to 1029º and remained around that level until it was finally discontinued in 1940. The war had essentially done for Porter. Sales slumped and continued to fall every year until its final demise.

At the start of the war, Drybrough's XXX looked quite similar to Whitbread's SS and SSS, apart from lighter hopping. Unlike Whitbread, however, Drybrough brought their strong Stout back after war's end.

Averaging around 7lbs of hops per quarter, Whitbread's Stouts were more heavily hopped than Usher's and Drybrough's, which averaged about 5 lbs. I'm surprised the difference isn't bigger. Usher seem to have stuck with heavier hopping than some Scottish breweries. Some of William Younger's Stouts had less than 2 lbs of hops per quarter.

Looking at Usher's Stout grists, the very high percentage of sugar leaps out. Which is pretty weird when you see the very poor attenuation. You'd expect a beer that's 25% sugar to attenuate better than 50%.

Thomas Usher Stout grists 1914 - 1919

Date	Year	Beer	OG	pale malt	brown malt	black malt	crystal malt	flaked maize	sugar
25th Aug	1914	48/-	1046	55.81%	9.30%	6.98%		4.65%	23.26%
25th Aug	1914	54/-	1056	55.81%	9.30%	6.98%		4.65%	23.26%
25th Feb	1916	48/-	1046	56.93%		8.76%	8.76%	4.38%	21.17%
25th Feb	1916	XP	1058	56.93%		8.76%	8.76%	4.38%	21.17%
25th Feb	1916	54/-	1055	56.93%		8.76%	8.76%	4.38%	21.17%
13th Jun	1917	54/- St	1048	58.41%		7.96%	5.31%		28.32%
29th Jan	1918	54/- St	1046	61.86%		9.28%	6.19%		22.68%
13th May	1919	Stout	1049	70.59%		8.82%	5.88%		14.71%
24th Jun	1919	St 60/-	1047	64.29%		8.04%	5.36%		22.32%
30th Jul	1919	Stout	1049	65.45%		5.45%	5.45%		23.64%
Source: Thomas Usher brewing record held at the Scottish Brewing Archive, document number TU/6/1/5.									

The sugar isn't as simple as it appears in the table. Every grist contained Penang, which I assume is a sort of cane sugar. They also contained a further three of four types of proprietary sugar: DL, CDM, Durax, Maltosan and Oatine. The latter sounds like something specifically designed for Oatmeal Stout. Something listed as Greenock – which I think is an invert sugar – appears occasionally, too.

Amongst the malts, the only significant change was swapping in crystal malt for brown. Dropping the small amount of flaked maize used at the start of the war was probably due to supply problems rather than out of choice.

Drybrough's Stout grists are some of the weirdest I've ever seen. Especially in the early war years. Somehow they managed to brew a Stout that contained zero roasted malts

Drybrough Stout grists 1915 - 1919

Date	Year	Beer	OG	pale malt	flaked maize	No. 4 invert	other sugar	caramel
9th Jul	1915	XXX	1087.0	77.79%	6.67%	5.91%	4.45%	5.19%
11th Jan	1916	XXX	1086.0	78.26%	6.52%	6.52%	4.35%	4.35%
21st Jul	1916	XXX	1057.0	77.27%	6.82%	6.82%	4.55%	4.55%
21st Jul	1916	XX	1055.0	77.27%	6.82%	6.82%	4.55%	4.55%
19th Jan	1917	XXX	1064.4	72.26%	13.14%	6.57%	3.65%	4.38%
19th Jan	1917	XX	1054.2	72.26%	13.14%	6.57%	3.65%	4.38%
8th Feb	1918	XX	1045.0	84.27%	3.37%	3.37%	3.37%	5.62%
8th Mar	1918	XX	1045.0	84.27%	3.37%	3.37%	3.37%	5.62%
13th Aug	1918	XX	1039.0	84.17%		4.32%	4.32%	7.19%
29th Oct	1918	XX	1040.0	85.40%			7.30%	7.30%
7th Feb	1919	XX	1040.0	85.71%			7.14%	7.14%
8th Jul	1919	XX	1042.0	87.34%			5.06%	7.59%

Source:
Drybrough brewing record held at the Scottish Brewing Archive, document number D/6/1/1/3.

There was such a big change in the grists in 1919 that I've had to split the table into two parts. It looks as if the No. 4 invert sugar and the caramel were what gave these beers their stoutiness. The other sugar doesn't, as you might expect, include proprietary sugars designed for Stout. It's just various combinations of No 1, No. 2 and No. 3 invert.

From October 1919 Drybrough's Stout grists looked very different.

Drybrough Stout grists 1919 - 1920

Date	Year	Beer	OG	pale malt	black malt	amber malt	crystal malt	flaked maize	sugar	caramel
21st Oct	1919	XX	1070.0	73.33%		6.67%		3.33%	11.67%	5.00%
16th Jan	1920	XXX	1075.0	74.29%	5.71%		5.71%		14.29%	
16th Jan	1920	XX	1045.0	74.29%	5.71%		5.71%		14.29%	
22nd Jul	1920	BS XXX	1074.0	52.94%	5.88%	8.82%	8.82%		17.65%	5.83%
21st Oct	1920	BS	1074.0	53.73%	5.97%			14.93%	22.39%	2.99%

Source:
Drybrough brewing record held at the Scottish Brewing Archive, document number D/6/1/1/3.

Now there was the roasted malt that you would expect. The No. 4 invert had been dropped, but there was still loads of caramel in some versions. The sugars were no longer numbered inverts, but proprietary sugars, principally something called Durax. The sugar and adjunct content of the final BS, at getting on for 40%, is very high. Almost as bad as William Younger with their grits.

I haven't repeated all the Whitbread beers because of the parti-gyling. It's pointless showing the grists for both F and LS, as they were always parti-gyled together. As were SS and SSS.

Whitbread Porter and Stout grists 1914 - 1920

Date	Year	Beer	OG	pale malt	brown malt	black malt	amber malt	oats	no. 3 sugar	other sugar
19th Aug	1914	SSS	1096.1	50.52%	13.02%	5.89%	17.36%		13.22%	
10th Aug	1914	Exp S	1065.4	48.29%	10.24%	7.32%	14.63%		19.51%	
9th Jul	1914	P	1051.0	72.45%	9.18%	9.86%		0.34%	8.16%	
17th Jul	1914	ES	1066.8	56.90%	9.05%	6.47%	15.52%	0.00%	12.07%	
6th May	1915	P	1051.8	75.79%	12.63%	11.05%		0.53%		
19th May	1915	SSS	1094.5	65.73%	13.29%	5.59%	2.80%		12.59%	
26th Jan	1916	SSS	1091.5	58.59%	13.41%	5.65%	10.59%			11.76%
26th Jan	1916	P	1049.3	69.39%	12.59%	9.86%				8.16%
14th Mar	1917	SSS	1092.2	67.44%	12.50%	6.10%			13.95%	
2nd Aug	1917	P	1049.0	66.42%	13.07%	10.34%			10.16%	
2nd Aug	1917	Imp.	1077.6	66.42%	13.07%	10.34%			10.16%	
11th Jan	1918	Imp.	1074.4	60.87%	18.63%	10.56%			9.94%	
11th Jan	1918	P	1050.7	60.87%	18.63%	10.56%			9.94%	
21st Oct	1918	P	1037.6	66.92%	15.38%	11.54%			6.15%	
24th Feb	1919	P	1042.9	60.37%	14.29%	10.60%			14.75%	
19th Dec	1919	P	1044.8	63.62%	14.06%	10.04%		0.67%	11.61%	
19th Dec	1919	OS	1049.6	63.62%	14.06%	10.04%		0.67%	11.61%	
30th Dec	1919	S	1059.4	64.10%	14.06%	9.84%			12.00%	
30th Dec	1919	ES	1055.0	64.10%	14.06%	9.84%			12.00%	
7th Jun	1920	P	1041.4	63.01%	14.00%	10.50%		0.35%	12.14%	
8th Jun	1920	S	1061.0	64.04%	14.23%	9.96%			11.76%	
8th Jun	1920	ES	1055.3	64.04%	14.23%	9.96%			11.76%	

Source:
Whitbread brewing records held at the London Metropolitan Archives, document numbers LMA/4453/D/09/109, LMA/4453/D/09/110, LMA/4453/D/09/111, LMA/4453/D/09/112 and LMA/4453/D/09/113.

Whitbread used about half the amount of sugar in their Stouts that Usher did. Though the pale malt percentage wasn't much different due to the large amount of brown malt Whitbread threw in, usually 13-14%, at least. Whitbread were a little heavier with the black malt, too. The combined roast malt percentage of over 20% is very high. That it continued at the same level throughout the war demonstrates malt roasting wasn't banned during the war, as the myth on the death of Porter goes.

1921 - 1939

Usher continued to brew Stout after WW I, but in pretty tiny quantities. Very occasional brews of just 30 to 40 barrels, while they regularly brewed 200-300 barrel batches of their big seller, PA 60/-.

Thomas Usher Stout 1928 - 1931

Date	Year	Beer	OG	FG	ABV	App. Attenuation	lbs hops/ qtr	hops lb/brl
18th Jan	1928	Stout	1045	1021.5	3.11	52.22%	7.00	1.27
2nd Oct	1931	Stout 80/-	1052	1023	3.84	55.77%	3.75	0.80

Source:
Thomas Usher brewing record held at the Scottish Brewing Archive, document number TU/6/1/6.

Not much there to draw any conclusions from there. Other than a continuing poor rate of attenuation. It's the story of Scottish beer.

William Younger, possibly because they had a large trade outside Scotland, were more enthusiastic Stout brewers:

Year	Beer	OG	FG	ABV	App. Atten- uation	lbs hops/ qtr	hops lb/brl
1921	MBS	1055	1017.5	4.96	68.18%	9.00	1.94
1921	Btg DBS	1060	1019	5.42	68.33%	10.65	2.63
1921	DBS	1060	1025	4.63	58.33%	3.89	0.92
1921	XXS	1050	1020	3.97	60.00%	3.89	0.77
1922	XXS	1045.8	1023.4	2.97	48.98%	4.55	1.51
1923	XXS	1049	1025	3.18	48.98%	4.21	1.62
1923	DBS	1058	1029	3.84	50.00%	4.21	1.67
1933	DBS Btg	1066.0	1025.0	5.42	62.12%	9.31	2.14
1939	DBS Btg	1066	1023.0	5.69	65.15%	6.06	1.59
Sources: William Younger brewing records held at the Scottish Brewing Archive, document numbers WY/6/1/2/63, WY/6/1/2/70 and WY/6/1/2/76.							

Younger had two Stouts of different strengths DBS and XXS, both will fairly reasonable gravities. Later in this chapter we'll learn just how watery some Scottish Stouts were between the wars. Younger's stayed at least reasonable.

The two versions of DBS, the standard and bottling, differed a little in gravity but mostly in the level of hopping. XXS and the standard DBS were only hopped at around 4 lbs per quarter. Which is low, even for Scotland. Especially in the stronger DBS.

Let's see how these Scottish Stouts stack up against those of our old friend Whitbread.

Whitbread Porter and Stout 1921 - 1939

Year	Beer	OG	FG	ABV	App. Attenuation	lbs hops/ qtr	hops lb/brl
1921	P	1028.3	1008.0	2.68	71.69%	6.93	0.87
1921	LS	1046.1	1012.0	4.51	73.98%	6.93	1.42
1921	S	1054.1	1015.0	5.18	72.29%	8.02	2.00
1921	ES	1054.1	1015.0	5.18	72.29%	8.02	2.00
1925	P	1028.0	1009.0	2.52	67.89%	8.52	1.07
1925	CS	1052.1	1016.0	4.77	69.28%	8.52	1.99
1925	S	1056.8	1022.0	4.61	61.30%	6.13	1.59
1925	LS	1057.0	1020.0	4.89	64.88%	7.95	2.00
1925	ES	1057.0	1020.0	4.89	64.88%	7.95	2.00
1930	P	1028.0	1007.0	2.78	74.98%	9.17	1.04
1930	LS	1054.3	1016.5	5.00	69.61%	9.16	2.09
1930	ES	1054.3	1016.5	5.00	69.61%	9.16	2.09
1930	S	1054.3	1016.5	5.00	69.61%	9.16	2.09
1939	P	1029.7	1007.5	2.94	74.75%	6.89	0.83
1939	LS	1045.2	1013.5	4.19	70.13%	6.89	1.26
1939	MS	1051.2	1017.5	4.46	65.82%	6.89	1.43
1939	ES	1055.4	1017.0	5.08	69.31%	6.94	1.59
1939	SSS	1110.3	1045.0	8.64	59.20%	7.40	3.44

Sources:
Whitbread brewing records held at the London Metropolitan Archives, document numbers LMA/4453/D/09/114, LMA/4453/D/09/118, LMA/4453/D/09/123 and LMA/4453/D/09/126.

A little explanation of the names is in order. P is Porter, S is Stout, LS is London Stout, ES is Extra Stout, CS is Country Stout and MS is Mackeson Stout. There were also beer in the brewing record called LOS (London Oatmeal Stout) and COS (Country Oatmeal Stout). As these were identical to LS and CS respectively, I didn't bother to include them in the table.

An obvious difference is the continued presence of Porter. Now a low-gravity beer with sales that fell every year, but it was still knocking around. William Younger's DBS Btlg is the only Scottish Stout with a level of hopping comparable to Whitbread's. Though even there the hoping had slipped a little from its 1930 level, falling from 9 lbs per quarter of malt to 7 lbs.

Whitbread's beers average about 70% apparent attenuation. Much higher than the Scottish Stouts, other than Younger's DBS and MBS.

It shouldn't come as any surprise that Whitbread brewed a larger range of Black Beers. Porter was the beer that brewery had been built on. And Stout was still very popular in its home town. LS (London Stout) in the table above was available both in bottle and on draught. At a time when very little draught Stout was sold anywhere in England outside London.

The different scale of Stout brewing in London and Scotland isn't visible in the tables. The largest Scottish batch was 126 barrels of William Younger's DBS Btlg. The smallest batch at Whitbread was

65 barrels. And that was Porter, a dying product. The Stouts were brewed in batches up to 700 barrels. And that's just one beer of a parti-gyle. A total brew could be as much as 1,000 barrels.

William Younger's Stout grists were weird and atypical at the same time:

William Younger Stout 1921-1939

Year	Beer	OG	pale malt	black malt	amber malt	crystal malt	grits	roast barley	caramel	lactose
1921	MBS	1055	50.85%	5.08%	5.08%		35.59%		3.39%	
1921	Btg DBS	1060	47.80%	3.30%	6.59%		37.91%		4.40%	
1921	DBS	1060	50.94%	5.66%	5.66%		33.96%		3.77%	
1921	XXS	1050	50.94%	5.66%	5.66%		33.96%		3.77%	
1923	XXS	1045.8	52.63%			5.26%	36.84%	5.26%		
1923	DBS	1058	52.63%			5.26%	36.84%	5.26%		
1933	DBS Btlg	1066.0	50.53%	3.16%		3.16%	34.74%		4.21%	4.21%
1939	DBS Btlg	1066	53.83%	3.19%		3.19%	19.15%		4.26%	6.38%

Sources:
William Younger brewing records held at the Scottish Brewing Archive, document numbers WY/6/1/2/63, WY/6/1/2/70 and WY/6/1/2/76.

For a Scottish brewery, that's a lot of different types of malt. Another big difference with normal Scottish practice is the small amount of sugar use. In some none at all, in others just caramel and in some caramel and lactose. At over a third of the grist the grits content is very high, though not as bad as some of William Younger's other beers.

Over at Usher, the grists were typically weird.

Thomas Usher Stout grists 1928 - 1931

Date	Year	Beer	OG	pale malt	black malt	crystal malt	flaked maize	other sugar
18th Jan	1928	Stout	1045	57.97%	1.45%	5.80%	5.80%	28.99%
2nd Oct	1931	Stout 80/-	1052	64.29%		7.14%		28.57%

Source:
Thomas Usher brewing record held at the Scottish Brewing Archive, document number TU/6/1/6.

The Stout 80/- is another example of a Stout with no roast malt. Not that there's a great deal in the Stout from 1928. Both recipes used lots of different types of sugar. The 1928 Stout included cane, Penang, Oatine and Maltosan. In the later beer, it was cane, Penang, CDM, Caramax and DF. I'm guessing that most of the Stout character came from one or more of the proprietary sugars.

Looking at Whitbread's grists it's clear how much Scottish and London Stout had diverged.

Whitbread Porter and Stout grists 1921 - 1939										
Year	Beer	OG	pale malt	brown malt	black malt	choc. Malt	mild malt	oats	no. 3 sugar	Duttson sugar
1921	P	1028.3	59.01%	13.19%	12.53%			0.33%	14.95%	
1921	LS	1046.1	59.01%	13.19%	12.53%			0.33%	14.95%	
1921	S	1054.1	65.96%	14.90%	11.10%				8.03%	
1921	ES	1054.1	65.96%	14.90%	11.10%				8.03%	
1925	P	1028.0	62.23%	14.09%	3.52%	11.74%		0.59%	7.83%	
1925	CS	1052.1	62.23%	14.09%	3.52%	11.74%		0.59%	7.83%	
1925	S	1056.8	65.85%	14.63%		11.71%			7.80%	
1925	LS	1057.0	65.05%	14.56%		12.14%		0.49%	7.77%	
1925	ES	1057.0	65.05%	14.56%		12.14%		0.49%	7.77%	
1930	P	1028.0	71.22%	8.78%		8.78%		0.49%	8.46%	2.28%
1930	LS	1054.3	71.45%	8.81%		8.81%		0.49%	8.48%	1.96%
1930	ES	1054.3	71.45%	8.81%		8.81%		0.49%	8.48%	1.96%
1930	S	1054.3	71.45%	8.81%		8.81%		0.49%	8.48%	1.96%
1939	P	1029.7	71.47%	7.85%		7.85%		0.79%	8.38%	3.66%
1939	LS	1045.2	71.47%	7.85%		7.85%		0.79%	8.38%	3.66%
1939	MS	1051.2	71.47%	7.85%		7.85%		0.79%	8.38%	3.66%
1939	ES	1055.4	59.69%	7.85%		7.85%	11.78%	0.79%	8.38%	3.66%
1939	SSS	1110.3	72.22%	7.94%		7.94%		0.79%	8.47%	2.65%

Sources:
Whitbread brewing records held at the London Metropolitan Archives, document numbers LMA/4453/D/09/114, LMA/4453/D/09/118, LMA/4453/D/09/123 and LMA/4453/D/09/126.

Whitbread remained faithful to a typical London combination of pale, brown and black malt. Though they did later swap the black for chocolate malt. Brown malt seems to have been dropped completely in Scotland around WW I, though some breweries had stopped using it much earlier.

The sugar content is quite low at mostly just 11-12%. My guess is that the Duttson was a proprietary sugar specifically for Stout. Its introduction coincides with a reduction in the roast malt percentage from almost 27% to 17.5%. Plus Duttson only appears in Whitbread Porter and Stout grists.

Stout in Scotland

Milk Stout, popularised by Mackeson, was a big hit in England after WW I. Sweetened with unfermentable lactose, it was all the rage. Though drier Stouts continued to be brewed. The Scots went one step further, brewing ridiculously sweet Stouts, with very low degrees of attenuation and very little alcohol. This type of beer still exists today in the form of Sweetheart Stout. Originally brewed by George Younger in Alloa, it's one of those hardy brands that has survived its parent brewery by several decades.

Not all Scottish Stouts were sweet. There was a huge diversity both in terms of strength and degree of attenuation. I've divided them into three groups to make them easier to analyse.

These are examples of Sweet Stouts, some them so barely fermented that they must have tasted very sweet indeed:

Scottish Sweet Stout 1920 - 1937						
Year	Brewer	Beer	OG	FG	ABV	App. Attenuation
1933	Tennent	Nourishing Stout	1024	1015	1.16	37.50%
1933	Dryborough	Nourishing Stout	1031	1019	1.54	38.71%
1937	Younger, Geo	Cream Double Stout	1045.5	1025.5	2.56	43.96%
1933	Murray	Milk Stout	1036	1018	2.31	50.00%
1932	Morrison	Stout	1033	1016	2.19	51.52%
1933	Tennent	Nourishing Stout	1029	1014	1.93	51.72%
1930	McLennan & Urquhart	Dalkeith Stout	1040.5	1019.5	2.70	51.85%
1928	Usher	Stout	1045	1021.5	3.11	52.22%
1931	Younger, Geo	Milk Stout	1044	1020	3.09	54.55%
1933	Tennent	Light Stout	1032	1014	2.32	56.25%
1931	McEwan	Special Stout Red Label	1043.8	1019	3.19	56.62%
1920	Usher	Stout	1048	1020.7	3.52	56.87%
1937	Murray	Milk Stout	1044.8	1019.2	3.30	57.14%
1931	Dryborough	Nourishing Stout	1033	1014	2.45	57.58%
1924	Ballingall	Imperial Stout Special Quality	1038.7	1016.4	2.87	57.62%
1933	Tennent	Nourishing Stout	1031	1013	2.32	58.06%
1931	Tennent	Nourishing Stout	1039	1016	2.97	58.97%
1923	Bernard	Imperial Stout	1057.59	1023.49	4.40	59.21%

Sources:
Thomas Usher brewing record document TU/6/16 held at the Scottish Brewing Archive.
Thomas Usher Gravity Book document TU/6/11 held at the Scottish Brewing Archive
Younger, Wm. & Co Gravity Book document WY/6/1/1/19 held at the Scottish Brewing Archive
Whitbread Gravity book held at the London Metropolitan Archives, document number LMA/4453/D/02/001.

The next set were neither sweet nor dry. More fobly-mobey.

Scottish Middling Stout 1920 - 1939

Year	Brewer	Beer	OG	FG	ABV	App. Attenuation
1932	Tennent	Nourishing Stout	1030	1012	2.32	60.00%
1939	Calder	Milk Stout	1052.5	1021	4.06	60.00%
1937	Calder	Milk Stout	1055.8	1022.3	4.32	60.09%
1931	Caler	Milk Stout	1059	1023	4.65	61.02%
1932	Jeffrey	Nourishing Stout	1031	1012	2.45	61.29%
1928	Tennent	Nourishing Stout	1039	1015	3.10	61.54%
1924	McEwan	Double Imperial Stout	1056.5	1021.7	4.49	61.59%
1928	Wright (Perth)	Stout XXX	1035	1013	2.84	62.86%
1920	Usher	Export Stout	1067	1024.4	5.51	63.58%
1929	Murray	Oatmeal Stout	1044	1016	3.62	63.64%
1939	Younger, Wm.	Milk Stout (Monk Export Brand)	1065.8	1023.9	5.42	63.68%
1927	Tennent	Nourishing Stout	1039	1014	3.23	64.10%
1923	Wright (Perth)	Crown Stout	1050	1017	4.27	66.00%
1922	Usher	Extra Stout (Belgian sample)	1069.2	1021.8	6.15	68.50%
1921	Brown (Coldstream Brewery)	Stout	1050.8	1016	4.51	68.50%

Sources:
Thomas Usher Gravity Book document TU/6/11 held at the Scottish Brewing Archive
Younger, Wm. & Co Gravity Book document WY/6/1/1/19 held at the Scottish Brewing Archive
Whitbread Gravity book held at the London Metropolitan Archives, document number LMA/4453/D/02/001.

The final set has something like normal attenuation.

Scottish Dry Stout 1922 - 1939						
Year	Brewer	Beer	OG	FG	ABV	App. Attenuation
1925	Tennent	Nourishing Stout	1037	1011	3.37	70.27%
1937	Younger, Wm.	Milk Stout	1068	1020	6.24	70.59%
1939	Younger, Wm.	Milk Stout	1065.5	1019	6.04	70.99%
1924	Tennent	Nourishing Stout	1038.3	1010.8	3.56	71.80%
1932	Bernard	Double Brown Stout	1035.5	1009.5	3.37	73.24%
1924	McEwan	Double Imperial Stout	1078	1020	7.57	74.36%
1929	Younger, Geo	XXX Stout	1047.5	1012	4.61	74.74%
1938	Bernard	Milk Stout	1057	1013.6	5.65	76.14%
1936	Younger, Wm.	Milk Stout	1063	1014.7	6.30	76.67%
1932	Reid	Special Stout	1051.5	1012	5.14	76.70%
1929	McEwan	Imperial Stout	1044	1010	4.42	77.27%
1922	Calder	Stout	1053.0	1011	5.47	79.24%
1936	McEwan	Milk Stout	1064.4	1013.1	6.70	79.66%
1923	Henderson, Alloa	Stout	1040	1008	4.16	80.00%

Sources:
Thomas Usher Gravity Book document TU/6/1 held at the Scottish Brewing Archive
Younger, Wm. & Co Gravity Book document WY/6/1/1/19 held at the Scottish Brewing Archive
Whitbread Gravity book held at the London Metropolitan Archives, document number LMA/4453/D/02/001.

It's clear that there was an enormous variation in Scottish Stouts both in terms of OG, ABV and rate of attenuation. While some had equivalents in England, the ones with attenuation below 50% were unique to Scotland.

Strong/Scotch Ale

Two main types of Strong Ale were brewed between the wars. The commonest type had an OG of around 1080º and was sold both in the UK and abroad. William Younger's No. 1 and the Strong Ales from Lorimer & Clark, Drybrough, Maclay and William Younger's No. 1 were of this type.

The second rarer type is represented by William Younger's No 3, which, with a gravity of 1055º, filled the same slot as Burton in London. It was sold in both draught and bottled form. It's another survivor which, despite being discontinued several times, is still around.

Drybrough produced one of the stronger types of Scotch Ale, called Burns Ale:

Drybrough Strong/Scotch Ale 1933 - 1936

Year	Beer	OG	FG	ABV	App. Atten-uation	lbs hops/qtr	hops lb/brl
1933	Burns	1084.0	1027.0	7.54	67.86%	6.29	2.51
1935	Burns	1084.0	1033.0	6.75	60.71%	5.99	2.49
1935	Burns	1084.0	1033.0	6.75	60.71%	6.30	2.25
1936	Burns	1084.0	1030.0	7.14	64.29%	6.30	2.48

Source:
Drybrough brewing record held at the Scottish Brewing Archive, document number D/6/1/1/4.

As was the case at most Scottish breweries, Burns Ale was parti-gyled with Drybrough's Pale Ales. How was that possible? Because we know that Scotch Ale was dark. How could you parti-gyle it with Pale Ale? Easy. By the use of primings or caramel at racking time. That's how Scottish brewers made their beers dark. Nothing crazy like adding dark malts to the grist.

Two of these next three breweries also produced their Strong Ale from a part-gyle with Pale Ales. Lorimer & Clark being the exception in brewing theirs single-gyle.

Thomas Usher, Lorimer & Clark and Maclay Strong Ale 1928 - 1939

Year	Brewer	Beer	OG	FG	ABV	App. Atten-uation	lbs hops/qtr	hops lb/brl
1928	Thomas Usher	OSA	1085	1026	7.81	69.41%	7.50	2.30
1938	Maclay	SA	1075	1028	6.22	62.67%	5.00	1.65
1933	Lorimer & Clark	SA	1096	1025	9.39	73.96%	14.88	6.45
1939	Maclay	SA	1089	1030	7.81	66.29%	5.00	1.90
1939	Maclay	SA	1082	1022	7.94	73.17%	6.00	2.12

Sources:
Thomas Usher brewing record held at the Scottish Brewing Archive, document number TU/6/1/6.
Lorimer & Clark brewing record held at Caledonian Brewery
Maclay brewing records held at the Scottish Brewing Archive, document numbers M/6/1/1/3 and M/6/1/1/4.

The Strong Ales from Maclay and Usher look pretty similar: an OG of around 1080º an a hopping rate of around 6lbs per quarter of malt. Lorimer & Clark's is a little stronger and much more heavily hopped. Therein lay the advantage of brewing it single-gyle. It's a big beer and with its decent rate of attenuation it weighs in at over 9% ABV. It must have tasted very different to its rivals. Could it have been intended for export?

William Younger, as always, did things differently.

Mini Book Series volume XXVIII: Scotland! FG

William Younger Strong Ales 1922 - 1939

Year	Beer	OG	FG	ABV	App. Attenuation	lbs hops/ qtr	hops lb/brl
1922	1	1082	1029	7.01	64.63%	7.37	2.35
1922	3	1053.5	1015.15	5.07	71.67%	4.55	1.05
1929	1	1087	1032	7.28	63.22%	5.26	1.80
1929	3	1054.5	1014.55	5.29	73.33%	4.55	0.95
1933	1	1085.0	1033.0	6.88	61.18%	5.26	1.79
1933	3	1055.0	1015.5	5.23	71.82%	5.20	1.11
1933	3 pale	1055.0	1016.0	5.16	70.91%	6.25	1.28
1939	1	1084.0	1033.5	6.68	60.12%	4.74	1.58
1939	3	1053.0	1017.0	4.76	67.92%	3.00	0.61

Sources:
William Younger brewing records held at the Scottish Brewing Archive, document numbers WY/6/1/2/63, WY/6/1/2/68, WY/6/1/2/70 and WY/6/1/2/76.

As well as the usual Scotch Ale with a gravity in the 1080's they also produced a weaker one, called No. 3. This was sold on draught as well as in bottle. Whereas the stronger No. 1 was a purely bottled product.

Down in London, the upper end of the dark beer spectrum was occupied by Burton Ales. Usually designated by K's within the brewery, in a system analogous to that with X's for Mild Ales.

Barclay Perkins Burton Ales 1921 - 1940

Year	Beer	OG	FG	ABV	App. Attenuation	lbs hops/ qtr	hops lb/brl
1921	KK (bottling)	1070.2	1024.5	6.05	65.10%	13.00	3.78
1923	KK	1055.2	1016.0	5.19	71.01%	10.00	2.24
1924	KK (bottling)	1070.0	1019.0	6.75	72.86%	14.00	3.95
1924	KKK	1082.1	1028.0	7.16	65.90%	14.00	4.75
1926	KK	1055.5	1015.0	5.35	72.96%	9.00	1.91
1928	KK bottling	1069.4	1021.5	6.34	69.04%	11.00	2.99
1928	KKKK	1078.6	1027.0	6.82	65.64%	11.00	3.45
1936	KK (bottling)	1068.6	1022.0	6.17	67.95%	10.54	2.92
1940	KK	1051.3	1015.5	4.74	69.79%	8.50	1.86

Sources:
Barclay Perkins brewing records held at the London Metropolitan Archives, document numbers ACC/2305/01/608, ACC/2305/01/611, ACC/2305/01/614, ACC/2305/01/621 and ACC/2305/01/623.

Barclay Perkins' KK – a draught beer called simply "Burton" in the pub – had a similar profile to Younger's No. 3. The bottling version of KK – sold as Southwarke Olde Ale – wasn't quite up to the Strong Scotch Ales, but wasn't far off. KKK and KKKK were extra strong beers sold around Christmas, if the adverts are to be believed, from a wooden pin on top of the bar.

It's hard to miss the enormous difference in the hopping. Barclay Perkins' K Ales were Stock Ales in origin. Beers meant for storing were always hopped heavily. All but draught KK were still being aged.

Heavy hopping was logical. Per quarter, it's double or more the rate amongst the Scottish examples. Other than Lorimer & Clark's. Which has a similar level of hopping to Barclay Perkins' Burtons.

Drybrough's recipe wasn't particularly exciting:

Drybrough Strong/Scotch Ale grists 1933 - 1936							
Year	Beer	OG	pale malt	black malt	flaked maize	malt extract	sugar
1933	Burns	1084.0	74.18%	1.97%	15.90%	0.88%	7.07%
1935	Burns	1084.0	74.55%	1.45%	12.85%	0.86%	10.28%
1935	Burns	1084.0	77.20%	1.51%	13.31%	0.89%	7.10%
1936	Burns	1084.0	77.20%	1.51%	13.31%	0.89%	7.10%
Source: Drybrough brewing record held at the Scottish Brewing Archive, document number D/6/1/1/4.							

Only the touch of black malt and the malt extract are a little unusual. Otherwise it's the standard combination of pale malt, maize and sugar in the usual proportions.

The outlier is easy to spot in these grists from three different breweries:

Thomas Usher, Lorimer & Clark and Maclay Strong Ale 1928 - 1939								
Year	Brewer	Beer	OG	pale malt	flaked maize	no. 2 sugar	malt extract	Invert sugar
1928	Thomas Usher	OSA	1085	77.84%	11.35%			10.81%
1938	Maclay	SA	1075	77.42%	9.68%	12.90%		
1933	Lorimer & Clark	SA	1096	90.00%			6.67%	3.33%
1939	Maclay	SA	1089	77.42%	9.68%	12.90%		
1939	Maclay	SA	1082	77.42%	9.68%	12.90%		
Sources: Thomas Usher brewing record held at the Scottish Brewing Archive, document number TU/6/1/6. Lorimer & Clark brewing record held at Caledonian Brewery Maclay brewing records held at the Scottish Brewing Archive, document numbers M/6/1/1/3 and M/6/1/1/4.								

The Usher and Maclay have very similar grists, with near identical proportions of pale malt, flaked maize and invert sugar. Lorimer & Clark on the other hand went for mostly malt and just a bit of sugar and malt extract.

William Younger, gritting their own cycle path as usual, had rather different recipes:

William Younger Strong Ale grists 1922 - 1939

Year	Beer	OG	pale malt	crystal malt	MA malt	grits	lactose
1922	1	1082	69.70%			30.30%	
1922	3	1053.5	69.86%			30.14%	
1929	1	1087	69.70%			30.30%	
1929	3	1054.5	68.28%			31.72%	
1933	1	1085.0	67.35%			28.57%	4.08%
1933	3	1055.0	67.44%			32.56%	
1933	3 pale	1055.0	65.85%			34.15%	
1939	1	1084.0	74.29%	5.71%	2.86%	13.33%	3.81%
1939	3	1053.0	88.73%			11.27%	

Sources:
William Younger brewing records held at the Scottish Brewing Archive, document numbers WY/6/1/2/63, WY/6/1/2/68, WY/6/1/2/70 and WY/6/1/2/76.

Pretty straightforward: pale malt and loads of grits. Typical William Younger. The lactose in No. 1 is an unusual touch. Lactose was usually reserved for Stout. I've not seen it in any other Strong Scotch Ale.

In London, though the Burton Ales were of a similar hue to Strong Scotch Ales, the origin of their colour was quite different:

Barclay Perkins Burton Ale grists 1921 - 1940

Year	Beer	OG	pale malt	crystal malt	mild malt	SA malt	flaked maize	flaked rice	sugar	malt extract
1921	KK (bottling)	1070.2		6.05%	18.81%	55.76%	8.06%		11.32%	
1923	KK	1055.2	21.61%	4.63%		50.95%	9.26%		13.55%	
1924	KK (bottling)	1070.0	18.32%	6.30%		55.53%	6.87%		12.98%	
1924	KKK	1082.1	21.81%	5.13%		60.29%			12.77%	
1926	KK	1055.5	26.45%	4.81%	24.04%	24.04%	9.62%		11.05%	
1928	KK bottling	1069.4	18.73%	6.02%	18.06%	32.11%	8.03%		15.27%	1.78%
1928	KKKK	1078.6	28.87%	7.06%		51.33%			11.03%	1.71%
1936	KK (bottling)	1068.6	68.71%	6.00%			8.01%		15.50%	1.78%
1940	KK (trade)	1051.3	8.29%	4.15%	51.81%	16.58%		8.29%	10.88%	

Sources:
Barclay Perkins brewing records held at the London Metropolitan Archives, document numbers ACC/2305/01/608, ACC/2305/01/611, ACC/2305/01/614, ACC/2305/01/621 and ACC/2305/01/623.

So many more different malts compared to Scotland. Even different base malts, mild malt and SA (Stock or Strong Ale) malt. Along with crystal malt. And, obviously, the usual maize and sugar. Though the malt content at Barclay Perkins was generally higher.

Strong Ale in Scotland and Belgium
You can see both types of Strong Ale (William Younger No. 1 and No. 3 types) in this table:

Scotch Ale 1920 - 1933

Year	Brewer	Beer	OG	FG	ABV	App. Atten- uation
1920	Usher	Old Scotch Ale	1080.7	1026	7.11	67.78%
1920	Usher	Old Scotch Ale	1078	1008	9.24	89.74%
1920	Usher	Old Scotch Ale	1078	1022	7.30	71.79%
1921	McEwan	Old Scotch Ale	1086	1028	7.54	67.44%
1925	Younger, Wm.	No.1 Strong Scotch Ale	1084.7	1013.8	9.34	83.71%
1925	Younger, Wm.	No.3 Scotch Ale	1053.8	1009.3	5.81	82.71%
1928	McEwan	Scotch Ale	1069.6	1017.2	6.83	75.29%
1932	Younger, Wm.	Scotch Ale	1051	1011.8	5.10	76.86%
1932	Younger, Wm.	Scotch Ale	1048	1010.2	4.92	78.75%
1932	Younger, Wm.	Scotch Ale	1050	1012.6	4.86	74.80%
1933	Usher	Old Scotch Ale	1096	1022	9.72	77.08%

Sources:
Whitbread Gravity book held at the London Metropolitan Archives, document number LMA/4453/D/02/001.
Thomas Usher Gravity Book document TU/6/11

After WW I a considerable trade built up for Scotch Ale in Belgium. As you can see in the table, these were around 8.5% ABV.

Scotch Ales for the Belgian market 1920 - 1923

Year	Brewer	Beer	OG	FG	ABV	App. Atten- uation
1922	McEwan	Old Scotch Ale	1090	1025	8.49	72.22%
1922	Usher	Old Scotch Ale	1071			
1922	Usher	Old Scotch Ale	1072.8			
1923	Usher	Old Scotch Ale	1082	1016	8.66	80.49%
1923	Usher	Old Scotch Ale	1083	1017	8.66	79.52%
1923	Usher	Old Scotch Ale	1082	1016	8.66	80.49%

Source:
Thomas Usher Gravity Book document TU/6/11

Beers similar to these are still available in Belgium now mostly, but not exclusively, brewed locally.

Lager

Very few breweries in the UK were brewing Lager between the wars. There were a couple of 100% dedicated Lager breweries – Red Tower in Manchester and the Wrexham Lager Brewery – and a handful brewing Lager as a sideline. The latter group included Barclay Perkins in London and four breweries in Scotland: Tennent, McEwan, Jeffrey and the Alloa Brewery. The latter had picked up Allsopp's Lager kit after the Burton brewer had been placed in receivership in 1913.

Lager, though available in a surprising number of pubs, was still very much a minority drink. Scotland was the first region where it began to break through into the mainstream. That could account for why relatively more brewers produced Lagers there than in the rest of the UK.

Scottish Lager 1931 - 1939

Year	Brewer	Beer	OG	FG	ABV	App. Attenuation	colour
1931	Tennent	Lager Beer	1043.1	1009.3	4.39	78.42%	8
1932	Jeffrey	Pilsener	1052	1007.8	5.77	85.00%	9
1933	Alloa Brewery	Graham's Golden Lager	1044.5	1010.5	4.42	76.40%	
1933	McEwan	Pilsener Beer	1044	1010	4.42	77.27%	8
1934	McEwan	Pilsener Beer	1049.6	1009.6	5.21	80.65%	
1936	Jeffrey	Lager	1046.4	1013.1	4.32	71.77%	
1937	Tennent	Pilsener Beer	1051.2	1010.8	5.26	78.91%	
1939	Alloa Brewery	Graham's Golden Lager	1045.2	1008.6	4.77	80.97%	8.5

Sources:
Whitbread Gravity book held at the London Metropolitan Archives, document number LMA/4453/D/02/001.
Thomas Usher Gravity Book document TU/6/11 held at the Scottish Brewing Archive
Younger, Wm. & Co Gravity Book document WY/6/1/1/19 held at the Scottish Brewing Archive

At the time British-brewed Lagers were still brewed to gravities similar to those on the continent. This would change after WW II.

Graham's Golden Lager was widely-available throughout the UK and probably the most famous Lager brand in the country. We'll learn in the next chapter what happened to it after WW II.

Recipes

1914 Thomas Usher 80/- MA

At the outbreak of WW I Thomas Usher still brewed a decent range of Mild Ales. 44/-, 50/-, 60/-, 80/- and 100/-, varying in gravity from 1032º to 1065º. The war would put paid to that. In the 1920's User brewed just a single Mild.

In London, there were no Mild Ales as weak as this before WW II. But out in the English provinces, there were Milds of 1040º, or even less. In 1914, for example, Adnams had an X Ale at 1033º and XX Ale at 1042º. London X Ales were a minimum of 1050º.

The recipe doesn't look that dissimilar to an English Mild of the same period. Pale and crystal malt, flaked maize and sugar. The original doesn't include No. 3 invert, but a dark proprietary sugar called DL. At least I think it's dark, based on the type of beers it's used in and the fact that the first letter of its name is a "D".

The hopping, unsurprisingly, is fairly modest. I've guessed English hops. It could just as easily have a mixture of North American, English and even continental hops. Use any combination of those, if you're so inclined.

1914 Thomas Usher 80/- MA		
pale malt	7.00 lb	73.68%
crystal malt	0.50 lb	5.26%
flaked maize	0.50 lb	5.26%
No. 3 invert sugar	0.75 lb	7.89%
cane sugar	0.75 lb	7.89%
Fuggles 120 min	0.75 oz	
Fuggles 60 min	0.50 oz	
Fuggles 30 min	0.50 oz	
OG	1046	
FG	1016.5	
ABV	3.90	
Apparent attenuation	64.13%	
IBU	22	
SRM	10	
Mash at	150º F	
Sparge at	170º F	
Boil time	120 minutes	
pitching temp	60º F	
Yeast	WLP028 Edinburgh Ale	

1917 Thomas Usher 100/-

When this beer was brewed in July 1917, the first restrictions on beer gravity were just coming into force.

Its effect is evident in this version of 100/-, which has a gravity 8 points lower than the pre-war version. The old type of Shilling Ales were pretty much killed off by the war. As were most types of Mild Ale in Scotland. It was a sad end to a long tradition. When the dust had settled after the war, Pale ale was totally dominant.

Other than the drop in gravity, the only change from the pre-war version is the lack of flaked maize. That's a change that was undoubtedly the result of the war. No maize was grown in the UK at the time, meaning it needed to be important. Something that was problematic once the German U boat campaign really kicked off at the start of 1917.

The sugars in the original were 2.5 cwt. DL and 8 cwt. Cane. I'm pretty sure that the former is some sort of dark proprietary sugar. No. 3 invert seems a reasonable enough substitute.

The war is also the reason why the hops arte all English. Though I'll admit that is just a guess. Usher's brewing records of this period make no mention of hops at all, other than the rate per quarter of malt. Which is a bit annoying.

1917 Thomas Usher 100/-		
pale malt	9.25 lb	78.72%
crystal malt 60L	0.75 lb	6.38%
cane sugar	1.25 lb	10.64%
No. 3 invert sugar	0.50 lb	4.26%
Fuggles 120 min	0.50 oz	
Fuggles 90 min	0.50 oz	
Fuggles 60 min	0.50 oz	
Fuggles 30 min	0.50 oz	
OG	1056	
FG	1025	
ABV	4.10	
Apparent attenuation	55.36%	
IBU	24	
SRM	10	
Mash at	148° F	
Sparge at	170° F	
Boil time	120 minutes	
pitching temp	60° F	
Yeast	WLP028 Edinburgh Ale	

1918 Thomas Usher GA

As you seemed to enjoy last week's Government Ale recipe, here's another. This time from Scotland. There's two boxes ticked: WW I and Scotland.

If you thought the Truman GA was watery, take a look at this baby. It's not even 2% ABV. Why is this beer weaker? Because it's from a year later, when brewing restrictions were even stricter. Strictly speaking, this isn't really from WW I, as it was brewed on the 13th November 1918, two days after the armistice.

You can the war biting in the grist. Pre-war and during its early years, Usher's beers contained flaked maize. But this became unavailable as it had to be imported. Which caused the malt content to increase. There's still sugar in the recipe, though. Sugar was scarce during the war, but not totally impossible to get hold of.

Considering the crazily low OG, it's reasonably well hopped. Talking of gravity, note how high the FG is. One of the unusual features of Scottish brewing is how similar the FG's are of beers with very different OG's. It strikes me that Scottish drinkers expected a certain amount of body, no matter how strong the beers were. It would also have made Scottish beers appear sweeter than English equivalents.

The hops are a guess. By this time only English hops were being used in British brewing. Fuggles is the most likely variety, just because that was the one grown the most. You can substitute some Goldings or other old English varieties if it takes your fancy.

It must have been fun drinking this stuff down the pub. You'd never, ever get pissed. Probably be safe to drive after a gallon or more.

1918 Thomas Usher GA

pale malt	5.00 lb	90.91%
glucose	0.25 lb	4.55%
No. 2 invert sugar	0.25 lb	4.55%
Fuggles 90 min	0.50 oz	
Fuggles 60 min	0.50 oz	
Fuggles 30 min	0.25 oz	
OG	1025	
FG	1010	
ABV	1.98	
Apparent attenuation	60.00%	
IBU	18	
SRM	4	
Mash at	149° F	
Sparge at	170° F	
Boil time	90 minutes	
pitching temp	60° F	
Yeast	WLP028 Edinburgh Ale	

1920 Drybrough 60/- Mild

Very little Mild was brewed in Scotland after WW I. And those that were had mostly disappeared by the time the next war rolled around.

Not that this beer is what I'd describe as a genuine Mild Ale. It's actually exactly the same beer as PI 60/-. Really exactly the same, as this beer was parti-gyled with it. But there was one teeny-weeny difference: the Mild only received a quarter of the dry hops of the Pale Ale. Not sure how noticeable that would have been to your average drinker. It's another indication of how arbitrary style designations could be.

At this point Drybrough's recipes were about as simple as possible: pale malt, flaked maize and No. 3 invert sugar. The latter is slightly odd in a Pale Ale. Usually No. 3 appears in darker beers like Mild. I've gradually come to the conclusion that it's the signature flavour of the Dark Milds I grew up with. All-malt versions just never taste right.

It doesn't look like Drybrough brewed this Mild very often of for long. This is the only sighting of it in the photographs I have of their brewing records. Odd how everyone suddenly lost interest in Mild in Scotland.

In terms of gravity, it's similar to a standard London Mild in the early 1920's, which were in the 1040-1043º range. Which is basically the gravity range for a beer retailing at 7d per pint in the last set of price controls, which were in force from April 1920 to August 1921.

1920 Drybrough 60/- Mild		
pale malt	7.50 lb	83.33%
flaked maize	1.00 lb	11.11%
no. 3 sugar	0.50 lb	5.56%
Cluster 90 min	0.75 oz	
Goldings 60 min	0.75 oz	
Goldings 30 min	0.75 oz	
Goldings dry hop	0.125 oz	
OG	1040	
FG	1013	
ABV	3.57	
Apparent attenuation	67.50%	
IBU	38	
SRM	6	
Mash at	148º F	
Sparge at	175º F	
Boil time	105 minutes	
pitching temp	60º F	
Yeast	WLP028 Edinburgh Ale	

1933 William Younger XX

Hope you're not getting bored of the Scottish recipes. Because there are loads more to come.

Yes, it's coming along nicely. Scotland! vol. II, I mean. The results of my poll were quite confusing. 250 recipes came top with a third of the votes. So I've decided to go for 300, the only option that received no votes. That's just the way I am. A contrary bastard.

Mild seems to have just melted away in Scotland after WW I. Replaced by 60/- Pale Ale, which may have been coloured up to look like Dark Mild. Though William Younger do seem to have stuck with brewing Mild longer than most.

Bizarrely – especially as Younger wasn't much into the technique, in contrast to every other brewery in Scotland – this was parti-gyled with Expt, a strong Pale Ale. Though they were hopped separately, only sharing pre-boil worts.

You've probably noticed how dull Younger's recipes were. Most don't stretch any further than pale malt and grits. Lots and lots of luvverly grits. They must have had quite a grits silo, the quantities they used. And a big cooker, given the percentage of grits in every recipe.

Grits aside, this has a similar profile to an English Ordinary Mild in terms of ABV and bitterness levels. Not in terms of colour. Though, it being a Scottish beer, they probably coloured to every imaginable shade of brown.

1933 William Younger XX		
pale malt	4.75 lb	55.88%
grits	3.75 lb	44.12%
Cluster 90 min	0.75 oz	
Fuggles 30 min	0.75 oz	
Goldings dry hops	0.50 oz	
OG	1037	
FG	1011	
ABV	3.44	
Apparent attenuation	70.27%	
IBU	27	
SRM	3	
Mash at	156° F	
Sparge at	160° F	
Boil time	165 minutes	
pitching temp	61° F	
Yeast	WLP028 Edinburgh Ale	

1931 Thomas Usher Brown Ale

This is a real rarity: a beer explicitly called Brown Ale in the brewing records.

Brown Ales are rare in English brewing records because of the way most breweries produced them. They weren't brewed as beer in their own right, with a few exceptions, but were tweaked versions of another beer, usually Dark Mild. The only difference would be in the primings.

Up in Scotland, where Mild Ale was already uncommon in the 1930's, that wasn't an option for many breweries. I assume that instead they used their weakest Pale Ale as a base for Brown Ale. Unless it was one of the stronger Scottish versions, in which case I assume the base was Export, the strongest Pale Ale.

The sugars are similar, but not identical, to those used in their 80/- Stout from the same year. 2 cwt. invert, 2 cwt. Barbados, 1 cwt. CDM, 1 cwt. Caramax, 2 cwt. of something illegible. I've gone with No. 3 and No. 4 invert again as substitutes.

This particular batch was carti-gyled with a weaker Mild Ale. With a gravity in the mid-1050's, it's definitely in Double Brown Ale territory. Though it's reasonably heavily hopped for the style. In character, it must have been very different to the main sort of Brown Ale sold in England, which was the weaker, Dark Mild-based style.

The hops are a pure guess. Though probably at least 50% would have been English.

1931 Thomas Usher Brown Ale		
pale malt	8.75 lb	77.78%
crystal malt 60 L	0.50 lb	4.44%
No. 3 invert sugar	1.50 lb	13.33%
No. 4 invert sugar	0.50 lb	4.44%
Fuggles 105 min	1.25 oz	
Fuggles 60 min	1.25 oz	
Fuggles 30 min	1.25 oz	
OG	1055	
FG	1016.5	
ABV	5.09	
Apparent attenuation	70.00%	
IBU	43	
SRM	20	
Mash at	148° F	
Sparge at	170° F	
Boil time	105 minutes	
pitching temp	60° F	
Yeast	WLPC28 Edinburgh Ale	

1915 Drybrough XXX Stout

WW I drove breweries to rationalise their product range. The losers being the less popular styles. There were fewer post-war examples of Mild Ales in particular, but also of Stouts.

Drybrough XXX is an example of a full-strength Stout, before the war wiped out most beers of this type. It was parti-gyled with a weaker XX Stout. Surprisingly, both survived the war. But not for long. By 1933 there's no Stout of any description in Drybrough's brewing records. They did still sell one, as I have an analysis from that year of a beer called Nourishing Stout with an OG of just 1031º. It looks like it's a version of P 54/- with different primings.

If you look at the grist of this beer, that's not so surprising. Because this contains no coloured malt of any description. Instead, it has almost a full set of numbered invert sugars. The very large quantity of No. 4 – the darkest of the numbered inverts – is presumably what gave this beer its Stoutiness. And, coupled with a huge amount of caramel, make for a very black finished beer.

This is completely unlike any London Stout grist I've ever seen and I can't think of a similar example from anywhere in England. A London Stout would usually contain both black and brown malt, while English provincial versions made do with just black malt mostly.

1915 Drybrough XXX Stout		
pale malt	8.50 lb	47.89%
flaked maize	3.00 lb	16.90%
no. 1 sugar	1.00 lb	5.63%
no. 2 sugar	1.00 lb	5.63%
no. 4 sugar	2.25 lb	12.68%
caramel	2.00 lb	11.27%
Fuggles 120 min	1.00 oz	
Goldings 60 min	0.75 oz	
Goldings 30 min	0.75 oz	
OG	1082	
FG	1026	
ABV	7.41	
Apparent attenuation	68.29%	
IBU	25	
SRM	66	
Mash at	146º F	
Sparge at	176º F	
Boil time	120 minutes	
pitching temp	60º F	
Yeast	WLP028 Edinburgh Ale	

1917 Thomas Usher 54/- Stout

You can probably guess where I've got to with Thomas Usher's brewing logs. Currently I'm knee-deep in WW I mud.

1917 was a funny year in British brewing. At its start, gravities hadn't changed much since the war began. They'd dropped a few points but nothing too significant. Once the unrestricted U-boat campaign started to bite, the government took drastic action and gravities began to tumble. The second half of the year saw changes to strength and recipes almost on a weekly basis.

It's a nightmare for me when I'm researching. In a normal year, little changes at a brewery. A dozen or so snaps is sufficient to capture all the beers and recipe variations. The later years of WW II demand far more photos to make sure nothing is missed. It quadruples my work, at least.

For a Scottish beer, this has a very complicated grist. Three types of malt and five types of sugar. As usual, I've substituted invert sugars for proprietary sugars. The original contained 2.5 cwt Durax, 2.5 cwt CDM, 2 cwt maltosan. 2.5 cwt DL and 6.5 cwt Penang. The Penang is easy – that's a type of cane sugar. I know that CDM is a pretty dark proprietary sugar and that DL is a very dark one. The Durax, DCDM and maltosan I replaced with No. 3 invert, DL with No. 4 invert.

The poor attenuation was becoming typical of Scottish Stouts. It rarely poked its head much over the 50% parapet. The resulting ABV – just over 3% in this case – is pretty pathetic for a beer of 1048º.

The hopping has been greatly reduced from the pre-war version, which had roughly three times as many hops. Which, coupled with the poor attenuation, must have left a very sweet, sticky beer. The variety of hops is a pure guess. By the latter stages of the war pretty much only English hops were used. For a beer like this, Fuggles are the obvious choice.

After the war, Scottish Stouts would become even more poorly attenuated, lower in gravity and just about unintoxicating.

1917 Thomas Usher 54/- Stout		
pale malt	5.50 lb	57.89%
black malt	0.75 lb	7.89%
crystal malt 60L	0.50 lb	5.26%
cane sugar	1.00 lb	10.53%
No. 3 invert sugar	1.25 lb	13.16%
No. 4 invert sugar	0.50 lb	5.26%
Fuggles 180 min	0.50 oz	
Fuggles 60 min	0.50 oz	
Fuggles 30 min	0.50 oz	
OG	1048	
FG	1024.5	
ABV	3.11	
Apparent attenuation	48.96%	
IBU	19	
SRM	34	
Mash at	148° F	
Sparge at	170° F	
Boil time	180 minutes	
pitching temp	60° F	
Yeast	WLP028 Edinburgh Ale	

1921 William Younger MBS

I've already mentioned that William Younger was a bit odd with their beer range. Nowhere was that more true than with their Stouts.

In first half of the 19th century they brewed Stouts that looked very much like those from London. And different from Younger's Scottish-style beers in that the rate of attenuation was significantly higher. In the 1870's they started a new range of Stouts, much more lightly hopped and with a poorer degree of attenuation. Sometimes they contained no fresh hops at, just spent hops from previous brews.

MBS, which appeared just before WW I, seems to combine attributes of the two older sets of Stout. It had a reasonable degree of attenuation, but was lightly hopped and used spent hops. It seems to have been discontinued in the 1930's

This post WW I version is rather more heavily and thankfully without spent hops. It's a nightmare writing a recipe with lots of spent hops in it. I've assumed, for recipe purposes, that spent hops have a tenth of the power of unused hops. No idea how accurate that is.

For William Younger, the recipe is incredibly complicated, with three different sorts of malt and caramel. Obviously, there's a shitload of grits, too. Though not quite as many as it some of their other beers.

The hopping, in terms of varieties, is exactly the same as for all their other beers of this period: Kent, Saaz, British Columbia and Pacific. Not quite sure what Saaz was bringing to the part as the amount used was always pretty small.

For a compare and contrast exercise, next I'll give you the recipe for DBS, the most long-lived of Younger's Stouts. And the most normal-looking one.

1921 William Younger MBS		
pale malt	6.25 lb	50.00%
black malt	0.75 lb	6.00%
amber malt	0.75 lb	6.00%
grits	4.25 lb	34.00%
caramel 500 SRM	0.50 lb	4.00%
Cluster 90 min	1.25 oz	
Cluster 60 min	1.25 oz	
Saaz 30 min	0.50 oz	
Fuggles 30 min	1.00 oz	
Goldings dry hops	1.00 oz	
OG	1055	
FG	1017.5	
ABV	4.96	
Apparent attenuation	68.18%	
IBU	67	
SRM	34	
Mash at	152° F	
Sparge at	160° F	
Boil time	150 minutes	
pitching temp	60° F	
Yeast	WLP028 Edinburgh Ale	

1921 William Younger Btg DBS

As promised, here's the longest-lived of William Younger's Stouts, DBS.

Which I assume stands for Double Brown Stout. It was brewed from at least 1851 to 1949. Which a decent run for any beer. Despite what brewers may want you to believe, few beers I've for centuries. A single century is rare enough.

How does it differ from MES? It's a little bit stronger, for one thing. And more heavily hopped. The grists are pretty similar: pale, black and amber malts, grits and caramel. Rather a lot of caramel, so it can't be the 15,000 SRM kind. 500 SRM is a random-ish guess, purely based on getting the colour about right. They're not that different. It makes you wonder why they bothered with both.

This is right in the middle of Younger's grits period. Between 1913 and 1933 they used crazily large percentages of it in all their beers. Up to as much as 45% of the grist. Sometime later in the 1930's the proportion of grits was greatly reduced. Just after the war they were using none at all, instead going for flaked barley as an adjunct.

This wasn't voluntary. The use of maize products – which had to be imported – stopped during WW II. Brewers were told to use first flaked oats and later flaked barley instead. Restrictions continued in the immediate post-war years but by the early 1950's maize, usually in the form of flakes, was once again a very common ingredient.

1921 William Younger Btg DBS		
pale malt	6.50 lb	48.15%
black malt	0.50 lb	3.70%
amber malt	1.00 lb	7.41%
grits	5.00 lb	37.04%
caramel 500 SRM	0.50 lb	3.70%
Cluster 90 min	1.75 oz	
Cluster 60 min	1.75 oz	
Saaz 30 min	0.50 oz	
Fuggles 30 min	1.50 oz	
Goldings dry hops	1.00 oz	
OG	1060	
FG	1019	
ABV	5.42	
Apparent attenuation	68.33%	
IBU	90	
SRM	30	
Mash at	156° F	
Sparge at	160° F	
Boil time	120 minutes	
pitching temp	60° F	
Yeast	WLP028 Edinburgh Ale	

1931 Thomas Usher Stout 80/-

In the 1930's, genuine Scottish Stouts began to fade away as breweries concentrated almost exclusively on brewing Pale Ales.

This had some odd results. With some pretty strange Stouts gracing the brewing logs. This is an example of one.

It's mostly to do with the grist. You may imagine that at least one type of roasted malt was essential to the flavour profile of a Stout. Not so in Scotland. They made do with pale malt and a load of sugar, sometimes, as in this case, with a little crystal malt included.

I've done some interpretation in terms of the sugars. These were the ones used in the original: 6 cwt. cane, 2 cwt. Penang, 2cwt. CDW, 1 cwt. Caramax, 1 cwt. DF. The first two sound like simple sugars. The next two are types of dark proprietary sugars, the last, I've no idea. A combination of No. 3 and No. 4 invert should come somewhere close.

As always with Thomas Usher 20th-century recipes, the hops are a total guess as there are no details in the brewing record. Substituting something like Cluster for the 120 minute addition wouldn't be out of place.

1931 Thomas Usher Stout 80/-		
pale malt	6.00 lb	61.54%
crystal malt 60 L	0.75 lb	7.69%
No. 3 invert sugar	1.75 lb	17.95%
No. 4 invert sugar	1.25 lb	12.82%
Fuggles 120 min	0.50 oz	
Fuggles 60 min	0.50 oz	
Fuggles 30 min	0.50 oz	
OG	1052	
FG	1023	
ABV	3.84	
Apparent attenuation	55.77%	
IBU	18	
SRM	30	
Mash at	148° F	
Sparge at	170° F	
Boil time	120 minutes	
pitching temp	60° F	
Yeast	WLP028 Edinburgh Ale	

1914 Drybrough Pl

On the outbreak of war, Drybrough brewed three Pale Ales, in ascending order of strength: IP 48/-, IP and IP 60/-.

With a fairly modest gravity in the mid-1040's, Drybrough's Pl was the equivalent of an English AK. Though it wasn't as heavily hopped, as was becoming the case with all Scottish Pale Ales. Fullers AK, for example, also had an OG of 1044 in 1914. That had 1.36 lbs of hops per barrel while Drybrough Pl had only 0.91 lbs. That's a significant difference.

The grist is much like an English Pale Ale of the period: pale malt, flaked maize and sugar. The flaked rice is unusual, however. It does turn up occasionally in beers, mostly just after the 1880 Free mash Tun Act. Barclay Perkins, for example, used it for a while before switching to maize. I assume price was the reason for preferring maize.

The sugar in the original really was No. 1 and No. 2. Though there was also a very small amount of something described as "Dxt". It's probably dextrose, but the quantity is so small – 28 lbs spread over 132 barrels – that it's not really worth worrying about.

1914 Drybrough Pl		
pale malt	8.25 lb	82.50%
flaked maize	0.50 lb	5.00%
flaked rice	0.50 lb	5.00%
no. 1 sugar	0.25 lb	2.50%
no. 2 sugar	0.50 lb	5.00%
Fuggles 120 min	0.50 oz	
Goldings 60 min	0.50 oz	
Goldings 30 min	0.50 oz	
Goldings dry hop	0.50 oz	
OG	1044	
FG	1015	
ABV	3.84	
Apparent attenuation	65.91%	
IBU	20	
SRM	6	
Mash at	149° F	
Sparge at	175° F	
Boil time	120 minutes	
pitching temp	60° F	
Yeast	WLP028 Edinburgh Ale	

1917 Drybrough PI

WW I was a weird time for brewing. In the first 3 years, other than output being limited and some imported ingredients becoming scarce, nothing much happened.

Gravities had fallen a point or two, but not a great deal. Drybrough PI, for example, 1044º in 1914, had an OG of 1041º in January 1917.

The real turmoil began in July 1917, when the first restrictions on beer gravity were introduced. Half of the beer a brewery produced had to have an OG under 1036º. So it's no surprise that when this beer was brewed on August 14th 1917, it's gravity had been cut to 1035º. PI was one Drybrough's biggest sellers. It would have been very difficult for them to leave it over 1036º.

In terms of the grist, the only changes from 1914 were a reduction in the percentage of flaked maize and the introduction of caramel. The former change was almost certainly caused by the wartime situation. Not sure of the reason behind the second.

1917 Drybrough PI		
pale malt	6.50 lb	85.02%
flaked maize	0.50 lb	6.54%
no. 1 sugar	0.125 lb	1.64%
no. 2 sugar	0.50 lb	6.54%
caramel	0.02 lb	0.26%
Strisselspalt 120 min	0.25 oz	
Fuggles 60 min	0.50 oz	
Fuggles 30 min	0.25 oz	
Goldings dry hop	0.50 oz	
OG	1035	
FG	1010	
ABV	3.31	
Apparent attenuation	71.43%	
IBU	14	
SRM	5	
Mash at	148° F	
Sparge at	175° F	
Boil time	120 minutes	
pitching temp	60° F	
Yeast	WLP028 Edinburgh Ale	

1932 Lorimer & Clark XXP 6

Had enough of watery Scottish Pale Ales? I thought so. But I'm going to publish another one anyway.

If only because this makes this week that little bit easier. I already have the recipe lying around and all I need to do is wrap a little bollocks around it and I'm done. No real work or effort required. Which is just how I like things.

I though a quick comparison with some similar-strength English Pale Ales might be instructive. So I had a quick look in my mega table of analyses. And could find bugger all. I've only got 7 English Pale Ales that have a gravity even vaguely similar. And two of them are the same beer. It was hard to find anything English under 1040º. Though I did find some other Scottish Pales Ales around 1030º. Obviously a Scottish thing.

All but one of the English beers is in bottled format. They look to me as if they were probably sold as Light Ale or Light Dinner Ale. To makes things even more confusing, the Whitbread beer is their IPA.

Low-gravity English Pale Ales in 1932

Brewer	Beer	Price	package	OG	FG	ABV	App. Attenuation
Ind Coope	Pale Ale	12d	draught	1035.3			
John Smith	Dinner Ale		bottled	1036	1010.8	3.26	70.00%
Northampton Brewery	Pale Ale	11d	bottled	1032	1007.2	3.22	77.50%
Taylor Walker	Pale Ale	8d	bottled	1031	1007.8	3.01	74.84%
Taylor Walker	Pale Ale	8d	bottled	1032	1007.4	3.19	76.88%
Truman	Sparkling Ale	7d	bottled	1029	1006.4	2.93	77.93%
Whitbread	Pale Ale		bottled	1034	1008	3.37	76.47%

Source:
Whitbread Gravity book held at the London Metropolitan Archives, document number LMA/4453/D/02/001.
Thomas Usher Gravity Book document TU/6/11

XXP 6 isn't even Lorimer & Clarke's weakest Pale Ale. There's also XXP 5, weighing in at a mighty 1027º.

As for the recipe, note the high proportion of dry hops. All their Pale Ales got the same dose of dry hops, no matter what the strength of the beer. In such a light beer, I guess they were going to be pretty noticeable.

Everything else is just like the XXP 7 and 8. Just in slightly smaller amounts.

1932 Lorimer & Clark XXP 6		
pale malt	5.00 lb	74.07%
flaked barley	0.75 lb	11.11%
malt extract	0.50 lb	7.41%
No. 2 invert sugar	0.50 lb	7.41%
Fuggles 90 min	0.50 oz	
Fuggles 60 min	0.50 oz	
Goldings 30 min	0.50 oz	
Goldings dry hops	0.50 oz	
OG	1031	
FG	1007.5	
ABV	3.11	
Apparent attenuation	75.81%	
IBU	22	
SRM	5	
Mash at	154° F	
Sparge at	160° F	
Boil time	90 minutes	
pitching temp	62° F	
Yeast	WLP028 Edinburgh Ale	

1932 Lorimer & Clark XXP 7

I had a great piece of luck earlier this week at the Caledonian Brewery in Edinburgh I stumbled on a brewing book.

I wasn't going to pass up a chance like that and quickly snapped some snaps. This is a recipe from the very first photograph. It's an interwar Lorimer & Clark Pale Ale, with the snappy name of XXP 7. I think I understand that. XXP means Pale Ale – William Younger used the name, too – and 7 is just the price, 7d per pint. They loved naming beers after their price, the Scots.

It's another very straightforward beer: pale malt, invert sugar, flaked maize and malt extract. The type of draught Bitter that was brewed both sides of the border. An English beer would probably have had more sugar instead of the malt extract, but otherwise be very similar. At least in terms of grist. The hopping rate is lower than in England.

Let's make a quick comparison with Whitbread's beers of the same era. For reference purposes, XXP & was hopped at 4.81 lbs per quarter, 0.75 lbs per barrel.

Whitbread Ales in 1932							
Beer	Style	OG	FG	ABV	App. Atten- uation	lbs hops/ qtr	hops lb/brl
LA	Mild	1026.0	1006.5	2.58	75.00%	8.50	0.93
X	Mild	1032.6	1009.0	3.12	72.39%	8.26	1.11
IPA	IPA	1035.2	1009.0	3.47	74.43%	11.00	1.64
XX	Mild	1039.0	1012.5	3.51	67.95%	8.26	1.33
XXX	Strong Ale	1045.2	1015.5	3.93	65.71%	7.49	1.45
PA	Pale Ale	1046.1	1013.0	4.38	71.80%	8.00	1.58
Ex PA	Pale Ale	1046.4	1016.0	4.02	65.52%	8.00	1.59
DB	Brown Ale	1057.8	1014.0	5.79	75.78%	9.96	2.23
Source: Whitbread brewing book held at the London Metropolitan Archives, document number LMA/4453/D/01/098.							

You can see that XXP 7 was less heavily hopped than even LA, Whitbread's low-gravity Mild. And at only half the rate of IPA, a beer of about the same strength. It's pretty clear that XXP 7 was much less bitter than an equivalent English beer. Meaning it probably drank more like a Light Mild than a Bitter.

Nothing else I can really say. A simple, light, mild Bitter.

1932 Lorimer & Clark XXP 7		
pale malt	6.00 lb	75.00%
flaked barley	1.00 lb	12.50%
malt extract	0.50 lb	6.25%
No. 2 invert sugar	0.50 lb	6.25%
Fuggles 90 min	0.50 oz	
Fuggles 60 min	0.50 oz	
Goldings 30 min	0.50 oz	
Goldings dry hops	0.50 oz	
OG	1037	
FG	1010	
ABV	3.57	
Apparent attenuation	72.97%	
IBU	22	
SRM	5	
Mash at	154° F	
Sparge at	160° F	
Boil time	90 minutes	
pitching temp	61° F	
Yeast	WLP028 Edinburgh Ale	

1932 Lorimer & Clark XXP 8

Here's another of Lorimer & Clark's Pale Ales, this time the top of the range 8d one.

You may have noticed something with these pre-war Pale Ales. 6d, 7d and 8d are about the same gravity as post-war 60/-, 70/- and 80/-, respectively. Funny that. I'm still not convinced that 60/-, 70/- and 80/- were ever really the hogshead price of the beers bearing the name. Were they just totally random?

There isn't much I can say about the recipe that didn't bring up when discussing XXP 7. Because their four Pale Ales were all parti-gyled together. So this is just like the XXP 7, but with a little more of everything. Except for the dry hops. All four Pale Ales have the same quantity of dry hops. Odd that. Usually the dry-hopping is proportionate to the strength.

Best Bitter is how I'd describe this. Though with fewer hops than an English version. Er, I'm really running out of stuff to say. Malty, I would guess. Don't believe me? Brew it up and write in and call me an idiot if it's different.

1932 Lorimer & Clark XXP 8		
pale malt	7.75 lb	77.50%
flaked barley	1.25 lb	12.50%
malt extract	0.50 lb	5.00%
No. 2 invert sugar	0.50 lb	5.00%
Fuggles 90 min	0.75 oz	
Fuggles 60 min	0.75 oz	
Goldings 30 min	0.50 oz	
Goldings dry hops	0.50 oz	
OG	1045	
FG	1011	
ABV	4.50	
Apparent attenuation	75.56%	
IBU	28	
SRM	5	
Mash at	154° F	
Sparge at	160° F	
Boil time	90 minutes	
pitching temp	62.5° F	
Yeast	WLP028 Edinburgh Ale	

1933 Drybrough P80/-

You can never have too many watery Scottish Pale Ale recipes, that's what I say. But that's not what you're getting.

Instead it's a full-strength, top-of-the-range Pale Ale. Obviously, though, it being Scotland, Drybrough used the same recipe for all their beers.

You know how the standard line is that Scottish Ales get all their colour from either being boiled to gloop or roast barley? I've found fuck all evidence of this. Dark grains of any variety are rare in any Scottish beer other than Stout. So I was slightly surprised to discover Drybrough adding a touch of black malt to their beers in the 1930's. I assume it's there purely to add a little colour. Strange that they didn't use caramel like everyone else.

Other than the pale and black malt, there's also flaked maize, malt extract (very popular in the 1930's) and a proprietary sugar called Avona. As I haven't the foggiest what that is, I've substituted No. 1 invert. Though I could just as easily plumped for No. 2 invert.

As usual, there's a good bit of guessing in the hops. All I know for sure is that they were all English. Making Fuggles and Golding a safe choice.

English Pale Ales in 1933							
Brewer	Beer	Price per pint d	package	OG	FG	ABV	App. Attenuation
Barclay Perkins	Pale Ale	7	draught	1049.1			
Bass	Pale Ale		bottled	1055	1007	6.28	87.27%
Bass	Blue Label		bottled	1057.5	1014	5.66	75.65%
Charrington	PA	7	draught	1048	1012.4	4.62	74.17%
Courage	PA	8	draught	1057	1010.5	6.07	81.58%
Hoare	PA	7	draught	1043	1007.8	4.58	81.86%
Hoare & Co	Pale Ale	7	draught	1044.9			
Ind Coope	Draught Ale	8	draught	1056	1009	6.14	83.93%
Lees	B			1047.0	1009.0	5.03	80.85%
Mann	Pale Ale	7	draught	1052.6			
Meux	Pale Ale	7	draught	1043.9			
Morgans	Pale Ale	9	bottled	1048	1018.4	3.82	61.67%
Taylor Walker	Pale Ale	7	draught	1044	1008.8	4.58	80.00%
Tetley	Bitter	8	draught	1048	1008.6	5.14	82.08%
Truman	PA	7	draught	1050	1005.7	5.80	88.60%
Watney	Pale Ale	7	draught	1050	1015.7	4.44	68.60%
Whitbread	PA	7	draught	1048.8	1012.2	4.75	75.00%
Sources: Truman Gravity Book held at the London Metropolitan Archives, document number B/THB/C/252. Whitbread Gravity book held at the London Metropolitan Archives, document number LMA/4453/D/02/001. Thomas Usher Gravity Book document TU/6/11 Lees brewing records							

Going into compare and contrast mode, P80/- looks very much like and English 7d Pale Ale, or Best Bitter. Though most of the English examples have a much higher degree of attenuation, mostly over 80%. Though you can that Bass was stronger and not that far off the classic 1065º pre-WW I OG.

1933 Drybrough P80/-		
pale malt	7.50 lb	70.62%
black malt	0.06 lb	0.56%
flaked maize	1.75 lb	16.48%
No. 1 invert sugar	1.25 lb	11.77%
malt extract	0.06 lb	0.56%
Fuggles 120 min	1.00 oz	
Fuggles 60 min	0.75 oz	
Goldings 30 min	0.75 oz	
Goldings dry hops	0.25 oz	
OG	1049	
FG	1015	
ABV	4.50	
Apparent attenuation	69.39%	
IBU	31	
SRM	8	
Mash at	152º F	
Sparge at	167º F	
Boil time	120 minutes	
pitching temp	59º F	
Yeast	WLP028 Edinburgh Ale	

1933 William Younger XXPS

Finding a beer that I once drank myself in a brewing book always causes a certain frisson. Which Younger XXPS, a beer I drank many times, certainly does.

For much of the 20th century XXPS was William Younger's bread and butter Pale Ale, making up a considerable percentage of their output. After WW II it was called a variety of names in the trade. In Scotland, it was 70/- or simply Heavy. In England, it was usually referred to as Scotch Bitter.

It was a descendant of the stronger of William Younger's two original Pale Ales, XP and XXP. As such it had a very long history, lasting right up to the end of the 20th century, even surviving the closure of the Holyrood Brewery. In keg form, it was marketed as Tartan or Tartan Bitter. A beer with not the greatest of reputations.

It's a simple, but strange recipe. Betraying Younger love affair with grits. They make up over 40% of the grist, which was pretty typical for Younger at this time. Other than that, there are just American and Kent hops in fairly modest quantities. Leaving a very pale beer (at least, as brewed) without a too overpowering hop character. A easy drinker, basically.

1933 William Younger XXPS		
pale malt	6.75 lb	58.70%
grits	4.75 lb	41.30%
Cluster 90 min	1.00 oz	
Fuggles 30 min	1.00 oz	
Goldings dry hops	0.25 oz	
OG	1049	
FG	1014	
ABV	4.63	
Apparent attenuation	71.43%	
IBU	33	
SRM	4	
Mash at	154° F	
Sparge at	160° F	
Boil time	105 minutes	
pitching temp	60° F	
Yeast	WLP028 Edinburgh Ale	

1939 Maclay PA 6d

Maclay was another brewery which after WW I just brewed a single Pale Ale recipe to various strengths.

They had three Pale Ales: PA 5d (1032º), PA 6d (1038º) and Fa 7d (1043º), plus a Strong Ale (1089º). They were all parti-gyled together in every possible combination.

The recipe isn't hugely complicated: a single malt, flaked maize and invert sugar. That's about the minimum number of ingredients you'd see in the British beer of this period. Most of the hops in this brew were English, but 7 of the 70 lbs were British Columbian. Too small an amount to bother with, really. If you're so inclined, knock down the Fuggles and add 0.125 oz. of Cluster.

The 6d in the name is the price per pint. Weirdly, this beer continued to the called PA 6d in the brew house right through into the 1990's. When, obviously, a pint cost much more than 6d. That wasn't what drinkers called it, however. The trade name for this beer after WW II was 60/-. What I used to think was a Dark Mild.

The two mashing temperatures are because Maclay were underlet mashers. The first temperature is for the main infusion, the second for after the underlet.

1939 Maclay PA 6d		
pale malt	6.00 lb	77.42%
flaked maize	0.50 lb	6.45%
No. 2 invert sugar	1.25 lb	16.13%
Fuggles 90 min	1.00 oz	
Goldings 30 min	0.75 oz	
Goldings dry hops	0.25 oz	
OG	1038	
FG	1014	
ABV	3.18	
Apparent attenuation	63.16%	
IBU	23	
SRM	7	
Mash at	149/157° F	
Sparge at	170° F	
Boil time	90 minutes	
pitching temp	61° F	
Yeast	WLP028 Edinburgh Ale	

1918 Thomas Usher X 60/-

To prove that WW I wasn't all doom and gloom, here's a Mild that's not so watery.

The date is important, mind. The Government Ale recipe from Usher also dates from 1918. But it's from November, while X 60/- is from January. A lot had happened between those two dates. Ironically, the watery GA, which was brewed on 13th November, is technically a post-war beer. In April 1918 the average gravity of all beer brewed by brewery was limited to $1030º$[59]. I wonder if drinkers realised what was about to happen to their beer at the start of 1918?

What is a Mild? It's a question I often ask myself, especially when looking at Scottish beer. Why do I classify this as a Mild? Because of the X in the name, really. But it all gets messy when you consider what this was parti-gyled with: PA. A beer that's pretty obviously supposed to be a Pale Ale. Even more confusingly PA was weaker than X 60/-.

One reason I wanted to share this recipe with you is that it's about the last period Mild was being brewed in any quantity in Scotland. Unusually, Usher continued to brew small quantities of a beer called MA until at least the 1930's. Most other breweries produced nothing but Pale Ale, Strong Ale and the odd Stout.

It's another very simple grist. The sugar type is a guess. It's something called Greenock in the records. No idea what that was. But, as it's in pretty much all their beers, I doubt it was a very dark type of sugar.

The hop variety is a guess, too. Usher didn't bother specifying the hops in their logs at this point. Which is a bit frustrating. But by the late war years just about exclusively English hops were being used as there were more than enough to go around.

1918 Thomas Usher X 60/-		
pale malt	8.75 lb	92.11%
No. 2 invert sugar	0.75 lb	7.89%
Fuggles 90 min	0.75 oz	
Fuggles 60 min	0.75 oz	
Fuggles 30 min	0.75 oz	
OG	1043	
FG	1014.5	
ABV	3.77	
Apparent attenuation	66.28%	
IBU	27	
SRM	6	
Mash at	152º F	
Sparge at	170º F	
Boil time	90 minutes	
pitching temp	60º F	
Yeast	WLP028 Edinburgh Ale	

---

[59] "The Brewers' Almanack 1928" page 100.

1928 Thomas Usher OSA

When Scottish brewers went over to brewing pretty much nothing but Pale Ales between the wars, they started brewing their Strong Ales a different way. Rather than being the top end of their Shilling Ale range, they were just a super- strong version of their Pale Ale recipe.

Usher OSA is a great example of that kind of beer. This particular example was parti-gyled with PA 60/-, a beer the slightly less than half OSA's OG. It also look rather like the type of beer sold as Scotch Ale in Belgium.

Usher didn't go in for complicated recipes. There really three ingredients in the grist: pale malt, flaked maize and invert sugar. It doesn't specify exactly what type of invert in the brewing record. I've guessed at No. 2, but it could also have been No. 1.

My guess is that, as sold, Old Scotch Ale as the brewery called it, was much darker than the colour I give below in the recipe. I know that after in 1953 it was 30 EBC, about 15 SRM.

As with all Usher's beers of this period the hop varieties can only be a guess.

1928 Thomas Usher OSA		
pale malt	4.25 lb	78.08%
flaked maize	2.00 lb	10.96%
No. 2 invert sugar	2.00 lb	10.96%
Goldings 105 min	1.50 oz	
Goldings 60 min	1.50 oz	
Goldings 30 min	1.50 oz	
OG	1085	
FG	1026	
ABV	7.81	
Apparent attenuation	69.41%	
IBU	46	
SRM	10	
Mash at	150° F	
Sparge at	170° F	
Boil time	105 minutes	
pitching temp	60.5° F	
Yeast	WLP028 Edinburgh Ale	

1933 William Younger No. 1

In the first half of the 20th century, William Younger bashed out two Scotch Ales, No. 3 and the more powerful No. 1.

Both had been around since the 1850's at least and managed to survive two world wars. Unlike the other Ales completing the set, No. 2 and No. 4. While No.3 was often sold on draught and filled a similar niche to Burton, No. 1 was more in the tradition of Scotch Ales sold in Belgium. It was dark and pretty powerful. I believe it was discontinued in the 1950's or early 1960's.

This is so exciting. Because here's a Younger's beer that has more ingredients than just pale malt and grits. It has that super-secret exciting ingredient you wouldn't expect in a Scotch Ale: lactose. It's about the only example of the use of lactose in a beer other than a Stout that I can recall. I assume it was a way of simulating the high FG beers of this type had in the 19th century.

It has one of the highest percentages of malt for a Younger's beer of this period: almost 60%. That shows how special it was. The hopping is more heavy than style Nazis would have you believe was normal in Scotland. But compared to earlier version, it looks positively restrained at just 50 IBUs.

Once again, this would have been coloured up with caramel at racking time. Just pick your shade, as I'm sure it came in several, depending on where it was being sold.

1933 William Younger No. 1		
pale malt	11.25 lb	58.44%
grits	7.25 lb	37.66%
lactose	0.75 lb	3.90%
Cluster 90 min	1.75 oz	
Fuggles 30 min	1.75 oz	
Goldings dry hops	0.25 oz	
OG	1085	
FG	1033	
ABV	6.88	
Apparent attenuation	61.18%	
IBU	50	
SRM	5	
Mash at	156° F	
Sparge at	160° F	
Boil time	150 minutes	
pitching temp	57° F	
Yeast	WLP028 Edinburgh Ale	

1933 William Younger No. 3

You've probably noticed that I have a bit of a thing about Younger's No. 3. Probably because it was a beer I quite liked.

I drank it regularly at a couple of places in the 1980's. The Burley Liberal Club in Leeds. And the pub just around the corner from my office on Gloucester Place in London. In my head, I was thinking strong Dark Mild. Which wasn't totally far off the mark.

It was a nice alternative to Younger's IPA. At the time it had an OG of 1043º, ever so slightly higher than the IPA's 1042.2º. A few pints at lunchtime set me up nicely for an afternoon snooze back at work. By the time I'd woken up it would be time to return to the pub for a few more pints before heading home.

You've probably noticed that the beer below is pretty pale. It always seems to have come in a variety of shades, though dark was most popular after WW I. The colour presumably coming from caramel added at racking time. Fee free to colour this up any way you like.

There's not really much to say about the grist. As with most Younger's beers in the 20th century. There's pale malt, loads and loads of grits and that's it. I have the feeling that all that limited grits to just 40% of the total was maintaining enough malt to convert the starch. They'd probably have happily used 70% grits, if t had been practical. Their beers have the highest levels of adjuncts I've seen anywhere.

1933 William Younger No. 3		
pale malt	7.50 lb	58.82%
grits	5.25 lb	41.18%
Cluster 90 min	1.25 oz	
Fuggles 30 min	1.25 oz	
Goldings dry hops	0.25 oz	
OG	1055	
FG	1015.5	
ABV	5.23	
Apparent attenuation	71.82%	
IBU	39	
SRM	4	
Mash at	154º F	
Sparge at	160º F	
Boil time	135 minutes	
pitching temp	59º F	
Yeast	WLP028 Edinburgh Ale	

1933 Lorimer & Clark SA

I did contemplate going through the whole set of Pale Ales. But, as they're just different-strength versions of the same basic beer, I thought that might be a little dull.

Instead I've plucked out SA, the beer that isn't like the others. Which, I'll admit, was quite a surprise. I'd expected SA to be like the Strong Ales produced at other breweries like Drybrough or Maclay. Just a super-strong version of their Pale Ale recipe. But that's not the case. It's not parti-gyled with a Pale Ale and the recipe is quite different.

For a start there's no flaked maize. And there's less sugar and one extra ingredient: caramel. Also it was boiled for much longer, 3 hours rather than 1.5 and 2 hours. But the biggest difference is the hopping. It's so out of whack with their other beers that I just cross-checked the numbers to make sure I hadn't made a mistake. It really is hopped at three times the rate of their Pale Ales: 14.88 lbs per quarter compared to 4.88 lbs.

Which leaves this beer looking very 19th century. The combination of high gravity and heavy hopping is reminiscent of William Younger's 140/- and 160/- from the end of the 1800's. Other Scottish Strong Ales of the 1930's look very different. Their hopping is much more restrained. A quick look at this table shows how much of an Outlier Lorimer & Clark's SA was:

Scottish Strong Ales of the 1930's

Year	Brewer	Beer	OG	FG	ABV	App. Attenuation	lbs hops/qtr	hops lb/brl
1933	Drybrough	Burns	1084.0	1027.0	7.54	67.86%	6.29	2.51
1933	Wm. Younger	1	1085.0	1033.0	6.88	61.18%	5.26	1.79
1938	Maclay	SA	1075	1028	6.22	62.67%	5.00	1.65
1932	Lorimer & Clark	SA	1096	1025	9.39	73.96%	14.88	6.45

Sources:
Drybrough brewing record held at the Scottish Brewing Archive, document number D/6/1/1/4.
William Younger brewing record held at the Scottish Brewing Archive, document number WY/6/1/2/70.
Maclay brewing record held at the Scottish Brewing Archive, document number M/6/1/1/3.

As to what SA might mean, I won't commit myself without seeing some labels. Based on other breweries, such as William Younger, it might have been called Strong Ale north of the border and Scotch Ale south of it.

1933 Lorimer & Clark SA		
pale malt	18.75 lb	88.24%
malt extract	1.50 lb	7.06%
caramel	0.25 lb	1.18%
No. 2 invert sugar	0.75 lb	3.53%
Fuggles 90 min	5.00 oz	
Fuggles 60 min	4.00 oz	
Goldings 30 min	4.00 oz	
OG	1096	
FG	1025	
ABV	9.39	
Apparent attenuation	73.96%	
IBU	123	
SRM	55	
Mash at	154° F	
Sparge at	165° F	
Boil time	180 minutes	
pitching temp	59.5° F	
Yeast	WLP028 Edinburgh Ale	

1933 Drybrough Burns Ale

By 1933, Drybrough's range of beers was very simple. They had a single recipe from which they parti-gyled all their beers in various combinations.

In essence, it was a Pale Ale recipe with its strength adjusted to suit. There were three Pale Ales, P 54/-, P 60/- and P 80/- plus a Strong Ale, Burns Ale. This type of beer was produced by several Scottish brewers. I can understand why they'd brew it this way. Given the quantities of it they brewed, there wasn't a huge demand.

The vast majority of Drybrough's output was a single beer, the mid-strength Pale Ale P 60/-, which amounted for around 90% of what they brewed:

Drybrough output July 1934		
	barrels	%
54/-	245.72	8.97%
60/-	2430.44	88.76%
80/-	54.64	2.00%
Burns	7.31	0.27%
total	*2738.11*	
Source: Drybrough brewing record held at the Scottish Brewing Archive, document number D/6/1/1/4.		

The amount of Burns Ale produced was tiny. About the largest batch I've seen was 50 barrels. Interestingly, parti-gyles which included Burns Ale contained about double the quantity of black compared to other brews. They were clearly after a dark colour for their Strong Ale.

In this case the dry hops are a guess. Based on the records where the dry hopping is recorded, I'm sure this was dry hopped. After all, they even dry hopped their Mild. In their Pale Ales, it was always the same amount, no matter what the strength of the beer: the equivalent of half an ounce in 5 UK/6 US barrels. Though it's possible this could have contained more.

1933 Drybrough Burns Ale		
pale malt	13.75 lb	74.00%
black malt	0.33 lb	1.78%
flaked maize	3.00 lb	16.15%
No. 1 invert sugar	1.25 lb	6.73%
malt extract	0.25 lb	1.35%
Fuggles 120 min	1.75 oz	
Fuggles 60 min	1.75 oz	
Goldings 30 min	1.75 oz	
Goldings dry hops	0.50 oz	
OG	1084	
FG	1027	
ABV	7.54	
Apparent attenuation	67.86%	
IBU	51	
SRM	17	
Mash at	152° F	
Sparge at	167° F	
Boil time	120 minutes	
pitching temp	67.5° F	
Yeast	WLP028 Edinburgh Ale	

1939 – 1970 Austerity to Prosperity (and oblivion)

Introduction

A second global war, inevitably, but pressure on the supply of brewing materials. Scotland – as the rest of the UK – was dependent on foreign ingredients. Barley from California, the Middle East and South America; hops from anywhere they were grown. The war changed all that.

The UK government had learned from the first war. They expected a U-boat campaign would restrict imports and tried to make Britain less dependent on foreign ingredients. The production of barley soared and enough English hops were around, after the blip when 30% of the 1940 crop was destroyed in an early raid of the London Blitz, to just about cover demand.

During the war and its immediate aftermath, brewers were encumbered with limited access to raw materials and all sorts of restrictions on what they could brew. The main victim were strong beers, something that had been a speciality of the Scots.

Beer production

After a difficult time in the immediate aftermath of WW II, beer production began to slowly rise in the late 1950's, before really taking off in the 1960's.

Beer output in the UK and Scotland 1951 - 1975 (bulk barrels)		
Year	UK	Scotland	% Scotland
1951	24,891,746	2,000,000	8.03%
1952	25,156,489	2,019,000	8.03%
1953	24,883,227	2,106,000	8.46%
1954	24,582,303	1,981,000	8.06%
1955	23,934,215	2,068,000	8.64%
1956	24,551,158	2,086,000	8.50%
1957	24,506,524	2,156,000	8.80%
1958	24,647,978	2,111,000	8.56%
1959	23,783,833	2,226,000	9.36%
1960	26,115,012	2,347,000	8.99%
1961	27,098,240	2,507,000	9.25%
1962	27,495,836	2,501,000	9.10%
1963	27,813,506	2,611,000	9.39%
1964	28,964,230	2,707,000	9.35%
1965	29,528,050	2,742,000	9.29%
1966	29,987,533	2,800,000	9.34%
1967	30,418,232	2,933,000	9.64%
1968	30,528,513	3,096,000	10.14%
1969	31,554,274	3,353,000	10.63%
1970	32,940,567	3,855,000	11.70%
1971	34,360,000	4,306,000	12.53%
1972	34,969,310	4,474,000	12.79%
1973	35,338,345	4,835,000	13.68%
1974	37,893,753	5,046,000	13.32%
1975	38,238,657	5,413,000	14.16%
Sources: Brewers' Almanack 1955, p. 50; Brewers' Almanack 1962, p. 48; Brewers' Almanack 1971, p. 45; "The Brewers' Society Statistical Handbook 1988" page 7; "A History of the Brewing Industry in Scotland" by Ian Donnachie, 1998, page 237. Statistical Handbook of the British Beer & Pub Association 2005, p. 7			

Despite a dramatic reduction in the number of breweries, the amount of beer brewed in Scotland rose considerably after 1960, more than doubling between then and 1975. This was well above the 46% rise in output of the UK as a whole. It is reflected in Scotland's share of beer production rising from 8% to 14%.

[examples of the decline/disappearance of Strong Ales]

Breweries

The number of breweries continued its long-term decline during and after WW II. By the end of the 1960's only a handful remained.

Scottish beer out and no. breweries 1939 - 1975			
Year	Output barrels	Number of Brewers	average output per brewery
1939		40	0
1945		36	0
1950		35	0
1951	2,000,000	36	55,556
1952	2,019,000	34	59,382
1953	2,106,000	34	61,941
1954	1,981,000	33	60,030
1955	2,068,000	41	50,439
1956	2,086,000	31	67,290
1957	2,156,000	33	65,333
1958	2,111,000	30	70,367
1959	2,226,000	30	74,200
1960	2,347,000	30	78,233
1961	2,507,000		
1962	2,501,000		
1963	2,611,000	20	130,550
1964	2,707,000	17	159,235
1965	2,742,000	15	182,800
1966	2,800,000	15	186,667
1967	2,933,000	14	209,500
1968	3,096,000		
1969	3,353,000		
1970	3,855,000		
1971	4,306,000		
1972	4,474,000		
1973	4,835,000		
1974	5,046,000		
1975	5,413,000		
Source: "A History of the Brewing Industry in Scotland" by Ian Donnachie, 1998, page 234. Brewer's Almanack 1955, page 85. Brewer's Almanack 1962, page 83. Brewer's Almanack 1971, page 80.			

The 1950's and 1960's were a period of consolidations and closures in the UK brewing industry. But the concentration in production took a more dramatic form in Scotland, with only a handful of brewing companies surviving. Most either ended up in the Scottish Brewers conglomerate set up by William Younger and William McEwan or were gobbled up by one of the emerging national brewers.

In Scotland two brewing groups drove the rationalisation process: Scottish Brewers (becoming Scottish & Newcastle later) and Eddie Taylor's United Breweries (the first foundation of the mighty Bass Charrington empire). All the other UK Big Six brewers, except for Courage, grabbed a share. The last scraps were scrapped over by Whitbread and Watney, who were a little slow off the mark. Vaux, a regional brewer from the Northeast of England, who already had commercial interests in Scotland, did surprisingly well, picking up four breweries. Including the only Edinburgh brewery of this period that's still open: Caledonian.

How the Scottish brewing industry disappeared							
Company	Brewery	Town	Total Capital £	Takeover Company	Date of Takeover	closed	Brewery group
Aitchison	Canongate	Edinburgh	400,000	Hammonds UBs.	1959	1961	Bass Charrington
Aitken	Falkirk	Falkirk	927,000	United Bs.	1960	1966	Bass Charrington
Arrol	Alloa	Alloa		Allsopp	1930	1998	Allied
Ballingall	Park, Pleasance	Dundee	75,000			1964	
Bernard	New Edinburgh	Edinburgh	1 075,000	Scottish Bs.	1960	1960	Scottish & Newcastle
Blair	Townhead	Alloa	200,000	G. Younger	1959	1959	Bass Charrington
Calder	Shore	Alloa	525,000	United Bs.	1960	1961 (1921)	Bass Charrington
Campbell, Hope & King	Argyle	Edinburgh	250,000	Whitbread	1967	1970	Whitbread
James Deuchar	Lochside	Montrose		Newcastle Bs.	1956	1956	Scottish & Newcastle
Robert Deuchar	Duddingston	Edinburgh		Newcastle Bs.	1954	1961	Scottish & Newcastle
Drybrough	Edinburgh	Edinburgh	300,000	Watney Mann	1965	1987	Watney
Dudgeon	Belhaven	Dunbar	-				
Fowler	Prestonpans	Prestonpans	300,000	United Bs.	1960	1962	Bass Charrington
Gordon & Blair	Craigwell	Edinburgh		Mackay	1954	1953	Watney
Jeffrey	Heriot	Edinburgh	280,000	United Bs.	1960	1992	Bass Charrington
Lorimer & Clark	Caledonian	Edinburgh	100,000	Vaux	1947		Vaux
Mackay	St.Leonard's	Edinburgh		Watney Mann	1963	1963	Watney
Maclay	Thistle	Alloa	50,000			1999	
Maclachlan	Castle	Edinburgh	600,000	Tennent	1960	1956	Bass Charrington
MacLennan & Urquhart	Dalkeith	Dalkeith	-	Aitchison	1955	1958	Bass Charrington
McEwan	Fountain	Edinburgh	1,000,000	Scottish Bs.	1931	2005	Scottish & Newcastle
Morison	Edinburgh	Edinburgh	-	Scottish Bs.	1960	1960	Scottish & Newcastle
Murray	Craigmillar	Edinburgh	375,000	United Bs.	1960	1963	Bass Charrington
Steel, Coulson	Croft-an-Righ	Edinburgh	140,000	Vaux	1959	1960	Vaux
Tennent	Wellpark	Glasgow	2,250,000	Charrington	1963		Bass Charrington
Wright	Perth	Perth	-	Vaux	1961	1961	Vaux
Young	Ladywell	Musselburgh	30,000	Whitbread	1968	1969	Whitbread
G. Younger	Candleriggs	Alloa	750,000	United Bs.	1960	1963	Bass Charrington
R. Younger	St. Ann's	Edinburgh	530,000	Scottish Bs.	1960	1961	Scottish & Newcastle
W. Younger	Abbey, Holyrood	Edinburgh	1,000,000	Scottish Bs.	1931	1986	Scottish & Newcastle
Usher	Park	Edinburgh	400,000	Vaux	1960	1981	Vaux

Sources:
Brewery Manual 1955, 1960, 1965 (via "A History of the Brewing Industry in Scotland" by Ian Donnachie, 1998, page 240.)
"A Century of British Brewers", Barber, 2005.
Scottish Brewing Archive website

At the end of the 1960's, only two Scottish remained independent: Maclay and Belhaven. Of these two, only the latter still brews, now owned the large English firm, Greene King, who bought it in 2005. Maclays stopped brewing in 1999, become a pub company, which in turn has disappeared. A sad end to brewing in Alloa.

There's one firm in the table that wasn't taken over: Ballingall. They just gave up brewing in 1964, though continued to supply their 7 pubs with beer from Drybrough until finally closing the business in 1968.

William Younger

Even the largest Edinburgh breweries were fairly modest affairs. William Younger's Abbey brewery, one of the largest in Scotland brewed far less than the large English breweries, which by this time were producing over 1 million barrels a year.

William Younger overview 1940 - 1950

year	malt (qtrs)	sugar (qtrs)	total (qtrs)	copper hops (lbs)	dry hops (lbs)	Total hops (lbs)	barrels in tuns	hops lbs/ brl	hops lbs/ qtr	average OG
1940	27,805	544	28,349	114,221	25,447	139,668	173,630	0.80	4.93	1043.47
1950	21,064	1,800	22,864	105,285	11,845	117,130	141,864	0.83	5.12	1042.23

Sources:
William Younger brewing records documents WY/6/1/2/76 and WY/6/1/2/88 held at the Scottish Brewing Archive.

Though William Younger did have a second plant, the Holyrood Brewery, in addition to the Abbey Brewery.

Ingredients

The biggest impact of WW II on British brewing was becoming self-sufficient in raw materials. A combination of weaker beer, reduced beer consumption and a boost to domestic production left the UK with more than sufficient home-grown brewing materials. It was quite a change. The UK hadn't been able to produce enough materials for brewing since the 1840's.

Malt

During WW II British barley production increased enormously. For the first time in around a century British brewing was no longer dependent on foreign grain.

Wartime shortages prompted the government to force materials on brewers that they would have preferred not to employ. A bumper oats crop in 1942 caused the government to insist brewers include 10% of it in all their grists. From 1943 onwards brewers were compelled to use a percentage of flaked barley. The reasoning being that using flakes saved the energy need for malting. An important factor when coal was in short supply.

After the war, intensive breeding programmes meant that new, improved barley varieties were coming onto the market more quickly than ever. A corollary to this was than malting barleys disappeared more quickly than before, too. Soon all the traditional varieties had disappeared. Not always to the delight of brewers. The new varieties were designed with the farmer rather than the brewer in mind and concentrated on characteristics such as disease resistance or yield rather than flavour or ease of use in the brewery.

Sugar

Brewers, through government restrictions, were forced to reduce their sugar usage during the war. With sugar rationing lasting until the early 1950's, it wasn't until the middle of that decade that brewers were free to use as much sugar as they wanted.

Numbered invert sugars were still around, though increasingly brewers both in England and Scotland used proprietary brewing sugars which were often designed to be used in specific types of beer, such as Oatmeal Stout. Cane sugar and straight sucrose mostly disappeared.

Adjuncts

The war badly obstructed the import of maize from the USA and in the later war years brewers used flaked barley in its place. Once supplies were resumed, everyone went back to using flaked maize or grits.

A bumper oats crop in 1942 led the government to force brewers to use 10% in all their grists. It wasn't greatly appreciated by brewers, especially ones filling their mash tuns to capacity. Oats take up a greater volume than barley, reducing the mash tun's capacity.

Maclay, for example, had around 7% flaked maize in their grists until 1940, after which they used no adjuncts. In 1943, flaked oats appeared as a substitute for maize. But there was also 10% malted oats in the mash. Flaked barley replaced the flaked oats in 1944, though the malted oats remained[60].

---

[60] Maclay brewing records held at the Scottish Brewing Archive, document numbers M/6/1/1/4 and M/6/1/1/13.

Hops

WW II prevented brewers from buying American hops. After the war, with the UK self-sufficient in hops, there was no longer a need to import them. Only tiny quantities, mostly top-quality continental hops like Saaz and Hallertau, though some Styrian Goldings were imported as well.

New hop varieties had been developed earlier in the century, such as Brewer's Gold (1919), Bramling Cross (1927) and Northern Brewer (1934). However, in the 1950's the vast majority of hops grown in England were either Fuggles or the whitebines collectively referred to as Goldings.

Water

Edinburgh's breweries were mostly grouped around two locations, the Royal Mile in the city centre and Duddingston on its periphery. One of the principal reasons for breweries selecting these locations was the availability of a good supply of brewing water through wells on the premises.

But some breweries in the city centre were getting in the way of the town planners. They eyed their prime central locations with envy. In the 1950's there were schemes to move some of the centrally-located breweries.

Starting in 1950, when it was proposed to remove the breweries from the Canongate area (part of the Royal Mile) and replace them with residential accommodation. The plan included William Younger's Abbey and Holyrood breweries, which were amongst the largest in Scotland. To overcome the brewery's objections to the loss of their water supply the council proposed moving them to Duddingston[61]. For whatever reason, the plan never went ahead and William Younger remained on the Royal mile until their closure.

In 1954, it was the turn of Campbell, Hope & King to be threatened with eviction. The brewery's main objection to the plan was that they would lose their well, claiming that a suitable supply of water was only available in a few locations in the city[62]. Like the earlier plan, nothing ever came of it. Campbell, Hope & King remained at the same location until their closure in 1970.

---

[61] The Scotsman - Tuesday 04 July 1950, page 6.
[62] Dundee Courier - Wednesday 07 April 1954, page 2.

Techniques

Mashing

With their simple as cymbals system of mashing, there wasn't much for the Scots to rationalise.

Initially, at least, they didn't at William Younger:

William Younger 1949 XXP mashing scheme	
strike heat	161° F
time mashed	8 minutes
time stood	2 hours
mash temperature	153° F
1st sparge heat	160° F
2nd sparge heat	160° F
1st tap heat	148° F
2nd tap heat	150° F
3rd tap heat	154° F
Source: William Younger brewing record held at the Scottish Brewing Archive, document number WY/6/1/2/88.	

Comparing that scheme directly with the one from 1933, nothing much had changed since the war:

William Younger mashing schemes		
	1933 XXP	1949 XXP
strike heat	160° F	161° F
time mashed	7 minutes	8 minutes
time stood	2 hours	2 hours
mash temperature	152° F	153° F
1st sparge heat	160° F	160° F
2nd sparge heat	160° F	160° F
1st tap heat	150° F	148° F
2nd tap heat	153° F	150° F
3rd tap heat	155° F	154° F
Source: William Younger brewing records held at the Scottish Brewing Archive, document numbers WY/6/1/2/70 and WY/6/1/2/88.		

A degree warmer at the start of the mash in 1949. In it's nothing huge.

Boiling

Just like the previous war, WW II had an impact on boiling practices in the UK. The spur to reduce boiling times was exactly the same: a need to conserve fuel in a time of coal shortages.

At William Younger the cutting of the boil time is quite clear:

William Younger boiling times 1939 - 1949

Year	Beer	Style	OG	boil 1	boil 2
1939	XXX	Mild	1037	1.75	2.25
1939	XXPS	Pale Ale	1046	1.75	2.25
1939	3	Strong Ale	1053	1.75	2.25
1939	DBS Btlg	Stout	1066	2.5	3
1939	*Average*			*1.94*	*2.44*
1949	XXX	Mild	1030.5	1.25	1.75
1949	Pale XXPS	Pale Ale	1037	1.25	1.75
1949	Btlg DBS	Stout	1046	1.5	2
1949	3 Btg	Strong Ale	1047	1.25	1.75
1949	*Average*			*1.31*	*1.81*

Sources:
William Younger brewing records documents WY/6/1/2/76 and WY/6/1/2/88 held at the Scottish Brewing Archive.

There was a reduction of more than 30 minutes for both the first and second coppers.

At Maclay the reduction was even more extreme:

Maclay boiling times 1939 - 1951

Year	Beer	Style	OG	boil 1	boil 2
1939	PA 6d	Pale Ale	1038	2.50	2
1939	SA	Strong Ale	1082	2.50	2
1939	*Average*			*2.50*	*2.00*
1951	PA 6d	Pale Ale	1031	0.75	1.25
1951	SPA	Pale Ale	1038	2.00	
1951	Exp	Pale Ale	1043	1.83	0.75
1951	SA	Strong Ale	1076	0.75	1.25
1951	*Average*			*1.33*	*1.08*

Sources:
Maclay brewing records held at the Scottish Brewing Archive, document numbers M/6/1/1/4 and M/6/1/1/28.

Here the reduction was around an hour for each copper. Oddly, that left the average boil time for the first copper almost exactly the same at both breweries. Though the second copper was boiled for considerably longer at William Younger.

Over at Robert Younger, boiling times remained long even after the war:

Robert Younger boiling times in 1957

Beer	Style	OG	boil 1	boil 2	boil 3
60/-	Pale Ale	1030	2	2	2
70/-	Pale Ale	1035	2	2	2
80/-	Pale Ale	1043	2	2	2
SS	Stout	1030	2	2	2

Source:
Robert Younger brewing record held at the Scottish Brewing Archive, document number RY/6/1/2.

A two-hour boil was unusually long in the UK after WW II.

In London, the war also impacted Whitbread's boiling practices:

Whitbread boiling times 1939 - 1951					
Year	Beer	Style	OG	boil 1	boil 2
1939	X	Mild	1033.9	1.25	1
1939	LS	Stout	1045.2	1.25	1.42
1939	PA	Pale Ale	1048.2	1.17	1.08
1939	33	Strong Ale	1061	1.25	1
1939	*Average*			*1.23*	*1.13*
1951	Best Ale	Mild	1031.8	1	0.75
1951	WS	Stout	1038.6	1	0.75
1951	PA	Pale Ale	1039.5	1.08	1.25
1939	*Average*			*1.03*	*0.92*
Sources: Whitbread brewing records held at the London Metropolitan Archives, document numbers LMA/4453/D/01/107, LMA/4453/D/01/119, LMA/4453/D/05/126 and LMA/4453/D/09/131.					

The reduction was less than 15 minutes for each copper in this case, though Whitbread had started with shorter boils. At only around an hour for each copper, there wasn't much room for further reduction.

At Fuller, the war seemed to have no impact at all on their copper timings:

Fuller's boiling times 1939 - 1951					
Year	Beer	Style	OG	boil 1	boil 2
1939	X	Mild	1032.3	1.5	1.75
1939	PA	Pale Ale	1051.1	1.5	1.75
1939	BO	Strong Ale	1055.5	1.5	1.75
1939	*Average*			*1.5*	*1.75*
1958	X	Mild	1031.3	1.5	1.75
1958	PA	Pale Ale	1033.4	1.5	1.75
1958	OBE	Strong Ale	1049.4	1.5	1.75
1958	*Average*			*1.5*	*1.75*
Source: Fullers brewing records held at the brewery.					

Pulling all of that information together, it's interesting to note that by the 1950's, though they had started from very different places, the boiling times of William Younger and Fuller were remarkably similar:

English and Scottish boiling times 1939 - 1958

Year	Brewery	boil 1	boil 2
1939	Wm. Younger	1.94	2.44
1949	Wm. Younger	1.31	1.81
1939	Maclay	2.5	2
1951	Maclay	1.33	1.08
1939	Whitbread	1.23	1.13
1951	Whitbread	1.03	0.92
1939	Fuller	1.5	1.75
1958	Fuller	1.5	1.75

Sources:
William Younger brewing records documents WY/6/1/2/76 and WY/6/1/2/88 held at the Scottish Brewing Archive.
Maclay brewing records held at the Scottish Brewing Archive, document numbers M/6/1/1/4 and M/6/1/1/28.
Whitbread brewing records held at the London Metropolitan Archives, document numbers LMA/4453/D/01/107, LMA/4453/D/01/119, LMA/4453/D/09/126 and LMA/4453/D/09/131.
Fullers brewing records held at the brewery.

The same was also true, to some extent, of Maclay and Whitbread.

Fermentation

Nothing much had changed with William Younger's fermentation profiles. The y still kicked off in the low 60's F, rose to a peak of around 70º F on the second day, then fell to the high 50's F for the final part of the fermentation.

William Younger fermentations in 1949

Beer	OG	Pitch heat	day 1 AM	day 1 PM	day2 AM	day2 PM	day 3 AM	day 3 PM	day 4 AM	day 4 PM
Btlg XXP	1031	62° F	65° F	66.5° F	68° F	64.5° F	58° F	58° F	58.5° F	58° F
XXPs	1037	62° F	66° F	68° F	69° F	66° F	59° F	59° F	58° F	
3 Btlg	1047	61° F	68° F	70.5° F	64° F	60° F	58° F	58° F	58° F	

Source:
William Younger brewing record held at the Scottish Brewing Archive, document number WY/6/1/2/88.

At fellow Edinburgh brewer Drybrough, the profile looked quite different:

Drybrough fermentations in 1960

Beer	OG	Pitch heat	day 1 AM	day 1 PM	day2 AM	day2 PM	day 3 AM	day 3 PM	day 4 AM	day 4 PM	day 5 AM	day 5 PM
60/-	1031	61° F	62.5° F	63.5° F	64.5° F	65.5° F	66° F	66.5° F	67° F	67° F	66.5° F	
KH	1037	62° F	63.5° F	64° F	66.5° F	67.5° F	69° F	70° F	71° F	71.5° F	72° F	72.5° F
XXP	1042	62° F	63.5° F	64° F	66.5° F	68° F	69.5° F	70.5° F	71.5° F	72.5° F	73° F	74° F

Source:
Drybrough brewing record held at the Scottish Brewing Archive, document number D/6/1/1/8.

Rather than rising quickly at the start of the process then falling again quickly at Younger, at Drybrough the fermentation temperature rose slowly and continued to rise until the end.

At Robert Younger, also in Edinburgh, the fermentation looked different again:

Robert Younger fermentations in 1957										
		Pitch	day 1		day 2		day 3		day 4	
Beer	OG	heat	AM	PM	AM	PM	AM	PM	AM	PM
60/-	1030	60° F	61° F	61.5° F	64° F	64.5° F	59° F			
70/-	1035	60° F	61° F	63° F	65° F	66° F	63° F	59° F		
80/-	1043	60° F	61° F	63.5° F	65° F	67° F	68° F	65° F	62° F	
Source: Robert Younger brewing record held at the Scottish Brewing Archive, document number RY/6/1/2.										

Here the temperature rose slowly during the initial phases of fermentation, then fell again towards the end. The maximum temperature was considerably lower than at Drybrough and a few degrees cooler than at William Younger.

Comparing English and Scottish fermentation profiles presents one big difficulty: the English weren't so diligent in recording the details as the Scots.

Only a few English breweries could be arsed. Fullers in London, for example:

Fuller's fermentations in 1949										
		Pitch	day 1		day 2		day 3		day 4	
Beer	OG	heat	AM	PM	AM	PM	AM	PM	AM	PM
BO	1044	62° F	67° F	70° F	70° F	70° F	69° F	67° F	59° F	
X	1030	62° F	65° F	66.5° F	68° F	68° F	67.5° F	67.5° F	60° F	
SPA	1042	61° F	69° F	70° F	70° F	70° F	69° F	69° F	60° F	
Source: Fullers brewing record held at the brewery.										

The main difference with what was happening at William Younger is that the maximum temperature was held for longer at Fuller. The profile looks similar to Robert Younger, but with higher temperatures.

Comparing three beers of similar gravity from the four breweries makes everything clearer:

English and Scottish fermentations 1949 - 1960												
		Pitch	day 1		day 2		day 3		day 4		day 5	
Beer	OG	heat	AM	PM	AM	PM	AM	PM	AM	PM	AM	PM
Wm. Younger 3 Btlg	1047	61° F	68° F	70.5° F	64° F	60° F	58° F	58° F	58° F			
Fuller SPA	1042	61° F	69° F	70° F	70° F	70° F	69° F	69° F	60° F			
Drybrough XXP	1042	62° F	63.5° F	64° F	66.5° F	68° F	69.5° F	70.5° F	71.5° F	72.5° F	73° F	74°
Rbt. Younger 80/-	1043	60° F	61° F	63.5° F	65° F	67° F	68° F	65° F	62° F			
Sources :												
William Younger brewing record held at the Scottish Brewing Archive, document number WY/6/1/2/88.												
Fullers brewing record held at the brewery.												
Drybrough brewing record held at the Scottish Brewing Archive, document number D/6/1/1/8.												
Robert Younger brewing record held at the Scottish Brewing Archive, document number RY/6/1/2.												

All the fermentation profiles are different. Strangely, Robert Younger had not only the warmest fermentation but also the longest. It's difficult to see any particular pattern of differences between England and Scotland. More that each brewery fermented its own particular way.

William Younger and Robert Younger must have been actively cooling the wort with attemperators to achieve the profile that they did. While Drybrough appear to have just let the fermentation rip.

Dry hopping

Scottish brewers continued to dry hop certain types of beer. In particular Pale Ales, but also some beers in other styles such as Stout or Strong Ale.

In the early 1950's, Drybrough were still dry hopping at approximately the same rate – 4 oz. per barrel – as they had in WW I.

Drybrough dry hopping 1954 – 1960 (oz. per barrel)						
Year	B 60/-	60/-	XXP	B XXP	Export	Burns
1954	4.30	4.28	5.59		1.96	7.86
1960	0.00	2.99	4.06	2.73	0.98	1.55
Source: Drybrough brewing record held at the Scottish Brewing Archive, document number D/6/1/1/7.						

However, that had been considerably reduced by 1960, the drop in the strong Burns Ale being particularly drastic. Less than 2 oz. is a very small amount for a beer with an OG in the 1070's.

A similar fall in dry hopping rates was also occurring across Edinburgh at William Younger:

William Younger dry hopping 1939 - 1949 (oz. per barrel)								
Year	1	3 Btg	3 Pale	DBS Btlg	Pale XXPS	Ext	XXP Btlg	LAE
1939	2.25		2.08	3.05	2.92	2.09	2.02	4.16
1949	2.15	2.88	2.86	0.77	2.03	1.28	0	2.89
Source: William Younger brewing records held at the Scottish Brewing Archive, document numbers WY/6/1/2/76 and WY/6/1/2/88.								

Though over the period 1939 – 1949 some of the fall may be accounted for by a reduction in beer gravity. 1 and 3 were Strong Ales, DBS Btlg a Stout and the others are all Pale Ales. Dry hopping at less than an ounce per barrel seems pretty pointless.

Parti-gyling

William Younger excepted, Scottish brewers parti-gyled just about everything. It wasn't difficult with the narrow range of beers most produced. Three strengths of Pale Ale and a Strong Ale could easily be brewed from the same grist, in any required combination.

Stout was the only difficulty and brewers even managed to get around that. Either by adding all the darker materials to one of the worts in the parti-gyle or simply by adding coloured primings at racking time.

Colouring

Scottish brewers were masters of colouring beer to different shades with caramel. Producing multiple variations of the same beer.

In 1960, Scottish Brewers (William Younger and William McEwan) sold their draught beers in a variety of colour variations, some achieved through the recipe, others with caramel colour adjustments.

Scottish Brewers Draught Beer Colours							
Younger				McEwan			
XXPS (P. 70/-)		XXP (P. 60/-)		P. 70/-		P. 60/-	
Brewery shade	Tint.	Brewery shade	Tint.	Brewery shade	Tint.	Brewery shade	Tint.
C	21	C	21	2P	24	2P	24
F Shade *	25	F *	25			4D	56
J Shade *	26	J *	36			10D	88
		Q	47				
		V	77				
Source: A document at the Scottish Brewing Archive. Note: Colours as brewed unless marked with an *							

In the above table, only the ones marked with an asterisk were the result of caramel additions, while all of this wet were:

Scottish Brewers other shades beers were coloured to			
Shade	Tint.	Shade	Tint.
2 Pale	24	5 Dark	62
1 Pale	29	6 Dark	67
Standard	35	7 Dark	72
1 Dark	40	8 Dark	78
2 Dark	45	9 Dark	83
3 Dark	51	10 Dark	88
4 Dark	56		
Source: A document at the Scottish Brewing Archive.			

A note at the end of the document says "Every effort should be made to take beer as brewed." The colours are given in º L, which is approximately double EBC.

But Scottish Brewers were by no means the most extreme. At Jeffrey's Heriot Brewery around the same time things were really out of hand:

> "FJC [Jim Collinson] found that at Heriot they had gone much further, for be discovered they had no less than 117 different coloured beers, to meet the historical requirements of their free trade customers, and the help of memory men within the brewery was essential to ensure each customer got his variation; plus, of course, a massive amount of administration and manual labour. He set about reducing the colours to three - dark, light and twilight - and found to his considerable surprise that the brewery received not one complaint from the trade when it was done."

"The Brewing Industry 1950 - 1990", by Anthony Avis, 1997, page 73.

Totally and utterly crazy and, as it turns out, totally unnecessary.

Another Edinburgh brewer, T & J Bernard, coloured one of their beers, No. 3 quality, their equivalent of 60/-, to a wide range of different shades for different regions:

Bernard No. 3 quality draught beer colours	
place	tint
3 customers in Dundee & 1 in Aberdeen	25
Dundee	32
Edinburgh	32
Fife	58
Inverness	150
Borders	45
East Coast	45
Glasgow 25%	45
........50%	58
........12.5%	80
........12.5%	150
Newcastle	32
Source: A document in the Scottish Brewing Archive.	

That's a huge variation in colour, from pale amber to near black.

Styles

The number of different beers produced at UK breweries was reduced by WW II. In Scotland the effect was even more pronounced, with many breweries cutting back to a set of parti-gyled Pale Ales.

After WW II the terms 60/-, 70/- and 80/-, as well as the colloquial names Light, Heavy and Export, came into use. Before WW II Heavy had been used as a synonym for "strong" and had mostly been used to describe Strong Ales. In the same period Export was used much was after the war, that is to refer to a brewery's strongest Pale Ale.

Pale Ale

Over 90% of what was brewed in Scotland was some form of Pale Ale. Most brewers produced parti-gyled Pale Ales at three strengths, and sometimes spun a Strong Ale out of the same basic recipe. It's all pretty dull.

Most breweries produced three strengths of Pale Ale, usually parti-gyled from a single recipe, though that wasn't the case at William Younger, who had always preferred to brew most of their beers single-gyle.

Most Scottish breweries produced a range of three Pale Ales, often referred to as 60/-, 70/- and 80/- by the brewery and Light, Heavy and Export by drinkers. Robert Younger, a relatively small Edinburgh brewer, had a larger range than most, producing a total of five.

Robert Younger Pale Ales in 1957

Date	Year	Beer	OG	FG	ABV	App. Atten-uation	lbs hops/qtr	hops lb/brl
8th Aug	1957	54/-	1028	1010	2.38	64.29%	4.92	0.58
7th Aug	1957	60/-	1030	1011	2.51	63.33%	4.92	0.58
6th Aug	1957	70/-	1035	1011	3.18	68.57%	4.93	0.67
6th Aug	1957	80/-	1043	1012	4.10	72.09%	4.93	0.83
7th Aug	1957	Ex	1045	1012	4.37	73.33%	4.92	0.87

Source:
Robert Younger brewing record held at the Scottish Brewing Archive, document number RY/6/1/2.

Note that, in typically Scottish fashion, there's almost no difference between the FGs of the different strength beers. The hopping is very light, especially for Pale ales. As can be seen by a comparison with Whitbread's Ales from the same year:

Whitbread's Ales in 1957

Date	Beer	Style	OG	FG	ABV	App. Atten-uation	lbs hops/qtr	hops lb/brl
11th Jan	Best Ale	Mild	1030.4	1010.0	2.70	67.11%	5.56	0.71
31st Jan	FB	Brown Ale	1033.9	1007.0	3.56	79.35%	5.27	0.74
7th Jan	IPA	IPA	1035.8	1006.5	3.88	81.84%	8.53	1.26
14th Feb	PA	Pale Ale	1039.6	1008.5	4.11	78.54%	5.59	0.93

Source:
Whitbread brewing record held at the London Metropolitan Archives document number LMA/4453/D/01/124.

Robert Younger's Pale Ales were hopped at a lower rate than even Whitbread's Mild and Brown Ales.

At Whitbread Best Ale, IPA and PA filled the same gravity slots as Robert Younger 60/-, 70/- and 80/-. Which demonstrates that, while 60/- wasn't technically speaking a Mild Ale, it played the same role as it in Scotland.

Drybrough's Pale Ales look very similar to Robert Younger's:

Drybrough Pale Ales 1954 - 1960							
Year	Beer	OG	FG	ABV	App. Atten- uation	lbs hops/ qtr	hops lb/brl
1954	B 60/-	1031.0	1011.0	2.65	64.52%	4.48	0.57
1954	60/-	1032.0	1011.0	2.78	65.63%	4.42	0.57
1954	XXP	1043.0	1011.5	4.17	73.26%	4.42	0.79
1954	Export	1045.0	1013.5	4.17	70.00%	4.48	0.83
1960	B 60/-	1030.0	1012.0	2.38	60.00%	4.48	0.56
1960	60/-	1031.0	1012.0	2.51	61.29%	4.51	0.58
1960	B XXP	1037.0	1014.0	3.04	62.16%	4.49	0.69
1960	KH	1037.0	1014.0	3.04	62.16%	4.49	0.63
1960	XXP	1042.0	1014.0	3.70	66.67%	4.51	0.73
1960	Export	1044.0	1015.0	3.84	65.91%	4.48	0.82
Source: Drybrough brewing record held at the Scottish Brewing Archive, document number D/6/1/1/7.							

A slightly worse rate of attenuation, but filling similar gravity slots and with a similar level of hopping. You'll see that the names for the different strengths weren't identical at Robert Younger and Drybrough. Both called the strongest Export and the one around 1030º 60/-. But the middle beer was 70/- at Robert Younger and KH – Keg Heavy – at Drybrough.

Here are even more dull Pale Ales from the 1950's:

Bernard Pale Ales in 1958							
Year	Beer	OG	FG	ABV	App. Atten- uation	lbs hops/ qtr	hops lb/brl
1958	Pale 1/1	1031.0	1011.5	2.58	62.90%	3.47	0.46
1958	Pale 1/2	1036.0	1011.5	3.24	68.06%	3.47	0.54
1958	Sp Ext	1043.0	1012.0	4.10	72.09%	3.47	0.55
Source: Bernard brewing record held at the London Metropolitan Archives, document number TJB/6/1/1.							

1/1 and 1/2 are, again, names derived from prices. 13d and 14d, obviously the retail price per pint. Those crazy Scots, eh? The beers fit into the gravity slots we've seen elsewhere. The three standard strengths of draught beer found throughout the UK.

With fewer than 4 lbs of hops per quarter of malt, these are the most lightly hopped Pale Ales we've seen yet.

Compared to earlier Scottish Pale Ales, the use of black malt, presumably for colour, jumps out in these grists:

Drybrough Pale Ale grists 1954 - 1960

Year	Beer	OG	pale malt	black malt	enzymic malt	flaked maize	flaked barley	malt extract	sugar
1954	B 60/-	1031.0	75.87%	2.30%	0.38%	5.75%	5.75%	0.77%	9.20%
1954	60/-	1032.0	76.37%	2.31%	0.48%	5.79%	5.79%	0.77%	8.49%
1954	XXP	1043.0	72.76%	2.60%	0.39%	6.50%	6.50%	0.87%	10.39%
1954	Export	1045.0	75.87%	2.30%	0.38%	5.75%	5.75%	0.77%	9.20%
1960	B 60/-	1030.0	74.81%	0.75%	0.30%	12.07%		0.80%	11.26%
1960	60/-	1031.0	75.53%	0.12%	0.50%	11.93%			11.93%
1960	B XXP	1037.0	74.82%	0.63%		12.86%		0.78%	10.91%
1960	KH	1037.0	74.82%	0.63%		12.86%		0.78%	10.91%
1960	XXP	1042.0	75.53%	0.12%	0.50%	11.93%			11.93%
1960	Export	1044.0	74.81%	0.75%	0.30%	12.07%		0.80%	11.26%

Source:
Drybrough brewing record held at the Scottish Brewing Archive, document number D/6/1/1/7.

Throwing in a bit of enzymic malt and malt extract is very 1950's. Not sure why it was so popular other than fashion. Otherwise, there's the classic mix of around 75% malt and 25% adjunct/sugar. It's almost as if it were a law.

Robert Younger's grists were somewhat simpler:

Robert Younger Pale Ale grists in 1957

Year	Beer	OG	pale malt	flaked maize	other sugar	malt extract	caramel
1957	54/-	1028	73.73%	16.38%	8.74%	1.09%	0.06%
1957	60/-	1030	73.73%	16.38%	8.74%	1.09%	0.06%
1957	70/-	1035	75.69%	14.56%	8.73%	0.97%	0.05%
1957	80/-	1043	75.69%	14.56%	8.73%	0.97%	0.05%
1957	Ex	1045	73.73%	16.38%	8.74%	1.09%	0.06%

Source:
Robert Younger brewing record held at the Scottish Brewing Archive, document number RY/6/1/2.

The pale malt content was pretty similar, but, while Drybrough used similar amounts of sugar and flaked maize, Robert Younger used far more maize than sugar. Both beers contain some malt extract, something which was common both sides of the border after WW I. I'm not totally sure of its purpose, but I suspect it's for extra enzymes.

Whitbread's grists look very different:

Whitbread's Ales in 1957

Date	Beer	Style	OG	PA malt	mild malt	crystal malt	sugar
31st Jan	FB	Brown Ale	1033.9		78.97%	7.18%	13.85%
7th Jan	IPA	IPA	1035.8	83.33%		5.56%	11.11%
11th Jan	Best Ale	Mild	1030.4		79.44%	6.27%	14.29%
14th Feb	PA	Pale Ale	1039.6	75.47%		5.66%	18.87%

Source:
Whitbread brewing record held at the London Metropolitan Archives document number LMA/4453/D/01/124.

For a start, Whitbread didn't use the same base malt in all their beers. The Pale Ales, logically enough, contained PA malt, while Mild and Brown Ale had mild malt. PA malt was a pale malt of the highest quality. Whereas mild malt was made from slightly lower quality barley and kilned slightly darker.

Highly significant is the complete lack of crystal malt in the Scottish Pale Ales. Crystal malt was originally designed in the 19th century for use in Mild Ales. Before WW I its use was almost totally limited to Mild and Stout. Whitbread themselves didn't include any in their Pale Ale grists until 1929[63].

The other big difference with Whitbread's grists is the use of adjuncts. Though Whitbread was atypical in avoiding their use.

Despite the different names, both Drybrough and Robert Younger were brewing beers that fitted very much in with those down in England in terms of gravity. 60/- filling in for Mild, while 70/- (Heavy) and Export imitated Ordinary and Best Bitter. Before 1914, English and Scottish beers didn't match up quite so well on gravity.

One of the weird effects of WW I was a much greater standardisation of beer strengths. Probably because of the price controls in effect between 1917 and 1921. They linked gravity and price in a way that was cemented for the whole interwar period, more or less. The old regional differences in beer strengths mostly disappeared.

Which is clear when you look at Maclay's beers:

---

[63] Whitbread brewing record held at the London Metropolitan Archives document number LMA/4453/D/01/92.

Maclay Pale Ale 1951 - 1971

Year	Beer	OG	FG	ABV	App. Attenuation	lbs hops/qtr	hops lb/brl
1951	PA 6d	1030	1011	2.51	63.33%	5.33	0.67
1951	SPA	1037	1015	2.91	59.46%	5.26	0.87
1951	Export	1042	1016	3.44	61.90%	5.33	0.93
1956	PA 6d	1030	1010	2.65	66.67%	6.00	0.77
1956	SPA	1035	1011	3.18	68.57%	6.49	0.98
1956	Exp	1040	1012	3.70	70.00%	6.49	1.12
1965	PA 6d	1030	1012	2.38	60.00%	6.05	0.74
1965	SPA	1035	1012	3.04	65.71%	6.05	0.88
1965	Exp	1040	1013	3.57	67.50%	6.05	1.00
1971	PA 6d	1030	1008	2.91	73.33%	5.08	0.64
1971	SPA	1035	1009	3.44	74.29%	5.08	0.75
1971	Exp	1040	1010	3.97	75.00%	5.08	0.86

Source: Maclay brewing records held at the Scottish Brewing Archive, document numbers M/6/1/1/28, M/6/1/1/35, M/6/1/1/44 and M/6/1/1/46.

Another three different strength Pale Ales of similar gravities. And, like the previous Drybrough and Robert Younger examples, all parti-gyled together.

You might imagine that parti-gyled beers would all taste pretty similar. I suggest comparing Fuller's London Pride, ESB and Golden Pride. All parti-gyled, but by no means identical. Having drunk all three of Maclay's Pale Ales, I know that they were just as different. Especially after colouring up with caramel. I'd have sworn their 60/- (PA 6d) was a Dark Mild.

Maclay employed typical, if rather dull, Scottish grists:

Maclay Pale Ale 1951 - 1971

Year	Beer	OG	pale malt	flaked maize	no. 1 sugar	malt extract	caramel	DCS sugar
1951	PA 6d	1030	91.14%		5.79%		0.18%	2.89%
1951	SPA	1037	94.12%		5.88%			
1951	Export	1042	91.14%		5.79%		0.18%	2.89%
1956	PA 6d	1030	74.82%	11.51%	7.67%	1.92%	0.24%	3.84%
1956	SPA	1035	74.91%	11.52%	7.68%	1.92%	0.12%	3.84%
1956	Exp	1040	74.91%	11.52%	7.68%	1.92%	0.12%	3.84%
1965	PA 6d	1030	74.82%	11.51%	7.67%	1.92%	0.24%	3.84%
1965	SPA	1035	75.00%	11.54%	7.69%	1.92%		3.85%
1965	Exp	1040	75.00%	11.54%	7.69%	1.92%		3.85%
1971	PA 6d	1030	79.18%	11.31%	5.66%	1.89%	0.08%	1.89%
1971	SPA	1035	79.21%	11.32%	5.66%	1.89%	0.05%	1.89%
1971	Exp	1040	79.21%	11.32%	5.66%	1.89%	0.05%	1.89%

Source: Maclay brewing records held at the Scottish Brewing Archive, document numbers M/6/1/1/28, M/6/1/1/35, M/6/1/1/44 and M/6/1/1/46.

Maclay's are some of the dullest brewing records I've seen. For most of the post-war period they brewed just three different strength Pale Ales, all parti-gyled together. And used the same one recipe for decades on end. It must have been dead exciting working as a brewer there.

Scottish Pale Ale turns sweet

Around WW I the hopping rate of William Younger's beers plummeted. There was another big drop in the 1930's. The result was Pale Ales with the very the low levels of bitterness that is associated with Scotland today. For this table I've used brewing software to calculate the IBU level. I wouldn't take the numbers as gospel, but they do give a good indication of the trend.

William Younger Pale Ale bitterness 1851 - 1949			
Year	Beer	OG	IBU
1851	XP	1058	180
1851	XXP	1072	217
1858	Ex Pale Ale	1063	142
1868	XP	1051	73
1868	XXP	1052	73
1879	XP	1052	99
1879	2XP	1046	76
1885	XP	1054	100
1885	XP Scotch	1055	87
1898	XP Scotch	1053	80
1913	LAE	1045	78
1914	SLE	1055	83
1921	XXPS	1046	36
1933	XXP	1043	34
1933	Expt	1054	53
1933	XXPS	1049	33
1039	XXPS	1046	13
1940	XP Btlg	1033	18
1949	XXP Btlg	1031	14
1949	XXPS	1037	21
1949	XXP	1031.5	19
Sources			
William Younger brewing records held at the Scottish Brewing Archive, document numbers WY/6/1/2/3, WY/6/1/2/28, WY/6/1/2/31, WY/6/1/2/45, WY/6/1/2/58, WY/6/1/2/63, WY/6/1/2/70, WY/6/1/2/76 and WY/6/1/2/88.			

In a century, XXP went from over 200 IBUs to just 19, while the gravity more than halved. It just show the changes time can wreak on a beer.

Mild Ale

True Mild Ale had disappeared, but weak Pale Ale coloured up with caramel in the form of 60/- was able to perform a passable imitation. Though even in England, as the popularity of Mild began to plummet, some brewers simply started colouring their Ordinary Bitter with caramel at racking time to "create" a Mild.

Scottish Brewers marketed a beer called Tartan Mild, but this seems to have been exclusively for the market in England where, before 1970, there was still a strong demand for Mild.

William Younger Milds – Tartan Mild and its predecessors – look suspiciously similar to Younger's weakest Pale Ale, XXP. Though I know from their brewing records that they were brewed as separate recipes.

Scottish Mild Ales 1939 - 1972							
Year	Brewer	Beer	OG	FG	ABV	App. Atten-uation	colour
1939	Murray	Light Ale	1035.8	1008.7	3.52	75.70%	42
1939	Younger, Geo.	Light Ale	1033.6	1005.8	3.61	82.74%	44
1939	Wm. Younger	Light Ale	1030.6	1004.5	3.39	85.29%	160
1951	Wm. Younger	X	1029.98				72
1952	Wm. Younger	X	1031.23				80
1952	Wm. Younger	X	1033.48				92
1953	Wm. Younger	X	1033.31				82
1955	Wm. Younger	X	1030.24				96
1961	Wm. Younger	Mild	1029.2	1004.5	3.21	84.59%	75
1972	Wm. Younger	Tartan Mild	1029.6	1008	2.80	72.97%	
Sources: Whitbread Gravity book held at the London Metropolitan Archives, document number LMA/4453/D/02/001. Whitbread Gravity book held at the London Metropolitan Archives, document number LMA/4453/D/02/002. Truman Gravity Book document B/THB/C/252 held at the London Metropolitan Archives. Daily Mirror July 10th 1972, page 15							

Younger XXP had an OG of 1031º in 1949[64] and 1030.4º in 1959[65]. I rest my case. I'd be 100% certain, if it weren't William Younger, who did all sorts of odd things and brewed loads of stuff single-gyle.

Younger's post-war Mild looks much like most English Mild of the period: 1030-1034º, 3% ABV, dark.

---

[64] William Younger brewing record held at the Scottish Brewing Archive, document number WY/6/1/2/88.
[65] Whitbread Gravity book held at the London Metropolitan Archives, document number LMA/4453/D/02/002.

London Mild Ale 1939 - 1960

Year	Brewer	Beer	OG	FG	ABV	App. Attenuation	colour
1939	Barclay Perkins	X	1037.9	1009	3.75	76.25%	90
1939	Charrington	X	1035.9	1011.7	3.13	67.41%	95
1939	Courage	X	1035.4	1012	3.03	66.10%	85
1939	Whitbread	X	1038.2	1013	3.26	65.97%	90
1948	Barclay Perkins	XX	1031.4	1009.4	2.85	70.06%	90
1949	Charrington	MA	1029.4	1010.3	2.47	64.97%	130
1949	Courage	MA	1028.3	1008.2	2.60	71.02%	95
1949	Whitbread	Best Ale	1032.5	1009	3.04	72.31%	100
1957	Barclay Perkins	XX	1031.4	1005.8	3.33	81.53%	100
1957	Charrington	Mild Ale	1032.6	1007.4	3.27	77.30%	110
1957	Courage	Mild Ale	1032.5	1006.4	3.39	80.31%	115
1957	Whitbread	Best Ale	1032.4	1011.4	2.71	64.81%	95
1960	Whitbread	Mild	1031.4	1011.3	2.60	64.01%	

Sources:
Whitbread Gravity book held at the London Metropolitan Archives, document number LMA/4453/D/02/002.
Which Beer Report, 1960, pages 171 - 173.

London Mild was a little darker, for the most part, than Scottish versions. Once again, Scottish examples are showing a greater variation in colour than London ones. The explanation might be that London Milds were mostly being drunk in one market: London. Of course they'd be generally similar. As the Scots coloured their beer differently for different markets, what colour they were would depend on where you collected the sample.

Brown Ale

Just as down south in Sassenachland, Brown Ale was extremely popular in Scotland after WW I. Though the beers sold under that name don't appear to have been exactly the same.

With a couple of exceptions, mostly in the Northeast, English Brown Ales were watery after WW II. While before the war they'd been about average gravity (low 1040's), they were at the bottom end after it. Which meant an OG Of 1027-1032º and ABV as low as 2.5%.

Some of the examples in the table clearly fall into that category. Though there are also ones in the mid-1040's or even 1050's. Much stronger than most English Brown Ales of the period

Scottish Brown Ales 1947 - 1958							
Year	Brewer	Beer	OG	FG	ABV	App. Attenuation	colour
1947	Steel Coulson	Brown Ale	1028.5	1005	3.05	82.46%	
1949	McEwan	Nut Brown Ale	1029.5	1006	3.05	79.66%	
1949	Murray	Brown Ale	1037.8	1010	3.60	73.54%	115
1949	Wm. Younger	Brown Ale	1033.6	1011.2	2.90	66.67%	115
1949	Wm. Younger	Brown Ale	1033	1014	2.45	57.58%	
1950	Calder	Nut Brown Ale	1034.3	1011.4	2.96	66.76%	70
1950	Murray	Brown Ale	1057.1	1013.4	5.69	76.53%	83
1950	Wm. Younger	Brown Ale	1032.6	1011.4	2.74	65.03%	180
1953	Steel Coulson	Brown Ale B. 60/-	1030				
1954	Wm. Younger	Double Century Ale	1056.6	1023.3	4.29	58.83%	80
1956	Aitchison	Gold Seal Brown Ale	1041.6	1013.9	3.58	66.59%	50
1956	Wm. Younger	"Wee Willie" Brown Ale	1033.5	1009.6	3.10	71.34%	70
1956	Wm. Younger	Edinburgh Brown Ale	1046.8	1013.2	4.36	71.79%	75
1957	Ushers	Brown Export Ale	1044.4	1017.3	3.50	61.04%	130
1957	Wm. Younger	Edinburgh Brown Ale	1046.6	1013.1	4.34	71.89%	55
1958	Bernard	Double Brown Ale (D.B. Ale)	1043	1013	3.89	69.77%	
1958	Blair	Brown Ale	1034.1	1011.7	2.80	65.69%	125

Sources:
Whitbread Gravity book held at the London Metropolitan Archives, document number LMA/4453/D/02/002.
Thomas Usher Gravity Book document TU/6/11 held at the Scottish Brewing Archive.
T & J Bernard's brewing records held at the Scottish Brewing Archive
document from the Steel Coulson archive held at the Scottish Brewing Archives

The weaker versions I'm sure are the brewery's lowest-strength Pale Ale caramelled up. The ones in the 1040's, same thing, just with Export. Not sure about those over 1050º.

Down in London, Brown Ales were far weaker on average. In the late 1940's, most hovered either side of 1030º.

London Brown Ales 1947 - 1956							
Year	Brewer	Beer	OG	FG	ABV	App. Attenuation	colour
1947	Barclay Perkins	Doctor Brown Ale	1030.7	1006.6	3.13	78.50%	95
1947	Beasley	Brown Ale	1029	1009.3	2.55	67.93%	85
1947	Charrington	Brown Ale	1028.9	1011	2.31	61.94%	90
1947	Hammerton	Nut Brown Ale	1027.6	1003.9	3.08	85.87%	80
1947	Mann Crossman	Brown Ale	1033.6	1008.4	3.27	75.00%	83
1947	Taylor Walker	Brown Ale	1030.3	1007.3	2.98	75.91%	85
1947	Truman	Trubrown	1032.7	1006.7	3.38	79.51%	95
1947	Watney	Brown Ale	1028.3	1010.3	2.33	63.60%	90
1947	Whitbread	Double Brown	1043	1010.1	4.27	76.51%	100
1947	Whitbread	Forest Brown	1028.9	1006.5	2.91	77.51%	83
1956	Barclay Perkins	Doctor Brown Ale	1032.9	1009.9	2.98	69.91%	100
1956	Charrington	Brown Ale	1032.1	1009.4	2.94	70.72%	110
1956	Courage	Nut Brown Ale	1032.2	1011.9	2.62	63.04%	100
1956	Fullers	Brown Ale	1031.7	1009.4	2.89	70.35%	90
1956	Mann Crossman	Brown Ale	1035.5	1013.2	2.88	62.82%	115
1956	Meux	Nut Brown Ale	1030.9	1012.6	2.36	59.22%	120
1956	Taylor Walker	Nut Brown Ale	1032.4	1009.9	2.91	69.44%	95
1956	Truman	Trubrown	1034.9	1016.5	2.37	52.72%	95
1956	Watney	Brown Ale	1032.2	1011.1	2.73	65.53%	120
1954	Whitbread	Forest Brown	1034.8	1012.2	2.92	64.94%	95

Source:
Whitbread Gravity book held at the London Metropolitan Archives, document number LMA/4453/D/02/002.

There's only a single beer over 1040º, Whitbread Double Brown, which was discontinued in the mid-1950's. Though the average colour of both the English and Scottish example is 96º EBC, the four palest are all Scottish. As are the two darkest, meaning the Scottish Brown Ales have a wider diversity in colour.

Shilling Ales

A new set of Shilling Ales, completely unconnected with those of the 19th century, emerged after WW II. 60/-, 70/- and 80/- filled the same roles as Mild Ale, Ordinary Bitter and Best Bitter in England, though all were really types of Pale Ale.

Though there is one example of a 200/- Ale from William Younger in 1949. It really was the last hurrah for this venerable style.

With its massive OG, I can only conclude that 200/- Ale was intended for export:

William Younger 200/- Ale in 1949							
Year	Beer	OG	FG	ABV	App. Atten-uation	lbs hops/ qtr	hops lb/brl
1949	200/-	1099	1028	9.39	71.72%	7.37	2.62
Source: William Younger brewing record held at the Scottish Brewing Archive, document number WY/6/1/2/88.							

It was an extremely powerful beer for the period. I'm racking my brains to think of any English beer that at that time was vaguely similar.

The grist for 200/- is quite simple:

William Younger 200/- Ale in 1949						
Year	Beer	OG	pale malt	crystal malt	mild malt	flaked maize	sugar
1949	200/-	1099	71.19%	2.54%	2.54%	20.34%	3.39%
Source: William Younger brewing record held at the Scottish Brewing Archive, document number WY/6/1/2/88.						

A consistent theme at William Younger in the 20th century was their sparing use of sugar and their enthusiasm for unmalted grain. 10% flaked maize is rather on the high side. Still, it's better than having the grist almost half grits.

Stout

Most Scottish Stouts that survived WW II were of the sweet type. Though the style in general was getting thin on the ground. Brewers rarely brewed more than one. And sometimes not even that. Though they may have labelled one of their beers "Stout".

The way some brewers made Stout was, to say the least unconventional. No Stout appears in Drybrough's brewing records, but they did market one. It appears to have been created from their weakest Pale Ale, presumably by the addition of sugar and caramel after primary fermentation. Lovely.

Scottish Stout 1939 - 1966

Year	Brewer	Beer	OG	FG	ABV	App. Attenuation	lbs hops/ qtr	hops lb/brl
1939	Younger, Wm	DBS Btlg	1066	1023	5.69	65.15%	6.06	1.59
1949	Younger, Wm	Btlg DBS	1046	1019	3.57	58.70%	6.30	1.16
1957	Younger, Robert	SS	1030	1014.5	2.05	51.67%	4.34	0.57
1966	Maclay	OMS	1035	1012	3.04	65.71%	4.10	0.75
1958	Bernard	Stout	1040	1009.5	4.03	76.25%	2.63	0.48

Sources:
William Younger brewing records held at the Scottish Brewing Archive, document numbers WY/6/1/2/76 and WY/6/1/2/88.
Robert Younger brewing record held at the Scottish Brewing Archive, document number RY/6/1/2.
Maclay brewing record held at the Scottish Brewing Archive, document number M/6/1/1/44.
Bernard brewing record held at the Scottish Brewing Archive, document number TJB 6/1/1/1.

William Younger's DBS continues to look pretty much like a Stout in terms of hopping. And does at least try with attenuation. Bernard's is a bizarre one. Reasonably attenuated, but with minimal hopping. When we get onto the grists you'll see just how atypical its flavour profile must have been.

To say that Scottish Stout grists were diverse is something of an understatement.

Scottish Stout grists 1939 - 1966

Year	1939	1949	1957	1966	1958
Brewer	Younger, Wm.	Younger, Wm.	Younger, Robert	Maclay	Bernard
Beer	DBS Btlg	Btlg DBS	SS	OMS	Stout
OG	1066	1046	1030	1035	1040
pale malt	63.83%	56.25%	76.43%	43.84%	71.32%
black malt	3.19%		0.68%	8.22%	13.18%
crystal malt	3.19%	4.69%			
mild malt		4.69%			
flaked maize			13.65%		3.10%
grits	19.15%				
roast barley		9.38%			
flaked barley		9.38%			
malted oats				32.88%	
malt extract			0.91%		
no. 3 sugar					4.13%
caramel	4.26%	3.13%	0.15%	0.46%	
lactose	3.38%	12.50%			
other sugar			8.19%	14.61%	8.27%

Sources:
William Younger brewing records held at the Scottish Brewing Archive, document numbers WY/6/1/2/76 and WY/6/1/2/88.
Robert Younger brewing record held at the Scottish Brewing Archive, document number RY/6/1/2.
Maclay brewing record held at the Scottish Brewing Archive, document number M/6/1/1/44.
Bernard brewing record held at the Scottish Brewing Archive, document number TJB 6/1/1/1.

Other than pale malt, there's no ingredient common to all these Stouts, not even black malt.

William Younger were probably forced to drop grits during WW II because of supply problems. Flaked barley was the adjunct preferred by the government because it could be grown in the UK. Their 1949 Btlg DBS is a rum bugger, with almost 10% roast barley and 12.5 lactose. It must have resulted in a beer that was both very roasty and sweet. The 1939 version also contained liquorice.

The only one of these beers to look even vaguely normal is Bernard's Stout. And even that contains way in excess of 10% black malt. While Robert Younger's SS has almost no roast in the grist. The Stout character presumably deriving from proprietary sugars and caramel. Maclay OMS, on the other hand, is one third malted oats, an insanely high percentage.

London Stout 1939 - 1964								
Year	Brewer	Beer	OG	FG	ABV	App. Atten-uation	lbs hops/ qtr	hops lb/brl
1946	Barclay Perkins	IBS (Scot.)	1043.8	1019.5	3.21	55.48%	7.53	1.54
1946	Barclay Perkins	BS	1037.6	1014.8	3.02	60.77%	7.50	1.21
1946	Barclay Perkins	LS	1029.4	1010.0	2.57	65.99%	7.50	0.94
1947	Barclay Perkins	VS	1034.4	1014.0	2.70	59.30%	5.83	1.41
1939	Whitbread	ES	1055.4	1017.0	5.08	69.31%	6.93	1.62
1939	Whitbread	P	1029.9	1009.0	2.76	69.90%	6.89	0.85
1939	Whitbread	LS	1045.5	1013.0	4.30	71.43%	6.89	1.29
1939	Whitbread	LOS	1045.5	1013.0	4.30	71.43%	6.89	1.29
1939	Whitbread	MS	1051.4	1015.0	4.82	70.82%	6.89	1.46
1949	Whitbread	MS	1041.3	1015.0	3.48	63.68%	6.66	1.15
1949	Whitbread	ES	1055.1	1018.0	4.91	67.33%	6.66	1.54
1949	Whitbread	WS	1037.4	1013.5	3.16	63.90%	8.30	1.34
1956	Whitbread	MS	1042.4	1013.5	3.82	68.16%	5.54	0.98
1956	Whitbread	ES	1055.4	1016.0	5.21	71.12%	5.54	1.29
1956	Whitbread	WOS	1038.8	1013.5	3.35	65.21%	8.58	1.43
1964	Whitbread	WOS	1037.2	1008.8	3.76	76.34%	8.84	1.39
1964	Whitbread	MS	1041.4	1010.5	4.09	74.64%	5.78	1.01
1964	Whitbread	ES	1055.6	1013.5	5.57	75.72%	5.78	1.35

Sources:
Barclay Perkins brewing record held at the London Metropolitan Archives, document number ACC/2305/01/627.
Whitbread brewing records held at the London Metropolitan Archives, document numbers LMA/4453/D/09/126, LMA/4453/D/09/130, LMA/4453/D/09/134 and LMA/4453/D/09/138.

Among the Whitbread beers, MS is Mackeson, ES is Extra Stout, LS London Stout and WS is Whitbread Stout. The O in the middle of some indicates an oatmeal version. For Barclay Perkins, IBS = Imperial Stout, BS = Brown Stout, LS = London Stout and VS = Victory Stout.

After WW II, London Stouts were pretty weak for the most part. Whitbread Extra Stout, brewed for the Belgian market is one example of a stronger version. As was the full-strength version of Barclay Perkins Imperial Stout, which returned in the 1950's.

The hopping rate of the London beers, 6 to 8 lbs per quarter of malt, is significantly greater than all the Scottish examples, save those of William Younger.

Though not quite as crazy as in Scotland, Whitbread's grists contained a large number of different ingredients:

Whitbread Stout grists 1939 - 1964

Year	Beer	OG	pale malt	mild malt	brown malt	choc. Malt	oats	malted oats	no. 3 sugar	other sugar
1939	ES	1055.4	59.69%	10.99%	7.85%	7.85%	1.57%		8.38%	3.66%
1939	P	1029.9	71.47%		7.85%	7.85%	0.79%		8.38%	3.66%
1939	LS	1045.5	71.47%		7.85%	7.85%	0.79%		8.38%	3.66%
1939	LOS	1045.5	71.47%		7.85%	7.85%	0.79%		8.38%	3.66%
1939	MS	1051.4	71.47%		7.85%	7.85%	0.79%		8.38%	3.66%
1949	MS	1041.3		75.42%	7.63%	8.47%			4.52%	3.95%
1949	ES	1055.1		75.42%	7.63%	8.47%			4.52%	3.95%
1949	WS	1037.4		73.58%	5.66%	8.49%		0.94%	7.55%	3.77%
1956	MS	1042.4		73.45%	7.43%	8.25%			8.25%	2.61%
1956	ES	1055.4		73.45%	7.43%	8.25%			8.25%	2.61%
1956	WOS	1038.8		68.52%	7.41%	8.33%		4.63%	8.64%	2.47%
1964	WOS	1037.2		75.08%	9.23%	9.23%			4.31%	2.15%
1964	MS	1041.4		77.98%	7.57%	8.41%			3.37%	2.66%
1964	ES	1055.6		77.98%	7.57%	8.41%			3.37%	2.66%

Sources:
Whitbread brewing records held at the London Metropolitan Archives, document numbers LMA/4453/D/09/126, LMA/4453/D/09/130, LMA/4453/D/09/134 and LMA/4453/D/09/138.

Missing from the Mackeson (MS) grist is the lactose which was only added after the end of primary fermentation. After WW II lactose was a common ingredient in Stouts throughout the UK as the market for Sweet Stout increased.

The tiny percentage of oats used by Whitbread was typical of London Oatmeal Stouts. The quantity seems to be a token one, presumably so they could throw the word "oatmeal" on the label without any legal repercussions. Quite a contrast with the massive percentage of oats in Maclay's Stout.

London brewers remained very loyal to brown malt, using it in their Stouts until the bitter end. Whitbread combined it with chocolate malt rather than the black malt or roast barley you might expect. After the war Whitbread changed from pale malt to mild malt as a base for their Stouts, presumably on cost grounds.

In the 20th century London brewers employed four different base malts: standard pale malt, PA (Pale Ale) malt, mild malt and SA (Strong/Stock Ale) malt. I've never come across anything other than pale malt as a base in Scotland.

Barclay Perkins used all four base malts in their Stouts:

Barclay Perkins Stout grists 1946 - 1947

Year	Beer	OG	mild malt	SA malt	PA malt	brown malt	amber malt	crystal malt	roast barley	no. 3 sugar	caramel
1946	IBS (Scot.)	1043.8		32.14%	32.14%	10.71%	10.71%		7.14%	7.14%	4.46%
1946	BS	1037.6		60.83%		11.06%	5.53%	6.91%	8.29%	7.37%	4.84%
1946	LS	1029.4		60.83%		11.06%	5.53%	6.91%	8.29%	7.37%	4.84%
1947	VS	1034.4	9.74%	31.17%		11.69%	6.82%	6.82%	9.09%	24.68%	4.55%

Sources:
Barclay Perkins brewing record held at the London Metropolitan Archives, document number ACC/2305/01/627.

Not only did Barclay Perkins stick with brown malt, they also continued to use amber malt in their Stouts. This type of malt had been fairly common in Stouts in the 19th century but had gradually fallen out of favour. They were an exception in using roast barley rather than black malt. Most English breweries continued to use the latter.

Stout in Scotland

Below are some examples of Sweet Stouts, in some cases ludicrously sweet:

Scottish Sweet Stout 1947 - 1967

Year	Brewer	Beer	OG	FG	ABV	App. Atten-uation	colour
1955	Younger, Geo.	Sweetheart Stout	1036.4	1024.5	1.52	32.69%	225
1967	Tennent	Sweetheart Stout	1035.7	1024	1.46	32.77%	280
1959	Younger, Geo.	Sweetheart Stout	1036.4	1024.4	1.53	32.97%	275
1956	Younger, Geo	Sweetheart Stout	1037.6	1024.6	1.66	34.57%	225
1967	Campbell, Hope & King	Sweet Stout	1036	1023	1.63	36.11%	250
1964	Tennent	Sweet Stout	1032.7	1019.9	1.60	39.14%	425
1947	Tennent	Stout	1030.7	1018.18	1.61	40.78%	1 + 11.5
1959	Aitchison & Co	Dalkeith Sweet Stout	1037.3	1021.3	2.05	42.90%	600
1959	Aitken	Stout	1039.4	1022.3	2.19	43.40%	250
1961	Aitken	Stout (no lactose)	1038.9	1022	2.11	43.44%	275
1961	Tennent	Stout (no lactose)	1033.6	1019	1.82	43.45%	300
1955	Tennent	Stout	1034.7	1019.3	1.98	44.38%	325
1949	Tennent	Stout	1032	1017.5	1.86	45.31%	
1951	Younger, Wm. & Co	Sweet Stout	1035.7	1019.5	2.08	45.38%	150
1954	Jeffrey & Co	Nourishing Stout	1036.1	1019.3	2.16	46.54%	250
1954	McEwan	Sweet Stout	1036.1	1019.3	2.16	46.54%	350
1954	McLennan & Urquhart	Dalkeith Stout	1037.1	1019.7	2.23	46.90%	450
1949	Tennent	Stout	1034.9	1018.3	2.13	47.56%	200
1949	Aitken	Stout	1038.5	1020	2.38	48.05%	
1948	Tennent	Stout	1030	1015.5	1.86	48.33%	
1961	Dudgeon & Co.	Milk Stout (lactose)	1048.4	1025	2.93	48.35%	374
1959	Younger, R	Sweet Stout	1035.5	1018.3	2.21	48.45%	250

Scottish Sweet Stout 1947 - 1967

Year	Brewer	Beer	OG	FG	ABV	App. Attenuation	colour
1967	Tennent	Sweet Stout	1033.2	1017.1	2.01	48.49%	280
1954	Aitken	A Stout	1041.4	1021.2	2.59	48.79%	375
1959	Calders	Scotch Stout	1042.2	1021.5	2.66	49.05%	300
1953	Dudgeon & Co	Bellhaven Heavy Stout	1059	1029.6	3.77	49.83%	300
1955	Younger, Wm. & Co	Sweet Stout	1034.9	1017.5	2.24	49.86%	200
1966	Tennent	Sweet Stout	1034	1016.9	2.14	50.29%	300
1966	Dudgeon & Co. (Belhaven)	Dunbar Sweet Stout	1038.2	1018.9	2.41	50.52%	280
1959	Younger, Wm. & Co	Capital Stout	1043.7	1021.6	2.84	50.57%	376
1960	Younger, Wm. & Co	Sweet Stout (lactose present)	1034.8	1016.9	2.24	51.44%	250
1955	McEwan	Sweet Stout	1038.4	1018.6	2.55	51.56%	375
1955	J Aitken	Stout	1040.3	1019.5	2.67	51.61%	325
1953	Younger, Robert	Sweet Stout	1035.7	1017.2	2.38	51.82%	200
1954	Younger, Geo.	Extra Stout	1037.5	1018	2.51	52.00%	600
1948	Younger, Geo	Extra Stout	1036.5	1017.5	2.44	52.05%	
1961	Calders	Stout (no lactose)	1041.3	1019.8	2.69	52.06%	250
1954	Younger, Wm. & Co	Nourishing Stout	1046.3	1021.6	3.18	53.35%	275
1959	Murray, Wm	Extra Sweet Stout	1039.6	1018.3	2.74	53.79%	175
1949	Blair	Invalid Stout	1035	1016	2.45	54.29%	
1959	Deuchar, R	Edinburgh Sweet Stout	1043.5	1019.7	3.06	54.71%	275
1967	Younger, Wm. & Co	Sweet Stout	1034	1015.3	2.34	55.00%	300
1954	Steel Coulson	Elephant Stout	1038.9	1017.5	2.76	55.01%	325
1949	Belhaven	No. 1 Stout	1035.5	1015.5	2.58	56.34%	
1949	McEwan	Imperial Stout	1039.5	1017	2.90	56.96%	
1950	Calder Alloa	Milk Stout	1069.3	1029.7	5.10	57.14%	250
1961	Mackays	Stout (no lactose)	1037.9	1016.2	2.71	57.26%	250
1954	Younger, Wm. & Co	Capital Stout (Lactose present)	1046.5	1019.7	3.45	57.63%	250
1955	Maclachlan	Extra Sweet Stout	1035.8	1014.8	2.71	58.66%	225
1955	Younger, Geo.	Extra Stout	1038.5	1015.8	2.93	58.96%	575

Sources:
Thomas Usher Gravity Book document TU/6/11 held at the Scottish Brewing Archive
Whitbread Gravity book held at the London Metropolitan Archives, document number LMA/4453/D/02/002.

It's significant that the group with a moderate degree of attenuation is much, much smaller. And there are only four after 1955.

Scottish Middling Stout 1947 - 1964

Year	Brewer	Beer	OG	FG	ABV	App. Attenuation	colour
1948	McEwan	Imperial Stout	1047	1018.5	3.68	60.64%	
1959	Younger, Wm. & Co	Sweet Stout	1033.3	1013.1	2.61	60.66%	300
1956	Deuchar R	Edinburgh Sweet Stout	1042.9	1016.8	3.37	60.84%	300
1954	Calder	Scotch Stout	1040.9	1015.9	3.23	61.12%	250
1948	Calder Alloa	Stout	1039.5	1015	3.16	62.03%	
1964	Tennent	Milk Stout	1061.8	1023	4.85	62.78%	250

Scottish Middling Stout 1947 - 1964

Year	Brewer	Beer	OG	FG	ABV	App. Attenuation	colour
1957	Tennent	???? Brand Stout	1059.4	1020.8	4.99	64.98%	300
1949	McEwan & Co.	Manx Oyster Stout	1040.5	1014	3.43	65.43%	
1955	J & J Morison	Sweet Stout	1035.7	1012.3	3.02	65.55%	325
1954	Steel Coulson	Elephant Sweet Stout	1041.7	1014.1	3.57	66.19%	350
1949	Calder Alloa	Stout	1038.5	1013	3.30	66.23%	
1950	McEwan	Imperial Stout	1043	1014.4	3.70	66.51%	
1955	Blair & Co	Sweet Stout	1033.1	1010.9	2.87	67.07%	300
1947	Campbell, Hope & King	Draught Stout	1032.5	1010.5	2.85	67.69%	
1958	Bernard	Export Stout	1046.4	1014.7	3.96	68.32%	225
1950	Tennent	Milk Stout (Export)	1063.2	1020	5.60	68.35%	300
1948	Belhaven	No. 1 Stout	1035	1011	3.11	68.57%	
1949	McEwan & Co.	Imperial Stout	1046.4	1014.4	4.14	68.97%	275
1950	J & T Bernard Ltd Edinburgh	Stout (Export)	1045.5	1014.1	4.07	69.01%	150
1949	McEwan & Co.	Manx Oyster Stout	1046.4	1014.3	4.16	69.18%	260
1954	Bernard	Export Stout	1043.9	1013.3	3.96	69.70%	250

Sources:
Thomas Usher Gravity Book document TU/6/11 held at the Scottish Brewing Archive
Whitbread Gravity book held at the London Metropolitan Archives, document number LMA/4453/D/02/002.

The group with attenuation over 70% is tiny and all but one is from the 1940's:

Scottish Dry Stout 1947 - 1959

Year	Brewer	Beer	OG	FG	ABV	App. Attenuation	colour
1948	Maclachlan	Stout	1032	1009.5	2.91	70.31%	
1948	Ballingall & Son	Angus Stout	1037.6	1011.09	3.43	70.51%	350
1947	Younger, Robert	Stout	1028	1007.5	2.66	73.21%	
1949	Bernard	Export Stout	1040	1010	3.89	75.00%	
1955	Murray W	Export Stout	1064.6	1015.8	6.36	75.54%	350
1947	Jeffrey & Co	XXX Stout	1064.5	1014.5	6.52	77.52%	
1947	McEwan	Stout	1030.5	1006	3.18	80.33%	
1947	Jeffrey & Co	Double Stout	1076.5	1004.5	9.53	94.12%	

Sources:
Thomas Usher Gravity Book document TU/6/11 held at the Scottish Brewing Archive
Whitbread Gravity book held at the London Metropolitan Archives, document number LMA/4453/D/02/002.

Strong/Scotch Ale

Scottish brewers remained famous for their Strong Ales both at home and abroad. They brewed some of the strongest beers regularly produced during the 1950's, when anything over 5% ABV was regarded as strong and anything over 7% ABV dangerously strong.

The naming remained schizophrenic. The same beer, for example William Younger No. 1, being sold as Strong Ale North of the border and Scotch Ale elsewhere.

Drybrough brewed a Strong Ale the classic 20th-century way: parti-gyled with their Pale Ales.

Drybrough Strong Ale 1954 - 1960							
Year	Beer	OG	FG	ABV	App. Attenuation	lbs hops/ qtr	hops lb/brl
1954	Burns	1073.0	1032.5	5.36	55.48%	4.67	1.40
1960	Burns	1073.0	1033.5	5.23	54.11%	4.78	1.45
Source: Drybrough brewing record held at the Scottish Brewing Archive, document number D/6/1/1/7.							

Maclay brewed a similar Strong Ale in the 1950's but had discontinued it by the mid 1960's. Though they had rather a better rate of attenuation than Drybrough:

Maclay Strong Ale 1951 - 1956							
Year	Beer	OG	FG	ABV	App. Attenuation	lbs hops/ qtr	hops lb/brl
1951	SA	1075	1026	6.48	65.33%	5.30	1.65
1956	SA	1075	1017	7.67	77.33%	6.32	2.06
Source: Maclay brewing records held at the Scottish Brewing Archive, document numbers M/6/1/1/28 and, M/6/1/1/35.							

The hopping rates for both the Drybrough and Maclay Strong Ale is obviously low. They couldn't help but be as they were parti-gyled with their lightly-hopped Pale Ales.

Ever the contrarians, William Younger brewed two different Strong/Scotch Ales that were brewed single gyle. I shouldn't complain. Scottish brewing would be dead dull without them.

William Younger Strong Ales 1939 - 1949							
Year	Beer	OG	FG	ABV	App. Attenuation	lbs hops/ qtr	hops lb/brl
1939	1	1084.0	1033.5	6.68	60.12%	4.74	1.58
1949	3 Btg	1047.0	1012.0	4.63	74.47%	4.58	0.82
1949	3 Pale	1044.0	1012.0	4.23	72.73%	4.57	0.78
1949	1	1074.0	1023.0	6.75	68.92%	4.72	1.34
Source: William Younger brewing records held at the Scottish Brewing Archive, document numbers WY/6/1/2/76 and WY/6/1/2/88.							

Decent enough attenuation, but very sparse hopping. No. 1 was clearly filling the same slot as the Drybrough and Maclay beers as they all have near identical gravities. You'll see in a while why the attenuation of No. 3 was better than No. 1. The hopping, at around 5 lbs per quarter of malt is much the same for all of them.

For much of the 1940's and 1950's, there were very few English beers with a gravity to match Scottish Strong Ales. In England, there were rather more of the Burton type. These, particularly in London, were often draught beers.

English Strong Ale (Burton type) 1939 - 1964

Year	Brewer	Beer	OG	FG	ABV	App. Atten- uation	lbs hops/ qtr	hops lb/brl
1940	Barclay Perkins	KK (trade)	1051.3	1015.5	4.74	69.79%	8.50	1.86
1946	Barclay Perkins	KK (bottling)	1047.4	1018.3	3.86	61.50%	8.85	1.81
1947	Barclay Perkins	KK (trade)	1042.5	1015.0	3.64	64.71%	7.83	1.33
1964	Eldridge Pope	XXXX	1053.2	1017.2	4.76	67.71%	5.77	1.25
1939	Fullers	BO	1055.5	1015.2	5.32	72.54%	7.01	1.63
1958	Fullers	OBE	1049.4	1013.3	4.78	73.11%	4.51	0.91
1953	Lees	"C" Ale	1052.0				4.21	0.93
1939	Whitbread	33	1061.0	1020.0	5.42	67.21%	8.49	2.15
1946	Whitbread	XXXX	1043.3	1008.5	4.60	80.37%	5.75	1.07
1958	Whitbread	KKKK	1050.5	1011.5	5.16	77.23%	7.75	1.68

Sources:
Barclay Perkins brewing records held at the London Metropolitan Archives, document numbers ACC/2305/01/623 and ACC/2305/01/627.
Eldridge Pope brewing record.
Fullers brewing records held at the brewery.
Lees brewing record held at the brewery.
Whitbread brewing records held at the London Metropolitan Archives, document numbers LMA/4453/D/01/107, LMA/4453/D/01/113 and LMA/4453/D/09/126.

Scottish Strong Ales averaged around 5 lbs of hops per quarter. Many of the English ones rack up double that. In fact, although they're much weaker, some of the English examples contain more hops per barrel. For example, Barclay Perkins KK (bottling) from 1946 has 1.86 lbs per barrel, while the far stronger William Younger No. 1 for 1949 only has 1.34 lbs.

The one Scottish beer with a strength similar to a Burton, William Younger No. 3, was much more lightly hopped than most of the English beers.

English Barley Wines look much more like Scottish Strong Ales, with gravities 1075-1090º.

English Strong Ale (Barley Wine type) 1939 - 1968

Year	Brewer	Beer	OG	FG	ABV	App. Atten-uation	lbs hops/qtr	hops lb/brl
1939	Tetley	XXX	1090.9	1030.2	8.03	66.77%	4.72	1.76
1954	Lees	Golden Brew	1078.0				3.41	1.37
1964	Eldridge Pope	Dorset Special	1074.8	1024.1	6.71	67.78%	5.10	1.52
1967	Eldridge Pope	BW	1085.3	1029.4	7.40	65.58%	5.81	1.95
1968	Whitbread	FSA	1079.6	1012.4	8.89	84.42%	6.88	2.35

Sources:
Tetley brewing record held at the West Yorkshire Archives, document number WYL756/ACC3349/557.
Lees brewing record held at the brewery.
Eldridge Pope brewing record.
Whitbread brewing record held at the London Metropolitan Archives, document number LMA/4453/D/01/137.

In terms of lbs per quarter of malt, this type was less heavily-hopped than the Burton type. When compared with the stronger Scottish beers, the hopping level both in lbs per quarter of malt and pounds per barrel are roughly similar.

As Drybrough's and Maclay's beers were parti-gyled with Pale Ales, the grists are obviously identical. But I'm going to repeat them, anyway.

Drybrough Strong Ale grists 1954 - 1960

Year	Beer	OG	pale malt	black malt	enzymic malt	flaked maize	flaked barley	malt extract	sugar
1954	Burns	1073.0	75.04%	0.76%	2.42%	6.05%	6.05%	1.61%	8.07%
1960	Burns	1073.0	75.79%	1.13%		11.76%		1.74%	9.58%

Source:
Drybrough brewing record held at the Scottish Brewing Archive, document numberD/6/1/1/7.

Enzymic malt and malt extract were both very popular in the 1950's. They turn up regularly in English beers, too.

Maclay's grists were pretty similar, just without the black malt, enzymic malt and flaked barley.

Maclay Strong Ale grists 1951 - 1956

Year	Beer	OG	pale malt	flaked maize	no. 1 sugar	malt extract	caramel	DCS sugar
1951	SA	1075	86.33%		9.59%		0.24%	3.84%
1956	SA	1075	73.24%	11.27%	9.39%	1.88%	0.47%	3.76%

Source:
Maclay brewing records held at the Scottish Brewing Archive, document numbers M/6/1/1/23 and, M/6/1/1/35.

Without William Younger, this would be as boring as Bognor on a wet weekend. See how much more fun their grists are:

| \multicolumn{8}{l}{**William Younger Strong Ales 1939 - 1949**} |
Year	Beer	OG	pale malt	crystal malt	mild malt	grits	flaked barley	lactose
1939	1	1084.0	69.64%	5.36%	2.68%	18.75%		3.57%
1949	3 Btg	1047.0	87.50%				12.50%	
1949	3 Pale	1044.0	86.96%				13.04%	
1949	1	1074.0	79.25%	2.83%	2.83%		11.32%	3.77%

Source:
William Younger brewing records held at the Scottish Brewing Archive, document numbers WY/6/1/2/76 and WY/6/1/2/88.

Not sure if that was really mild malt. Just the only type of malt I can think of that could be abbreviated to "M". Flaked barley is a wartime thing. Brewers were forced to use it by the government. For most brewers this was to replace flaked barley. But for William Younger, it was grits.

The secret ingredient in No. 1 is lactose. Something usually associated with Milk Stout. Obviously it's there to add sweetness. Which earlier Scottish brewers achieved just through crap attenuation.

You have to wonder, given how different the recipes are, how similar No. 1 tasted to the Drybrough and Maclay Strong Ales.

The grists of English Strong Ales were, to say the least, diverse:

English Strong Ale (Burton type) grists 1939 - 1964

Year	1940	1946	1947	1964	1939	1958	1953	1939	1946	1958
Brewer	Barclay Perkins			Eldridge Pope	Fullers	Fullers	Lees	Whitbread		
Beer	KK (trade)	KK (bottling)	KK (trade)	XXXX	BO	OBE	"C" Ale	33	XXXX	KKKK
OG	1051.3	1047.4	1042.5	1053.2	1055.5	1049.4	1052	1061	1043.3	1050.5
pale malt	8.29%			71.68%	31.66%	81.06%	73.56%	25.27%		
brown malt							1.44%		1.58%	
black malt							1.44%			
amber malt			4.69%							
choc. Malt							1.44%		1.98%	0.90%
crystal malt	4.15%	5.44%	7.03%	13.94%			2.88%	2.45%	2.37%	
MA malt	51.81%									
SA malt	16.58%		72.66%							
PA malt		73.47%						52.17%	63.72%	82.23%
flaked maize					13.87%	9.01%				
flaked rice	8.29%									
wheat flour				4.65%						
flaked barley		5.44%	4.69%						12.66%	
malt extract				3.54%						
no. 1 sugar		14.51%								
no. 2 sugar						4.80%				
no. 3 sugar			0.94%						16.89%	14.46%
caramel	1.21%	1.13%								
glucose					3.08%		3.85%			
other sugar	9.67%			6.19%	1.39%	5.14%	15.38%	20.11%	0.79%	2.41%

Sources:
Barclay Perkins brewing records held at the London Metropolitan Archives, document numbers ACC/2305/01/623 and ACC/2305/01/627.
Eldridge Pope brewing record.
Fullers brewing records held at the brewery.
Lees brewing record held at the brewery.
Whitbread brewing records held at the London Metropolitan Archives, document numbers LMA/4453/D/01/107, LMA/4453/D/01/113 and LMA/4453/D/09/126.

About the only type of malt not used was lager malt. A large variety of coloured malts were employed. The only English beers to contain none were Fullers BO and OBE. Whereas in Scotland the Drybrough beers had a little black malt and Younger's No. 1 some crystal malt, but

The sugar content was generally higher amongst the English beers. The highest percentage in the Scots beers was 9.5%. Only two English beers, Eldridge Pope XXXX and Barclay Perkins BO contained less than 10% sugar.

In Scotland, unmalted adjuncts averaged around 12% of the grist. While in England it varied from 0% in some Whitbread beers to 14% in Fullers BO.

The grist of the stronger English type weren't quite so crazy:

English Strong Ale (Barley Wine type) grists 1939 - 1968					
Year	1939	1954	1964	1967	1968
Brewer	Tetley	Lees	Eldridge Pope	Eldridge Pope	Whitbread
Beer	XXX	Golden Brew	DSp	BW	FSA
OG	1090.9	1078	1074.8	1085.3	1079.6
pale malt	82.25%	81.66%	76.49%	54.27%	87.86%
choc. Malt					3.47%
crystal malt			5.97%	8.74%	
lager malt				21.11%	
enzymic malt		1.78%			
wheat flour			4.88%	11.46%	
malt extract			3.25%	4.42%	
no. 1 sugar					8.67%
other sugar	17.75%	16.57%	9.40%		
Sources: Tetley brewing record held at the West Yorkshire Archives, document number WYL756/ACC3349/557. Lees brewing record held at the brewery. Eldridge Pope brewing record. Whitbread brewing record held at the London Metropolitan Archives, document number LMA/4453/D/01/137.					

The grists also look more like Scottish Strong Ales, with only Whitbread FSA containing any roasted malt

Scotch Ale in Scotland

Here are some example of Scotch Ales:

Scotch Ales 1939 - 1967

Year	Brewer	Beer	OG	FG	ABV	App. Attenuation	colour
1939	McEwan	Scotch Ale	1086.2	1019.6	8.73	77.26%	55
1941	Younger, Wm.	Scotch Ale	1046.3	1013	4.32	71.92%	40
1947	Usher	Old Scotch Ale	1073.5	1020.5	6.90	72.11%	
1948	Calder Alloa	Scotch Strong Ale	1065.5	1019	6.04	70.39%	
1948	Gordon & Blair	"Unique" Scotch Ale	1043.5	1016.5	3.49	62.07%	
1948	Steel Coulson	Elephant Brand Scotch Ale	1044	1011.5	4.22	73.36%	
1949	Younger, Wm.	Scotch Ale	1041.7	1011	3.98	73.62%	52
1950	Aitchison	Scotch Ale	1080	1020.8	7.73	74.00%	55
1950	Campbell	Royal Scotch Ale	1080.1	1014.2	8.66	82.27%	77
1950	Younger, Wm.	Double Scotch Ale	1057.7	1018.4	5.09	68.11%	80
1950	Younger, Wm.	Scotch Ale	1088	1022.6	8.56	74.32%	65
1950	Younger, Wm.	Scotch Ale	1087.6	1017.5	9.21	80.02%	60
1952	Campbell	Royal Edinburgh Scotch Ale	1080.3	1011.1	9.12	86.18%	50
1952	McEwan	Scotch Ale	1090.3	1023.1	8.80	74.42%	62
1952	Younger, Wm.	Scotch Ale	1083.5	1021.7	8.07	74.01%	70
1955	Younger, Wm.	No. 1 Strong Ale	1071.4	1024.3	6.11	65.97%	80
1966	Younger, Wm.	No.3 Scotch Ale	1044.8	1011.9	4.11	73.44%	65
1967	Scottish Brewers	No. 3	1041.6	1006.2	4.61	85.10%	80

Sources:
Whitbread Gravity book held at the London Metropolitan Archives, document number LMA/4453/D/02/001.
Whitbread Gravity book held at the London Metropolitan Archives, document number LMA/4453/D/02/002.

Note the two main types: beers in the 1040º's and ones around 1080º. The latter group look very much like pre-WW II examples.

Belgium remained a good market for strong Scotch Ale and several Scottish breweries resumed shipments across the channel after the end of WW II. And, as you can see in the table, it wasn't just Scottish breweries getting in on the act. John Smith, a very English brewery, also made a Scotch Ale exclusively for Belgium.

| Scotch Ales for the Belgian market 1950 - 1955 ||||||||
Year	Brewer	Beer	OG	FG	ABV	App. Atten-uation	colour
1950	Younger, Geo.	Gordon Highland Scotch Ale	1091.2	1031.1	7.81	65.90%	45
1950	Younger, Geo.	Gordon Xmas Ale (bottled in Antwerp)	1090.7	1032.3	7.58	64.39%	48
1952	Younger, Geo.	Gordon Highland Scotch Ale	1081.8	1026.5	7.19	67.60%	50
1954	Younger, Geo.	Gordon Highland Scotch Ale (purchased in Belgium)	1090.9	1028	8.20	69.20%	60
1954	John Smith	Scotch Ale (purchased in Belgium)	1072.6	1022.1	6.56	69.56%	95
1955	John Smith	Scotch Ale (purchased in Belgium)	1072.3	1022	6.54	69.57%	75
1955	McEwan	Scotch Ale (purchased in Belgium)	1088.2	1020.2	8.92	77.10%	65
1955	Truman	Scotch Ale (purchased in Belgium)	1083.4	1025.6	7.52	69.30%	80
Source: Whitbread Gravity book held at the London Metropolitan Archives, document number LMA/4453/D/02/002.							

Though the popularity of these imports encouraged Belgian brewers to make Scotch Ales their own. Currently most examples of the style on sale in Belgium are locally brewed.

Lager

During the 1950's Lager began its rise to dominance in the UK beer market. And Scotland was at the vanguard.

In the same way that Scotland had preceded England in the move from Mild Ale to Pale Ale, it also led the way in the move to Lager. Why Scottish drinkers were ahead of the game in this way, I've no idea.

Scottish Lager 1947 - 1967

Year	Brewer	Beer	OG	FG	ABV	App. Attenuation	colour
1947	Unknown	Pilsner	1035	1010	3.24	71.43%	
1950	Alloa Brewery	Light Lager	1043.4	1009.1	4.46	79.03%	7 B
1950	Alloa Brewery	Graham's Golden Lager	1040.6	1010.6	3.89	73.89%	9 B
1952	Alloa Brewery	Graham's Golden Lager	1039.2	1014.3	3.22	63.52%	15 B
1954	Steel Coulson	Lager Beer	1032	1004.3	3.60	86.56%	11
1955	Tennent	Lager	1036.1	1007.7	3.69	78.67%	9
1957	Alloa Brewery	Graham's Golden Lager	1030.4	1007.3	3.00	75.99%	11
1957	McEwan & Wm Younger	"MY" Export Lager	1033.6	1006.3	3.55	81.25%	13
1957	McEwan & Wm Younger	"MY" Export Lager	1035.2	1007.3	3.62	79.26%	13
1957	McEwan & Wm Younger	"MY" Export Lager	1033.8	1010.9	2.96	67.75%	13
1957	Tennent	Lager Beer	1040.6	1008.6	4.16	78.82%	11
1958	McEwan & Younger	MY Export Lager	1034.3	1010.5	2.97	69.39%	9
1960	Tennent	Tennent's Lager	1036.3	1008.55	3.60	76.45%	
1960	Alloa Brewery	Skol Pilsner Lager	1033.4	1007	3.30	79.04%	8
1961	McEwan	MY Export Lager	1032.9	1010.1	2.85	69.30%	10
1961	Tennant Bros.	Lager	1036	1007.6	3.55	78.89%	7.5
1963	Tennent	Lager	1036.9	1007.8	3.64	78.86%	7.5
1967	Ind Coope	Skol Lig??? Lager	1071.4	1013.7	7.55	80.81%	10

Sources:
Whitbread Gravity book held at the London Metropolitan Archives, document number LMA/4453/D/02/002.
Thomas Usher Gravity Book document TU/6/11 held at the Scottish Brewing Archive
Which Beer Report, 1960, pages 171 - 173.

In 1960, the Alloa Brewery, which had been bashing out Lager for forty years on Allsopp's old kit, became part of national group Allied Breweries. Around the same their most famous product, Graham's Golden Lager, was renamed Skol and launched not just as a national but as an international brand.

Tennent, another long-term Lager producer was absorbed into Bass Charrington, the biggest brewing group in the UK. Access to around 10,000 pubs gave its Lager a huge boost.

Recipes

1939 William Younger XX

I hope you're not getting bored of William Younger recipes. Because there are going to be quite a few more.

Including that rarest of beasts, a post-WW I Scottish Mild Ale. Which is what I've got for you here. A real Mild, too, not just a watery Pale Ale coloured up. Though I suspect this was coloured darker than it was brewed, the base recipe isn't a Pale Ale. Rather it's a very watered down version of No. 1 Ale.

If you've viewed the pale malt and grits recipes with increasing apathy, this recipe will knock you for six. Because it has a whole six ingredients in the grist. Exciting or what? Including Younger's special super-secret ingredient: lactose.

Younger's XXX is the equivalent of an English 4d Ale. And that's probably what it cost in the pub: 4d a pint. Most London brewers made one, though the quantities were often quite small. That wasn't a big deal, as they could parti-gyle with standard Mild, X Ale.

I just checked the Whitbread Gravity Book analyses and found something called Light Ale that looks like it could be this beer. The gravity is about the same – it's 1031º - and it's dark brown in colour. Though it cost 6d a pint, which is expensive for a beer this weak. Weird for a beer that's dark to be billed as a Light Ale, isn't it? But remember the analysis was performed by Whitbread. And their watery Dark Mild was called Light Ale.

This question pops into my mind: why did a Scottish brewer make a beer of this type? I think I might know the answer. It's because they already owned pubs in London. And Mild was still incredibly popular in the capital, probably accounting for 50% of sales in most pubs. Come to think of it, the London trade might also explain No. 3, a beer without an equivalent at other Scottish brewers I've researched. No.3 was similar to a London Burton Ale.

What I give as mild malt was probably something else. But I can't think of another malt beginning with the letter "M", which is how it's described in the brewing log. Given the small quantity, it might have been some sort of diastatic malt or even malt extract.

Liquorice is another off ingredient in anything but a Stout. Combine it with lactose and an extremely low level of hopping and you must have got something quite distinctive. And pretty sweet.

All in all. One of Younger's most interesting recipes.

1939 William Younger XX		
pale malt	5.00 lb	68.97%
crystal malt 60L	0.50 lb	6.90%
mild malt	0.13 lb	1.72%
grits	1.25 lb	17.24%
invert sugar	0.13 lb	1.72%
lactose	0.25 lb	3.45%
liquorice	0.25 oz	
Fuggles 90 min	0.50 oz	
Fuggles 30 min	0.25 oz	
Goldings dry hops	0.25 oz	
OG	1032	
FG	1011.5	
ABV	2.71	
Apparent attenuation	64.06%	
IBU	11	
SRM	6	
Mash at	154° F	
Sparge at	160° F	
Boil time	105 minutes	
pitching temp	62.5° F	
Yeast	WLP028 Edinburgh Ale	

1939 William Younger XXX

Now I've started I may as well do the set of William Younger 1939 Mild Ales. This is the stronger version, XXX.

I'm not going to pretend that it's hugely different from XX. It contains exactly the same ingredients, though the proportions are slightly different. Slightly less pale malt and a little more of everything else. It's not a massive difference.

This beer slips perfectly into what I would call the Ordinary Mild slot. A beer that would have cost 5d a pint in London. In the late 1930's, there were three types of Mild in London. 4d Ale at 1030º at 4d per pint; Mild at 1037º at 5d per pint and Best Mild at 1043º at 6d per pint. With the middle one being the most popular. Though not every brewery made all three types.

The crappy degree of attenuation – the lactose won't help – leaves XXX at just over 3% ABV. So it must have been quite a full-bodied beer. An FG of 1014º is high for a beer with a relatively low OG. But clearly that's what the brewery was aiming for. As I mentioned for XX, this is really a watered-down No. 1 Strong Ale. The grists are very similar, except there's no invert sugar in the No. 1.

Again I assume that this was primarily sold south of the border. This class of beer didn't exist in Scotland. At least I haven't found another similar Scottish beer. William Younger seems to have stuck with brewing proper Milds – not just a low-gravity Pale Ale with added sugar – much longer than anyone else in Scotland. Extensive trade in England (not just the Northeast of England where many Scottish brewers were active and Mild was also a rarity) is the most obvious explanation.

Even by the standards of Mild the hopping rate is very low. Barclay's X, a beer of a similar gravity, contained three times the volume of hops. While Whitbread X contained four times as many. Younger XX and XXX are some of the most lightly-hopped British beers I've ever come across.

1939 William Younger XXX

pale malt	5.25 lb	64.42%
crystal malt 60L	0.50 lb	6.13%
mild malt	0.40 lb	4.91%
grits	1.25 lb	15.34%
invert sugar	0.25 lb	3.07%
lactose	0.50 lb	6.13%
liquorice	0.25 oz	
Fuggles 90 min	0.50 oz	
Fuggles 30 min	0.25 oz	
Goldings dry hops	0.25 oz	
OG	1037	
FG	1014	
ABV	3.04	
Apparent attenuation	62.16%	
IBU	11	
SRM	6	
Mash at	154° F	
Sparge at	160° F	
Boil time	105 minutes	
pitching temp	61° F	
Yeast	WLP028 Edinburgh Ale	

1949 William Younger XXX

The beers from just after the war bring so much joy. Of the I'm-really-happy-I-didn't-live-back-then kind.

Younger, contrary bastards that they were, still brewed Mild after WW II. Unlike most Scottish brewers. Look back and you'll find an XXX recipe from 1939. When the gravity was a good bit higher, at 1037º. But don't blame Younger for this version being weaker. Blame Hitler.

This may look puny, but there were weaker ones. This is just about intoxicating. And doesn't have too much crap in it. No grits, while in 1939 they were 15% of the grist. Though, to be honest, the ingredients they used probably weren't under the brewer's full control.

This being a Scottish beer, you can colour to choice. A fun experiment would be to colour this beer a couple of different shades at racking time. Then get people to try them all without saying it's basically the same beer. I'm sure it would catch me out.

1949 William Younger XXX		
pale malt	5.25 lb	72.41%
crystal malt	0.50 lb	6.90%
mild malt	0.50 lb	6.90%
flaked barley	0.50 lb	6.90%
No. 2 invert sugar	0.50 lb	6.90%
Fuggles 90 min	0.25 oz	
Fuggles 60 min	0.25 oz	
Fuggles 30 min	0.25 oz	
OG	1030.5	
FG	1008	
ABV	2.98	
Apparent attenuation	73.77%	
IBU	11	
SRM	7	
Mash at	153º F	
Sparge at	160º F	
Boil time	75 minutes	
pitching temp	62º F	
Yeast	WLP028 Edinburgh Ale	

1970 Drybrough M Special Mild

Drybrough seems to have become much more adventurous after becoming part of Watney Mann. Which is the opposite of what I would have expected.

I was particularly surprised to come across what looks like a genuine Mild Ale. Was this because after their takeover they were supplying pubs in the North of England? By 1970 there was virtually no market left for Mild.

In their new recipes Drybrough often left out the flaked maize. Here its place is taken by either torrefied wheat or torrefied barley. The brewing record doesn't specify which, unfortunately, so take your pick. The No. 3 invert is a substitute for something called BME. Which could either be a proprietart sugar or some sort of malt extract.

The colour of the finished beer was probably darker, if I know Scotland. They most likely coloured it up to around 20 SRM after primary.

1970 Drybrough M Special Mild		
pale malt	5.50 lb	73.33%
crystal malt 60 L	0.75 lb	10.00%
torrefied barley	0.75 lb	10.00%
No. 2 invert sugar	0.25 lb	3.33%
No. 3 invert sugar	0.25 lb	3.33%
Fuggles 90 min	0.50 oz	
Goldings 30 min	0.25 oz	
Goldings dry hops	0.50 oz	
OG	1034.3	
FG	1008	
ABV	3.48	
Apparent attenuation	76.68%	
IBU	13	
SRM	9	
Mash at	146° F	
Sparge at	165° F	
Boil time	90 minutes	
pitching temp	62° F	
Yeast	WLP028 Edinburgh Ale	

1949 William Younger Double Century Ale

To celebrate a rather dubious 200 year anniversary – the brewery had really been founded a couple of decades later - William Younger introduced a new beer.

Unlike the most other Scottish breweries, William Younger had more than one recipe. Not that every beer had its own one, but they did vary things around more than most. The crazy bastards had four or five different ones.

Their two Strong/Scotch Ale, No. 1 and No. 3, had quite different recipes. Unlike No. 1, No. 3 contained no crystal malt and no lactose. Double Century, does. So what we're looking at here is a lower-gravity version of No. 1.

Lactose in beers other than Stout is pretty rare. Especially in a – what style is this? Brown ale? An analysis I have for 1954 gives the colour as 20 SRM. Or is it a weaker Scottish Strong Ale. Given the grist, I'd go with the latter. But it's all arbitrary.

1949 William Younger Double Century Ale		
pale malt	10.00 lb	75.47%
crystal malt 60L	1.50 lb	11.32%
mild malt	0.50 lb	3.77%
flaked barley	0.50 lb	3.77%
lactose	0.75 lb	5.66%
Fuggles 90 min	1.00 oz	
Fuggles 60 min	0.50 oz	
Fuggles 30 min	0.50 oz	
Goldings dry hops	0.25 oz	
OG	1057	
FG	1017	
ABV	5.29	
Apparent attenuation	70.18%	
IBU	25	
SRM	7	
Mash at	152° F	
Sparge at	160° F	
Boil time	90 minutes	
pitching temp	60° F	
Yeast	WLP028 Edinburgh Ale	

1958 Bernard Double Brown Ale

I'm so glad that I have photographs of T & J Bernard's last brewing book. It's quite a shock to see a Scottish brewery with more than one recipe.

Especially as one is a Double Brown Ale, a fairly rare type of beer and one I have very few brewing records for. In fact, I've very few brewing records for any sort of Brown Ale, other than Whitbread's Forest Brown and Double Brown. Most breweries just fiddled with their Mild Ale post-fermentation. Or, in the case of Scottish brewers, fiddled with their 60/- Pale Ale,

Not that there's anything very exciting the recipe. It's the usual combination of pale malt, flaked maize and sugar. Though there is a touch of black malt thrown in. You may have noticed how, despite the claims of some, roast barley was almost never used in Scotland, other than occasionally in Stouts.

I've substituted No. 2 invert for the two sugars in the original, invert and Avona. The hops are just guesswork. The only thing that I know for certain is that they were English and from the 1957 season, making them just shy of a year old (the original was brewed in July 1958).

You'll need to add caramel to get the right colour. As brewed, it's just 7.5 SRM.

1958 Bernard Double Brown Ale		
pale malt	6.50 lb	78.13%
black malt	0.07 lb	0.84%
flaked maize	1.25 lb	15.02%
No. 2 invert sugar	0.50 lb	6.01%
Fuggles 105 min	1.25 oz	
Goldings 30 min	1.25 oz	
OG	1043	
FG	1012	
ABV	4.10	
Apparent attenuation	72.09%	
IBU	31	
SRM	20	
Mash at	148° F	
Sparge at	167° F	
Boil time	105 minutes	
pitching temp	61° F	
Yeast	WLP028 Edinburgh Ale	

1966 Drybrough MBA Brown Ale

Drybrough went all exotic after their takeover by Watney Mann in 1965. They started using all sorts of exotic ingredients, like crystal malt. And brewing more than one recipe.

A real Brown Ale recipe was one of the results. At least that's what I think this is, mostly on the BA in the name. It also contains some typical Brown Ale ingredients, such as crystal malt and No. 3 invert. Torrefied barley is also a new departure for Drybrough. Though it could be torrefied wheat as record just says "torrefied".

I've adjusted the sugar a bit. There was really some No. 3 invert in the original recipe, but also something called BME. I've just added that to the No. 3 quantity.

As per usual, all I know about the hops is that they were English. I don't even know how long they boiled for, so I plumped for a middle-of-the-road 90 minutes.

1966 Drybrough MBA Brown Ale		
pale malt	4.25 lb	57.90%
black malt	0.09 lb	1.23%
crystal malt 60 L	1.75 lb	23.84%
torrefied barley	0.50 lb	6.81%
No. 3 invert sugar	0.50 lb	6.81%
caramel 500 SRM	0.25 lb	3.41%
Fuggles 90 min	0.50 oz	
Goldings 30 min	0.50 oz	
OG	1034	
FG	1012	
ABV	2.91	
Apparent attenuation	64.71%	
IBU	13	
SRM	21	
Mash at	145 / 158° F	
Sparge at	165° F	
Boil time	90 minutes	
pitching temp	62° F	
Yeast	WLP028 Edinburgh Ale	

1949 William Younger Bt g DBS

Scottish Stouts can be pretty odd. Especially in the 20th century. I'm still trying to get my head around them.

You have the incredibly sweet, barely fermented type like Sweetheart Stout. Robert Younger who parti-gyled one with Ordinary Bitter. And Drybrough who somehow magicked one from their single Pale Ale recipe, presumably by dumping a load of caramel in at racking time.

Then there's this beer.

Stouts came and went at William Younger, but DBS had real longevity. My first spotting of it in their brewing records is 1851. At that time it was highly-attenuated and heavily-hopped. Very unlike the Scottish-style beers that they brewed. In the 1870's it was joined by a group of weaker, less well-attenuated Stouts with minimal hopping. As time went on, these Stouts became even less well-attenuated and even more minimally hopped. They must have been incredibly sweet.

DBS remained much the same until WW I, though the attenuation and OG both fell a bit. The weak Stouts didn't survive the war. Maybe that's why the attenuation of DBS fell to 50% in the 1920's. Though it continued to have reasonably decent hopping. In the 1930's, attenuation and hopping increased again. And liquorice and lactose added to the ingredients. This is so confusing.

Which brings us to this incarnation. With it's odd combination of quite heavy hopping, low attenuation, lots of roast barley and lots of lactose. There must have been quite a clash of flavours, with both malts and hop bitterness battling it out with the sweetness from the lactose. Which had me really intrigued. What would it taste like? I suspect not much like anything on the market today. Maybe like Mackeson XXX, a beer I really rated but no longer see around.

1949 William Younger Btlg DBS		
pale malt	6.00 lb	57.14%
crystal malt 60L	0.50 lb	4.76%
mild malt	0.50 lb	4.76%
roast barley	1.00 lb	9.52%
flaked barley	1.00 lb	9.52%
caramel	0.25 lb	2.38%
lactose	1.25 lb	11.90%
Fuggles 90 min	0.75 oz	
Fuggles 60 min	0.75 oz	
Fuggles 30 min	0.75 oz	
Goldings dry hops	0.125 oz	
OG	1046	
FG	1019	
ABV	3.57	
Apparent attenuation	58.70%	
IBU	29	
SRM	27	
Mash at	151° F	
Sparge at	160° F	
Boil time	90 minutes	
pitching temp	60° F	
Yeast	WLP028 Edinburgh Ale	

1957 Robert Younger SS

Post-WW II Scottish brewing can be pretty weird. Mostly the result of brewers just having one recipe.

SS is one of the oddest Stouts I've come across. Because it was parti-gyled with 60/- and Export, two Pale Ales. It's identical to 60/-, save for what happened in the copper. It's a sort of hybrid parti-gyle as one of the coppers has the wort intended for the Stout, while the other two coppers were blended the usual way to produce Export and 60/-.

The SS copper has a couple of extra ingredients: liquorice and black malt. And more "colour" which is presumably some sort of caramel. I'm not totally sure that the black malt went into the copper, but that's definitely the suggestion, given the way the record is laid out. There were also far more hops than you would usually find in the third copper. A sure sign they were doing something different.

It's not clear how the gyles were blended. The quantities fermented (278 barrels) add up to more than the volume out of the coppers (203 barrels). I assume water must have been added to make up the volumes.

It's all very strange.

1957 Robert Younger SS		
pale malt	5.00 lb	73.42%
black malt	0.50 lb	7.34%
flaked maize	1.00 lb	14.68%
No. 2 invert sugar	0.25 lb	3.67%
malt extract	0.06 lb	0.88%
caramel	enough to hit the colour	
liquorice	0.50 oz	
Fuggles 120 min	1.25 oz	
Goldings 30 min	1.25 oz	
OG	1030	
FG	1007	
ABV	3.04	
Apparent attenuation	76.67%	
IBU	21	
SRM	40	
Mash at	151° F	
Sparge at	170° F	
Boil time	120 minutes	
pitching temp	60° F	
Yeast	WLP028 Edinburgh Ale	

1958 Bernard Export Stout

Bernard's records are dead exciting compared to most Scottish ones from the 1950's. Because they actually had more than one recipe.

Their Stout had its own recipe and was brewed single gyle. Something that seems to have been rare. Not that the ingredients are particularly strange. It's a fairly standard combination of pale malt, black malt, flaked maize and sugar. The No. 4 invert is my substitution for something called "S.K.". As that sugar only appears in the Stout, I think it's safe to assume that it's quite dark.

Even for post-war Scotland, the hopping is extremely light, just 2.63 lbs. per quarter of malt. There's no indication as to what variety the hops might have been, just the growers, in this case White and Marchant. I've gone with my usual guess of Fuggles and Goldings. Bramling Cross or Northern Brewer would be equally valid.

I've a couple of analyses of this beer – which was marketed as Export Stout – and in both the OG and FG are approximately 5 points higher. A specification from Bernard themselves also list the OG as 1045º. While the ABV from the analyses and in the brewing records is 4%. My guess is that some sort of priming was added after primary fermentation. Probably lactose.

I've added lactose to get it to fit with the analyses. Leave it out if you'd prefer to have it as brewed.

1958 Bernard Stout		
pale malt	6.50 lb	63.41%
black malt	1.25 lb	12.20%
flaked maize	0.25 lb	2.44%
No. 3 invert sugar	0.50 lb	4.88%
No. 4 invert sugar	0.75 lb	7.32%
lactose	1.00 lb	9.76%
Fuggles 105 min	0.50 oz	
Goldings 30 min	0.50 oz	
OG	1045	
FG	1015	
ABV	3.97	
Apparent attenuation	66.67%	
IBU	12	
SRM	41	
Mash at	148º F	
Sparge at	167º F	
Boil time	105 minutes	
pitching temp	61º F	
Yeast	WLP028 Edinburgh Ale	

1966 Maclay Oat Malt Stout

The brewers must have rejoiced when Maclay revived Oat Malt Stout in 1966. They had been brewing exactly the same recipe every day for a decade. Finally something different.

Maclay were the inventors of Oat Stout in the late 19th century, but for a long period in the 20th didn't produce one. This may have been an isolated brew. I can't find it again in the brewing records until 1992, when it had a slightly more reasonable gravity of 1044, but a much lower percentage of oats.

A distinguishing feature of the first version was the high percentage of oats in the grist, over 20%. In the revived version, it was even more, a full third of the fermentables. Which is pretty oaty. It's obvious why they've gone with malted rather than flaked oats: they would have struggled to have enough enzymes. Plus they dead call it Oat **Malt** Stout.

Also in common with the original beer is the use of liquorice. It's an ingredient that's been used intermittently – and before 1880, illegally – in Porter and Stout for a long time. It pops up in English Stouts sometimes, though I can't remember seeing it in one from London.

No. 3 invert is a substitution for a proprietary sugar called DCS. You'll also need to add caramel to get the colour in the recipe below.

The hop varieties are a guess. Though they were English.

1966 Maclay Oat Malt Stout		
pale malt	3.50 lb	46.67%
black malt	0.50 lb	6.67%
malted oats	2.50 lb	33.33%
No. 3 invert	1.00 lb	13.33%
liquorice	0.50 oz	
Fuggles 90 min	0.50 oz	
Fuggles 60 min	0.50 oz	
Goldings 30 min	0.50 oz	
OG	1035	
FG	1012	
ABV	3.04	
Apparent attenuation	65.71%	
IBU	19	
SRM	40	
Mash at	145/154° F	
Sparge at	165° F	
Boil time	90 minutes	
pitching temp	62° F	
Yeast	WLP028 Edinburgh Ale	

1949 William Younger 200/-

After a couple of decades' absence, a Shilling Ale suddenly appears in Younger's brewing records. Odd. The last example I have before this is from the 1920's.

I've no idea what prompted Younger to brew a strong Shilling Ale again. But I'm not complaining. It's a chance to see how these beers would have been brewed in the middle of the 20th century. Interestingly, it was all packaged in hogsheads. That says to me that it was intended for bottling. No pub would take a hogshead of such a strong beer.

The recipe is very similar to No. 1, with one difference: instead of lactose there are two types of sugar, invert and CWA. I've substituted No. 2 invert, but you could also try half No.2 invert and half No. 3.

The most unusual feature of this beer is the level of hopping, which is much higher than for any of their other beers. Younger's Pale Ales were hopped at about 4.5 lbs per quarter of malt. 200/- had almost 7.5 lbs per quarter. Giving it the highest IBU figure for a Younger's beer for a very long time.

1949 William Younger 200/-		
pale malt	16.50 lb	71.74%
crystal malt 60L	0.50 lb	2.17%
mild malt	0.50 lb	2.17%
flaked barley	4.75 lb	20.65%
No. 2 invert	0.75 lb	3.26%
Fuggles 90 min	2.00 oz	
Fuggles 60 min	2.00 oz	
Fuggles 30 min	1.75 oz	
Goldings dry hops	0.50 oz	
OG	1099	
FG	1028	
ABV	9.39	
Apparent attenuation	71.72%	
IBU	54	
SRM	10	
Mash at	153° F	
Sparge at	170° F	
Boil time	90 minutes	
pitching temp	56° F	
Yeast	WLP028 Edinburgh Ale	

1939 William Younger LAE

William Younger brewed a baffling range of Pale Ales before WW II. While most Scottish brewers would have three, Younger had loads.

At Maclay it was 5d, 6d and 7d PA. Beers which would after the war become 60/-, 70/- and 80/-. At Drybrough it was P 54/-, P 60/- and P 80/-. While Younger has P, XP, XP Btlg, XXP, XXP Btlg, XXPS, Ext, LAE and MXP E. Don't ask me what the hell they all were and why they needed so many.

LAE comes second in the gravity pecking order after Ext. I'm fairly certain it was a bottled beer. Partly by gut feeling. But also because there's another beer at the same gravity called XXPS which I know was a draught beer. Because I drank it myself. It was another name for Younger's Scotch or 70/-, a beer that was fairly common in the 1970's and 1980's.

The recipe is, as usual, remarkably subtle and complex. Like hell it is. Just another of Younger's pale malt and grits specials. It is untypical, in fact, of interwar Scottish Pale Ales. By this time most other brewers were using healthy doses of sugar and rather less in the way of maize. The more I research William Younger the more realise how untypical they were in general. Just as well I've looked at other brewers' records, too and haven't based all my conclusions on William Younger. I'd be coming out with the sort of crap Horst Dornbusch does.

Sometime in the late 1930's Younger seem to have gone over to all English hops. The records are no more specific than "Kent". My guess is Fuggles. But Goldings wouldn't be crazy, either.

Younger was a big fan of dry hopping. Pretty much all of their beers were dry hopped, including the weediest Milds. Other brewers could have been as keen, but most don't bother recording dry hops on their brewing logs. Lazy bastards (I'm looking at you Whitbread).

1939 William Younger LAE

pale malt	7.75 lb	73.81%
grits	2.75 lb	26.19%
Fuggles 90 min	1.00 oz	
Fuggles 30 min	1.00 oz	
Goldings dry hops	0.50 oz	
OG	1046	
FG	1013	
ABV	4.37	
Apparent attenuation	71.74%	
IBU	26	
SRM	4	
Mash at	156° F	
Sparge at	160° F	
Boil time	105 minutes	
pitching temp	61.5° F	
Yeast	WLP028 Edinburgh Ale	

1940 William Younger P Btlg

Let's move to the other end of Pale Ale spectrum at William Younger. With a luvverly watery beer, P. But not just any P, the bottling version of P.

You know what it looks like to me? A post-war 60/-. They were usually around 1030º. And pretty lightly hopped. Both of which characteristics this beer shares. During the first half of the 20th century Scottish brewers really knocked down their hopping rates. Leaving their beers much less hoppy than those from south of the border.

Whitbread's XX Mild Ale from the same year contained almost twice as many hops, while having only a slightly higher OG (1031.5º). The same was true of Barclay Perkins weaker Mild, A and X (1029º and 1032º) which had around 50% more hops than P. And remember that these beers are Mild, not Pale Ales.

You may have already spotted one unusual feature of this beer. It's all malt. There's a simple explanation for that. Pre-war, Younger's recipes were mostly just pale malt and grits. The war made all maize products unobtainable, as it needed to be imported. At the time there was no maize grown in the UK. Later in the war brewers used either oats or flaked barley as a replacement for maize.

I assume the relatively high OG is to stop the beer tasting too thin. It also means you've got zero chance of getting pissed on it. It's not even 2.5% ABV.

Do let me know if you brew this. I'd love to know how it tastes.

1940 William Younger P Btlg		
pale malt	6.50 lb	100.00%
Fuggles 90 min	0.50 oz	
Fuggles 30 min	0.50 oz	
Goldings dry hops	0.125 oz	
OG	1028	
FG	1010	
ABV	2.38	
Apparent attenuation	64.29%	
IBU	14	
SRM	3	
Mash at	154.5º F	
Sparge at	160º F	
Boil time	105 minutes	
pitching temp	63.5º F	
Yeast	WLP028 Edinburgh Ale	

1939 William Younger Ext

Another Scottish beer, but this time probably more like what you would expect.

Ext – which probably stands for Export – was William Younger's top of the range Pale Ale. I'm still struggling to make sense of their beer range. There seem to be far more beers that necessary. But this one I think I can place. It's not a million miles away from Drybrough 80/- of the same year. That had an OG of 1050 and was the forerunner of their post-war Export.

The term "Export" for a strong Pale Ale seems to have come into use before the war. While "Light" and "Heavy" I've only seen used after the war. At least in terms of Pale Ale. Heavy was sometimes used for Strong Ales – like Fowler's Wee Heavy – earlier, but not for a mid-strength Pale Ale.

The recipe is pretty dull, just pale malt and grits. And one type of hops, plus dry hops. At least it's only 20% grits this time. Not too crazy.

For a Scottish beer the attenuation is pretty reasonable at over 70%. Leaving a beer with over 5% ABV. The FG should be much easier to achieve than with the under-attenuated ones.

I don't have much more to add, other than that you can colour it darker with caramel, if the fancy takes you. I doubt it was always – if ever – sold as brewed. That's the Scots for you. They loved their caramel.

1939 William Younger Ext		
pale malt	10.00 lb	80.00%
grits	2.50 lb	20.00%
Fuggles 90 min	1.25 oz	
Fuggles 30 min	1.25 oz	
Goldings dry hops	0.25 oz	
OG	1054	
FG	1015	
ABV	5.16	
Apparent attenuation	72.22%	
IBU	30	
SRM	4	
Mash at	153° F	
Sparge at	160° F	
Boil time	105 minutes	
pitching temp	60° F	
Yeast	WLP028 Edinburgh Ale	

1949 William Younger LAE

Here's a post-war version of William Younger's LAE, allowing us to compare and contrast with the 1939 version. I always get a kick out of that. Now I think of it, there's also that 1913 version to look at, too.

I'm surprised to see how little the gravity changed over the years. 1045º in 1913, 1046º in 1939 and 1041º in 1949. That's quite unusual. I'd have expected the OG to be under 1040º. And because the degree of attenuation increased, the ABV of the 1949 version is barely lower than the other twentieth-century versions.

There were some big changes to the beer over time. Most of them involuntary. Younger didn't drop the grits and start using flaked barley from choice. Maize, which was imported mostly from the USA, became unavailable during WW II. And the government forced brewers to use flaked barley. Barley production increased enormously during the war, meaning there were reasonable supplies for brewers. The idea behind using flakes was to save the fuel expended in the malting process.

The war is also the reason for the change in hops. During both wars supplies of US hops dried up. But, due to the fall in gravity, the UK became self-sufficient in hops. This continued after WW II meaning there was no need to import hops.

If you look at the chart below you'll see one truly massive change: the level of bitterness. Which fell dramatically between 1898 and 1913 and again between 1913 and 1939. Though remember these are just calculated IBU numbers. Even so, the quantity of hops used was hugely reduced which must have had a big impact on the bitterness of the beer.

Younger LAE 1898 - 1949

Year	grist	hops	OG	FG	ABV	App. atten-uation	IBU
1898	85% pale malt, 15% grits	Cluster and Fuggles	1051	1014	4.89%	72.55%	160
1913	56% pale malt, 44% grits	Cluster and Fuggles	1045	1013	4.23%	71.11%	78
1921	58% pale malt, 42% grits	Cluster, Saaz and Fuggles	1047	1013	4.50%	72.34%	68
1933	57% pale malt, 43% grits	Cluster and Fuggles	1046	1013	4.37%	71.74%	51
1939	74% pale malt, 26% grits	Fuggles	1046	1013	4.37%	71.74%	26
1949	91% pale malt, 9% flaked barley	Fuggles	1041	1010	4.10%	75.61%	24

1949 William Younger LAE		
pale malt	7.75 lb	91.18%
flaked barley	0.75 lb	8.82%
Fuggles 90 min	0.75 oz	
Fuggles 60 min	0.50 oz	
Fuggles 30 min	0.50 oz	
Goldings dry hops	0.50 oz	
OG	1041	
FG	1010	
ABV	4.10	
Apparent attenuation	75.61%	
IBU	24	
SRM	4	
Mash at	155.5° F	
Sparge at	160° F	
Boil time	75 minutes	
pitching temp	60.5° F	
Yeast	WLP028 Edinburgh Ale	

1949 William Younger Pale XXPS

Another exciting beer from the colourful late 1940's. Only joking. I realise the period was as grey as its beers were watery.

This is so exciting. Because this is a beer I drank quite often, it being one of Younger's main cask beers. Though it was sold under different names: 70/- in Scotland, Scotch in England. It seems to have been introduced just after WW I, possibly as a reaction to the drop in gravity of their former flagship Pale Ale, XXP. Post-war, XXP became 60/-. So a beer which had originally been an IPA, ended up as Dark Mild. Now there's a weird transformation. But I digress.

On paper, this looks very similar to the beer I drank in the 1970's and 1980's. The gravity, 1037º, is identical. Though I suspect the recipe was rather different by then. I can't imagine that they continued to use flaked barley. I wonder if they went back to grits when maize became available again?

I know from a 1960 document that XXPS came in three different colours: 5, 6 and 9 SRM. The first was the as-brewed number, which is pretty close to the figure BeerSmith spat out.

Not much else to say, other than that this looks like an archetypal post-war Ordinary Bitter. Maybe the bitterness is a little below average.

1949 William Younger Pale XXPS		
pale malt	7.25 lb	85.29%
flaked barley	1.25 lb	14.71%
Fuggles 90 min	0.50 oz	
Fuggles 60 min	0.50 oz	
Fuggles 30 min	0.50 oz	
Goldings dry hops	0.25 oz	
OG	1037	
FG	1011	
ABV	3.44	
Apparent attenuation	70.27%	
IBU	21	
SRM	4	
Mash at	153º F	
Sparge at	160º F	
Boil time	75 minutes	
pitching temp	62º F	
Yeast	WLP028 Edinburgh Ale	

1954 Drybrough Export

After WW II, Drybrough carried on much as before. They still basically only had a single recipe and all their beers were different strength versions of it.

From the outside, Scottish brewing looked much more complicated than it really was. To all appearances multiple styles were being brewed: Pale Ale, Mild Ale, Stout, Brown Ale and Strong Ale. The sad truth was in the case of brewers like Drybrough it was all really Pale Ale under the covers. Just either brewed to a different strength or fiddled with after primary fermentation.

Recognisable names are starting to appear. Like Export, which was usually a brewery's strongest Pale Ale and was the rough equivalent of an English East Bitter. Oddly, at this period Drybrough didn't brew a Heavy – the equivalent of an English Ordinary Bitter. Oddly, they had another beer, XXP, which had an OG just 2º less than Export. Their other Pale Ale, 60/-, was, at 1032º, too weak for Ordinary Bitter and more like a Mild in terms of strength.

It may not look like it both types of sugar. In 1954 there were no fewer than 5 types of sugar: 2 cwt. Fison, 4 cwt. invert, 2 cwt. Avona[66], 2 cwt. Hydrol and 2 cwt. CME. The last two are the new ones. I've randomly selected No. 2 invert as a substitute. You could replace a bit of that with No. 3 invert, if the fancy takes you.

The hops are only listed by grower, not type or even region. All I know is that they were English. So the chances are they were Goldings, Fuggles or something similar.

The FG I've given is lower than in the brewing record. It's a guess based on analyses I've seen of Drybrough beers which have significantly lower FGs than in the logs.

1954 Drybrough Export		
pale malt	7.50 lb	76.30%
black malt	0.25 lb	2.54%
flaked maize	0.50 lb	5.09%
flaked barley	0.50 lb	5.09%
No. 2 invert sugar	1.00 lb	10.17%
malt extract	0.08 lb	0.81%
Fuggles 90 min	1.00 oz	
Goldings 30 min	0.75 oz	
Goldings dry hops	0.25 oz	
OG	1045	
FG	1011	
ABV	4.50	
Apparent attenuation	75.56%	
IBU	22	
SRM	14	
Mash at	148º F	
Sparge at	170º F	
Boil time	90 minutes	
pitching temp	65º F	
Yeast	WLP028 Edinburgh Ale	

---

[66] "Avona - the superlative copper sugar" Journal of the Institute of Brewing: Volume 46, 1940.

1957 Robert Younger 60/-

If you're starting to think that 1950s Scottish recipes are a bit dull, you're not far off track. Robert Younger won't disappoint. They're another one recipe brewery.

Obviously it's a Pale Ale recipe. With the standard combination of Pale malt, flaked maize and sugar. With a tiny amount of malt extract thrown in, presumably for enzymes. On the home brewing level, it's probably irrelevant. I've include it for historical accuracy.

Only two sugars this time: 5 cwt. invert, 4 cwt. Hydrol. I've substituted No. 2 invert. There was also a small amount of something called "colour", presumably some sort of caramel for colour adjustment. They probably coloured their beers up all sorts of ways at racking time, too. You can colour it anyway you want, really.

Robert Younger was another Scottish underlet brewer. An underlet at 180º raised the mash temperature to 153º F. I'm now wondering how many other Scottish brewers mashed this way. I've found three so far.

The hops are only described as English in the brewing record. Fuggles and Goldings Are what I always guess. Any hop grown in England at the time is a reasonable substitute for either.

I've adjusted the FG – give as 1011º in the brewing record – based on analyses I have from other sources.

Almost forgot – is this Pale Ale or, as I always considered 60/-, a Mild Ale? Who knows?

1957 Robert Younger 60/-		
pale malt	4.75 lb	75.28%
flaked maize	0.75 lb	11.89%
No. 2 invert sugar	0.75 lb	11.89%
malt extract	0.06 lb	0.95%
Fuggles 120 min	0.50 oz	
Goldings 30 min	0.50 oz	
Goldings dry hops	0.25 oz	
OG	1030	
FG	1007	
ABV	3.04	
Apparent attenuation	76.67%	
IBU	14	
SRM	5	
Mash at	151° F	
Sparge at	170° F	
Boil time	120 minutes	
pitching temp	60° F	
Yeast	WLP028 Edinburgh Ale	

1958 Bernard Pale 1/1

Bernard were certainly different from most of their Scottish colleagues. Not only did they have more than one recipe, they even had two recipes for the same beer.

Like everyone else in Scotland, Bernard brewed several Pale Ales of different strength. And, as you would expect, they parti-gyled them in various combination. The weakest, Pale 1/1, however, was sometimes brewed single gyle. When it was, the recipe was different from when it was parti-gyled with a stronger Pale Ale.

The difference lies in the adjuncts. Flaked maize is the only adjunct in the posher Pale Ale recipe. While the cheap recipe for Pale 1/1 also includes grits and corn grits. I've never seen a beer with both grits and flaked maize. Nor one with rice grits. It's all a bit odd, because it means that the mashing scheme for single-gyle Pale 1/1 would have to include an extra step to gelatinise the grits.

Why did they brew it this way? To save money, I would guess. That it's only for their cheapest beer is a clue.

Bernard took light hopping to a new extreme. At just over 3 lbs per quarter of malt, it's the fewest hops I've ever seen in a beer that's technically a Pale Ale.

The hops are a guess. That they're English is all I know. There's also no mention of dry hops, so that's a guess, too. But, based what I've seen at other Scottish breweries, I'd expect this beer to have been dry hopped.

And as for the co our . . . . refer back to the section on colouring. This is Bernard's No. 3 quality Pale Ale. Which means you can colour anything up to 35 SRM. Oddly, the colour calculated from the recipe is 15 SRM. Darker than the palest colour variant.

1958 Bernard Pale 1/1		
pale malt	5.25 lb	71.62%
black malt	0.33 lb	4.50%
flaked maize	0.25 lb	3.41%
grits	0.50 lb	6.82%
rice grits	0.50 lb	6.82%
No. 2 invert sugar	0.50 lb	6.82%
Fuggles 105 min	0.50 oz	
Goldings 30 min	0.25 oz	
Goldings dry hops	0.25 oz	
OG	1031	
FG	1007	
ABV	3.18	
Apparent attenuation	77.42%	
IBU	11	
SRM	any colour you like	
Mash at	149° F	
Sparge at	167° F	
Boil time	105 minutes	
pitching temp	61° F	
Yeast	WLP028 Edinburgh Ale	

1965 Maclay SPA

Maclay's records are easily the dullest I've ever come across. For a decade – 1956 to 1966 – they brewed exactly the same recipe every day. The same ingredients in the same quantities. From which they parti-gyled three Pale Ales and a Strong Ale.

It must have been so exciting for the brewers in 1966 when they brought back Oat Malt Stout. Or maybe it made the brewers nervous, suddenly having to do something different.

SPA was Maclay's 70/-, a beer I drank often enough in the 1970's and 1980's. Basically a middle of the road Ordinary Bitter, but a very tasty drink. The grist is much the same as for all Scottish Pale Ales after the war: pale malt, flaked maize and sugar. Though there's also the 1950's favourite, malt extract, thrown in.

The No. 3 invert is a substitution for a proprietary sugar called DCS. I've chosen No. 3 purely on the basis of the "D", assuming it stands for dark. There was also a little caramel in the original recipe.

As usual, I know very little about the hops, other than that almost all were English. With 10 lbs. of the 112 lbs. total being Styrian I thought it was too small an amount to worry about, but feel free to use a few if you have them. The boiling time is also a guess. I doubt it would have been any shorter, but it might have been 15 – 20 minutes longer.

1965 Maclay SPA		
pale malt	5.75 lb	76.67%
flaked maize	0.75 lb	10.00%
malt extract	0.25 lb	3.33%
No. 1 invert	0.50 lb	6.67%
No. 3 invert	0.25 lb	3.33%
Northern Brewer 90 min	0.75 oz	
Fuggles 60 min	0.50 oz	
Goldings 30 min	0.50 oz	
Goldings dry hops	0.25 oz	
OG	1035	
FG	1010	
ABV	3.31	
Apparent attenuation	71.43%	
IBU	33	
SRM	5	
Mash at	148/158° F	
Sparge at	165° F	
Boil time	90 minutes	
pitching temp	62° F	
Yeast	WLP028 Edinburgh Ale	

1957 Robert Younger Old Edinburgh Ale

From their one recipe, Robert Younger brewed four Pale Ales, a Stout – somehow – a Strong Ale and also something billed as an Old Ale.

I don't know what the colour of the beer when it hit the pub or shop. But my bet would be on something a fair bit darker than the colour as brewed.

The level of hopping in Robert Younger's beers, even for 1950's Scotland, is low. Even this, one of their higher-gravity beers, can't crawl its way up to 20 IBU.

English brewers haven't been averse to colouring up beers to produce an Old Ale. Like Harvey's. I'm pretty sure their Old Ale is just Sussex Best with caramel. Just like this is basically Robert Younger's 80/- (Export) probably coloured up.

1957 Robert Younger Old Edinburgh Ale		
pale malt	7.25 lb	75.52%
flaked maize	1.50 lb	15.63%
No. 2 invert sugar	0.75 lb	7.81%
malt extract	0.10 lb	1.04%
Fuggles 120 min	0.75 oz	
Goldings 30 min	0.75 oz	
Goldings dry hops	0.50 oz	
OG	1044	
FG	1007	
ABV	4.89	
Apparent attenuation	72.73%	
IBU	19	
SRM	6	
Mash at	148° F	
Sparge at	170° F	
Boil time	120 minutes	
pitching temp	60° F	
Yeast	WLP028 Edinburgh Ale	

1949 William Younger No 1

No. 1 emerged from WW II relatively unscathed, with the gravity only dropping a little, from 1085º to 1074º.

There was, however, a pretty significant change to the recipes. Out went the grits, so beloved by William Younger in the first part of the 20th century, replaced by flaked barley. This wasn't a voluntary change. Wartime restrictions demanded that brewers use flaked barley from 1943 onwards. Grits or even flaked maize became impossible to obtain because they needed to be imported.

The lactose is still there, though. Presumably to boost body. I'm really not sure about the mild malt. There's something simply called "M" in the brewing record. The only type of malt I can think of that starts with that letter is mild malt. But I somehow doubt that's what it is, given the small quantity. You can just boost the pale malt a little and leave it out if you want.

The hops are only indicated as being from Kent. The chances are they were Fuggles or Goldings, which made up the vast majority of hops grown in the UK at the time.

The colour I've taken from an analysis made in the mid-1950's. As brewed it comes out to about 7 SRM. You'll need – just as Younger did – to add caramel after primary fermentation to get the correct colour.

1949 William Younger No. 1		
pale malt	13.50 lb	78.26%
crystal malt 60L	0.50 lb	2.90%
mild malt	0.50 lb	2.90%
flaked barley	2.00 lb	11.59%
lactose	0.75 lb	4.35%
Fuggles 90 min	1.00 oz	
Fuggles 60 min	1.00 oz	
Fuggles 30 min	0.75 oz	
Goldings dry hops	0.25 oz	
OG	1074	
FG	1023	
ABV	6.75	
Apparent attenuation	68.92%	
IBU	29	
SRM	20	
Mash at	152° F	
Sparge at	160° F	
Boil time	90 minutes	
pitching temp	57.5° F	
Yeast	WLP028 Edinburgh Ale	

1949 William Younger No. 3 Btlg

No. 3 is a personal favourite of mine. Having drunk when it was still brewed by William Younger has left me with a lingering affection for the beer.

Which explains why I keep bothering you with recipes for it. I'm hoping eventually I'll get some in my glass. Though this is quite a tame looking version, what with its low level of hopping and modest OG.

As I've been explaining, foreign hops disappeared for the most part from British beer after WW II. For the simple reason that they weren't required any more. The UK was capable of growing all the hops it needed. Which certainly hadn't been true for the second half of the 19th century and some of the early 20th. You occasionally see classy continental hops like Saaz or Hallertau, but US hops had disappeared entirely from British beer.

It's strange that Younger's grists actually appear to have improved in quality due to government restrictions. The 1933 version of No. 3 contained 41% grits. I wonder if drinkers noticed? If they did, they'd probably have complained that the beer didn't taste like it used to. During the whole interwar period Younger's beers had crazy levels of grits in them. People must have got used to it.

I wouldn't pay too much attention to the colour listed. Third-party analyses I have of the beer put the colour somewhere in the 20's on the SRM scale.

1949 William Younger No. 3 Btlg		
pale malt	9.75 lb	88.64%
flaked barley	1.25 lb	11.36%
Fuggles 90 min	0.75 oz	
Fuggles 60 min	0.50 oz	
Fuggles 30 min	0.50 oz	
Goldings dry hops	0.25 oz	
OG	1047	
FG	1012	
ABV	4.63	
Apparent attenuation	74.47%	
IBU	22	
SRM	4	
Mash at	153° F	
Sparge at	160° F	
Boil time	75 minutes	
pitching temp	61° F	
Yeast	WLP028 Edinburgh Ale	

1954 Drybrough Burns Ale

In the 1950's, Scottish brewers continued to make small amounts of pretty strong beer. Certainly stronger than most of the beer you'd find in England. That's the weird thing about Scottish brewing. Often its beers were both weaker and stronger than in England.

It's a recurring theme in Scottish Beer. It was exactly the same in the middle of the 19th century, when brewers were turning out incredibly high-gravity beers as well as pretty weak Table Beers. In London, the beers tended to occupy more the middle ground, say 1050-1080º.

Burns Ale was, of course, just a very strong version of Drybrough's Pale Ale recipe. The only one they had.

It's quite odd that Drybrough were still using flaked barley. It was forced on brewers by the government during WW II as a replacement for flaked barley. Most dropped it again as soon as supplies of maize were restored. Maybe Drybrough liked it. On the other hand, they did stop using it in the late 1950s.

1954 Drybrough Burns Ale		
pale malt	12.75 lb	77.86%
black malt	0.125 lb	0.76%
flaked maize	1.00 lb	6.11%
flaked barley	1.00 lb	6.11%
No. 2 invert sugar	1.25 lb	7.63%
malt extract	0.25 lb	1.53%
Fuggles 90 min	1.50 oz	
Goldings 30 min	1.50 oz	
Goldings dry hops	1.00 oz	
OG	1073	
FG	1024	
ABV	6.48	
Apparent attenuation	67.12%	
IBU	31	
SRM	12	
Mash at	147º F	
Sparge at	170º F	
Boil time	90 minutes	
pitching temp	62º F	
yeast	WLP028 Edinburgh Ale	

1958 Robert Younger Strong Ale

Most Scottish brewers seem to have produced roughly similar Strong Ales after WW II. Usually brewed in a parti-gyle with Pale Ale. Which is exactly how Robert Younger made theirs.

The grist is typically post-war: pale malt, flaked maize and sugar. The latter being invert and Hydrol, for which I've substituted No. 2 invert. Just as a guess. There is, however, one ingredient which doesn't feature in the purely Pale Ale gyles: liquorice. Which is a little strange. It's something that usually only turns up in Stout.

Having an analysis of this beer from roughly the same dead was very useful. It's allowed me to adjust the FG down from what's in the brewing record and to increase the colour from that calculated based on the ingredients. As there was clearly a colour adjustment after primary fermentation.

1958 Robert Younger Strong Ale		
pale malt	11.00 lb	72.61%
flaked maize	2.75 lb	18.15%
No. 2 invert sugar	1.25 lb	8.25%
malt extract	0.15 lb	0.99%
caramel	0.35 oz	
liquorice	0.07 oz	
Fuggles 120 min	1.25 oz	
Goldings 30 min	1.25 oz	
Goldings dry hops	0.50 oz	
OG	1070	
FG	1018	
ABV	6.88	
Apparent attenuation	74.29%	
IBU	27	
SRM	26	
Mash at	148° F	
Sparge at	170° F	
Boil time	120 minutes	
pitching temp	61.5° F	
Yeast	WLP028 Edinburgh Ale	

1971 Maclay Strong Ale

Maclay, like most Scottish brewers, produced a Strong Ale. But they discontinues it sometime in the late 1950's or early 1960's. It returned in the early 1970's, but only seems to have been brewed intermittently.

As you would expect, it was just a very strong version of their Pale Ale parti-gyle. The only recipe they used. It's exactly what you would expect: pale malt, flaked maize and sugar. Note how little crystal malt was used in Scotland. Pale Ales usually contained no other malt than the base pale malt. Even in England, crystal malt was rare in Pale Ales before WW II.

Just like with the other Maclay beers, I've replaced proprietary sugar DCS with No. 3 invert. And guessed about the hops and dry hopping. As brewed the colour is much paler and you'll need to add caramel to hit 20 SRM. The real FG might well have been lower, around 1020º, so don't get too worried if it ferments out past 1029º

1971 Maclay Strong Ale

pale malt	12.75 lb	76.12%
flaked maize	1.75 lb	10.45%
malt extract	0.50 lb	2.99%
No. 1 invert	1.25 lb	7.46%
No. 3 invert	0.50 lb	2.99%
Fuggles 90 min	1.00 oz	
Fuggles 60 min	1.00 oz	
Goldings 30 min	1.00 oz	
Goldings dry hops	0.75 oz	
OG	1077	
FG	1029	
ABV	6.35	
Apparent attenuation	62.34%	
IBU	30	
SRM	20	
Mash at	147/156º F	
Sparge at	165º F	
Boil time	90 minutes	
pitching temp	61º F	
Yeast	WLP028 Edinburgh Ale	

1970 Drybrough Continental Lager

This beer started as a bit of a puzzle. Mostly because I couldn't read the name. Something ending in "–tal" was about all I could make. I had to go through just about every photograph before I found a legible one.

Looking in the ingredients, it was obviously a Lager. Which was dead pleasing, as I'm a bit short on Scottish Lager recipes. It's the watery, bland type of Lager I avoided like the plague in my youth. But which now fascinates me.

Drybrough really changed the way they brewed in the late 1960's. They stopped parti-gyling and they started brewing multiple recipes. Funnily enough, it's just after the company was acquired by Watney Mann. I'm sure the two events can't have ben unconnected.

They also started brewing some new beers: a Brown Ale, what looks like a Mild Ale and this Lager. Quite a big change for a brewery that had basically only brewed Pale Ale for three or four decades. They also simplified their recipes, doing away with most proprietary sugars.

There's not a lot to this recipe. Just lager malt, flaked maize and English hops. Oddly, some of their other beers brewed around this time contained Hallertau. While the Lager had all English hops. I've guessed the varieties. You can substitute any English hop that was around then, like Northern Brewer or Bramling Cross.

As for the mashing scheme, I've reproduced it exactly as in the brewing record. It lists four temperatures which are presumably a complex step mash. I'm not sure they had the right equipment to decoct. If you fancy having a go at a decoction, please do.

This period of Drybrough's records don't give any fermentation details. My guess is that they pitched in the mid 50's F and cooled it down. Though given that the fermentation only lasted 6 days, they might have fermented it quite warm.

1970 Drybrough Continental Lager		
lager malt	6.25 lb	86.21%
flaked maize	1.00 lb	13.79%
Fuggles 90 min	0.50 oz	
Goldings 30 min	0.25 oz	
OG	1032.8	
FG	1007	
ABV	3.41	
Apparent attenuation	78.66%	
IBU	10	
SRM	3	
Mash at	120/146/165/210° F	
Sparge at	175° F	
Boil time	90 minutes	
pitching temp	54° F	
Yeast	WLP800 Pilsner Lager	

Appendix I - Let's Brew

William Younger
1840 - 1880

1847 William Younger 80/-		
pale malt	11.75 b	82.46%
table sugar	2.50 lb	17.54%
Goldings 90 min	1.50 oz	
Goldings 30 min	1.25 oz	
OG	1071	
FG	1030	
ABV	5.42	
Apparent attenuation	57.75%	
IBU	30	
SRM	6	
Mash at	149° F	
Sparge at	184° F	
Boil time	90 minutes	
pitching temp	59° F	
Yeast	WLP028 Edinburgh Ale	

1847 William Younger 120/-		
pale malt	22.50 lb	100.00%
Goldings 70 min	5.00 oz	
Goldings 30 min	4.00 oz	
OG	1099	
FG	1040	
ABV	7.81	
Apparent attenuation	59.60%	
IBU	77	
SRM	9	
Mash at	151° F	
Sparge at	184° F	
Boil time	70 minutes	
pitching temp	55° F	
Yeast	WLP028 Edinburgh Ale	

1847 William Younger 140/-			
pale malt	25.25 lb	100.00%
Goldings 50 min	7.50 oz	
Goldings 20 min	4.50 oz	
OG	1112	
FG	1046	
ABV	8.73	
Apparent attenuation	58.93%	
IBU	81	
SRM	9	
Mash at	152° F	
Sparge at	186° F	
Boil time	50 minutes	
pitching temp	54° F	
Yeast	WLP028 Edinburgh Ale	

1849 William Younger XS Stock Ale			
pale malt	24.75 lb	100.00%
Goldings 60 min	7.00 oz	
Goldings 30 min	5.00 oz	
Goldings dry hops	1.00 oz	
OG	1108	
FG	1036	
ABV	9.53	
Apparent attenuation	66.67%	
IBU	86	
SRM	9	
Mash at	152° F	
Sparge at	185° F	
Boil time	60 minutes	
pitching temp	55° F	
Yeast	WLP028 Edinburgh Ale	

1849 William Younger S Stock Ale			
pale malt	21.50 lb	100.00%
Goldings 60 min	6.00 oz	
Goldings 30 min	3.00 oz	
Goldings dry hops	0.75 oz	
OG	1095	
FG	1028	
ABV	8.86	
Apparent attenuation	70.53%	
IBU	74	
SRM	8	
Mash at	151° F	
Sparge at	185° F	
Boil time	60 minutes	
pitching temp	55° F	
Yeast	WLP028 Edinburgh Ale	

1851 William Younger 80/-

pale malt	26.25 lb	100.00%
Goldings 90 min	2.50 oz	
Goldings 60 min	2.00 oz	
Goldings 30 min	2.00 oz	
OG	1085	
FG	1034	
ABV	6.75	
Apparent attenuation	60.00%	
IBU	72	
SRM	8	
Mash at	154° F	
Sparge at	184° F	
Boil time	90 minutes	
pitching temp	56° F	
Yeast	WLP028 Edinburgh Ale	

1851 William Younger XXP

pale malt	16.75 lb	100.00%
Goldings 75 min	6.00 oz	
Goldings 45 min	6.00 oz	
Goldings 30 min	6.00 oz	
OG	1072	
FG	1018	
ABV	7.14	
Apparent attenuation	75.00%	
IBU	217	
SRM	6	
Mash at	153° F	
Sparge at	184° F	
Boil time	75 minutes	
pitching temp	56° F	
Yeast	WLP028 Edinburgh Ale	

1851 William Younger 60/-

pale malt	16.25 lb	100.00%
Goldings 105 min	1.00 oz	
Goldings 60 min	1.00 oz	
Goldings 30 min	1.00 oz	
OG	1072	
FG	1030	
ABV	5.56	
Apparent attenuation	58.33%	
IBU	36	
SRM	7	
Mash at	151° F	
Sparge at	184° F	
Boil time	105 minutes	
pitching temp	56° F	
Yeast	WLP028 Edinburgh Ale	

1851 William Younger S Stock Ale

pale malt	22.75 lb	100.00%
Goldings 75 min	4.00 oz	
Goldings 45 min	4.00 oz	
Goldings 30 min	4.00 oz	
OG	1098	
FG	1034	
ABV	8.47	
Apparent attenuation	65.31%	
IBU	121	
SRM	7	
Mash at	153° F	
Sparge at	184° F	
Boil time	75 minutes	
pitching temp	57° F	
Yeast	WLP028 Edinburgh Ale	

1851 William Younger 100/-

pale malt	24.25 lb	100.00%
Goldings 90 min	2.00 oz	
Goldings 60 min	2.00 oz	
Goldings 30 min	2.00 oz	
OG	1104	
FG	1039	
ABV	8.60	
Apparent attenuation	62.50%	
IBU	58	
SRM	8	
Mash at	153° F	
Sparge at	184° F	
Boil time	90 minutes	
pitching temp	58° F	
Yeast	WLP028 Edinburgh Ale	

1851 William Younger 42/-

pale malt	10.00 lb	100.00%
Goldings 75 min	2.00 oz	
Goldings 50 min	1.00 oz	
Goldings 20 min	1.00 oz	
OG	1043	
FG	1014	
ABV	3.84	
Apparent attenuation	67.44%	
IBU	57	
SRM	4	
Mash at	153° F	
Sparge at	184° F	
Boil time	75 minutes	
pitching temp	57° F	
Yeast	WLP028 Edinburgh Ale	

1851 William Younger XX Mild Ale

pale malt	19.00 lb	100.00%
Goldings 90 min	4.00 oz	
Goldings 60 min	3.00 oz	
Goldings 20 min	3.00 oz	
OG	1032	
FG	1029	
ABV	7.01	
Apparent attenuation	64.63%	
IBU	109	
SRM	6	
Mash at	155° F	
Sparge at	184° F	
Boil time	90 minutes	
pitching temp	56° F	
Yeast	WLP028 Edinburgh Ale	

1851 William Younger T Table Beer

pale malt	8.50 lb	100.00%
Goldings 75 min	1.50 oz	
Goldings 50 min	1.00 oz	
Goldings 20 min	1.00 oz	
OG	1037	
FG	1013	
ABV	3.18	
Apparent attenuation	64.86%	
IBU	55	
SRM	4	
Mash at	153° F	
Sparge at	184° F	
Boil time	75 minutes	
pitching temp	58° F	
Yeast	WLP028 Edinburgh Ale	

1851 William Younger BS Porter

pale malt	6.50 lb	43.33%
brown malt	4.75 lb	31.67%
black malt	3.75 lb	25.00%
Goldings 120 min	2.00 oz	
Goldings 60 min	2.00 oz	
Goldings 30 min	2.00 oz	
OG	1057	
FG	1017	
ABV	5.29	
Apparent attenuation	70.18%	
IBU	80	
SRM	77	
Mash at	149° F	
Sparge at	184° F	
Boil time	120 minutes	
pitching temp	64° F	
Yeast	WLP028 Edinburgh Ale	

1851 William Younger XXX Mild Ale

pale malt	21.50 lb	100.00%
Goldings 80 min	4.00 oz	
Goldings 50 min	3.00 oz	
Goldings 20 min	3.00 oz	
OG	1093	
FG	1034	
ABV	7.81	
Apparent attenuation	63.44%	
IBU	100	
SRM	7	
Mash at	153° F	
Sparge at	184° F	
Boil time	80 minutes	
pitching temp	56° F	
Yeast	WLP028 Edinburgh Ale	

1859 William Younger No. 3

pale malt	21.00 lb	100.00%
Goldings 80 min	5.00 oz	
Goldings 60 min	5.00 oz	
Goldings 20 min	5.00 oz	
Goldings dry hops	2.25 oz	
OG	1090	
FG	1028	
ABV	8.20	
Apparent attenuation	68.89%	
IBU	150	
SRM	7	
Mash at	154° F	
Sparge at	186° F	
Boil time	80 minutes	
pitching temp	56° F	
Yeast	WLP028 Edinburgh Ale	

1868 William Younger 46/-

pale malt	9.00 lb	100.00%
Cluster 90 min	1.50 oz	spent hops
Goldings dry hops	1.00 oz	
OG	1039	
FG	1013	
ABV	3.44	
Apparent attenuation	66.67%	
IBU	34	
SRM	4	
Mash at	154° F	
Sparge at	185° F	
Boil time	120 minutes	
pitching temp	61° F	
Yeast	WLP028 Edinburgh Ale	

1868 William Younger 50/-

pale malt	9.25 lb	100.00%
Saaz 90 min	2.00 oz	spent hops
Saaz dry hops	0.50 oz	
OG	1040	
FG	1011	
ABV	3.84	
Apparent attenuation	72.50%	
IBU	28	
SRM	4	
Mash at	154° F	
Sparge at	185° F	
Boil time	120 minutes	
pitching temp	61° F	
Yeast	WLP028 Edinburgh Ale	

1868 William Younger 60/-

pale malt	11.00 lb	100.00%
Goldings 90 min	1.50 oz	spent hops
OG	1047	
FG	1021	
ABV	3.44	
Apparent attenuation	55.32%	
IBU	23	
SRM	4	
Mash at	154° F	
Sparge at	185° F	
Boil time	120 minutes	
pitching temp	62° F	
Yeast	WLP028 Edinburgh Ale	

1868 William Younger 100/-

pale malt	17.75 lb	100.00%
Cluster 90 min	2.00 oz	
Saaz 60 min	2.00 oz	
Saaz 20 min	2.00 oz	
OG	1076	
FG	1034	
ABV	5.56	
Apparent attenuation	55.26%	
IBU	63	
SRM	6	
Mash at	154° F	
Sparge at	185° F	
Boil time	105 minutes	
pitching temp	57° F	
Yeast	WLP028 Edinburgh Ale	

1868 William Younger 120/-

pale malt	20.50 lb	100.00%
Goldings 90 min	2.50 oz	
Saaz 60 min	2.50 oz	
Saaz 20 min	2.50 oz	
Saaz dry hops	0.50 oz	
OG	1088	
FG	1037	
ABV	6.75	
Apparent attenuation	57.95%	
IBU	55	
SRM	7	
Mash at	154° F	
Sparge at	185° F	
Boil time	90 minutes	
pitching temp	57° F	
Yeast	WLP028 Edinburgh Ale	

1868 William Younger 140/-

pale malt	23.75 lb	100.00%
Goldings 90 min	3.00 oz	
Saaz 60 min	3.00 oz	
Saaz 20 min	3.00 oz	
Goldings dry hops	1.25 oz	
OG	1102	
FG	1043	
ABV	7.81	
Apparent attenuation	57.84%	
IBU	67	
SRM	7	
Mash at	154° F	
Sparge at	185° F	
Boil time	90 minutes	
pitching temp	56° F	
Yeast	WLP028 Edinburgh Ale	

1868 William Younger 160/-

pale malt	27.00 lb	100.00%
Goldings 80 min	4.00 oz	
Goldings 60 min	4.00 oz	
Saaz 20 min	4.00 oz	
Saaz dry hops	1.50 oz	
OG	1116	
FG	1053	
ABV	8.33	
Apparent attenuation	54.31%	
IBU	85	
SRM	8	
Mash at	154° F	
Sparge at	185° F	
Boil time	80 minutes	
pitching temp	57° F	
Yeast	WLP028 Edinburgh Ale	

1868 William Younger XP		
pale malt	11.75 lb	100.00%
Spalt 90 min	2.00 oz	
Spalt 60 min	2.00 oz	
Spalt 20 min	2.00 oz	
Spalt dry hops	1.375 oz	
OG	1051	
FG	1013	
ABV	5.03	
Apparent attenuation	74.51%	
IBU	67	
SRM	5	
Mash at	154° F	
Sparge at	185° F	
Boil time	120 minutes	
pitching temp	59° F	
Yeast	WLP028 Edinburgh Ale	

1868 William Younger XXP		
pale malt	11.75 lb	100.00%
Saaz 90 min	1.50 oz	
Saaz 60 min	1.50 oz	
Saaz 20 min	1.50 oz	
Saaz dry hops	1.75 oz	
OG	1052	
FG	1016	
ABV	4.76	
Apparent attenuation	69.23%	
IBU	73	
SRM	5	
Mash at	154° F	
Sparge at	185° F	
Boil time	120 minutes	
pitching temp	60° F	
Yeast	WLP028 Edinburgh Ale	

1868 William Younger X Mild Ale

pale malt	12.25 lb	100.00%
Goldings 90 min	1.00 oz	
Goldings 60 min	1.00 oz	
Goldings 30 min	1.00 oz	
OG	1053	
FG	1023	
ABV	3.97	
Apparent attenuation	56.60%	
IBU	41	
SRM	5	
Mash at	154° F	
Sparge at	185° F	
Boil time	120 minutes	
pitching temp	59° F	
Yeast	WLP028 Edinburgh Ale	

1868 William Younger XX Mild Ale

pale malt	12.25 lb	100.00%
Poperinge 90 min	1.00 oz	
Saaz 90 min	0.50 oz	
Saaz 60 min	1.50 oz	
Saaz 20 min	1.50 oz	
Saaz dry hops	0.50 oz	
OG	1057	
FG	1024	
ABV	4.37	
Apparent attenuation	57.89%	
IBU	41	
SRM	5	
Mash at	154° F	
Sparge at	185° F	
Boil time	120 minutes	
pitching temp	58° F	
Yeast	WLP028 Edinburgh Ale	

1869 William Younger XXXX Mild Ale		
pale malt	20.75 lb	100.00%
Strisselspalt 90 min	3.00 oz	
Strisselspalt 60 min	3.00 oz	
Goldings 30 min	3.00 oz	
OG	1089	
FG	1021	
ABV	9.00	
Apparent attenuation	76.40%	
IBU	84	
SRM	7	
Mash at	154° F	
Sparge at	185° F	
Boil time	105 minutes	
pitching temp	57° F	
Yeast	WLP028 Edinburgh Ale	

1868 William Younger S Stock Ale		
pale malt	18.00 lb	100.00%
Strisselspalt 90 min	0.75 oz	
Saaz 60 min	0.75 oz	
Saaz 20 min	0.75 oz	
Saaz dry hops	0.75 oz	
OG	1077	
FG	1032	
ABV	5.95	
Apparent attenuation	58.44%	
IBU	21	
SRM	6	
Mash at	154° F	
Sparge at	185° F	
Boil time	90 minutes	
pitching temp	58° F	
Yeast	WLP028 Edinburgh Ale	

1868 William Younger XXS Stock Ale

pale malt	23.75 lb	100.00%
Goldings 90 min	3.50 oz	
Saaz 20 min	3.50 oz	
Goldings dry hops	0.50 oz	
OG	1102	
FG	1045	
ABV	7.54	
Apparent attenuation	55.88%	
IBU	56	
SRM	7	
Mash at	154° F	
Sparge at	185° F	
Boil time	90 minutes	
pitching temp	56° F	
Yeast	WLP028 Edinburgh Ale	

1868 William Younger XXXS Stock Ale

pale malt	30.00 lb	100.00%
Strisselspalt 90 min	2.75 oz	
Goldings 90 min	2.00 oz	
Goldings 60 min	5.00 oz	
Spalt 20 min	4.00 oz	
Goldings dry hops	4.50 oz	
OG	1129	
FG	1066	
ABV	8.33	
Apparent attenuation	48.84%	
IBU	100	
SRM	9	
Mash at	154° F	
Sparge at	185° F	
Boil time	90 minutes	
pitching temp	55° F	
Yeast	WLP028 Edinburgh Ale	

1868 William Younger No. 1 Ale (London)		
pale malt	23.00 lb	100.00%
Strisselspalt 90 min	2.50 oz	
Strisselspalt 60 min	1.25 oz	
Goldings 60 min	1.25 oz	
Goldings 20 min	2.50 oz	
Goldings dry hops	0.75 oz	
OG	1099	
FG	1041	
ABV	7.67	
Apparent attenuation	58.59%	
IBU	63	
SRM	7	
Mash at	154° F	
Sparge at	185° F	
Boil time	105 minutes	
pitching temp	56° F	
Yeast	WLP028 Edinburgh Ale	

1868 William Younger No. 2 Ale (London)		
pale malt	20.50 lb	100.00%
Strisselspalt 90 min	1.50 oz	
Spalt 60 min	1.50 oz	
Goldings 60 min	1.50 oz	
Goldings 20 min	1.50 oz	
Goldings dry hops	0.75 oz	
OG	1088	
FG	1034	
ABV	7.14	
Apparent attenuation	61.36%	
IBU	58	
SRM	7	
Mash at	154° F	
Sparge at	185° F	
Boil time	90 minutes	
pitching temp	56° F	
Yeast	WLP028 Edinburgh Ale	

1869 William Younger No. 3 Ale (London)

pale malt	18.00 lb	100.00%
Strisselspalt 90 min	1.50 oz	
Goldings 60 min	2.50 oz	
Spalt 20 min	2.25 oz	
Goldings dry hops	0.75 oz	
OG	1077	
FG	1031	
ABV	6.09	
Apparent attenuation	59.74%	
IBU	72	
SRM	6	
Mash at	154° F	
Sparge at	185° F	
Boil time	105 minutes	
pitching temp	57° F	
Yeast	WLP028 Edinburgh Ale	

1868 William Younger Bottling Porter

pale malt	10.40 lb	93.27%
black malt	0.75 lb	6.73%
Goldings 90 min	1.50 oz	spent hops
OG	1046	
FG	1020	
ABV	3.44	
Apparent attenuation	56.52%	
IBU	25	
SRM	24	
Mash at	150° F	
Sparge at	185° F	
Boil time	120 minutes	
pitching temp	61° F	
Yeast	WLP028 Edinburgh Ale	

1879 William Younger T Table Beer

pale malt	7.00 lb	100.00%
Cluster 90 min	1.25 oz	
Goldings 20 min	0.75 oz	
Goldings dry hops	0.50 oz	
OG	1030	
FG	1005	
ABV	3.31	
Apparent attenuation	83.33%	
IBU	40	
SRM	3	
Mash at	154° F	
Sparge at	170° F	
Boil time	105 minutes	
pitching temp	61° F	
Yeast	WLP028 Edinburgh Ale	

1879 William Younger S 50/-

pale malt	9.75 lb	100.00%
Goldings 90 min	0.75 oz	spent hops
OG	1042	
FG	1012	
ABV	3.97	
Apparent attenuation	71.43%	
IBU	34	
SRM	4	
Mash at	154° F	
Sparge at	170° F	
Boil time	120 minutes	
pitching temp	62° F	
Yeast	WLP028 Edinburgh Ale	

1879 William Younger H 60/-

pale malt	9.25 lb	100.00%
Cluster 90 min	1.25 oz	
Goldings 30 min	1.25 oz	
Goldings dry hops	0.75 oz	
OG	1040	
FG	1004	
ABV	4.76	
Apparent attenuation	90.00%	
IBU	43	
SRM	4	
Mash at	150° F	
Sparge at	170° F	
Boil time	105 minutes	
pitching temp	61° F	
Yeast	WLP028 Edinburgh Ale	

1879 William Younger 80/-

pale malt	13.75 lb	100.00%
Cluster 90 min	2.50 oz	
Goldings 30 min	2.50 oz	
Goldings dry hops	0.125 oz	
OG	1059	
FG	1020	
ABV	5.16	
Apparent attenuation	66.10%	
IBU	75	
SRM	5	
Mash at	150° F	
Sparge at	170° F	
Boil time	90 minutes	
pitching temp	61° F	
Yeast	WLP028 Edinburgh Ale	

1879 William Younger 100/-

pale malt	16.25 lb	100.00%
Cluster 90 min	3.00 oz	
Goldings 30 min	3.00 oz	
OG	1070	
FG	1026	
ABV	5.82	
Apparent attenuation	62.86%	
IBU	88	
SRM	6	
Mash at	150° F	
Sparge at	170° F	
Boil time	90 minutes	
pitching temp	60° F	
Yeast	WLP028 Edinburgh Ale	

1879 William Younger 120/-

pale malt	19.25 lb	100.00%
Cluster 90 min	4.25 oz	
Goldings 30 min	4.25 oz	
Goldings dry hops	0.125 oz	
OG	1083	
FG	1032	
ABV	6.75	
Apparent attenuation	61.45%	
IBU	114	
SRM	6	
Mash at	149° F	
Sparge at	170° F	
Boil time	90 minutes	
pitching temp	60° F	
Yeast	WLP028 Edinburgh Ale	

1879 William Younger 140/-

pale malt	22.26 lb	100.00%
Cluster 90 min	4.25 oz	
Goldings 30 min	4.25 oz	
Goldings dry hops	0.125 oz	
OG	1096	
FG	1047	
ABV	6.48	
Apparent attenuation	51.04%	
IBU	95	
SRM	7	
Mash at	149° F	
Sparge at	170° F	
Boil time	90 minutes	
pitching temp	56° F	
Yeast	WLP028 Edinburgh Ale	

1879 William Younger XP		
pale malt	12.00 lb	100.00%
Cluster 90 min	2.75 oz	
Goldings 30 min	2.50 oz	
Spalt 30 min	0.75 oz	
Goldings dry hops	1.50 oz	
OG	1052	
FG	1016	
ABV	4.76	
Apparent attenuation	69.23%	
IBU	99	
SRM	5	
Mash at	150° F	
Sparge at	165° F	
Boil time	90 minutes	
pitching temp	60° F	
Yeast	WLP028 Edinburgh Ale	

1879 William Younger 2XP		
pale malt	10.75 lb	100.00%
Cluster 90 min	2.25 oz	
Goldings 30 min	1.50 oz	
Spalt 30 min	0.50 oz	
Goldings dry hops	2.00 oz	
OG	1046	
FG	1009	
ABV	4.89	
Apparent attenuation	80.43%	
IBU	76	
SRM	4	
Mash at	150° F	
Sparge at	170° F	
Boil time	90 minutes	
pitching temp	60° F	
Yeast	WLP028 Edinburgh Ale	

1879 William Younger X

pale malt	10.25 lb	100.00%
Cluster 90 min	1.50 oz	
Goldings 30 min	1.50 oz	
Goldings dry hops	1.00 oz	
OG	1044	
FG	1010	
ABV	4.50	
Apparent attenuation	77.27%	
IBU	54	
SRM	4	
Mash at	150° F	
Sparge at	170° F	
Boil time	90 minutes	
pitching temp	61° F	
Yeast	WLP028 Edinburgh Ale	

1879 William Younger XXX

pale malt	14.75 lb	100.00%
Cluster 90 min	2.50 oz	
Fuggles 60 min	1.25 oz	
Fuggles 30 min	1.25 oz	
Goldings dry hops	1.00 oz	
OG	1063	
FG	1030	
ABV	4.37	
Apparent attenuation	52.38%	
IBU	78	
SRM	5	
Mash at	150° F	
Sparge at	170° F	
Boil time	90 minutes	
pitching temp	59° F	
Yeast	WLP028 Edinburgh Ale	

1879 William Younger No. 3		
pale malt	17.25 lb	100.00%
Cluster 90 min	2.75 oz	
Cluster 60 min	2.75 oz	
Goldings 30 min	1.50 oz	
Goldings dry hops	1.50 oz	
OG	1074	
FG	1035	
ABV	5.16	
Apparent attenuation	52.70%	
IBU	115	
SRM	6	
Mash at	156° F	
Sparge at	165° F	
Boil time	90 minutes	
pitching temp	57.5° F	
Yeast	WLP028 Edinburgh Ale	

1879 William Younger S1		
pale malt	12.00 lb	69.57%
brown malt	3.50 lb	20.29%
black malt	1.75 lb	10.14%
Cluster 90 min	2.00 oz	
Goldings 30 min	1.25 oz	
OG	1071	
FG	1023	
ABV	6.35	
Apparent attenuation	67.61%	
IBU	53	
SRM	49	
Mash at	148° F	
Sparge at	165° F	
Boil time	90 minutes	
pitching temp	61° F	
Yeast	WLP028 Edinburgh Ale	

1879 William Younger S2		
pale malt	12.75 lb	82.26%
brown malt	1.75 lb	11.29%
black malt	1.00 lb	6.45%
Cluster 90 min	2.00 oz	
Goldings 30 min	1.00 oz	
Spalt 30 min	1.00 oz	
OG	1060	
FG	1020	
ABV	5.29	
Apparent attenuation	66.67%	
IBU	62	
SRM	34	
Mash at	148° F	
Sparge at	165° F	
Boil time	90 minutes	
pitching temp	61° F	
Yeast	WLP028 Edinburgh Ale	

1879 William Younger S3		
pale malt	7.50 lb	71.43%
brown malt	2.00 lb	19.05%
black malt	1.00 lb	9.52%
Cluster 90 min	1.00 oz	
Goldings 30 min	0.50 oz	
Spalt 30 min	0.50 oz	
OG	1043	
FG	1010	
ABV	4.37	
Apparent attenuation	76.74%	
IBU	36	
SRM	34	
Mash at	148° F	
Sparge at	165° F	
Boil time	90 minutes	
pitching temp	58.5° F	
Yeast	WLP028 Edinburgh Ale	

1879 William Younger DBS		
pale malt	15.00 lb	86.96%
brown malt	1.50 lb	8.70%
black malt	0.75 lb	4.35%
Fuggles 90 min	3.50 oz	
Goldings 60 min	3.50 oz	
Goldings 30 min	3.50 oz	
Goldings dry hops	1.75 oz	
OG	1073	
FG	1035	
ABV	5.03	
Apparent attenuation	52.05%	
IBU	126	
SRM	29	
Mash at	154° F	
Sparge at	165° F	
Boil time	90 minutes	
pitching temp	58° F	
Yeast	WLP028 Edinburgh Ale	

1880 - 1914

1880 William Younger PX Pils

pale malt	13.75 lb	100.00%
Cluster 90 min	0.50 oz	
Saaz 60 min	0.50 oz	
Saaz 30 min	0.50 oz	
OG	1059	
FG	1018	
ABV	5.42	
Apparent attenuation	69.49%	
IBU	20	
SRM	5	
Mash rest 1	100° F	
Mash rest 2	131° F	
Mash rest 3	142° F	
Mash rest 4	163° F	
Sparge at	164° F	
Boil time	150 minutes	
pitching temp	55° F	
fermentation temp	42° F	
Yeast	WLP800 Pilsner Lager	

1885 William Younger X

pale malt	11.25 lb	100.00%
Cluster 90 min	0.50 oz	
Spalt 60 min	0.50 oz	
Fuggles 30 min	1.25 oz	
OG	1048	
FG	1009	
ABV	5.16	
Apparent attenuation	81.25%	
IBU	31	
SRM	4	
Mash at	156° F	
Sparge at	163° F	
Boil time	90 minutes	
pitching temp	60° F	
Yeast	WLP028 Edinburgh Ale	

1885 William Younger XX		
pale malt	13.00 lb	100.00%
Cluster 90 min	1.00 oz	
Spalt 60 min	0.75 oz	
Fuggles 30 min	1.75 oz	
Goldings dry hops	0.50 oz	
OG	1056	
FG	1012	
ABV	5.82	
Apparent attenuation	78.57%	
IBU	48	
SRM	5	
Mash at	156° F	
Sparge at	163° F	
Boil time	90 minutes	
pitching temp	60° F	
Yeast	WLP028 Edinburgh Ale	

1885 William Younger XXX		
pale malt	15.00 lb	100.00%
Cluster 90 min	1.75 oz	
Spalt 60 min	1.50 oz	
Fuggles 30 min	0.75 oz	
Goldings dry hops	0.75 oz	
OG	1065	
FG	1021	
ABV	5.82	
Apparent attenuation	67.69%	
IBU	61	
SRM	5	
Mash at	156° F	
Sparge at	163° F	
Boil time	90 minutes	
pitching temp	58° F	
Yeast	WLP028 Edinburgh Ale	

1885 William Younger XXXX

pale malt	18.25 b	100.00%
Cluster 90 min	3.50 oz	
Spalt 60 min	3.50 oz	
Fuggles 30 min	3.00 oz	
Goldings dry hops	1.25 oz	
OG	1079	
FG	1020	
ABV	7.81	
Apparent attenuation	74.68%	
IBU	128	
SRM	6	
Mash at	156° F	
Sparge at	163° F	
Boil time	90 minutes	
pitching temp	52° F	
Yeast	WLP028 Edinburgh Ale	

1885 William Younger S1

pale malt	13.50 lb	77.14%
brown malt	3.00 lb	17.14%
black malt	1.00 lb	5.71%
Cluster 90 min	0.75 oz	
Spalt 60 min	0.75 oz	
Fuggles 30 min	0.75 oz	
Goldings dry hops	0.25 oz	
OG	1073	
FG	1033	
ABV	5.29	
Apparent attenuation	54.79%	
IBU	30	
SRM	36	
Mash at	156° F	
Sparge at	178° F	
Boil time	90 minutes	
pitching temp	57° F	
Yeast	WLP028 Edinburgh Ale	

1885 William Younger S2

pale malt	11.75 lb	75.81%
brown malt	2.75 lb	17.74%
black malt	1.00 lb	6.45%
Cluster 90 min	0.75 oz	
Spalt 60 min	0.75 oz	
Fuggles 30 min	0.75 oz	
OG	1064	
FG	1030	
ABV	4.50	
Apparent attenuation	53.13%	
IBU	32	
SRM	36	
Mash at	156° F	
Sparge at	178° F	
Boil time	90 minutes	
pitching temp	59° F	
Yeast	WLP028 Edinburgh Ale	

1885 William Younger 50/-

pale malt	8.25 lb	100.00%
Cluster 90 min	1.00 oz	
Spalt 60 min	0.50 oz	
Fuggles 30 min	0.50 oz	
Goldings dry hops	0.25 oz	
OG	1036	
FG	1011	
ABV	3.31	
Apparent attenuation	69.44%	
IBU	38	
SRM	4	
Mash at	156° F	
Sparge at	163° F	
Boil time	90 minutes	
pitching temp	61° F	
Yeast	WLP028 Edinburgh Ale	

1885 William Younger S 50/-		
pale malt	9.75 lb	100.00%
Fuggles 90 min	0.50 oz	
Fuggles 30 min	0.50 oz	
OG	1042	
FG	1018	
ABV	3.18	
Apparent attenuation	57.14%	
IBU	11	
SRM	4	
Mash at	156° F	
Sparge at	163° F	
Boil time	90 minutes	
pitching temp	61° F	
Yeast	WLP028 Edinburgh Ale	

1885 William Younger B 50/-		
pale malt	9.00 lb	94.74%
table sugar	0.50 lb	5.26%
Cluster 90 min	0.50 oz	
Spalt 60 min	0.50 oz	
Fuggles 30 min	0.50 oz	
Goldings dry hops	0.50 oz	
OG	1044	
FG	1016	
ABV	3.70	
Apparent attenuation	63.64%	
IBU	30	
SRM	4	
Mash at	156° F	
Sparge at	163° F	
Boil time	90 minutes	
pitching temp	61° F	
Yeast	WLP028 Edinburgh Ale	

1885 William Younger H 60/-

pale malt	9.50 lb	100.00%
Cluster 90 min	1.00 oz	
Spalt 60 min	1.00 oz	
Fuggles 30 min	0.50 oz	
Goldings dry hops	0.75 oz	
OG	1041	
FG	1011	
ABV	3.97	
Apparent attenuation	73.17%	
IBU	44	
SRM	4	
Mash at	156° F	
Sparge at	163° F	
Boil time	90 minutes	
pitching temp	60° F	
Yeast	WLP028 Edinburgh Ale	

1885 William Younger 60/-

pale malt	12.00 lb	100.00%
Cluster 90 min	0.75 oz	
Spalt 60 min	1.00 oz	
Fuggles 30 min	0.50 oz	
OG	1052	
FG	1023	
ABV	3.84	
Apparent attenuation	55.77%	
IBU	35	
SRM	5	
Mash at	156° F	
Sparge at	178° F	
Boil time	90 minutes	
pitching temp	60° F	
Yeast	WLP028 Edinburgh Ale	

1885 William Younger 80/-

pale malt	14.75 lb	100.00%
Cluster 90 min	1.25 oz	
Spalt 60 min	1.25 oz	
Fuggles 30 min	0.50 oz	
OG	1064	
FG	1027	
ABV	4.89	
Apparent attenuation	57.81%	
IBU	45	
SRM	5	
Mash at	154° F	
Sparge at	175° F	
Boil time	90 minutes	
pitching temp	58° F	
Yeast	WLP028 Edinburgh Ale	

1885 William Younger 100/-

pale malt	17.25 lb	100.00%
Cluster 90 min	1.25 oz	
Spalt 60 min	1.50 oz	
Fuggles 30 min	1.00 oz	
OG	1074	
FG	1030	
ABV	5.82	
Apparent attenuation	59.46%	
IBU	49	
SRM	6	
Mash at	155° F	
Sparge at	163° F	
Boil time	90 minutes	
pitching temp	57° F	
Yeast	WLP028 Edinburgh Ale	

1885 William Younger 120/-

pale malt	20.00 lb	100.00%
Cluster 90 min	2.00 oz	
Spalt 60 min	2.00 oz	
Fuggles 30 min	1.50 oz	
OG	1086	
FG	1040	
ABV	6.09	
Apparent attenuation	53.49%	
IBU	68	
SRM	7	
Mash at	154° F	
Sparge at	163° F	
Boil time	90 minutes	
pitching temp	55° F	
Yeast	WLP028 Edinburgh Ale	

1885 William Younger 140/-		
pale malt	19.75 lb	91.86%
table sugar	1.75 lb	8.14%
Cluster 90 min	2.75 oz	
Spalt 60 min	2.00 oz	
Fuggles 30 min	2.00 oz	
Goldings dry hops	0.50 oz	
OG	1099	
FG	1043	
ABV	7.41	
Apparent attenuation	56.57%	
IBU	77	
SRM	7	
Mash at	155° F	
Sparge at	163° F	
Boil time	90 minutes	
pitching temp	57° F	
Yeast	WLP028 Edinburgh Ale	

1885 William Younger 160/-		
pale malt	22.00 lb	88.89%
table sugar	2.75 lb	11.11%
Cluster 90 min	5.50 oz	
Saaz 60 min	3.00 oz	
Fuggles 30 min	3.00 oz	
OG	1115	
FG	1050	
ABV	8.60	
Apparent attenuation	56.52%	
IBU	120	
SRM	7	
Mash at	152° F	
Sparge at	163° F	
Boil time	90 minutes	
pitching temp	56° F	
Yeast	WLP028 Edinburgh Ale	

1885 William Younger T

pale malt	6.50 lb	100.00%
Cluster 90 min	0.50 oz	
Spalt 60 min	0.50 oz	
Fuggles 30 min	0.25 oz	
Goldings dry hops	0.50 oz	
OG	1028	
FG	1010	
ABV	2.38	
Apparent attenuation	64.29%	
IBU	27	
SRM	3	
Mash at	154° F	
Sparge at	163° F	
Boil time	90 minutes	
pitching temp	61° F	
Yeast	WLP028 Edinburgh Ale	

1885 William Younger DBS

pale malt	12.75 lb	71.83%
brown malt	4.00 lb	22.54%
black malt	1.00 lb	5.63%
Cluster 90 min	5.50 oz	
Spalt 60 min	3.50 oz	
Fuggles 30 min	2.50 oz	
Goldings dry hops	1.50 oz	
OG	1073	
FG	1025	
ABV	6.35	
Apparent attenuation	65.75%	
IBU	171	
SRM	38	
Mash at	154° F	
Sparge at	163° F	
Boil time	90 minutes	
pitching temp	56° F	
Yeast	WLP028 Edinburgh Ale	

1885 William Younger P		
pale malt	11.00 lb	100.00%
Cluster 90 min	1.50 oz	
Spalt 60 min	1.25 oz	
Fuggles 30 min	1.00 oz	
Goldings dry hops	1.50 oz	
OG	1047	
FG	1007	
ABV	5.29	
Apparent attenuation	85.11%	
IBU	61	
SRM	4	
Mash at	156° F	
Sparge at	163° F	
Boil time	90 minutes	
pitching temp	60° F	
Yeast	WLP028 Edinburgh Ale	

1885 William Younger XP		
pale malt	12.50 lb	100.00%
Cluster 90 min	2.50 oz	
Spalt 60 min	2.00 oz	
Goldings 30 min	1.75 oz	
Goldings dry hops	1.25 oz	
OG	1054	
FG	1013	
ABV	5.42	
Apparent attenuation	75.93%	
IBU	100	
SRM	5	
Mash at	155° F	
Sparge at	163° F	
Boil time	90 minutes	
pitching temp	59° F	
Yeast	WLP028 Edinburgh Ale	

1385 William Younger XP Scotch

pale malt	12.75 lb	100.00%
Cluster 90 min	2.00 oz	
Saalt 60 min	1.00 oz	
Goldings 30 min	2.75 oz	
Goldings dry hops	1.25 oz	
OG	1055	
FG	1016	
ABV	5.13	
Apparent attenuation	70.91%	
IBU	87	
SRM	5	
Mash at	152° F	
Sparge at	163° F	
Boil time	90 minutes	
pitching temp	59° F	
Yeast	WLP028 Edinburgh Ale	

1885 William Younger No. 1

pale malt	20.00 lb	89.89%
table sugar	2.25 lb	10.11%
Cluster 90 min	5.00 oz	
Saaz 60 min	5.00 oz	
Goldings 30 min	4.00 oz	
Goldings dry hops	2.25 oz	
OG	1103	
FG	1035	
ABV	9.00	
Apparent attenuation	66.02%	
IBU	150	
SRM	7	
Mash at	155° F	
Sparge at	163° F	
Boil time	90 minutes	
pitching temp	55.5° F	
Yeast	WLP028 Edinburgh Ale	

1885 William Younger No. 2

pale malt	17.50 lb	89.74%
table sugar	2.00 lb	10.26%
Cluster 90 min	3.00 oz	
Saaz 60 min	4.00 oz	
Goldings 30 min	3.00 oz	
Goldings dry hops	2.25 oz	
OG	1091	
FG	1024	
ABV	8.86	
Apparent attenuation	73.63%	
IBU	164	
SRM	6	
Mash at	155° F	
Sparge at	163° F	
Boil time	90 minutes	
pitching temp	55° F	
Yeast	WLP028 Edinburgh Ale	

1898 William Younger H 60/-

pale malt	10.25 lb	100.00%
Cluster 90 min	1.75 oz	
Fuggles 30 min	0.75 oz	
Goldings dry hops	0.75 oz	
OG	1044	
FG	1012	
ABV	4.23	
Apparent attenuation	72.73%	
IBU	50	
SRM	4	
Mash at	151° F	
Sparge at	160° F	
Boil time	90 minutes	
pitching temp	59° F	
Yeast	WLP028 Edinburgh Ale	

1899 William Younger 60/-

pale malt	10.25 lb	100.00%
Cluster 90 min	1.75 oz	
Fuggles 30 min	0.75 oz	
OG	1050	
FG	1023	
ABV	3.57	
Apparent attenuation	54.00%	
BU	47	
SRM	5	
Mash at	152° F	
Sparge at	160° F	
Boil time	90 minutes	
pitching temp	59° F	
Yeast	WLP028 Edinburgh Ale	

1899 William Younger 100/-

pale malt	15.25 lb	92.42%
glucose	1.25 lb	7.58%
Cluster 90 min	2.75 oz	
Goldings 30 min	1.25 oz	
OG	1073	
FG	1036	
ABV	4.89	
Apparent attenuation	50.68%	
IBU	65	
SRM	6	
Mash at	152° F	
Sparge at	160° F	
Boil time	90 minutes	
pitching temp	59° F	
Yeast	WLP028 Edinburgh Ale	

1898 William Younger 120/-

pale malt	17.75 lb	92.21%
glucose	1.50 lb	7.79%
Cluster 90 min	4.75 oz	
Fuggles 30 min	2.00 oz	
OG	1086	
FG	1038	
ABV	6.35	
Apparent attenuation	55.81%	
IBU	99	
SRM	6	
Mash at	151° F	
Sparge at	160° F	
Boil time	90 minutes	
pitching temp	57° F	
Yeast	WLP028 Edinburgh Ale	

1898 William Younger 160/-		
pale malt	22.75 lb	91.92%
glucose	2.00 lb	8.08%
Cluster 90 min	7.00 oz	
Fuggles 30 min	3.00 oz	
OG	1111	
FG	1042	
ABV	9.13	
Apparent attenuation	62.16%	
IBU	123	
SRM	7	
Mash at	151° F	
Sparge at	160° F	
Boil time	90 minutes	
pitching temp	56° F	
Yeast	WLP028 Edinburgh Ale	

1898 William Younger XXX		
pale malt	14.75 lb	92.19%
invert sugar	1.25 lb	7.81%
Cluster 90 min	4.00 oz	
Fuggles 30 min	2.00 oz	
Goldings dry hops	0.75 oz	
OG	1074	
FG	1018	
ABV	7.41	
Apparent attenuation	75.68%	
IBU	94	
SRM	5	
Mash at	155° F	
Sparge at	160° F	
Boil time	90 minutes	
pitching temp	57.5° F	
Yeast	WLP028 Edinburgh Ale	

1898 William Younger XXXX

pale malt	14.00 lb	82.35%
grits	1.50 lb	8.82%
glucose	1.50 lb	8.82%
Cluster 90 min	5.75 oz	
Fuggles 30 min	2.25 oz	
Goldings dry hops	2.00 oz	
OG	1076	
FG	1020	
ABV	7.41	
Apparent attenuation	73.68%	
IBU	126	
SRM	5	
Mash at	155° F	
Sparge at	160° F	
Boil time	90 minutes	
pitching temp	57° F	
Yeast	WLP028 Edinburgh Ale	

1898 William Younger SLE

pale malt	8.25 lb	73.33%
grits	1.25 lb	11.11%
invert sugar	1.75 lb	15.56%
Cluster 90 min	4.50 oz	
Fuggles 30 min	2.00 oz	
Goldings dry hops	1.50 oz	
OG	1054	
FG	1015	
ABV	5.16	
Apparent attenuation	72.22%	
IBU	118	
SRM	4	
Mash at	155° F	
Sparge at	160° F	
Boil time	90 minutes	
pitching temp	59.5° F	
Yeast	WLP028 Edinburgh Ale	

1898 William Younger SS1		
pale malt	9.25 lb	59.68%
black malt	2.00 lb	12.90%
amber malt	1.00 lb	6.45%
grits	1.75 lb	11.29%
glucose	1.50 lb	9.68%
Cluster 90 min	1.75 oz	
Fuggles 30 min	0.50 oz	
spent hops 120 min	1.50 oz	
OG	1068	
FG	1029	
ABV	5.16	
Apparent attenuation	57.35%	
IBU	69	
SRM	46	
Mash at	155º F	
Sparge at	160º F	
Boil time	180 minutes	
pitching temp	59º F	
Yeast	WLP028 Edinburgh Ale	

1898 William Younger MBS		
pale malt	8.50 lb	57.63%
black malt	2.00 lb	13.56%
amber malt	1.00 lb	6.78%
grits	1.75 lb	11.86%
glucose	1.50 lb	10.17%
Cluster 90 min	2.25 oz	
Fuggles 30 min	0.25 oz	
spent Cluster 120 min	1.00 oz	
Goldings dry hops	1.50 oz	
OG	1065	
FG	1025	
ABV	5.29	
Apparent attenuation	61.54%	
IBU	68	
SRM	46	
Mash at	155º F	
Sparge at	160º F	
Boil time	180 minutes	
pitching temp	59º F	
Yeast	WLP028 Edinburgh Ale	

1898 William Younger No. 1		
pale malt	9.75 b	72.22%
grits	2.25 b	16.67%
glucose	1.50 b	11.11%
Cluster 120 min	6.00 oz	
Cluster 90 min	6.00 oz	
Fuggles 30 min	6.00 oz	
Goldings dry hops	2.00 oz	
OG	1104	
FG	1030	
ABV	9.79	
Apparent attenuation	71.15%	
IBU	228	
SRM	7	
Mash at	155° F	
Sparge at	160° F	
Boil time	180 minutes	
pitching temp	55° F	
Yeast	WLP028 Edinburgh Ale	

1898 William Younger No. 3		
pale malt	15.75 lb	92.65%
glucose	1.25 lb	7.35%
Caramel	to get the righ colour	
Cluster 120 min	3.00 oz	
Cluster 90 min	3.50 oz	
Fuggles 30 min	3.00 oz	
Goldings dry hops	1.25 oz	
OG	1074	
FG	1019	
ABV	7.28	
Apparent attenuation	74.32%	
IBU	148	
SRM	22	
Mash at	155° F	
Sparge at	160° F	
Boil time	180 minutes	
pitching temp	57.5° F	
Yeast	WLP028 Edinburgh Ale	

1898 William Younger No. 3 pale

pale malt	14.00 lb	82.35%
grits	1.75 lb	10.29%
glucose	1.25 lb	7.35%
Cluster 120 min	3.25 oz	
Cluster 90 min	3.25 oz	
Fuggles 30 min	3.25 oz	
Goldings dry hops	1.25 oz	
OG	1075	
FG	1024	
ABV	6.75	
Apparent attenuation	68.00%	
IBU	150	
SRM	4	
Mash at	155° F	
Sparge at	160° F	
Boil time	180 minutes	
pitching temp	57° F	
Yeast	WLP028 Edinburgh Ale	

1898 William Younger XP Scotch

pale malt	10.75 lb	87.76%
grits	1.50 lb	12.24%
Cluster 90 min	1.50 oz	
Cluster 60 min	1.50 oz	
Fuggles 30 min	1.50 oz	
Goldings dry hops	1.25 oz	
OG	1053	
FG	1013	
ABV	5.29	
Apparent attenuation	75.47%	
IBU	80	
SRM	4	
Mash at	151° F	
Sparge at	160° F	
Boil time	120 minutes	
pitching temp	59.5° F	
Yeast	WLP028 Edinburgh Ale	

1898 William Younger LDA		
pale malt	9.00 lb	100.00%
Cluster 90 min	2.50 oz	
Cluster 60 min	2.50 oz	
Fuggles 30 min	1.50 oz	
Goldings dry hops	1.00 oz	
OG	1039	
FG	1010	
ABV	3.34	
Apparent attenuation	74.36%	
IBU	134	
SRM	4	
Mash at	151° F	
Sparge at	160° F	
Boil time	165 minutes	
pitching temp	60° F	
Yeast	WLP028 Edinburgh Ale	

1898 William Younger T		
pale malt	7.25 lb	100.00%
Cluster 90 min	0.75 oz	
Cluster 60 min	0.50 oz	
Fuggles 30 min	0.25 oz	
OG	1031	
FG	1008	
ABV	3.04	
Apparent attenuation	74.19%	
IBU	34	
SRM	3	
Mash at	151° F	
Sparge at	160° F	
Boil time	180 minutes	
pitching temp	61° F	
Yeast	WLP028 Edinburgh Ale	

1898 William Younger S2		
pale malt	7.75 lb	56.36%
black malt	2.00 lb	14.55%
amber malt	0.75 lb	5.45%
grits	1.75 lb	12.73%
glucose	1.50 lb	10.91%
Cluster 120 min spent hops	0.25 oz	
Cluster 90 min	0.25 oz	
Cluster 60 min	0.25 oz	
Fuggles 30 min	0.25 oz	
OG	1059	
FG	1029	
ABV	3.97	
Apparent attenuation	50.85%	
IBU	18	
SRM	46	
Mash at	152° F	
Sparge at	160° F	
Boil time	180 minutes	
pitching temp	59.5° F	
Yeast	WLP028 Edinburgh Ale	

1898 William Younger DBS		
pale malt	10.25 lb	64.06%
black malt	2.00 lb	12.50%
amber malt	0.75 lb	4.69%
grits	1.75 lb	10.94%
glucose	1.25 lb	7.81%
Cluster 90 min	1.75 oz	
Cluster 60 min	1.75 oz	
Goldings 30 min	1.25 oz	
Goldings dry hops	2.00 oz	
OG	1069	
FG	1023	
ABV	6.09	
Apparent attenuation	66.67%	
IBU	78	
SRM	46	
Mash at	155° F	
Sparge at	160° F	
Boil time	180 minutes	
pitching temp	59.5° F	
Yeast	WLP028 Edinburgh Ale	

1898 William Younger SE		
pale malt	13.00 lb	83.87%
grits	2.50 lb	16.13%
Cluster 90 min	3.00 oz	
Cluster 60 min	3.00 oz	
Fuggles 30 min	3.00 oz	
Goldings dry hops	1.50 oz	
OG	1037	
FG	1018	
ABV	6.48	
Apparent attenuation	73.13%	
IBU	142	
SRM	5	
Mash at	155° F	
Sparge at	160° F	
Boil time	180 minutes	
pitching temp	59° F	
Yeast	WLP028 Edinburgh Ale	

1898 William Younger LAE		
pale malt	10.00 lb	85.11%
grits	1.75 lb	14.89%
Cluster 90 min	2.00 oz	
Cluster 60 min	2.00 oz	
Fuggles 30 min	1.75 oz	
Goldings dry hops	1.50 oz	
OG	1051	
FG	1014	
ABV	4.89	
Apparent attenuation	72.55%	
IBU	160	
SRM	4	
Mash at	155° F	
Sparge at	160° F	
Boil time	180 minutes	
pitching temp	59.5° F	
Yeast	WLP028 Edinburgh Ale	

1898 William Younger B XPSc		
pale malt	10.25 lb	83.67%
grits	2.00 lb	16.33%
Cluster 90 min	1.75 oz	
Cluster 60 min	1.75 oz	
Goldings 30 min	1.75 oz	
Goldings dry hops	1.50 oz	
OG	1053	
FG	1014	
ABV	5.16	
Apparent attenuation	73.58%	
IBU	92	
SRM	4	
Mash at	154° F	
Sparge at	160° F	
Boil time	180 minutes	
pitching temp	59° F	
Yeast	WLP028 Edinburgh Ale	

1913 William Younger H 60/-		
pale malt	5.50 lb	55.00%
grits	4.50 lb	45.00%
Cluster 90 min	0.50 oz	
Cluster 60 min	0.50 oz	
Fuggles 30 min	0.25 oz	
Goldings dry hops	0.25 oz	
OG	1044	
FG	1013	
ABV	4.10	
Apparent attenuation	70.45%	
IBU	19.5	
SRM	3	
Mash at	151° F	
Sparge at	160° F	
Boil time	120 minutes	
pitching temp	60° F	
Yeast	WLP028 Edinburgh Ale	

1913 William Younger 60/-

pale malt	5.75 lb	53.49%
grits	4.75 lb	44.19%
glucose	0.25 lb	2.33%
Cluster 90 min	0.25 oz	
Cluster 60 min	0.25 oz	
Fuggles 30 min	0.25 oz	
OG	1047	
FG	1023	
ABV	3.18	
Apparent attenuation	51.06%	
IBU	14	
SRM	3	
Mash at	151° F	
Sparge at	160° F	
Boil time	105 minutes	
pitching temp	60° F	
Yeast	WLP028 Edinburgh Ale	

1913 William Younger 80/-

pale malt	6.50 lb	52.00%
grits	5.25 lb	42.00%
glucose	0.75 lb	6.00%
caramel	to get the right colour	
Cluster 90 min	0.75 oz	
Cluster 60 min	0.50 oz	
Fuggles 30 min	0.25 oz	
OG	1056	
FG	1027	
ABV	3.34	
Apparent attenuation	51.79%	
IBU	29	
SRM	20	
Mash at	151° F	
Sparge at	160° F	
Boil time	135 minutes	
pitching temp	59.5° F	
Yeast	WLP028 Edinburgh Ale	

1913 William Younger 100/-		
pale malt	7.75 lb	51.67%
grits	6.50 lb	43.33%
glucose	0.75 lb	5.00%
caramel	to get the right colour	
Cluster 90 min	0.75 oz	
Cluster 60 min	0.75 oz	
Fuggles 30 min	0.50 oz	
OG	1066	
FG	1032	
ABV	4.50	
Apparent attenuation	51.52%	
IBU	33	
SRM	20	
Mash at	151° F	
Sparge at	160° F	
Boil time	135 minutes	
pitching temp	58° F	
Yeast	WLP028 Edinburgh Ale	

1913 William Younger XX		
pale malt	7.00 lb	54.90%
grits	5.50 lb	43.14%
glucose	0.25 lb	1.96%
Cluster 90 min	0.75 oz	
Cluster 60 min	0.75 oz	
Fuggles 30 min	0.50 oz	
Goldings dry hops	0.25 oz	
OG	1055	
FG	1018	
ABV	4.89	
Apparent attenuation	67.27%	
IBU	36	
SRM	4	
Mash at	152° F	
Sparge at	160° F	
Boil time	135 minutes	
pitching temp	60° F	
Yeast	WLP028 Edinburgh Ale	

1913 William Younger XXX

pale malt	8.25 lb	55.93%
grits	6.25 lb	42.37%
glucose	0.25 lb	1.69%
Cluster 90 min	1.00 oz	
Cluster 60 min	1.00 oz	
Fuggles 30 min	0.50 oz	
Goldings dry hops	0.50 oz	
OG	1065	
FG	1021.5	
ABV	5.75	
Apparent attenuation	66.92%	
IBU	44	
SRM	4	
Mash at	153° F	
Sparge at	160° F	
Boil time	150 minutes	
pitching temp	60° F	
Yeast	WLP028 Edinburgh Ale	

1913 William Younger XXXX

pale malt	8.75 lb	55.56%
grits	6.50 lb	41.27%
No. 3 invert	0.50 lb	3.17%
Cluster 90 min	2.25 oz	
Cluster 60 min	2.25 oz	
Fuggles 30 min	1.50 oz	
Goldings dry hops	1.00 oz	
OG	1070	
FG	1024	
ABV	6.09	
Apparent attenuation	65.71%	
IBU	38	
SRM	7	
Mash at	154° F	
Sparge at	160° F	
Boil time	150 minutes	
pitching temp	59° F	
Yeast	WLP028 Edinburgh Ale	

1913 William Younger No. 3a

pale malt	8.75 lb	54.69%
grits	7.00 lb	43.75%
glucose	0.25 lb	1.56%
Cluster 90 min	1.00 oz	
Cluster 60 min	1.00 oz	
Fuggles 30 min	0.50 oz	
Goldings dry hops	0.375 oz	
OG	1072	
FG	1025	
ABV	6.22	
Apparent attenuation	65.28%	
IBU	42	
SRM	4	
Mash at	153° F	
Sparge at	160° F	
Boil time	1350 minutes	
pitching temp	59° F	
Yeast	WLP028 Edinburgh Ale	

1913 William Younger LDA

pale malt	4.50 lb	52.94%
grits	4.00 lb	47.06%
Cluster 90 min	0.50 oz	
Cluster 60 min	0.25 oz	
Fuggles 30 min	0.25 oz	
Goldings dry hops	0.375 oz	
OG	1037	
FG	1012	
ABV	3.31	
Apparent attenuation	67.57%	
IBU	21	
SRM	3	
Mash at	151° F	
Sparge at	160° F	
Boil time	150 minutes	
pitching temp	61.5° F	
Yeast	WLP028 Edinburgh Ale	

1913 William Younger S1

pale malt	6.00 lb	42.86%
black malt	0.75 lb	5.36%
choc. Malt	0.75 lb	5.36%
grits	4.50 lb	32.14%
caramel	0.50 lb	3.57%
glucose	1.00 lb	7.14%
No. 3 invert sugar	0.50 lb	3.57%
Cluster 120 min spent	0.25 oz	
Cluster 90 min	0.50 oz	
Cluster 60 min	0.50 oz	
Fuggles 30 min	0.25 oz	
OG	1065	
FG	1031	
ABV	4.50	
Apparent attenuation	52.31%	
IBU	32	
SRM	46	
Mash at	151° F	
Sparge at	160° F	
Boil time	120 minutes	
pitching temp	59.5° F	
Yeast	WLP028 Edinburgh Ale	

1913 William Younger S2

pale malt	5.50 lb	41.51%
black malt	1.00 lb	7.55%
choc. Malt	1.00 lb	7.55%
grits	4.25 lb	32.08%
caramel	0.50 lb	3.77%
glucose	0.50 lb	3.77%
No. 3 invert sugar	0.50 lb	3.77%
Cluster 120 min spent	0.25 oz	
Cluster 90 min	0.50 oz	
Cluster 60 min	0.25 oz	
Fuggles 30 min	0.25 oz	
OG	1059	
FG	1029	
ABV	3.97	
Apparent attenuation	50.85%	
IBU	28	
SRM	53	
Mash at	150° F	
Sparge at	160° F	
Boil time	135 minutes	
pitching temp	60° F	
Yeast	WLP028 Edinburgh Ale	

1913 William Younger DBS		
pale malt	6.00 lb	42.86%
black malt	0.75 lb	5.36%
choc. Malt	0.75 lb	5.36%
grits	4.75 lb	33.93%
caramel	0.50 lb	3.57%
No. 3 invert sugar	1.25 lb	8.93%
Cluster 90 min	2.00 oz	
Cluster 60 min	2.00 oz	
Fuggles 30 min	1.50 oz	
Goldings dry hops	1.00 oz	
OG	1065	
FG	1022	
ABV	5.69	
Apparent attenuation	66.15%	
IBU	92	
SRM	47	
Mash at	151° F	
Sparge at	160° F	
Boil time	135 minutes	
pitching temp	59.5° F	
Yeast	WLP028 Edinburgh Ale	

1913 William Younger MBS		
pale malt	7.25 lb	50.00%
black malt	0.75 lb	5.17%
choc. Malt	0.75 lb	5.17%
grits	4.75 lb	32.76%
caramel 500 SRM	0.50 lb	3.45%
No. 3 invert sugar	0.50 lb	3.45%
Cluster 120 min spent	1.00 oz	
Cluster 90 min	0.75 oz	
Cluster 60 min	0.50 oz	
Fuggles 30 min	0.25 oz	
Goldings dry hops	0.75 oz	
OG	1065	
FG	1020	
ABV	5.95	
Apparent attenuation	69.23%	
IBU	47	
SRM	46	
Mash at	155° F	
Sparge at	160° F	
Boil time	150 minutes	
pitching temp	60° F	
Yeast	WLP028 Edinburgh Ale	

1914 - 1939

1914 William Younger No. 2 Sc

pale malt	9.50 b	55.07%
grits	7.25 b	42.03%
No. 3 invert	0.25 b	1.45%
Glucose	0.25 b	1.45%
Cluster 90 min	2.25 oz	
Cluster 60 min	2.25 oz	
Fuggles 30 min	1.50 oz	
Goldings dry hops	1.00 oz	
OG	1076	
FG	1025	
ABV	6.75	
Apparent attenuation	67.11%	
IBU	94	
SRM	6	
Mash at	153° F	
Sparge at	160° F	
Boil time	150 minutes	
pitching temp	58° F	
Yeast	WLP028 Edinburgh Ale	

1914 William Younger SLE

pale malt	7.00 lb	54.90%
grits	5.75 lb	45.10%
Cluster 90 min	1.75 oz	
Cluster 60 min	1.75 oz	
Fuggles 30 min	1.00 oz	
Goldings dry hops	1.00 oz	
OG	1055	
FG	1014	
ABV	5.42	
Apparent attenuation	74.55%	
IBU	83	
SRM	4	
Mash at	154° F	
Sparge at	160° F	
Boil time	135 minutes	
pitching temp	59° F	
Yeast	WLP028 Edinburgh Ale	

1914 William Younger MM		
pale malt	6.00 lb	54.55%
grits	5.00 lb	45.45%
Cluster 90 min	0.75 oz	
Cluster 60 min	0.50 oz	
Fuggles 30 min	0.25 oz	
Goldings dry hops	0.375 oz	
OG	1048	
FG	1015	
ABV	4.37	
Apparent attenuation	68.75%	
IBU	30	
SRM	3	
Mash at	151° F	
Sparge at	160° F	
Boil time	135 minutes	
pitching temp	59° F	
Yeast	WLP028 Edinburgh Ale	

1921 William Younger LAE		
pale malt	6.25 lb	58.14%
grits	4.50 lb	41.86%
Cluster 90 min	1.25 oz	
Cluster 60 min	1.25 oz	
Saaz 30 min	0.25 oz	
Fuggles 30 min	1.00 oz	
Goldings dry hops	1.00 oz	
OG	1047	
FG	1013	
ABV	4.50	
Apparent attenuation	72.34%	
IBU	68	
SRM	3	
Mash at	154° F	
Sparge at	160° F	
Boil time	150 minutes	
pitching temp	60.5° F	
Yeast	WLP028 Edinburgh Ale	

1921 William Younger No. 1

pale malt	11.25 lb	60.00%
grits	7.50 lb	40.00%
Cluster 90 min	1.75 oz	
Cluster 60 min	1.75 oz	
Saaz 30 min	0.50 oz	
Fuggles 30 min	1.50 oz	
Goldings dry hops	0.50 oz	
OG	1082	
FG	1028	
ABV	7.14	
Apparent attenuation	65.85%	
BU	77	
SRM	8	
Mash at	155° F	
Sparge at	160° F	
Boil time	150 minutes	
pitching temp	57.5° F	
Yeast	WLP028 Edinburgh Ale	

1922 William Younger No. 2 Btg.

pale malt	10.00 lb	60.61%
grits	6.50 lb	39.39%
Cluster 90 min	1.75 oz	
Fuggles 60 min	2.25 oz	
Saaz 30 min	0.75 oz	
Fuggles 30 min	1.25 oz	
Goldings dry hops	1.00 oz	
OG	1072	
FG	1022	
ABV	6.31	
Apparent attenuation	69.44%	
BU	77	
SRM	5	
Mash at	155° F	
Sparge at	160° F	
Boil time	165 minutes	
pitching temp	56.5° F	
Yeast	WLP028 Edinburgh Ale	

1921 William Younger No. 3		
pale malt	7.50 lb	61.22%
grits	4.75 lb	38.78%
Cluster 90 min	0.75 oz	
Cluster 60 min	0.75 oz	
Saaz 30 min	0.25 oz	
Fuggles 30 min	0.50 oz	
Goldings dry hops	0.50 oz	
OG	1053.4	
FG	1013.4	
ABV	5.29	
Apparent attenuation	74.91%	
IBU	39	
SRM	4	
Mash at	155° F	
Sparge at	160° F	
Boil time	120 minutes	
pitching temp	60° F	
Yeast	WLP028 Edinburgh Ale	

1921 William Younger XX		
pale malt	5.00 lb	62.50%
grits	3.00 lb	37.50%
Cluster 90 min	0.50 oz	
Cluster 60 min	0.25 oz	
Saaz 30 min	0.125 oz	
Fuggles 30 min	0.25 oz	
Goldings dry hops	0.25 oz	
OG	1035	
FG	1009	
ABV	3.44	
Apparent attenuation	74.29%	
IBU	22	
SRM	3	
Mash at	152° F	
Sparge at	160° F	
Boil time	120 minutes	
pitching temp	61° F	
Yeast	WLP028 Edinburgh Ale	

1921 William Younger XXX		
pale malt	6.00 lb	61.54%
grits	3.75 lb	38.46%
Cluster 90 min	0.50 oz	
Cluster 60 min	0.50 oz	
Saaz 30 min	0.125 oz	
Fuggles 30 min	0.25 oz	
Goldings dry hops	0.25 oz	
OG	1042	
FG	1011	
ABV	4.10	
Apparent attenuation	73.81%	
IBU	27	
SRM	3	
Mash at	154° F	
Sparge at	160° F	
Boil time	120 minutes	
pitching temp	61° F	
Yeast	WLP028 Edinburgh Ale	

1921 William Younger 120/-		
pale malt	11.50 lb	61.33%
grits	7.25 lb	38.67%
Cluster 90 min	1.50 oz	
Cluster 60 min	1.50 oz	
Saaz 30 min	0.75 oz	
Fuggles 30 min	1.50 oz	
Goldings dry hops	0.50 oz	
OG	1082	
FG	1028	
ABV	7.14	
Apparent attenuation	65.85%	
IBU	70	
SRM	5	
Mash at	154° F	
Sparge at	160° F	
Boil time	150 minutes	
pitching temp	57° F	
Yeast	WLP028 Edinburgh Ale	

1922 William Younger 200/- B		
pale malt	13.00 lb	61.18%
grits	8.25 lb	38.82%
Cluster 90 min	2.25 oz	
Cluster 60 min	1.00 oz	
Fuggles 60 min	1.50 oz	
Saaz 30 min	0.75 oz	
Fuggles 30 min	1.75 oz	
Goldings dry hops	0.50 oz	
OG	1092	
FG	1032	
ABV	7.94	
Apparent attenuation	65.22%	
IBU	86	
SRM	5	
Mash at	156° F	
Sparge at	160° F	
Boil time	150 minutes	
pitching temp	56° F	
Yeast	WLP028 Edinburgh Ale	

1921 William Younger XXS		
pale malt	5.50 lb	48.89%
black malt	0.75 lb	6.67%
amber malt	0.75 lb	6.67%
grits	3.75 lb	33.33%
caramel	0.50 lb	4.44%
Cluster 90 min	0.50 oz	
Cluster 60 min	0.50 oz	
Saaz 30 min	0.25 oz	
Fuggles 30 min	0.50 oz	
OG	1050	
FG	1020	
ABV	3.97	
Apparent attenuation	60.00%	
IBU	29	
SRM	34	
Mash at	151° F	
Sparge at	160° F	
Boil time	150 minutes	
pitching temp	61° F	
Yeast	WLP028 Edinburgh Ale	

1921 William Younger XXPS		
pale malt	6.25 b	59.52%
grits	4.25 b	40.48%
Cluster 90 min	0.75 oz	
Cluster 60 min	0.50 oz	
Saaz 30 min	0.25 oz	
Fuggles 30 min	0.50 oz	
Goldings dry hops	0.50 oz	
OG	1046	
FG	1012	
ABV	4.50	
Apparent attenuation	73.91%	
IBU	36	
SRM	4	
Mash at	151° F	
Sparge at	160° F	
Boil time	120 minutes	
pitching temp	61° F	
Yeast	WLP028 Edinburgh Ale	

1922 William Younger LE		
pale malt	5.50 lb	56.41%
grits	4.25 lb	43.59%
Cluster 90 min	1.00 oz	
Cluster 60 min	1.00 oz	
Saaz 30 min	0.33 oz	
Fuggles 30 min	0.75 oz	
Goldings dry hops	1.00 oz	
OG	1042	
FG	1011	
ABV	4.10	
Apparent attenuation	73.81%	
IBU	57	
SRM	3	
Mash at	154° F	
Sparge at	160° F	
Boil time	150 minutes	
pitching temp	61° F	
Yeast	WLP028 Edinburgh Ale	

1922 William Younger SLE		
pale malt	7.25 lb	60.42%
grits	4.75 lb	39.58%
Cluster 90 min	1.25 oz	
Cluster 60 min	1.25 oz	
Fuggles 30 min	1.75 oz	
Goldings dry hops	1.00 oz	
OG	1052	
FG	1015	
ABV	4.89	
Apparent attenuation	71.15%	
IBU	71	
SRM	4	
Mash at	154° F	
Sparge at	160° F	
Boil time	150 minutes	
pitching temp	61° F	
Yeast	WLP028 Edinburgh Ale	

1922 William Younger SE		
pale malt	7.75 lb	59.62%
grits	5.25 lb	40.38%
Cluster 90 min	1.25 oz	
Cluster 60 min	1.25 oz	
Fuggles 30 min	2.00 oz	
Goldings dry hops	0.75 oz	
OG	1057	
FG	1015	
ABV	5.56	
Apparent attenuation	73.68%	
IBU	71	
SRM	4	
Mash at	152° F	
Sparge at	160° F	
Boil time	150 minutes	
pitching temp	60° F	
Yeast	WLP028 Edinburgh Ale	

1933 William Younger XXP		
pale malt	5.75 lb	57.50%
grits	4.25 lb	42.50%
Cluster 90 min	1.00 oz	
Fuggles 30 min	1.00 oz	
Goldings dry hops	0.25 oz	
OG	1043	
FG	1012	
ABV	4.10	
Apparent attenuation	72.09%	
IBU	34	
SRM	3	
Mash at	154° F	
Sparge at	160° F	
Boil time	135 minutes	
pitching temp	61° F	
Yeast	WLP028 Edinburgh Ale	

1933 William Younger LAE		
pale malt	6.00 lb	57.14%
grits	4.50 lb	42.86%
Cluster 90 min	1.50 oz	
Fuggles 30 min	1.50 oz	
Goldings dry hops	0.75 oz	
OG	1046	
FG	1013	
ABV	4.37	
Apparent attenuation	71.74%	
IBU	51	
SRM	3	
Mash at	156° F	
Sparge at	160° F	
Boil time	150 minutes	
pitching temp	60.5° F	
Yeast	WLP028 Edinburgh Ale	

1933 William Younger Expt		
pale malt	7.25 lb	58.00%
grits	5.25 lb	42.00%
Cluster 90 min	2.00 oz	
Fuggles 30 min	2.00 oz	
Goldings dry hops	1.00 oz	
OG	1054	
FG	1016	
ABV	5.03	
Apparent attenuation	70.37%	
IBU	53	
SRM	4	
Mash at	156° F	
Sparge at	160° F	
Boil time	165 minutes	
pitching temp	60° F	
Yeast	WLP028 Edinburgh Ale	

1933 William Younger XP Btlg		
pale malt	5.00 lb	55.56%
grits	4.00 lb	44.44%
Cluster 90 min	1.00 oz	
Fuggles 30 min	1.00 oz	
Goldings dry hops	0.25 oz	
OG	1039	
FG	1012	
ABV	3.57	
Apparent attenuation	69.23%	
IBU	35	
SRM	3	
Mash at	156° F	
Sparge at	160° F	
Boil time	135 minutes	
pitching temp	61° F	
Yeast	WLP028 Edinburgh Ale	

1933 William Younger XXP Btlg

pale malt	5.50 lb	55.00%
grits	4.50 lb	45.00%
Cluster 90 min	1.00 oz	
Fuggles 30 min	1.00 oz	
Goldings dry hops	0.25 oz	
OG	1043	
FG	1013	
ABV	3.97	
Apparent attenuation	69.77%	
IBU	34	
SRM	3	
Mash at	156° F	
Sparge at	160° F	
Boil time	135 minutes	
pitching temp	61° F	
Yeast	WLP028 Edinburgh Ale	

1933 William Younger P Btlg

pale malt	4.00 lb	55.17%
grits	3.25 lb	44.83%
Cluster 90 min	0.75 oz	
Fuggles 30 min	0.75 oz	
Goldings dry hops	0.25 oz	
OG	1032	
FG	1011	
ABV	2.78	
Apparent attenuation	65.63%	
IBU	28	
SRM	3	
Mash at	156° F	
Sparge at	160° F	
Boil time	135 minutes	
pitching temp	62° F	
Yeast	WLP028 Edinburgh Ale	

1933 William Younger XXX		
pale malt	5.75 lb	58.97%
grits	4.00 lb	41.03%
Cluster 90 min	0.75 oz	
Fuggles 30 min	0.75 oz	
Goldings dry hops	0.25 oz	
OG	1042	
FG	1014	
ABV	3.70	
Apparent attenuation	66.67%	
IBU	26	
SRM	3	
Mash at	154° F	
Sparge at	160° F	
Boil time	135 minutes	
pitching temp	61° F	
Yeast	WLP028 Edinburgh Ale	

1933 William Younger MXP E		
pale malt	6.25 lb	59.52%
grits	4.25 lb	40.48%
Cluster 90 min	1.00 oz	
Fuggles 30 min	1.00 oz	
Goldings dry hops	0.25 oz	
OG	1046	
FG	1013	
ABV	4.37	
Apparent attenuation	71.74%	
IBU	34	
SRM	3	
Mash at	156° F	
Sparge at	160° F	
Boil time	135 minutes	
pitching temp	60.5° F	
Yeast	WLP028 Edinburgh Ale	

1933 William Younger DBS Btlg

pale malt	7.50 lb	50.85%
black malt	0.50 lb	3.39%
crystal malt 60L	0.50 lb	3.39%
grits	5.25 lb	35.59%
caramel	0.50 lb	3.39%
lactose	0.50 lb	3.39%
Fuggles 90 min	2.25 oz	
Fuggles 30 min	2.25 oz	
Goldings dry hops	0.75 oz	
OG	1066	
FG	1025	
ABV	5.42	
Apparent attenuation	62.12%	
IBU	66	
SRM	30	
Mash at	154° F	
Sparge at	160° F	
Boil time	150 minutes	
pitching temp	60.5° F	
Yeast	WLP028 Edinburgh Ale	

1933 William Younger XX Sc

pale malt	6.50 lb	57.78%
grits	4.25 lb	37.78%
lactose	0.50 lb	4.44%
liquorice	0.50 oz	
Cluster 90 min	0.75 oz	
Fuggles 30 min	1.00 oz	
Goldings dry hops	0.50 oz	
OG	1050	
FG	1025	
ABV	3.31	
Apparent attenuation	50.00%	
IBU	27	
SRM	3	
Mash at	154° F	
Sparge at	160° F	
Boil time	120 minutes	
pitching temp	60° F	
Yeast	WLP028 Edinburgh Ale	

1939 – 1970

1939 William Younger XXPS

pale malt	9.00 lb	83.72%
grits	1.75 lb	16.28%
Fuggles 90 min	0.50 oz	
Fuggles 30 min	0.50 oz	
Goldings dry hops	0.25 oz	
OG	1046	
FG	1015	
ABV	4.10	
Apparent attenuation	67.39%	
IBU	13	
SRM	4	
Mash at	153° F	
Sparge at	160° F	
Boil time	105 minutes	
pitching temp	60.5° F	
Yeast	WLP028 Edinburgh Ale	

1939 William Younger DBS Btlg

pale malt	9.50 lb	64.41%
black malt	0.50 lb	3.39%
crystal malt 60L	0.50 lb	3.39%
grits	2.75 lb	18.64%
caramel	0.50 lb	3.39%
lactose	1.00 lb	6.78%
liquorice	0.25 oz	
Fuggles 90 min	1.00 oz	
Fuggles 60 min	1.00 oz	
Fuggles 30 min	1.00 oz	
Goldings dry hops	0.50 oz	
OG	1066	
FG	1023	
ABV	5.69	
Apparent attenuation	65.15%	
IBU	34	
SRM	30	
Mash at	155° F	
Sparge at	160° F	
Boil time	150 minutes	
pitching temp	60.5° F	
Yeast	WLP028 Edinburgh Ale	

1939 William Younger No. 3		
pale malt	10.25 lb	83.67%
grits	2.00 lb	16.33%
Fuggles 90 min	0.75 oz	
Fuggles 30 min	0.50 oz	
Goldings dry hops	0.25 oz	
OG	1053	
FG	1017	
ABV	4.76	
Apparent attenuation	67.92%	
IBU	16	
SRM	4	
Mash at	153° F	
Sparge at	160° F	
Boil time	105 minutes	
pitching temp	60° F	
Yeast	WLP028 Edinburgh Ale	

1939 William Younger No. 1		
pale malt	13.25 lb	68.83%
crystal malt 60L	1.00 lb	5.19%
mild malt	0.50 lb	2.60%
grits	3.75 lb	19.48%
lactose	0.75 lb	3.90%
Fuggles 90 min	1.50 oz	
Fuggles 60 min	1.00 oz	
Fuggles 30 min	1.00 oz	
Goldings dry hops	0.25 oz	
OG	1084	
FG	1033.5	
ABV	6.68	
Apparent attenuation	60.12%	
IBU	37	
SRM	10	
Mash at	157° F	
Sparge at	160° F	
Boil time	105 minutes	
pitching temp	57.5° F	
Yeast	WLP028 Edinburgh Ale	

1939 William Younger X

pale malt	4.25 lb	65.38%
crystal malt 60L	0.50 lb	7.69%
mild malt	0.25 lb	3.85%
grits	1.00 lb	15.38%
invert sugar	0.25 lb	3.85%
lactose	0.25 lb	3.85%
liquorice	0.25 oz	
Fuggles 90 min	0.25 oz	
Fuggles 30 min	0.25 oz	
Goldings dry hops	0.25 oz	
OG	1029	
FG	1012	
ABV	2.25	
Apparent attenuation	58.62%	
IBU	7	
SRM	5	
Mash at	154° F	
Sparge at	160° F	
Boil time	105 minutes	
pitching temp	62.5° F	
Yeast	WLP028 Edinburgh Ale	

1939 William Younger XXP Btlg

pale malt	7.75 lb	100.00%
grits		0.00%
Fuggles 90 min	0.75 oz	
Fuggles 30 min	0.75 oz	
Goldings dry hops	0.25 oz	
OG	1040	
FG	1013	
ABV	3.57	
Apparent attenuation	67.50%	
IBU	20	
SRM	4	
Mash at	153° F	
Sparge at	160° F	
Boil time	105 minutes	
pitching temp	61° F	
Yeast	WLP028 Edinburgh Ale	

1940 William Younger XP Btlg		
pale malt	7.75 lb	100.00%
Fuggles 90 min	0.75 oz	
Fuggles 30 min	0.50 oz	
Goldings dry hops	0.125 oz	
OG	1033	
FG	1011	
ABV	2.91	
Apparent attenuation	66.67%	
IBU	18	
SRM	3	
Mash at	154° F	
Sparge at	160° F	
Boil time	105 minutes	
pitching temp	63.5° F	
Yeast	WLP028 Edinburgh Ale	

1949 William Younger XXP Btlg		
pale malt	6.75 lb	93.10%
flaked barley	0.50 lb	6.90%
Fuggles 90 min	0.50 oz	
Fuggles 30 min	0.50 oz	
OG	1031	
FG	1008	
ABV	3.04	
Apparent attenuation	74.19%	
IBU	14	
SRM	3	
Mash at	256° F	
Sparge at	160° F	
Boil time	75 minutes	
pitching temp	62° F	
Yeast	WLP028 Edinburgh Ale	

1949 William Younger XXP

pale malt	6.75 lb	90.00%
flaked barley	0.75 lb	10.00%
Fuggles 90 min	0.50 oz	
Fuggles 60 min	0.50 oz	
Fuggles 30 min	0.25 oz	
Goldings dry hops	0.125 oz	
OG	1031.5	
FG	1011	
ABV	2.71	
Apparent attenuation	65.08%	
IBU	19	
SRM	3	
Mash at	155° F	
Sparge at	160° F	
Boil time	75 minutes	
pitching temp	61.5° F	
Yeast	WLP028 Edinburgh Ale	

1949 William Younger No. 3 Pale

pale malt	9.00 lb	87.80%
flaked barley	1.25 lb	12.20%
Fuggles 90 min	0.75 oz	
Fuggles 60 min	0.50 oz	
Fuggles 30 min	0.50 oz	
Goldings dry hops	0.50 oz	
OG	1044	
FG	1012	
ABV	4.23	
Apparent attenuation	72.73%	
IBU	23	
SRM	4	
Mash at	155° F	
Sparge at	160° F	
Boil time	75 minutes	
pitching temp	60.5° F	
Yeast	WLP028 Edinburgh Ale	

1949 William Younger Ext

pale malt	9.75 lb	88.64%
flaked barley	1.25 lb	11.36%
Fuggles 90 min	0.75 oz	
Fuggles 60 min	0.50 oz	
Fuggles 30 min	0.50 oz	
Goldings dry hops	0.125 oz	
OG	1047	
FG	1006.5	
ABV	5.36	
Apparent attenuation	86.17%	
IBU	23	
SRM	4	
Mash at	151° F	
Sparge at	160° F	
Boil time	120 minutes	
pitching temp	60° F	
Yeast	WLP028 Edinburgh Ale	

1949 William Younger No. 3

pale malt	13.50 lb	78.26%
crystal malt 60L	0.50 lb	2.90%
mild malt	0.50 lb	2.90%
flaked barley	2.00 lb	11.59%
lactose	0.75 lb	4.35%
Fuggles 90 min	1.00 oz	
Fuggles 60 min	1.00 oz	
Fuggles 30 min	1.00 oz	
Goldings dry hops	0.25 oz	
OG	1074	
FG	1023	
ABV	6.75	
Apparent attenuation	68.92%	
IBU	32	
SRM	8	
Mash at	155° F	
Sparge at	160° F	
Boil time	150 minutes	
pitching temp	57.5° F	
Yeast	WLP028 Edinburgh Ale	

Thomas Usher

1880 – 1913

1885 Thomas Usher IPA		
pale malt	10.75 lb	100.00%
Cluster 90 min	1.75 oz	
Spalt 30 min	1.75 oz	
Goldings dry hops	0.25 oz	
OG	1047	
FG	1013	
ABV	4.50	
Apparent attenuation	72.34%	
IBU	64	
SRM	2	
Mash at	156° F	
Sparge at	175° F	
Boil time	90 minutes	
pitching temp	58° F	
Yeast	WLP028 Edinburgh Ale	

1885 Thomas Usher PA		
pale malt	12.50 lb	100.00%
Cluster 90 min	2.00 oz	
Strisselspalt 30 min	2.00 oz	
Goldings dry hops	0.25 oz	
OG	1054	
FG	1015	
ABV	5.16	
Apparent attenuation	72.22%	
IBU	61	
SRM	5	
Mash at	154° F	
Sparge at	175° F	
Boil time	90 minutes	
pitching temp	59° F	
Yeast	WLP028 Edinburgh Ale	

1885 Thomas Usher X		
pale malt	11.50 lb	98.92%
black malt	0.125 lb	1.08%
Cluster 90 min	1.50 oz	
Strisselspalt 60 min	1.50 oz	
Strisselspalt 30 min	1.50 oz	
OG	1050	
FG	1013	
ABV	4.89	
Apparent attenuation	74.00%	
IBU	65	
SRM	9	
Mash at	155° F	
Sparge at	175° F	
Boil time	90 minutes	
pitching temp	58° F	
Yeast	WLP028 Edinburgh Ale	

1885 Thomas Usher 54/- M		
pale malt	12.25 lb	89.09%
cane sugar	1.50 lb	10.91%
Cluster 90 min	1.25 oz	
Cluster 60 min	1.25 oz	
Strisselspalt 30 min	0.75 oz	
OG	1064	
FG	1025	
ABV	5.16	
Apparent attenuation	60.94%	
IBU	55	
SRM	5	
Mash at	155° F	
Sparge at	175° F	
Boil time	120 minutes	
pitching temp	58° F	
Yeast	WLP028 Edinburgh Ale	

1885 Thomas Usher 80/-		
pale malt	10.75 lb	87.76%
cane sugar	1.50 lb	12.24%
Cluster 90 min	1.00 oz	
Cluster 60 min	1.00 oz	
Strisselspalt 30 min	0.50 oz	
OG	1058	
FG	1023	
ABV	4.63	
Apparent attenuation	60.34%	
IBU	45	
SRM	4	
Mash at	155° F	
Sparge at	175° F	
Boil time	120 minutes	
pitching temp	59° F	
Yeast	WLP028 Edinburgh Ale	

1885 Thomas Usher 60/- B		
pale malt	8.00 lb	88.89%
cane sugar	1.00 lb	11.11%
Cluster 90 min	0.75 oz	
Cluster 60 min	0.75 oz	
Strisselspalt 30 min	0.50 oz	
OG	1041.5	
FG	1015	
ABV	3.51	
Apparent attenuation	63.86%	
IBU	39	
SRM	4	
Mash at	155° F	
Sparge at	175° F	
Boil time	120 minutes	
pitching temp	59° F	
Yeast	WLP028 Edinburgh Ale	

1885 Thomas Usher 40/- B

pale malt	5.75 lb	88.46%
cane sugar	0.75 lb	11.54%
Cluster 90 min	0.50 oz	
Cluster 60 min	0.50 oz	
Strisselspalt 30 min	0.25 oz	
OG	1030	
FG	1011	
ABV	2.51	
Apparent attenuation	63.33%	
IBU	27	
SRM	3	
Mash at	155° F	
Sparge at	175° F	
Boil time	90 minutes	
pitching temp	57.5° F	
Yeast	WLP028 Edinburgh Ale	

1885 Thomas Usher XX

pale malt	12.75 lb	100.00%
Strisselspalt 90 min	3.25 oz	
Hallertau 30 min	3.25 oz	
Goldings dry hops	0.50 oz	
OG	1055	
FG	1015	
ABV	5.29	
Apparent attenuation	72.73%	
IBU	69	
SRM	5	
Mash at	155° F	
Sparge at	175° F	
Boil time	105 minutes	
pitching temp	58° F	
Yeast	WLP028 Edinburgh Ale	

1885 Thomas Usher 68/- M

pale malt	18.50 lb	100.00%
Strisselspalt 120 min	1.75 oz	
Strisselspalt 90 min	1.75 oz	
Hallertau 60 min	1.75 oz	
Hallertau 30 min	1.75 oz	
OG	1080	
FG	1025	
ABV	7.28	
Apparent attenuation	68.75%	
IBU	61	
SRM	6	
Mash at	153° F	
Sparge at	175° F	
Boil time	120 minutes	
pitching temp	58° F	
Yeast	WLP028 Edinburgh Ale	

1885 Thomas Usher KPA

pale malt	14.00 lb	100.00%
Strisselspalt 120 min	2.25 oz	
Strisselspalt 90 min	2.25 oz	
Hallertau 60 min	2.25 oz	
Hallertau 30 min	2.25 oz	
Goldings dry hops	0.50 oz	
OG	1060	
FG	1015	
ABV	5.95	
Apparent attenuation	75.00%	
IBU	89	
SRM	5	
Mash at	153° F	
Sparge at	175° F	
Boil time	135 minutes	
pitching temp	59° F	
Yeast	WLP028 Edinburgh Ale	

1888 Thomas Usher XXX		
pale malt	10.25 lb	89.13%
cane sugar	1.25 lb	10.87%
Hallertau 90 min	3.00 oz	
Fuggles 60 min	2.50 oz	
Fuggles 30 min	2.50 oz	
Goldings dry hops	0.25 oz	
OG	1054	
FG	1011	
ABV	5.69	
Apparent attenuation	79.63%	
IBU	87	
SRM	4	
Mash at	153° F	
Sparge at	175° F	
Boil time	105 minutes	
pitching temp	58° F	
Yeast	WLP028 Edinburgh Ale	

1888 Thomas Usher Expt		
pale malt	12.50 lb	100.00%
Hallertau 180 min	2.25 oz	
Hallertau 90 min	2.25 oz	
Fuggles 60 min	2.25 oz	
Fuggles 30 min	2.25 oz	
Goldings dry hops	0.50 oz	
OG	1054	
FG	1012	
ABV	5.56	
Apparent attenuation	77.78%	
IBU	105	
SRM	5	
Mash at	153° F	
Sparge at	175° F	
Boil time	180 minutes	
pitching temp	58° F	
Yeast	WLP028 Edinburgh Ale	

1888 Thomas Usher 50/- B		
pale malt	6.75 lb	90.00%
No. 2 invert sugar	0.75 lb	10.00%
Fuggles 120 min	0.50 oz	
Spalt 60 min	0.75 oz	
Fuggles 30 min	0.50 oz	
OG	1035	
FG	1009	
ABV	3.44	
Apparent attenuation	74.29%	
IBU	30	
SRM	6	
Mash at	150º F	
Sparge at	175º F	
Boil time	120 minutes	
pitching temp	60º F	
Yeast	WLP028 Edinburgh Ale	

1894 Thomas Usher PA		
pale malt	9.00 lb	85.71%
No. 2 invert sugar	1.50 lb	14.29%
Fuggles 90 min	1.50 oz	
Goldings 60 min	1.50 oz	
Goldings 30 min	1.50 oz	
Goldings dry hops	0.25 oz	
OG	1049	
FG	1015	
ABV	4.50	
Apparent attenuation	69.39%	
IBU	56	
SRM	8	
Mash at	150º F	
Sparge at	180º F	
Boil time	90 minutes	
pitching temp	58º F	
Yeast	WLP028 Edinburgh Ale	

1894 Thomas Usher 100/-

pale malt	10.00 lb	75.47%
No. 2 invert sugar	3.25 lb	24.53%
Fuggles 90 min	0.75 oz	
Fuggles 60 min	0.75 oz	
Goldings 30 min	1.25 oz	
OG	1068	
FG	1030	
ABV	5.03	
Apparent attenuation	55.88%	
IBU	29	
SRM	12	
Mash at	146° F	
Sparge at	170° F	
Boil time	90 minutes	
pitching temp	58° F	
Yeast	WLP028 Edinburgh Ale	

1894 Thomas Usher 80/-

pale malt	8.00 lb	76.19%
No. 2 invert sugar	2.50 lb	23.81%
Fuggles 90 min	0.50 oz	
Fuggles 60 min	0.50 oz	
Goldings 30 min	1.00 oz	
OG	1053	
FG	1020	
ABV	4.37	
Apparent attenuation	62.26%	
IBU	23	
SRM	10	
Mash at	146° F	
Sparge at	170° F	
Boil time	90 minutes	
pitching temp	60° F	
Yeast	WLP028 Edinburgh Ale	

1894 Thomas Usher 60/- Br		
pale malt	6.75 lb	87.10%
No. 2 invert sugar	1.00 lb	12.90%
Fuggles 90 min	0.75 oz	
Fuggles 60 min	0.75 oz	
Goldings 30 min	0.75 oz	
OG	1037	
FG	1010	
ABV	3.57	
Apparent attenuation	72.97%	
IBU	30	
SRM	6	
Mash at	150° F	
Sparge at	180° F	
Boil time	90 minutes	
pitching temp	59° F	
Yeast	WLP028 Edinburgh Ale	

1894 Thomas Usher 50/- Br		
pale malt	15.75 lb	94.03%
No. 2 invert sugar	1.00 lb	5.97%
Fuggles 90 min	0.50 oz	
Fuggles 60 min	0.50 oz	
Goldings 30 min	1.00 oz	
OG	1032	
FG	1009	
ABV	3.04	
Apparent attenuation	71.88%	
IBU	27	
SRM	6	
Mash at	150° F	
Sparge at	180° F	
Boil time	90 minutes	
pitching temp	60° F	
Yeast	WLP028 Edinburgh Ale	

1894 Thomas Usher Stout		
pale malt	5.50 lb	46.81%
brown malt	2.25 lb	19.15%
black malt	1.00 lb	8.51%
No. 4 invert	0.75 lb	6.38%
cane sugar	2.25 lb	19.15%
Fuggles 180 min	0.50 oz	
Fuggles 90 min	0.50 oz	
Fuggles 60 min	0.75 oz	
Goldings 30 min	0.75 oz	
OG	1058	
FG	1019	
ABV	5.16	
Apparent attenuation	67.24%	
IBU	32	
SRM	41	
Mash at	146° F	
Sparge at	170° F	
Boil time	180 minutes	
pitching temp	59° F	
Yeast	WLP028 Edinburgh Ale	

1894 Thomas Usher PA 60/-		
pale malt	9.75 lb	84.78%
No. 2 invert sugar	1.75 lb	15.22%
Fuggles 90 min	1.75 oz	
Fuggles 60 min	1.50 oz	
Goldings 30 min	1.50 oz	
Goldings dry hops	0.50 oz	
OG	1055	
FG	1015	
ABV	5.29	
Apparent attenuation	72.73%	
IBU	57	
SRM	9	
Mash at	150° F	
Sparge at	180° F	
Boil time	90 minutes	
pitching temp	58° F	
Yeast	WLP028 Ecinburgh Ale	

1894 Thomas Usher 3 XX		
pale malt	10.25 lb	95.35%
No. 2 invert sugar	0.50 lb	4.65%
Fuggles 90 min	1.75 oz	
Fuggles 60 min	1.75 oz	
Goldings 30 min	1.75 oz	
Goldings dry hops	0.50 oz	
OG	1049	
FG	1015	
ABV	4.50	
Apparent attenuation	69.39%	
IBU	66	
SRM	5	
Mash at	150° F	
Sparge at	180° F	
Boil time	90 minutes	
pitching temp	58° F	
Yeast	WLP028 Edinburgh Ale	

1912 Thomas Usher PA 60/-		
pale malt	9.25 lb	78.72%
flaked maize	1.25 lb	10.64%
No. 2 invert sugar	1.25 lb	10.64%
Fuggles 90 min	1.25 oz	
Fuggles 60 min	1.00 oz	
Goldings 30 min	1.00 oz	
Goldings dry hops	0.50 oz	
OG	1054	
FG	1016	
ABV	5.03	
Apparent attenuation	70.37%	
IBU	38	
SRM	8	
Mash at	149° F	
Sparge at	170° F	
Boil time	90 minutes	
pitching temp	60° F	
Yeast	WLP028 Edinburgh Ale	

1912 Thomas Usher PA

pale malt	8.25 lb	80.49%
flaked maize	1.00 lb	9.76%
No. 2 invert sugar	1.00 lb	9.76%
Fuggles 90 min	1.00 oz	
Fuggles 60 min	1.00 oz	
Goldings 30 min	1.00 oz	
Goldings dry hops	0.25 oz	
OG	1048	
FG	1015	
ABV	4.37	
Apparent attenuation	68.75%	
IBU	36	
SRM	7	
Mash at	149° F	
Sparge at	170° F	
Boil time	90 minutes	
pitching temp	60° F	
Yeast	WLP028 Edinburgh Ale	

1912 Thomas Usher Stout

pale malt	10.00 b	67.80%
brown malt	0.75 b	5.08%
choc. Malt	0.75 b	5.08%
crystal malt	0.75 b	5.08%
No. 3 invert	2.50 b	16.95%
Fuggles 90 min	1.50 oz	
Fuggles 60 min	1.50 oz	
Fuggles 30 min	1.50 oz	
OG	1070	
FG	1029	
ABV	5.42	
Apparent attenuation	58.57%	
IBU	52	
SRM	32	
Mash at	148° F	
Sparge at	170° F	
Boil time	240 minutes	
pitching temp	60° F	
Yeast	WLP028 Edinburgh Ale	

1912 Thomas Usher 54/- Stout

pale malt	7.75 lb	67.39%
brown malt	0.50 lb	4.35%
choc. Malt	0.75 lb	6.52%
crystal malt	0.75 lb	6.52%
No. 3 invert	1.75 lb	15.22%
Fuggles 90 min	1.25 oz	
Fuggles 60 min	1.25 oz	
Fuggles 30 min	1.00 oz	
OG	1054	
FG	1026	
ABV	3.70	
Apparent attenuation	51.85%	
IBU	44	
SRM	30	
Mash at	148° F	
Sparge at	170° F	
Boil time	240 minutes	
pitching temp	60° F	
Yeast	WLP028 Edinburgh Ale	

1912 Thomas Usher 60/- Br

pale malt	6.00 lb	80.00%
flaked maize	0.75 lb	10.00%
No. 2 invert sugar	0.75 lb	10.00%
Fuggles 90 min	0.75 oz	
Fuggles 60 min	0.50 oz	
Fuggles 30 min	0.50 oz	
OG	1034	
FG	1010	
ABV	3.18	
Apparent attenuation	70.59%	
IBU	23	
SRM	5	
Mash at	150° F	
Sparge at	170° F	
Boil time	90 minutes	
pitching temp	60° F	
Yeast	WLP028 Edinburgh Ale	

1912 Thomas Usher 50/- Br		
pale malt	5.25 lb	77.78%
flaked maize	0.75 lb	11.11%
No. 2 invert sugar	0.75 lb	11.11%
Fuggles 90 min	0.50 oz	
Fuggles 60 min	0.50 oz	
Fuggles 30 min	0.50 oz	
OG	1031	
FG	1009	
ABV	2.91	
Apparent attenuation	70.97%	
IBU	20	
SRM	5	
Mash at	150° F	
Sparge at	170° F	
Boil time	90 minutes	
pitching temp	60° F	
Yeast	WLP028 Edinburgh Ale	

1912 Thomas Usher 60/-		
pale malt	4.74 lb	63.28%
crystal malt 60L	0.50 lb	6.68%
flaked maize	0.50 lb	6.68%
No. 2 invert sugar	0.50 lb	6.68%
cane sugar	1.25 lb	16.69%
Fuggles 120 min	0.75 oz	
Fuggles 60 min	0.50 oz	
Fuggles 30 min	0.50 oz	
OG	1039	
FG	1015	
ABV	3.18	
Apparent attenuation	61.54%	
IBU	23	
SRM	7	
Mash at	148° F	
Sparge at	170° F	
Boil time	120 minutes	
pitching temp	60° F	
Yeast	WLP028 Edinburgh Ale	

1912 Thomas Usher 44/-		
pale malt	4.00 lb	60.79%
crystal malt	0.33 lb	5.02%
flaked maize	0.50 lb	7.60%
No. 2 invert sugar	0.50 lb	7.60%
cane sugar	1.25 lb	19.00%
Fuggles 120 min	0.50 oz	
Fuggles 60 min	0.50 oz	
Fuggles 30 min	0.50 oz	
OG	1034	
FG	1013	
ABV	2.78	
Apparent attenuation	61.76%	
IBU	20	
SRM	6	
Mash at	148° F	
Sparge at	170° F	
Boil time	120 minutes	
pitching temp	60° F	
Yeast	WLP028 Edinburgh Ale	

1912 Thomas Usher 80/-		
pale malt	5.75 lb	60.53%
crystal malt	0.50 lb	5.26%
flaked maize	0.75 lb	7.89%
No. 2 invert sugar	0.75 lb	7.89%
cane sugar	1.75 lb	18.42%
Fuggles 120 min	0.75 oz	
Fuggles 60 min	0.75 oz	
Fuggles 30 min	0.75 oz	
OG	1049	
FG	1018	
ABV	4.10	
Apparent attenuation	63.27%	
IBU	27	
SRM	8	
Mash at	148° F	
Sparge at	170° F	
Boil time	120 minutes	
pitching temp	60° F	
Yeast	WLP028 Edinburgh Ale	

1912 Thomas Usher X 60/-		
pale malt	9.25 lb	78.72%
flaked maize	1.75 lb	14.89%
No. 2 invert sugar	0.75 lb	6.38%
Fuggles 120 min	1.25 oz	
Fuggles 60 min	1.00 oz	
Fuggles 30 min	1.00 oz	
OG	1052	
FG	1016	
ABV	4.76	
Apparent attenuation	69.23%	
IBU	38	
SRM	6	
Mash at	150° F	
Sparge at	170° F	
Boil time	120 minutes	
pitching temp	60° F	
Yeast	WLP028 Edinburgh Ale	

1912 Thomas Usher X		
pale malt	7.75 lb	77.50%
flaked maize	1.50 lb	15.00%
No. 2 invert sugar	0.75 lb	7.50%
Fuggles 90 min	1.00 oz	
Fuggles 60 min	0.75 oz	
Fuggles 30 min	0.75 oz	
OG	1045	
FG	1014.5	
ABV	4.03	
Apparent attenuation	67.78%	
IBU	30	
SRM	6	
Mash at	150° F	
Sparge at	170° F	
Boil time	90 minutes	
pitching temp	60° F	
Yeast	WLP028 Edinburgh Ale	

1913 Thomas Usher 50/-

pale malt	3.75 lb	60.00%
crystal malt 80L	0.25 lb	4.00%
flaked maize	0.50 lb	8.00%
No. 2 invert sugar	0.50 lb	8.00%
cane sugar	1.25 lb	20.00%
Fuggles 120 min	0.50 oz	
Fuggles 60 min	0.50 oz	
Fuggles 30 min	0.50 oz	
OG	1033	
FG	1015	
ABV	2.38	
Apparent attenuation	54.55%	
IBU	20	
SRM	6	
Mash at	148° F	
Sparge at	170° F	
Boil time	120 minutes	
pitching temp	60° F	
Yeast	WLP028 Edinburgh Ale	

1913 Thomas Usher 40/-

pale malt	5.00 lb	80.00%
flaked maize	0.75 lb	12.00%
No. 2 invert sugar	0.50 lb	8.00%
Fuggles 120 min	0.50 oz	
Fuggles 60 min	0.50 oz	
Fuggles 30 min	0.50 oz	
OG	1029	
FG	1010	
ABV	2.51	
Apparent attenuation	65.52%	
IBU	21	
SRM	5	
Mash at	151° F	
Sparge at	170° F	
Boil time	90 minutes	
pitching temp	60° F	
Yeast	WLP028 Edinburgh Ale	

1914 – 1939

1914 Thomas Usher 50/- MA		
pale malt	5.75 lb	77.60%
crystal malt	0.33 lb	4.45%
flaked maize	0.33 lb	4.45%
No. 3 invert sugar	0.50 lb	6.75%
cane sugar	0.50 lb	6.75%
Fuggles 120 min	0.50 oz	
Fuggles 60 min	0.50 oz	
Fuggles 30 min	0.50 oz	
OG	1035	
FG	1013	
ABV	2.91	
Apparent attenuation	62.86%	
IBU	20	
SRM	8	
Mash at	150° F	
Sparge at	170° F	
Boil time	120 minutes	
Pitching temp	60° F	
Yeast	WLP028 Edinburgh Ale	

1914 Thomas Usher 44/- MA		
pale malt	5.00 lb	75.08%
crystal malt	0.33 lb	4.95%
flaked maize	0.33 lb	4.95%
No. 3 invert sugar	0.50 lb	7.51%
cane sugar	0.50 lb	7.51%
Fuggles 120 min	0.50 oz	
Fuggles 60 min	0.50 oz	
Fuggles 30 min	0.25 oz	
OG	1032	
FG	1012.5	
ABV	2.58	
Apparent attenuation	60.94%	
IBU	17	
SRM	8	
Mash at	150° F	
Sparge at	170° F	
Boil time	120 minutes	
pitching temp	60° F	
Yeast	WLP028 Edinburgh Ale	

1914 Thomas Usher 100/- MA

pale malt	9.75 lb	73.58%
crystal malt	0.75 lb	5.66%
flaked maize	0.75 lb	5.66%
No. 3 invert sugar	1.00 lb	7.55%
cane sugar	1.00 lb	7.55%
Fuggles 120 min	1.00 oz	
Fuggles 60 min	0.75 oz	
Fuggles 30 min	0.75 oz	
OG	1065	
FG	1027	
ABV	5.03	
Apparent attenuation	58.46%	
IBU	28	
SRM	13	
Mash at	150° F	
Sparge at	170° F	
Boil time	120 minutes	
pitching temp	60° F	
Yeast	WLP028 Edinburgh Ale	

1917 Thomas Usher 60/- Br

pale malt	5.00 lb	80.00%
flaked maize	0.50 lb	8.00%
No. 2 invert sugar	0.75 lb	12.00%
Fuggles 90 min	0.50 oz	
Fuggles 60 min	0.50 oz	
Fuggles 30 min	0.50 oz	
OG	1029	
FG	1009	
ABV	2.65	
Apparent attenuation	68.97%	
IBU	20	
SRM	5	
Mash at	149° F	
Sparge at	170° F	
Boil time	90 minutes	
pitching temp	60° F	
Yeast	WLP028 Edinburgh Ale	

1917 Thomas Usher PA		
pale malt	6.75 lb	79.41%
flaked maize	0.75 lb	8.82%
No. 2 invert sugar	1.00 lb	11.76%
Fuggles 90 min	0.75 oz	
Fuggles 60 min	0.75 oz	
Fuggles 30 min	0.50 oz	
OG	1040	
FG	1013	
ABV	3.57	
Apparent attenuation	67.50%	
IBU	25	
SRM	6	
Mash at	149° F	
Sparge at	170° F	
Boil time	90 minutes	
pitching temp	60° F	
Yeast	WLP028 Edinburgh Ale	

1917 Thomas Usher X		
pale malt	6.00 lb	77.42%
flaked maize	0.50 lb	6.45%
No. 2 invert sugar	1.25 lb	16.13%
Fuggles 90 min	0.75 oz	
Fuggles 60 min	0.50 oz	
Fuggles 30 min	0.50 oz	
OG	1038	
FG	1013	
ABV	3.31	
Apparent attenuation	65.79%	
IBU	23	
SRM	7	
Mash at	149° F	
Sparge at	170° F	
Boil time	90 minutes	
pitching temp	60° F	
Yeast	WLP028 Edinburgh Ale	

1917 Thomas Usher IP

pale malt	5.75 lb	79.31%
flaked maize	0.50 lb	6.90%
No. 2 invert sugar	1.00 lb	13.79%
Fuggles 105 min	0.75 oz	
Fuggles 60 min	0.50 oz	
Fuggles 30 min	0.50 oz	
OG	1035	
FG	1013	
ABV	2.91	
Apparent attenuation	62.86%	
IBU	23	
SRM	6	
Mash at	149° F	
Sparge at	170° F	
Boil time	105 minutes	
pitching temp	60° F	
Yeast	WLP028 Edinburgh Ale	

1917 Thomas Usher PA 60/-

pale malt	8.26 lb	80.51%
flaked maize	0.75 lb	7.31%
No. 2 invert sugar	1.25 lb	12.18%
Fuggles 105 min	0.75 oz	
Fuggles 60 min	0.75 oz	
Fuggles 30 min	0.75 oz	
OG	1048	
FG	1014	
ABV	4.50	
Apparent attenuation	70.83%	
IBU	27	
SRM	7	
Mash at	149° F	
Sparge at	170° F	
Boil time	105 minutes	
pitching temp	60° F	
Yeast	WLP028 Edinburgh Ale	

1917 Thomas Usher 60/-

pale malt	5.00 lb	78.99%
crystal malt 60L	0.33 lb	5.21%
cane sugar	0.75 lb	11.85%
No. 3 invert sugar	0.25 lb	3.95%
Fuggles 120 min	0.25 oz	
Fuggles 90 min	0.25 oz	
Fuggles 60 min	0.25 oz	
Fuggles 30 min	0.25 oz	
OG	1031	
FG	1014	
ABV	2.25	
Apparent attenuation	54.84%	
IBU	14	
SRM	6	
Mash at	148° F	
Sparge at	170° F	
Boil time	120 minutes	
pitching temp	60° F	
Yeast	WLP028 Edinburgh Ale	

1917 Thomas Usher 80/-

pale malt	6.00 lb	79.16%
crystal malt 60L	0.33 lb	4.35%
cane sugar	1.00 lb	13.19%
No. 3 invert sugar	0.25 lb	3.30%
Fuggles 120 min	0.50 oz	
Fuggles 90 min	0.25 oz	
Fuggles 60 min	0.25 oz	
Fuggles 30 min	0.25 oz	
OG	1038	
FG	1015	
ABV	3.04	
Apparent attenuation	60.53%	
IBU	18	
SRM	6	
Mash at	148° F	
Sparge at	170° F	
Boil time	120 minutes	
pitching temp	60° F	
Yeast	WLP028 Edinburgh Ale	

1918 Thomas Usher PA		
pale malt	7.25 lb	90.63%
No. 2 invert sugar	0.75 lb	9.38%
Fuggles 90 min	0.75 oz	
Fuggles 60 min	0.75 oz	
Fuggles 30 min	0.50 oz	
OG	1037	
FG	1014	
ABV	3.04	
Apparent attenuation	62.16%	
IBU	26	
SRM	6	
Mash at	152° F	
Sparge at	170° F	
Boil time	90 minutes	
pitching temp	60° F	
Yeast	WLP028 Edinburgh Ale	

1918 Thomas Usher MA		
pale malt	6.00 lb	88.89%
No. 2 invert sugar	0.75 lb	11.11%
Fuggles 90 min	0.50 oz	
Fuggles 60 min	0.50 oz	
Fuggles 30 min	0.25 oz	
OG	1032	
FG	1013	
ABV	2.51	
Apparent attenuation	59.38%	
IBU	17	
SRM	5	
Mash at	152° F	
Sparge at	170° F	
Boil time	90 minutes	
pitching temp	60° F	
Yeast	WLP028 Edinburgh Ale	

1918 Thomas Usher PA 60/-		
pale malt	10.00 lb	95.24%
No. 2 invert sugar	0.50 lb	4.76%
Fuggles 90 min	0.75 oz	
Fuggles 60 min	0.75 oz	
Fuggles 30 min	0.75 oz	
Goldings dry hop	0.25 oz	
OG	1047	
FG	1015	
ABV	4.23	
Apparent attenuation	68.09%	
IBU	27	
SRM	6	
Mash at	152° F	
Sparge at	170° F	
Boil time	90 minutes	
pitching temp	60° F	
Yeast	WLP028 Edinburgh Ale	

1918 Thomas Usher 60/-		
pale malt	4.75 lb	82.61%
crystal malt	0.25 lb	4.35%
No. 2 invert sugar	0.75 lb	13.04%
Fuggles 90 min	0.50 oz	
Fuggles 60 min	0.50 oz	
Fuggles 30 min	0.25 oz	
OG	1031	
FG	1015	
ABV	2.12	
Apparent attenuation	51.61%	
IBU	17	
SRM	6	
Mash at	148° F	
Sparge at	170° F	
Boil time	90 minutes	
pitching temp	60° F	
Yeast	WLP028 Edinburgh Ale	

1918 Thomas Usher 80/-		
pale malt	7.25 lb	87.03%
crystal malt	0.33 lb	3.96%
No. 2 invert sugar	0.75 lb	9.00%
Fuggles 90 min	0.50 oz	
Fuggles 60 min	0.50 oz	
Fuggles 30 min	0.50 oz	
OG	1038	
FG	1017	
ABV	2.78	
Apparent attenuation	55.26%	
IBU	16	
SRM	7	
Mash at	148° F	
Sparge at	170° F	
Boil time	90 minutes	
pitching temp	60° F	
Yeast	WLP028 Edinburgh Ale	

1918 Thomas Usher 100/-		
pale malt	9.75 lb	84.78%
crystal malt	0.50 lb	4.35%
No. 2 invert sugar	1.25 lb	10.87%
Fuggles 90 min	0.75 oz	
Fuggles 60 min	0.75 oz	
Fuggles 30 min	0.75 oz	
OG	1055	
FG	1026	
ABV	3.84	
Apparent attenuation	52.73%	
IBU	26	
SRM	9	
Mash at	148° F	
Sparge at	170° F	
Boil time	90 minutes	
pitching temp	60° F	
Yeast	WLP028 Edinburgh Ale	

1918 Thomas Usher 54/- St

pale malt	5.75 lb	60.53%
black malt	1.00 lb	10.53%
crystal malt 60 L	0.50 lb	5.26%
No. 3 invert sugar	1.25 lb	13.16%
No. 4 invert sugar	1.00 lb	10.53%
Fuggles 180 min	0.50 oz	
Fuggles 60 min	0.50 oz	
Fuggles 30 min	0.50 oz	
OG	1046	
FG	1025	
ABV	2.78	
Apparent attenuation	45.65%	
IBU	19	
SRM	43	
Mash at	148° F	
Sparge at	170° F	
Boil time	180 minutes	
pitching temp	60° F	
Yeast	WLP028 Edinburgh Ale	

1919 Thomas Usher IP

pale malt	5.25 lb	77.78%
flaked maize	0.50 lb	7.41%
No. 2 invert sugar	1.00 lb	14.81%
Goldings 90 min	0.75 oz	
Goldings 60 min	0.75 oz	
Goldings 30 min	0.75 oz	
Goldings dry hops	0.25 oz	
OG	1031	
FG	1014.5	
ABV	2.18	
Apparent attenuation	53.23%	
IBU	33	
SRM	6	
Mash at	153° F	
Sparge at	170° F	
Boil time	90 minutes	
pitching temp	60° F	
Yeast	WLP028 Edinburgh Ale	

1928 Thomas Usher PA 60/-		
pale malt	7.00 lb	77.78%
flaked maize	1.00 lb	11.11%
No. 2 invert sugar	1.00 lb	11.11%
Goldings 105 min	0.75 oz	
Goldings 60 min	0.75 oz	
Goldings 30 min	0.75 oz	
Goldings dry hops	0.25 oz	
OG	1041	
FG	1014	
ABV	3.57	
Apparent attenuation	65.85%	
IBU	31	
SRM	6	
Mash at	151° F	
Sparge at	170° F	
Boil time	105 minutes	
pitching temp	60° F	
Yeast	WLP028 Edinburgh Ale	

1928 Thomas Usher PA		
pale malt	5.75 lb	76.67%
flaked maize	1.00 lb	13.33%
No. 2 invert sugar	0.75 lb	10.00%
Goldings 105 min	0.75 oz	
Goldings 60 min	0.50 oz	
Goldings 30 min	0.50 oz	
Goldings dry hops	0.25 oz	
OG	1035	
FG	1013	
ABV	2.91	
Apparent attenuation	62.86%	
IBU	33	
SRM	5	
Mash at	149° F	
Sparge at	170° F	
Boil time	105 minutes	
pitching temp	60° F	
Yeast	WLP028 Edinburgh Ale	

1928 Thomas Usher PA 80/-

pale malt	9.25 lb	78.72%
flaked maize	1.25 lb	10.64%
No. 2 invert sugar	1.25 lb	10.64%
Goldings 105 min	1.00 oz	
Goldings 60 min	1.00 oz	
Goldings 30 min	1.00 oz	
Goldings dry hops	0.50 oz	
OG	1055	
FG	1015	
ABV	5.29	
Apparent attenuation	72.73%	
IBU	38	
SRM	7	
Mash at	151° F	
Sparge at	170° F	
Boil time	105 minutes	
pitching temp	61° F	
Yeast	WLP028 Edinburgh Ale	

1928 Thomas Usher PA 70/-

pale malt	8.00 lb	78.05%
flaked maize	1.25 lb	12.20%
No. 2 invert sugar	1.00 lb	9.76%
Goldings 105 min	1.00 oz	
Goldings 60 min	1.00 oz	
Goldings 30 min	0.75 oz	
Goldings dry hops	0.25 oz	
OG	1048	
FG	1014.5	
ABV	4.43	
Apparent attenuation	69.79%	
IBU	37	
SRM	7	
Mash at	150° F	
Sparge at	170° F	
Boil time	105 minutes	
pitching temp	60.5° F	
Yeast	WLP028 Edinburgh Ale	

1928 Thomas Usher Stout

pale malt	5.50 lb	58.67%
black malt	0.125 lb	1.33%
crystal malt 60 L	0.50 lb	5.33%
flaked maize	0.50 lb	5.33%
No. 3 invert sugar	1.50 lb	16.00%
No. 4 invert sugar	1.25 lb	13.33%
Fuggles 180 min	1.00 oz	
Fuggles 60 min	1.00 oz	
Fuggles 30 min	0.75 oz	
OG	1049	
FG	1024.5	
ABV	3.24	
Apparent attenuation	50.00%	
IBU	19	
SRM	31	
Mash at	147° F	
Sparge at	170° F	
Boil time	90 minutes	
pitching temp	60° F	
Yeast	WLP028 Edinburgh Ale	

1931 Thomas Usher MA

pale malt	5.75 lb	71.88%
crystal malt 60 L	0.50 lb	6.25%
No. 3 invert sugar	1.50 lb	18.75%
No. 4 invert sugar	0.25 lb	3.13%
Fuggles 120 min	0.50 oz	
Fuggles 60 min	0.50 oz	
Fuggles 30 min	0.25 oz	
OG	1040	
FG	1015.5	
ABV	3.24	
Apparent attenuation	61.25%	
IBU	17	
SRM	16	
Mash at	148° F	
Sparge at	170° F	
Boil time	120 minutes	
pitching temp	60° F	
Yeast	WLP028 Edinburgh Ale	

1931 Thomas Usher IPA

pale malt	5.00 lb	74.07%
flaked maize	1.00 lb	14.81%
No. 2 invert sugar	0.75 lb	11.11%
Goldings 120 min	0.50 oz	
Goldings 60 min	0.50 oz	
Goldings 30 min	0.50 oz	
Goldings dry hop	0.25 oz	
OG	1032	
FG	1011	
ABV	2.73	
Apparent attenuation	65.63%	
IBU	22	
SRM	5	
Mash at	152° F	
Sparge at	170° F	
Boil time	120 minutes	
pitching temp	60° F	
Yeast	WLP028 Edinburgh Ale	

Drybrough

1914 – 1939

1914 Drybrough Pl 60/-		
pale malt	9.50 lb	80.85%
flaked maize	1.00 lb	8.51%
no. 1 sugar	0.50 lb	4.26%
no. 2 sugar	0.75 lb	6.38%
Fuggles 120 min	0.75 oz	
Goldings 60 min	0.75 oz	
Goldings 30 min	0.75 oz	
Goldings dry hop	0.50 oz	
OG	1054	
FG	1018	
ABV	4.76	
Apparent attenuation	66.67%	
IBU	28	
SRM	7	
Mash at	148° F	
Sparge at	175° F	
Boil time	120 minutes	
pitching temp	60° F	
Yeast	WLP028 Edinburgh Ale	

1914 Drybrough Pl 48/-		
pale malt	7.25 lb	82.86%
flaked maize	0.75 lb	8.57%
no. 1 sugar	0.25 lb	2.86%
no. 2 sugar	0.50 lb	5.71%
Fuggles 120 min	0.50 oz	
Goldings 60 min	0.50 oz	
Goldings 30 min	0.50 oz	
Goldings dry hop	0.50 oz	
OG	1040	
FG	1014	
ABV	3.44	
Apparent attenuation	65.00%	
IBU	20	
SRM	5	
Mash at	148° F	
Sparge at	175° F	
Boil time	120 minutes	
pitching temp	60° F	
Yeast	WLP028 Edinburgh Ale	

1915 Drybrough 100/- m

pale malt	10.50 lb	81.84%
flaked maize	1.00 lb	7.79%
no. 1 sugar	0.33 lb	2.57%
no. 2 sugar	0.50 lb	3.90%
no. 3 sugar	0.50 lb	3.90%
Fuggles 120 min	0.75 oz	
Goldings 60 min	0.75 oz	
Goldings 30 min	0.75 oz	
OG	1060	
FG	1020	
ABV	5.29	
Apparent attenuation	66.67%	
IBU	27	
SRM	9	
Mash at	148° F	
Sparge at	175° F	
Boil time	120 minutes	
pitching temp	59.5° F	
Yeast	WLP028 Edinburgh Ale	

1917 Drybrough Pl 48/-

pale malt	5.75 lb	84.16%
flaked maize	0.50 lb	7.32%
no. 1 sugar	0.0625 lb	0.91%
no. 2 sugar	0.50 lb	7.32%
caramel	0.02 lb	0.29%
Strisselspalt 120 min	0.25 oz	
Fuggles 60 min	0.25 oz	
Fuggles 30 min	0.25 oz	
Goldings dry hop	0.50 oz	
OG	1031	
FG	1009	
ABV	2.91	
Apparent attenuation	70.97%	
IBU	11	
SRM	5	
Mash at	148° F	
Sparge at	175° F	
Boil time	120 minutes	
pitching temp	60° F	
Yeast	WLP028 Edinburgh Ale	

1918 Drybrough XX Stout

pale malt	9.00 lb	87.12%
flaked maize	0.33 lb	3.19%
cane sugar	0.125 lb	1.21%
no. 2 sugar	0.125 lb	1.21%
no. 4 sugar	0.25 lb	2.42%
caramel	0.50 lb	4.84%
Fuggles 120 min	0.75 oz	
Fuggles 60 min	0.75 oz	
Fuggles 30 min	0.50 oz	
OG	1045	
FG	1021	
ABV	3.18	
Apparent attenuation	53.33%	
IBU	28	
SRM	22	
Mash at	146° F	
Sparge at	175° F	
Boil time	120 minutes	
pitching temp	62° F	
Yeast	WLP028 Edinburgh Ale	

1918 Drybrough Pl

pale malt	6.00 lb	92.31%
cane sugar	0.125 lb	1.92%
no. 2 sugar	0.25 lb	3.85%
no. 4 sugar	0.125 lb	1.92%
Cluster 120 min	0.50 oz	
Fuggles 60 min	0.50 oz	
Fuggles 30 min	0.25 oz	
Goldings dry hop	0.50 oz	
OG	1030	
FG	1009	
ABV	2.78	
Apparent attenuation	70.00%	
IBU	23	
SRM	7	
Mash at	149° F	
Sparge at	175° F	
Boil time	90 minutes	
pitching temp	62° F	
Yeast	WLP028 Edinburgh Ale	

1918 Drybrough PI 48/-

pale malt	4.75 lb	90.48%
cane sugar	0.125 lb	2.38%
no. 2 sugar	0.25 lb	4.76%
no. 4 sugar	0.125 lb	2.38%
Cluster 90 min	0.50 oz	
Fuggles 60 min	0.25 oz	
Fuggles 30 min	0.25 oz	
Goldings dry hop	0.50 oz	
OG	1024	
FG	1007	
ABV	2.25	
Apparent attenuation	70.83%	
IBU	20	
SRM	7	
Mash at	149° F	
Sparge at	175° F	
Boil time	90 minutes	
pitching temp	62° F	
Yeast	WLP028 Edinburgh Ale	

1920 Drybrough PI 60/-

pale malt	7.25 lb	82.86%
flaked maize	1.00 lb	11.43%
no. 3 sugar	0.50 lb	5.71%
Cluster 90 min	0.75 oz	
Goldings 60 min	0.75 oz	
Goldings 30 min	0.75 oz	
Goldings dry hop	0.50 oz	
OG	1039	
FG	1008	
ABV	4.10	
Apparent attenuation	79.49%	
IBU	38	
SRM	6	
Mash at	148° F	
Sparge at	175° F	
Boil time	105 minutes	
pitching temp	60° F	
Yeast	WLP028 Edinburgh Ale	

1920 Drybrough 8d PA		
pale malt	10.50 lb	84.00%
flaked maize	1.25 lb	10.00%
no. 3 sugar	0.75 lb	6.00%
Cluster 90 min	1.00 oz	
Goldings 60 min	1.00 oz	
Goldings 30 min	1.00 oz	
Goldings dry hop	0.50 oz	
OG	1055	
FG	1012	
ABV	5.69	
Apparent attenuation	78.18%	
IBU	34	
SRM	8	
Mash at	148° F	
Sparge at	175° F	
Boil time	105 minutes	
pitching temp	60° F	
Yeast	WLP028 Edinburgh Ale	

1920 Drybrough Pl 54/-		
pale malt	6.25 lb	80.65%
flaked maize	1.00 lb	12.90%
no. 3 sugar	0.50 lb	6.45%
Cluster 90 min	0.75 oz	
Goldings 60 min	0.50 oz	
Goldings 30 min	0.50 oz	
Goldings dry hop	0.50 oz	
OG	1035	
FG	1007	
ABV	3.70	
Apparent attenuation	80.00%	
IBU	32	
SRM	6	
Mash at	148° F	
Sparge at	175° F	
Boil time	105 minutes	
pitching temp	60° F	
Yeast	WLP028 Edinburgh Ale	

1920 Drybrough XXX Stout

pale malt	12.75 lb	77.27%
black malt	1.00 lb	6.06%
crystal malt 60 L	1.00 lb	6.06%
no. 1 sugar	0.75 lb	4.55%
no. 3 sugar	1.00 lb	6.06%
Cluster 120 min	1.00 oz	
Goldings 60 min	1.00 oz	
Goldings 30 min	1.00 oz	
OG	1075	
FG	1020	
ABV	7.23	
Apparent attenuation	73.33%	
IBU	39	
SRM	35	
Mash at	146° F	
Sparge at	175° F	
Boil time	120 minutes	
pitching temp	61° F	
Yeast	WLP028 Edinburgh Ale	

1920 Drybrough XX Stout

pale malt	7.75 lb	79.49%
black malt	0.50 lb	5.13%
crystal malt	0.50 lb	5.13%
no. 1 sugar	0.50 lb	5.13%
no. 3 sugar	0.50 lb	5.13%
Cluster 120 min	0.75 oz	
Goldings 60 min	0.50 oz	
Goldings 30 min	0.50 oz	
OG	1045	
FG	1014	
ABV	4.10	
Apparent attenuation	68.89%	
IBU	29	
SRM	22	
Mash at	146° F	
Sparge at	175° F	
Boil time	120 minutes	
pitching temp	60° F	
Yeast	WLP028 Edinburgh Ale	

1920 Drybrough 80/-		
pale malt	8.25 lb	70.97%
flaked maize	2.25 lb	19.35%
malt extract	0.125 lb	1.08%
no. 2 sugar	1.00 lb	8.60%
Cluster 90 min	0.75 oz	
Strisselspalt 60 min	0.75 oz	
Goldings 30 min	0.75 oz	
Goldings dry hop	0.50 oz	
OG	1054	
FG	1014	
ABV	5.29	
Apparent attenuation	74.07%	
IBU	33	
SRM	7	
Mash at	152° F	
Sparge at	175° F	
Boil time	105 minutes	
pitching temp	60° F	
Yeast	WLP028 Edinburgh Ale	

1920 Drybrough 70/-		
pale malt	7.00 lb	70.89%
flaked maize	2.00 lb	20.25%
malt extract	0.75 lb	7.59%
no. 2 sugar	0.125 lb	1.27%
Cluster 90 min	0.75 oz	
Strisselspalt 60 min	0.50 oz	
Goldings 30 min	0.50 oz	
Goldings dry hop	0.50 oz	
OG	1045	
FG	1012	
ABV	4.37	
Apparent attenuation	73.33%	
IBU	29	
SRM	6	
Mash at	152° F	
Sparge at	175° F	
Boil time	105 minutes	
pitching temp	60° F	
Yeast	WLP028 Edinburgh Ale	

1920 Drybrough 60/-		
pale malt	5.75 lb	70.77%
flaked maize	1.50 lb	18.46%
malt extract	0.125 lb	1.54%
no. 2 sugar	0.75 lb	9.23%
Cluster 90 min	0.50 oz	
Strisselspalt 30 min	0.50 oz	
Goldings 30 min	0.50 oz	
Goldings dry hop	0.50 oz	
OG	1038	
FG	1008	
ABV	3.97	
Apparent attenuation	78.95%	
IBU	24	
SRM	6	
Mash at	152° F	
Sparge at	175° F	
Boil time	105 minutes	
pitching temp	60° F	
Yeast	WLP028 Edinburgh Ale	

1933 Drybrough P60/-		
pale malt	5.50 lb	70.06%
black malt	0.06 lb	0.76%
flaked maize	1.25 lb	15.92%
No. 1 invert sugar	1.00 lb	12.74%
malt extract	0.04 lb	0.51%
Fuggles 120 min	0.75 oz	
Fuggles 60 min	0.75 oz	
Saaz 30 min	0.75 oz	
Goldings dry hops	0.25 oz	
OG	1036	
FG	1008	
ABV	3.70	
Apparent attenuation	77.78%	
IBU	33	
SRM	7	
Mash at	152° F	
Sparge at	167° F	
Boil time	120 minutes	
pitching temp	58.5° F	
Yeast	WLP028 Edinburgh Ale	

1933 Drybrough P54/-

pale malt	2.50 lb	57.60%
black malt	0.05 lb	1.15%
flaked maize	1.00 lb	23.04%
No. 1 invert sugar	0.75 lb	17.28%
malt extract	0.04 lb	0.92%
Fuggles 120 min	0.75 oz	
Fuggles 60 min	0.50 oz	
Saaz 30 min	0.50 oz	
Goldings dry hops	0.25 oz	
OG	1030	
FG	1007	
ABV	3.04	
Apparent attenuation	76.67%	
IBU	25	
SRM	6	
Mash at	152° F	
Sparge at	167° F	
Boil time	120 minutes	
pitching temp	58.5° F	
Yeast	WLP028 Edinburgh Ale	

1933 Drybrough P80/-

pale malt	7.50 lb	70.62%
black malt	0.06 lb	0.56%
flaked maize	1.75 lb	16.48%
No. 1 invert sugar	1.25 lb	11.77%
malt extract	0.06 lb	0.56%
Fuggles 120 min	1.00 oz	
Fuggles 60 min	0.75 oz	
Goldings 30 min	0.75 oz	
Goldings dry hops	0.25 oz	
OG	1049	
FG	1012	
ABV	4.89	
Apparent attenuation	75.51%	
IBU	31	
SRM	8	
Mash at	152° F	
Sparge at	167° F	
Boil time	120 minutes	
pitching temp	59° F	
Yeast	WLP028 Edinburgh Ale	

1939 – 1970

1940 Drybrough P 54/-

pale malt	5.75 b	88.19%
black malt	0.04 b	0.61%
No. 1 invert sugar	0.66 b	10.12%
malt extract	0.07 b	1.07%
Fuggles 135 min	0.50 oz	
Fuggles 60 min	0.50 oz	
Goldings 30 min	0.25 oz	
Goldings dry hops	0.25 oz	
OG	1030	
FG	1011	
ABV	2.51	
Apparent attenuation	63.33%	
IBU	18	
SRM	6	
Mash at	152° F	
Sparge at	170° F	
Boil time	135 minutes	
pitching temp	60° F	
Yeast	WLP028 Edinburgh Ale	

1940 Drybrough Bottling

pale malt	6.50 lb	91.42%
black malt	0.04 lb	0.56%
No. 1 invert sugar	0.50 lb	7.03%
malt extract	0.07 lb	0.98%
Fuggles 135 min	0.50 oz	
Fuggles 60 min	0.50 oz	
Goldings 30 min	0.25 oz	
OG	1032	
FG	1010	
ABV	2.91	
Apparent attenuation	68.75%	
IBU	18	
SRM	6	
Mash at	154° F	
Sparge at	170° F	
Boil time	135 minutes	
pitching temp	59° F	
Yeast	WLP028 Edinburgh Ale	

1940 Drybrough P 60/-		
pale malt	7.00 lb	89.06%
black malt	0.04 lb	0.51%
No. 1 invert sugar	0.75 lb	9.54%
malt extract	0.07 lb	0.89%
Fuggles 135 min	0.50 oz	
Fuggles 60 min	0.50 oz	
Goldings 30 min	0.50 oz	
Goldings dry hops	0.25 oz	
OG	1036	
FG	1013	
ABV	3.04	
Apparent attenuation	63.89%	
IBU	20	
SRM	7	
Mash at	151° F	
Sparge at	170° F	
Boil time	135 minutes	
pitching temp	60° F	
Yeast	WLP028 Edinburgh Ale	

1940 Drybrough P 80/-		
pale malt	9.25 lb	89.55%
No. 1 invert sugar	1.00 lb	9.68%
malt extract	0.08 lb	0.77%
Fuggles 135 min	0.75 oz	
Fuggles 60 min	0.75 oz	
Goldings 30 min	0.50 oz	
Goldings dry hops	0.25 oz	
OG	1048	
FG	1013	
ABV	4.63	
Apparent attenuation	72.92%	
IBU	26	
SRM	5	
Mash at	152° F	
Sparge at	170° F	
Boil time	135 minutes	
pitching temp	60° F	
Yeast	WLP028 Edinburgh Ale	

1940 Drybrough Burns Ale

pale malt	16.75 lb	91.03%
black malt	0.25 lb	1.36%
No. 1 invert sugar	1.25 lb	6.79%
malt extract	0.15 lb	0.82%
caramel	to get the colour	
Fuggles 135 min	1.75 oz	
Fuggles 60 min	1.50 oz	
Goldings 30 min	1.50 oz	
Goldings dry hops	0.75 oz	
OG	1083	
FG	1026	
ABV	7.54	
Apparent attenuation	68.67%	
IBU	48	
SRM	20	
Mash at	152° F	
Sparge at	170° F	
Boil time	135 minutes	
pitching temp	60° F	
Yeast	WLP028 Edinburgh Ale	

1954 Drybrough 60/-

pale malt	5.00 lb	72.20%
black malt	0.125 lb	1.81%
flaked maize	0.50 lb	7.22%
flaked barley	0.50 lb	7.22%
No. 2 invert sugar	0.75 lb	10.83%
malt extract	0.05 lb	0.72%
Fuggles 90 min	0.50 oz	
Goldings 30 min	0.50 oz	
Goldings dry hops	0.50 oz	
OG	1032	
FG	1007	
ABV	3.31	
Apparent attenuation	78.13%	
IBU	13	
SRM	10	
Mash at	148° F	
Sparge at	170° F	
Boil time	90 minutes	
pitching temp	63° F	
Yeast	WLP028 Edinburgh Ale	

1954 Drybrough B 60/-

pale malt	4.75 lb	71.16%
black malt	0.125 lb	1.87%
flaked maize	0.50 lb	7.49%
flaked barley	0.50 lb	7.49%
No. 2 invert sugar	0.75 lb	11.24%
malt extract	0.05 lb	0.75%
Fuggles 90 min	0.50 oz	
Goldings 30 min	0.50 oz	
OG	1031	
FG	1007	
ABV	3.18	
Apparent attenuation	77.42%	
IBU	13	
SRM	10	
Mash at	148° F	
Sparge at	170° F	
Boil time	90 minutes	
pitching temp	63° F	
Yeast	WLP028 Edinburgh Ale	

1954 Drybrough XXP

pale malt	7.00 lb	75.03%
black malt	0.25 lb	2.68%
flaked maize	0.50 lb	5.36%
flaked barley	0.50 lb	5.36%
No. 2 invert sugar	1.00 lb	10.72%
malt extract	0.08 lb	0.86%
Fuggles 90 min	0.75 oz	
Goldings 30 min	0.75 oz	
Goldings dry hops	0.75 oz	
OG	1043	
FG	1010	
ABV	4.37	
Apparent attenuation	76.74%	
IBU	19	
SRM	14	
Mash at	148° F	
Sparge at	170° F	
Boil time	90 minutes	
pitching temp	63° F	
Yeast	WLP028 Edinburgh Ale	

Around 1960, Drybrough changes the way they mashed, moving to a step mash. Hence the two mashing temperatures.

1960 Drybrough 60/-

pale malt	5.00 lb	75.36%
black malt	0.01 lb	0.15%
flaked maize	0.75 lb	11.30%
No. 2 invert sugar	0.75 lb	11.30%
No. 3 invert sugar	0.13 lb	1.88%
Fuggles 90 min	0.50 oz	
Fuggles 60 min	0.50 oz	
Goldings 30 min	0.25 oz	
Goldings dry hops	0.50 oz	
OG	1031	
FG	1010	
ABV	2.78	
Apparent attenuation	67.74%	
BU	17	
SRM	10	
Mash at	144 / 159° F	
Sparge at	165° F	
Boil time	90 minutes	
pitching temp	61.5° F	
Yeast	WLP028 Edinburgh Ale	

1960 Drybrough XXP

pale malt	6.75 lb	77.05%
black malt	0.01 lb	0.11%
flaked maize	1.00 lb	11.42%
No. 2 invert sugar	0.75 lb	8.56%
No. 3 invert sugar	0.25 lb	2.85%
Fuggles 90 min	0.50 oz	
Fuggles 60 min	0.50 oz	
Goldings 30 min	0.50 oz	
Goldings dry hops	0.50 oz	
OG	1042	
FG	1012	
ABV	3.97	
Apparent attenuation	71.43%	
IBU	19	
SRM	11	
Mash at	144 / 159° F	
Sparge at	165° F	
Boil time	90 minutes	
pitching temp	61.5° F	
Yeast	WLP028 Edinburgh Ale	

1960 Drybrough B 60/-

pale malt	5.25 lb	81.08%
black malt	0.05 lb	0.77%
flaked maize	0.50 lb	7.72%
No. 2 invert sugar	0.50 lb	7.72%
No. 3 invert sugar	0.125 lb	1.93%
malt extract	0.05 lb	0.77%
Fuggles 90 min	0.50 oz	
Fuggles 60 min	0.25 oz	
Goldings 30 min	0.25 oz	
OG	1030	
FG	1010	
ABV	2.65	
Apparent attenuation	66.67%	
IBU	14	
SRM	10	
Mash at	145 / 159° F	
Sparge at	165° F	
Boil time	90 minutes	
pitching temp	61.5° F	
Yeast	WLP028 Edinburgh Ale	

1960 Drybrough Export

pale malt	7.50 lb	79.70%
black malt	0.08 lb	0.85%
flaked maize	0.75 lb	7.97%
No. 2 invert sugar	0.75 lb	7.97%
No. 3 invert sugar	0.250 lb	2.66%
malt extract	0.08 lb	0.85%
Fuggles 90 min	0.75 oz	
Fuggles 60 min	0.50 oz	
Goldings 30 min	0.50 oz	
Goldings dry hops	0.125 oz	
OG	1044	
FG	1009	
ABV	4.63	
Apparent attenuation	79.55%	
IBU	22	
SRM	9	
Mash at	145 / 159° F	
Sparge at	165° F	
Boil time	90 minutes	
pitching temp	61.5° F	
Yeast	WLP028 Edinburgh Ale	

1960 Drybrough B XXP

pale malt	6.00 lb	75.14%
black malt	0.05 lb	0.63%
flaked maize	1.00 lb	12.52%
No. 2 invert sugar	0.75 lb	9.39%
No. 3 invert sugar	0.125 lb	1.57%
malt extract	0.06 lb	0.75%
Fuggles 90 min	0.50 oz	
Fuggles 60 min	0.50 oz	
Goldings 30 min	0.25 oz	
Goldings dry hops	0.375 oz	
OG	1037	
FG	1007	
ABV	3.97	
Apparent attenuation	81.08%	
IBU	17	
SRM	8	
Mash at	146 / 158° F	
Sparge at	165° F	
Boil time	90 minutes	
pitching temp	62° F	
Yeast	WLP028 Edinburgh Ale	

1960 Drybrough Keg Light

pale malt	4.75 lb	73.99%
black malt	0.07 lb	1.09%
flaked maize	0.50 lb	7.79%
No. 2 invert sugar	0.75 lb	11.68%
No. 3 invert sugar	0.250 lb	3.89%
malt extract	0.10 lb	1.56%
Fuggles 90 min	0.50 oz	
Fuggles 60 min	0.25 oz	
Goldings 30 min	0.25 oz	
OG	1031	
FG	1010	
ABV	2.78	
Apparent attenuation	67.74%	
IBU	14	
SRM	9	
Mash at	146 / 158° F	
Sparge at	165° F	
Boil time	90 minutes	
pitching temp	61° F	
Yeast	WLP028 Edinburgh Ale	

1960 Drybrough Burns Ale

pale malt	12.00 lb	75.59%
black malt	0.125 lb	0.79%
flaked maize	2.00 lb	12.60%
No. 2 invert sugar	1.00 lb	6.30%
No. 3 invert sugar	0.500 lb	3.15%
malt extract	0.25 lb	1.57%
Fuggles 90 min	1.00 oz	
Fuggles 60 min	1.00 oz	
Goldings 30 min	1.00 oz	
Goldings dry hops	0.50 oz	
OG	1073	
FG	1024	
ABV	6.48	
Apparent attenuation	67.12%	
IBU	30	
SRM	14	
Mash at	146 / 158° F	
Sparge at	165° F	
Boil time	90 minutes	
pitching temp	59.5° F	
Yeast	WLP028 Edinburgh Ale	

1960 Drybrough Keg Heavy

pale malt	6.00 lb	75.14%
black malt	0.05 lb	0.63%
flaked maize	1.00 lb	12.52%
No. 2 invert sugar	0.75 lb	9.39%
No. 3 invert sugar	0.125 lb	1.57%
malt extract	0.06 lb	0.75%
Fuggles 90 min	0.50 oz	
Fuggles 60 min	0.50 oz	
Goldings 30 min	0.25 oz	
OG	1037	
FG	1007	
ABV	3.97	
Apparent attenuation	81.08%	
IBU	17	
SRM	8	
Mash at	146 / 158° F	
Sparge at	165° F	
Boil time	90 minutes	
pitching temp	62° F	
Yeast	WLP028 Edinburgh Ale	

1966 Drybrough XXP

pale malt	7.00 lb	75.51%
black malt	0.02 lb	0.22%
flaked maize	1.00 lb	10.79%
No. 2 invert sugar	0.75 lb	8.09%
No. 3 invert sugar	0.25 lb	2.70%
caramel 500 SRM	0.13 lb	1.35%
malt extract	0.13 lb	1.35%
Fuggles 90 min	0.75 oz	
Goldings 30 min	0.50 oz	
Goldings dry hops	0.125 oz	
OG	1042	
FG	1013.5	
ABV	3.77	
Apparent attenuation	67.86%	
IBU	16	
SRM	12	
Mash at	145 / 158° F	
Sparge at	165° F	
Boil time	90 minutes	
pitching temp	62° F	
Yeast	WLP028 Edinburgh Ale	

1970 Drybrough Keg Heavy

pale malt	6.00 lb	77.42%
flaked maize	1.00 lb	12.90%
No. 2 invert sugar	0.75 lb	9.68%
Fuggles 90 min	0.50 oz	
Hallertau 30 min	0.50 oz	
Goldings dry hops	0.50 oz	
OG	1036.8	
FG	1007	
ABV	3.94	
Apparent attenuation	80.98%	
IBU	12	
SRM	6	
Mash at	146° F	
Sparge at	165° F	
Boil time	90 minutes	
pitching temp	62° F	
Yeast	WLP028 Edinburgh Ale	

1970 Drybrough B 60/-

pale malt	5.00 lb	75.47%
black malt	0.125 lb	1.89%
flaked maize	0.75 lb	11.32%
No. 2 invert sugar	0.75 lb	11.32%
Fuggles 90 min	0.50 oz	
Hallertau 30 min	0.25 oz	
Goldings dry hops	0.375 oz	
OG	1030.8	
FG	1010	
ABV	2.75	
Apparent attenuation	67.53%	
IBU	10	
SRM	10	
Mash at	146° F	
Sparge at	165° F	
Boil time	90 minutes	
pitching temp	62° F	
Yeast	WLP028 Edinburgh Ale	

1970 Drybrough Export

pale malt	7.25 lb	80.20%
black malt	0.04 lb	0.44%
flaked maize	1.00 lb	11.06%
No. 2 invert sugar	0.75 lb	8.30%
Fuggles 90 min	0.50 oz	
Hallertau 30 min	0.50 oz	
Goldings dry hops	0.50 oz	
OG	1041.8	
FG	1009	
ABV	4.34	
Apparent attenuation	78.47%	
IBU	7	
SRM	11	
Mash at	146° F	
Sparge at	165° F	
Boil time	90 minutes	
pitching temp	62° F	
Yeast	WLP028 Edinburgh Ale	

Maclay

1880 – 1913

The two mashing temperatures are because Maclay were underlet mashers. The first temperature is for the main infusion, the second for after the underlet.

1909 Maclay Pl 54/-		
pale malt	5.50 lb	61.97%
amber malt	0.125 lb	1.41%
grits	2.25 lb	25.35%
No. 2 invert sugar	1.00 lb	11.27%
Cluster 120 min	0.50 oz	
Hallertau 60 min	0.50 oz	
Fuggles 30 min	1.00 oz	
Goldings dry hops	0.25 oz	
OG	1041	
FG	1015	
ABV	3.44	
Apparent attenuation	63.41%	
IBU	27	
SRM	6	
Mash at	147/153° F	
Sparge at	170° F	
Boil time	120 minutes	
pitching temp	61.5° F	
Yeast	WLP028 Edinburgh Ale	

1909 Maclay Pl 42/-		
pale malt	4.75 lb	64.41%
amber malt	0.125 lb	1.69%
grits	1.50 lb	20.34%
No. 2 invert sugar	1.00 lb	13.56%
Cluster 120 min	0.50 oz	
Hallertau 60 min	0.50 oz	
Fuggles 30 min	0.75 oz	
Goldings dry hops	0.25 oz	
OG	1035	
FG	1009	
ABV	3.44	
Apparent attenuation	74.29%	
IBU	26	
SRM	6	
Mash at	147/154° F	
Sparge at	170° F	
Boil time	120 minutes	
pitching temp	61.5° F	
Yeast	WLP028 Edinburgh Ale	

1909 Maclay Mild 42/-		
pale malt	4.50 lb	61.02%
amber malt	0.25 lb	3.39%
black malt	0.125 lb	1.69%
grits	1.50 lb	20.34%
No. 2 invert sugar	1.00 lb	13.56%
Cluster 120 min	0.50 oz	
Hallertau 60 min	0.50 oz	
Fuggles 30 min	1.00 oz	
OG	1034	
FG	1013	
ABV	2.78	
Apparent attenuation	61.76%	
IBU	28	
SRM	10	
Mash at	146/154° F	
Sparge at	170° F	
Boil time	120 minutes	
pitching temp	61° F	
Yeast	WLP028 Edinburgh Ale	

1909 Maclay DBS 54/-		
pale malt	5.25 lb	53.16%
black malt	1.00 lb	10.13%
amber malt	0.375 lb	3.80%
malted oats	2.00 lb	20.25%
caramel	0.25 lb	2.53%
No. 2 invert sugar	1.00 lb	10.13%
linseed	0.66 oz	
liquorice	0.33 oz	
Cluster 120 min	0.75 oz	
Hallertau 60 min	0.75 oz	
Goldings 30 min	1.50 oz	
OG	1044	
FG	1013	
ABV	4.10	
Apparent attenuation	70.45%	
IBU	55	
SRM	47	
Mash at	144° F	
Sparge at	170° F	
Boil time	120 minutes	
pitching temp	60.75° F	
Yeast	WLP028 Edinburgh Ale	

1914 – 1939

The two mashing temperatures are because Maclay were underlet mashers. The first temperature is for the main infusion, the second for after the underlet.

1939 Maclay PA 5d

pale malt	5.00 lb	76.92%
flaked maize	0.50 lb	7.69%
No. 2 invert sugar	1.00 lb	15.38%
Fuggles 90 min	0.75 oz	
Goldings 30 min	0.75 oz	
Goldings dry hops	0.25 oz	
OG	1032	
FG	1013	
ABV	2.51	
Apparent attenuation	59.38%	
IBU	20	
SRM	6	
Mash at	149/157° F	
Sparge at	170° F	
Boil time	90 minutes	
pitching temp	60° F	
Yeast	WLP028 Edinburgh Ale	

1939 Maclay PA 7d

pale malt	7.25 lb	78.38%
flaked maize	0.75 lb	8.11%
No. 2 invert sugar	1.25 lb	13.51%
Fuggles 90 min	0.75 oz	
Goldings 30 min	0.75 oz	
Goldings dry hops	0.25 oz	
OG	1043	
FG	1015	
ABV	3.70	
Apparent attenuation	65.12%	
IBU	18	
SRM	7	
Mash at	150/156° F	
Sparge at	170° F	
Boil time	90 minutes	
pitching temp	60° F	
Yeast	WLP028 Edinburgh Ale	

1939 Maclay SA Strong Ale		
pale malt	14.25 lb	77.03%
flaked maize	1.75 lb	9.46%
No. 2 invert sugar	2.50 lb	13.51%
Styrian Goldings 90 min	1.25 oz	
Fuggles 60 min	1.25 oz	
Goldings 30 min	1.25 oz	
Goldings dry hops	0.50 oz	
OG	1089	
FG	1030	
ABV	7.81	
Apparent attenuation	66.29%	
IBU	39	
SRM	11	
Mash at	147/152° F	
Sparge at	170° F	
Boil time	90 minutes	
pitching temp	60° F	
Yeast	WLP028 Edinburgh Ale	

1939 – 1970

1944 Maclay Export

pale malt	7.00 lb	80.00%
malted oats	0.50 lb	5.71%
flaked barley	0.50 lb	5.71%
No. 1 invert sugar	0.75 lb	8.57%
Fuggles 90 min	0.50 oz	
Fuggles 60 min	0.50 oz	
Goldings 30 min	0.25 oz	
Goldings dry hops	0.25 oz	
OG	1040	
FG	1015	
ABV	3.31	
Apparent attenuation	62.50%	
IBU	20	
SRM	5	
Mash at	147/155° F	
Sparge at	165° F	
Boil time	90 minutes	
pitching temp	60° F	
Yeast	WLP028 Edinburgh Ale	

1944 Maclay PA 6d

pale malt	5.75 lb	83.21%
malted oats	0.33 lb	4.78%
flaked barley	0.33 lb	4.78%
No. 1 invert sugar	0.50 lb	7.24%
Fuggles 90 min	0.50 oz	
Fuggles 60 min	0.25 oz	
Goldings 30 min	0.25 oz	
Goldings dry hops	0.25 oz	
OG	1032	
FG	1012.5	
ABV	2.53	
Apparent attenuation	60.94%	
IBU	14	
SRM	4	
Mash at	147/155° F	
Sparge at	165° F	
Boil time	90 minutes	
pitching temp	60° F	
Yeast	WLP028 Edinburgh Ale	

1951 Maclay PA 6d

pale malt	5.50 lb	85.21%
flaked rice	0.33 lb	5.11%
No. 1 invert sugar	0.50 lb	7.75%
No. 3 invert sugar`	0.125 lb	1.94%
Fuggles 90 min	0.50 oz	
Fuggles 60 min	0.50 oz	
Goldings 30 min	0.50 oz	
Goldings dry hops	0.25 oz	
OG	1030	
FG	1012	
ABV	2.38	
Apparent attenuation	60.00%	
IBU	21	
SRM	4	
Mash at	148/157° F	
Sparge at	165° F	
Boil time	90 minutes	
pitching temp	61° F	
Yeast	WLP028 Edinburgh Ale	

1951 Maclay SPA

pale malt	6.50 lb	82.54%
flaked rice	0.50 lb	6.35%
No. 1 invert sugar	0.75 lb	9.52%
No. 3 invert sugar	0.125 lb	1.59%
Fuggles 90 min	0.75 oz	
Fuggles 60 min	0.50 oz	
Goldings 30 min	0.50 oz	
Goldings dry hops	0.25 oz	
OG	1036	
FG	1012	
ABV	3.18	
Apparent attenuation	66.67%	
IBU	23	
SRM	5	
Mash at	148/157° F	
Sparge at	165° F	
Boil time	90 minutes	
pitching temp	61° F	
Yeast	WLP028 Edinburgh Ale	

1951 Maclay Export		
pale malt	7.50 lb	83.33%
flaked rice	0.50 lb	5.56%
No. 1 invert sugar	0.75 lb	8.33%
No. 3 invert sugar	0.25 lb	2.78%
Fuggles 90 min	0.75 oz	
Fuggles 60 min	0.75 oz	
Goldings 30 min	0.50 oz	
Goldings dry hops	0.25 oz	
OG	1041	
FG	1014	
ABV	3.57	
Apparent attenuation	65.85%	
IBU	26	
SRM	6	
Mash at	148/157° F	
Sparge at	165° F	
Boil time	90 minutes	
pitching temp	60° F	
Yeast	WLP028 Edinburgh Ale	

1951 Maclay Strong Ale		
pale malt	15.00 lb	85.71%
flaked rice	0.75 lb	4.29%
No. 1 invert sugar	1.25 lb	7.14%
No. 3 invert sugar	0.50 lb	2.86%
Fuggles 90 min	1.25 oz	
Fuggles 60 min	1.25 oz	
Goldings 30 min	1.25 oz	
Goldings dry hops	0.75 oz	
OG	1076	
FG	1028	
ABV	6.35	
Apparent attenuation	63.16%	
IBU	37	
SRM	9	
Mash at	148/157° F	
Sparge at	165° F	
Boil time	90 minutes	
pitching temp	60° F	
Yeast	WLP028 Edinburgh Ale	

1965 Maclay PA 6d		
pale malt	4.75 lb	30.80%
flaked maize	9.75 lb	63.23%
malt extract	0.17 lb	1.10%
No. 1 invert	0.50 lb	3.24%
No. 3 invert	0.25 lb	1.62%
Northern Brewer 90 min	0.50 oz	
Fuggles 60 min	0.50 oz	
Goldings 30 min	0.50 oz	
Goldings dry hops	0.25 oz	
OG	1030	
FG	1009	
ABV	2.78	
Apparent attenuation	70.00%	
IBU	27	
SRM	5	
Mash at	148/158° F	
Sparge at	165° F	
Boil time	90 minutes	
pitching temp	62° F	
Yeast	WLP028 Edinburgh Ale	

1965 Maclay Export		
pale malt	6.25 lb	73.62%
flaked maize	1.00 lb	11.78%
malt extract	0.25 lb	2.94%
No. 1 invert	0.66 lb	7.77%
No. 3 invert	0.33 lb	3.89%
Northern Brewer 90 min	0.75 oz	
Fuggles 60 min	0.75 oz	
Goldings 30 min	0.75 oz	
Goldings dry hops	0.25 oz	
OG	1040	
FG	1011	
ABV	3.84	
Apparent attenuation	72.50%	
IBU	38	
SRM	6	
Mash at	148/158° F	
Sparge at	165° F	
Boil time	90 minutes	
pitching temp	63.5° F	
Yeast	WLP028 Edinburgh Ale	

Robert Younger

1939 - 1970

1957 Robert Younger 70/-		
pale malt	5.75 lb	75.86%
flaked maize	1.00 lb	13.19%
No. 2 invert sugar	0.75 lb	9.89%
malt extract	0.08 lb	1.06%
Fuggles 120 min	0.75 oz	
Goldings 30 min	0.50 oz	
Goldings dry hops	0.25 oz	
OG	1035	
FG	1011	
ABV	3.18	
Apparent attenuation	68.57%	
IBU	17	
SRM	5	
Mash at	151º F	
Sparge at	170º F	
Boil time	120 minutes	
pitching temp	60º F	
Yeast	WLP028 Edinburgh Ale	

1957 Robert Younger 80/-		
pale malt	7.25 lb	77.62%
flaked maize	1.25 lb	13.38%
No. 2 invert sugar	0.75 lb	8.03%
malt extract	0.09 lb	0.96%
Fuggles 120 min	1.00 oz	
Goldings 30 min	0.75 oz	
Goldings dry hops	0.50 oz	
OG	1043	
FG	1012	
ABV	4.10	
Apparent attenuation	72.09%	
IBU	23	
SRM	6	
Mash at	151º F	
Sparge at	170º F	
Boil time	120 minutes	
pitching temp	60º F	
Yeast	WLP028 Edinburgh Ale	

1957 Robert Younger 54/-		
pale malt	4.50 lb	74.26%
flaked maize	1.00 lb	16.50%
No. 2 invert sugar	0.50 lb	8.25%
malt extract	0.06 lb	0.99%
Fuggles 120 min	0.50 oz	
Goldings 30 min	0.50 oz	
Goldings dry hops	0.25 oz	
OG	1028	
FG	1010	
ABV	2.38	
Apparent attenuation	64.29%	
IBU	14	
SRM	4	
Mash at	151° F	
Sparge at	170° F	
Boil time	120 minutes	
pitching temp	60° F	
Yeast	WLP028 Edinburgh Ale	

T & J Bernard

1939 – 1970

1958 Bernard Pale 1/2		
pale malt	6.25 lb	80.13%
black malt	0.05 lb	0.64%
flaked maize	0.75 lb	9.62%
No. 2 invert sugar	0.75 lb	9.62%
Fuggles 105 min	0.75 oz	
Goldings 30 min	0.50 oz	
Goldings dry hops	0.50 oz	
OG	1036	
FG	1012	
ABV	3.18	
Apparent attenuation	66.67%	
IBU	14	
SRM	7	
Mash at	148° F	
Sparge at	167° F	
Boil time	105 minutes	
pitching temp	61° F	
Yeast	WLP028 Edinburgh Ale	

1958 Bernard Pale 1/4		
pale malt	8.25 lb	82.01%
black malt	0.06 lb	0.60%
flaked maize	1.00 lb	9.94%
No. 2 invert sugar	0.75 lb	7.46%
Fuggles 105 min	0.75 oz	
Goldings 30 min	0.75 oz	
Goldings dry hops	0.50 oz	
OG	1046	
FG	1013	
ABV	4.37	
Apparent attenuation	71.74%	
IBU	13	
SRM	8	
Mash at	148° F	
Sparge at	167° F	
Boil time	105 minutes	
pitching temp	60.5° F	
Yeast	WLP028 Edinburgh Ale	

1958 Bernard Strong Ale		
pale malt	11.25 lb	76.27%
black malt	1.25 lb	8.47%
flaked maize	1.00 lb	6.78%
No. 2 invert sugar	1.25 lb	8.47%
Fuggles 105 min	1.00 oz	
Goldings 30 min	1.00 oz	
Goldings dry hops	0.75 oz	
OG	1066	
FG	1021	
ABV	5.95	
Apparent attenuation	68.18%	
IBU	21	
SRM	35	
Mash at	148° F	
Sparge at	167° F	
Boil time	105 minutes	
pitching temp	60.5° F	
Yeast	WLP028 Edinburgh Ale	

Not sure about the black malt percentage in this one. It looks way too high.

Appendix II – weights and measures

Not everyone went to school in pre-metric days as I did. So an overview of Imperial measure is in order.

Weight

16 oz (ounces) = 1 lb (pound)
112 lbs = 1 cwt (hundredweight)

1 lb = 0.4535 kilograms

Volume

8 gallons = 1 bushel
8 bushels = 1 quarter
1 quarter pale malt = approx. 324 lbs
1 quarter black malt = approx. 224 lbs
1 quarter brown malt = approx. 224 lbs

1 bushel = 36.369 litres

Liquid

20 fl. oz (fluid ounce) = 1 pint
8 pints = 1 gallon
36 gallons = 1 barrel
54 gallons = 1 hogshead

1 pint = .568 litre
1 barrel = 163.584 litres

Money

12d (pence) = 1s (shilling)
20s = 1 pound

Temperature

Fahrenheit to Celsius			
°F	°C	°F	°C
50	10	150	65.6
51	10.6	151	66.1
52	11.1	152	66.7
53	11.7	153	67.2
54	12.2	154	67.8
55	12.8	155	68.3
56	13.3	156	68.9
57	13.9	157	69.4
58	14.4	158	70.0
59	15.0	159	70.6
60	15.6	160	71.1
61	16.1	161	71.7
62	16.7	162	72.2
63	17.2	163	72.8
64	17.8	164	73.3
65	18.3	165	73.9
66	18.9	166	74.4
67	19.4	167	75.0
68	20.0	168	75.6
69	20.6	169	76.1
70	21.1	170	76.7
71	21.7	171	77.2
72	22.2	172	77.8
73	22.8	173	78.3
74	23.3	174	78.9
75	23.9	175	79.4
76	24.4	176	80.0

Index

100/-, 4, 5, 6, 23, 24, 26, 38, 39, 41, 50, 51, 66, 78, 80, 81, 84, 95, 96, 100, 101, 102, 103, 107, 112, 116, 152, 153, 154, 178, 179, 207, 208, 317, 321, 330, 342, 348, 359, 390, 401, 407, 414
120/-, 4, 23, 24, 26, 38, 39, 41, 50, 51, 66, 81, 84, 100, 101, 107, 183, 314, 321, 330, 342, 348, 368
140/-, 4, 5, 23, 24, 26, 38, 39, 41, 52, 66, 81, 84, 100, 101, 107, 115, 235, 315, 322, 330, 343
160/-, 4, 5, 23, 24, 26, 38, 39, 50, 55, 66, 81, 84, 100, 101, 107, 114, 117, 183, 235, 322, 343, 349
18th century, 30, 57, 59, 184
19th century, 12, 20, 21, 22, 30, 31, 35, 36, 45, 47, 48, 49, 51, 59, 63, 64, 66, 77, 86, 89, 93, 97, 104, 111, 112, 114, 115, 118, 123, 126, 131, 133, 147, 183, 216, 233, 235, 258, 264, 269, 294, 309, 310
20th century, 39, 59, 93, 101, 108, 127, 229, 233, 234, 265, 268, 290, 295, 297, 308
40/-, 52, 102, 103, 107, 115, 168, 169, 171, 315, 322, 330, 343, 386, 399
4d Ale, 181, 281, 283
50/-, 4, 24, 26, 39, 51, 54, 81, 85, 95, 96, 100, 101, 135, 178, 207, 320, 329, 339, 340, 389, 391, 396, 399, 400
54/-, 7, 38, 95, 96, 106, 107, 114, 127, 129, 143, 162, 164, 163, 175, 177, 188, 189, 191, 213, 214, 215, 237, 255, 257, 296, 384, 395, 408, 417, 421, 422, 432, 433, 441
60/-, 4, 5, 6, 7, 8, 16, 23, 24, 26, 31, 32, 38, 39, 43, 46, 49, 50, 51, 55, 81, 82, 84, 89, 90, 91, 95, 96, 97, 99, 100, 101, 102, 103, 113, 114, 117, 129, 131, 132, 133, 135, 137, 138, 152, 155, 156, 160, 162, 164, 166, 167, 168, 169, 171, 173, 174, 175, 176, 178, 179, 183, 188, 191, 193, 207, 210, 211, 220, 226, 230, 231, 232, 237, 247, 249, 250, 251, 252, 253, 255, 256, 257, 258, 259, 260, 263, 264, 288, 292, 296, 297, 301, 302, 303, 316, 321, 322, 329, 341, 343, 347, 348, 349, 357, 358, 385, 391, 392, 393, 395, 396, 398, 401, 403, 404, 406, 409, 413, 416, 420, 423, 424, 425, 426, 427, 431
70/-, 38, 173, 174, 226, 229, 247, 250, 252, 255, 256, 257, 258, 264, 296, 301, 306, 410, 419, 440

80/-, 4, 5, 6, 7, 16, 21, 23, 24, 26, 38, 39, 43, 49, 50, 53, 78, 80, 81, 84, 95, 96, 100, 101, 102, 103, 114, 118, 152, 154, 162, 164, 173, 174, 175, 177, 178, 179, 183, 193, 196, 207, 212, 219, 226, 227, 228, 237, 247, 250, 251, 255, 256, 257, 264, 296, 298, 307, 314, 316, 329, 342, 358, 385, 390, 397, 404, 407, 410, 419, 421, 423, 440
84/-, 31
90/-, 31, 32, 183
Abbey Brewery, 63, 86, 140, 243
Aberdeen, 72, 74, 253
Aitchison, 186, 242, 263, 269, 278
Aitken, 20, 186, 242, 269, 270
AK, 85, 132, 169, 170, 171, 172, 175, 176, 220
Ale, 4, 6, 7, 8, 14, 21, 22, 23, 24, 25, 26, 28, 29, 30, 32, 33, 34, 38, 39, 41, 42, 44, 45, 46, 47, 48, 49, 50, 51, 52, 53, 54, 55, 56, 58, 59, 60, 61, 62, 63, 64, 65, 67, 68, 69, 70, 78, 79, 83, 84, 85, 87, 89, 90, 91, 92, 93, 94, 95, 96, 97, 98, 99, 100, 102, 103, 107, 111, 112, 113, 114, 115, 116, 117, 118, 119, 120, 122, 124, 125, 126, 128, 129, 130, 131, 132, 133, 135, 136, 137, 138, 139, 140, 141, 142, 143, 145, 147, 150, 151, 153, 154, 157, 158, 159, 160, 161, 162, 163, 164, 165, 167, 170, 171, 173, 174, 176, 177, 178, 179, 180, 181, 182, 183, 184, 185, 186, 187, 188, 200, 201, 202, 203, 204, 205, 207, 208, 209, 210, 211, 212, 213, 215, 217, 218, 219, 220, 221, 222, 223, 224, 225, 226, 227, 228, 229, 230, 231, 232, 233, 234, 235, 236, 237, 238, 247, 248, 251, 252, 255, 256, 257, 258, 259, 260, 261, 262, 263, 264, 265, 268, 271, 272, 273, 274, 276, 277, 278, 279, 281, 282, 283, 284, 285, 286, 287, 288, 289, 290, 291, 292, 293, 294, 295, 296, 297, 298, 300, 301, 302, 303, 304, 305, 306, 307, 308, 309, 310, 311, 312, 313, 314, 315, 316, 317, 318, 319, 320, 321, 322, 323, 324, 325, 326, 327, 328, 329, 330, 331, 332, 333, 334, 335, 336, 337, 338, 339, 340, 341, 342, 343, 344, 345, 346, 347, 348, 349, 350, 351, 352, 353, 354, 355, 356, 357, 358, 359, 360, 361, 362, 363, 364, 365, 366, 367, 368, 369, 370, 371, 372, 373, 374, 375, 376, 377, 378, 379, 380, 381, 382, 383, 384, 385, 386, 387, 388, 389, 390, 391, 392, 393, 394, 395, 396, 397, 398, 399, 400, 401, 402, 403, 404, 405, 406, 407, 408, 409, 410, 411, 412, 413, 414,

415, 416, 417, 418, 419, 420, 421, 422, 423, 424, 425, 426, 427, 428, 429, 430, 431, 432, 433, 434, 435, 436, 437, 438, 439, 440, 441, 442, 443
Alloa, 12, 13, 16, 17, 197, 200, 205, 206, 242, 270, 271, 278, 280
Allsopp, 109, 205, 242, 280
amber malt, 36, 57, 58, 59, 75, 96, 105, 107, 111, 119, 120, 121, 122, 125, 126, 133, 143, 192, 193, 196, 217, 218, 269, 276, 351, 355, 369, 432, 433
American hops, 17, 34, 48, 114, 115, 144, 245
Amsterdam, 2
Anton Dreher, 42
Argentine, 15
Arrol, 242
Australia, 147
Ballingall, 198, 242, 243, 271
Barclay Perkins, 12, 21, 22, 46, 48, 57, 77, 79, 80, 87, 90, 91, 92, 93, 94, 96, 98, 99, 100, 106, 107, 118, 127, 132, 137, 153, 154, 155, 156, 161, 162, 165, 182, 184, 185, 186, 202, 204, 205, 220, 227, 262, 264, 267, 268, 269, 273, 276, 297
barley, 16, 43, 47, 48, 66, 68, 75, 115, 117, 150, 166, 196, 218, 223, 225, 226, 227, 239, 244, 257, 258, 266, 267, 268, 269, 274, 275, 276, 285, 286, 287, 288, 289, 290, 291, 295, 297, 299, 300, 301, 302, 308, 309, 310, 380, 381, 382, 424, 425, 436
Barnard, 77, 86, 87, 88
Bass, 12, 61, 62, 74, 108, 227, 228, 241, 242, 280
Bass Charrington, 241, 242, 280
Bavarian, 34, 63, 91
Beasley, 264
beer tax, 172
Belgium, 17, 76, 142, 143, 147, 204, 205, 232, 233, 278, 279
Bernard, 8, 186, 198, 200, 242, 253, 256, 263, 266, 267, 271, 288, 293, 304, 305, 442, 443
Best Mild, 283
bigg, 16, 30, 43
Bitter, 114, 129, 142, 154, 224, 226, 227, 228, 229, 258, 260, 264, 290, 301, 302, 306
BJCP, 134
black malt, 36, 37, 56, 57, 58, 59, 75, 96, 99, 104, 105, 107, 111, 119, 120, 122, 123, 124, 125, 126, 128, 177, 191, 192, 193, 196, 197, 203, 213, 215, 217, 218, 227, 228, 238, 257, 266, 267, 268, 269, 274, 276, 288, 289, 292, 293, 294, 302, 305, 310, 319, 328, 333, 334,

335, 338, 339, 344, 351, 355, 362, 363, 369, 376, 377, 384, 392, 408, 411, 418, 420, 421, 422, 423, 424, 425, 426, 427, 428, 429, 430, 431, 433, 442, 443, 444
Blair, 242, 263, 270, 271, 278
Bohemian, 17, 33, 34, 69, 142
Bohemian hops, 142
boiling, 29
bottled beer, 135, 142, 296
bottom-fermenting, 42, 144
Brazil, 15
British beer, 129, 145, 149, 151, 167, 230, 283, 309
British Lager, 42
Brown Ale, 6, 7, 8, 39, 134, 174, 184, 185, 186, 187, 212, 224, 255, 256, 258, 262, 263, 264, 288, 289, 302, 313
Brown Beer, 123
brown malt, 35, 36, 37, 56, 57, 59, 96, 99, 105, 106, 123, 124, 128, 191, 193, 197, 213, 268, 269, 276, 319, 333, 334, 335, 338, 339, 344, 392, 394, 395, 444
Brown Stout, 104, 200, 218, 267
BSt, 57
Burton, 11, 16, 18, 19, 28, 29, 30, 63, 66, 70, 77, 78, 108, 109, 142, 151, 162, 165, 200, 202, 204, 205, 233, 273, 274, 276, 281
Burton Ale, 77, 142, 165, 202, 204, 281
Calder, 186, 199, 200, 242, 263, 270, 271, 278
Californian, 34, 48, 68, 75, 77, 91, 115, 119
Campbell, Hope & King, 242, 245, 269, 271
Cannon, 186
Canongate, 242, 245
caramel, 49, 52, 105, 119, 126, 129, 140, 150, 166, 182, 185, 186, 192, 196, 201, 213, 216, 217, 218, 221, 227, 233, 234, 235, 236, 252, 257, 259, 260, 265, 266, 267, 269, 274, 276, 288, 289, 290, 291, 292, 294, 298, 303, 306, 307, 308, 311, 312, 358, 359, 362, 363, 369, 376, 377, 414, 415, 424, 430, 433
cask, 301
Charrington, 186, 227, 241, 242, 262, 264, 280
Cluster, 48, 54, 55, 63, 67, 68, 111, 112, 114, 115, 117, 118, 120, 122, 124, 125, 126, 130, 133, 136, 137, 138, 139, 141, 142, 143, 144, 210, 211, 217, 218, 219, 229, 230, 233, 234, 299, 320, 321, 328, 329, 330, 331, 332, 333, 334, 336, 337, 338, 339, 340, 341, 342, 343, 344, 345, 346, 347, 348, 349, 350, 351, 352, 353, 354, 355, 356, 357, 358, 359, 360, 361, 362, 363, 364, 365, 366, 367, 368, 369, 370,

371, 372, 373, 374, 375, 376, 383, 384, 385, 386, 415, 416, 417, 418, 419, 420, 432, 433
Country, 106, 127, 195
Courage, 156, 186, 227, 241, 262, 264
Craigmillar, 242
crystal malt, 75, 96, 99, 100, 103, 106, 116, 128, 150, 185, 191, 192, 196, 204, 207, 208, 212, 215, 219, 258, 265, 266, 269, 275, 276, 277, 282, 284, 285, 286, 287, 289, 291, 295, 308, 312, 376, 377, 378, 379, 382, 394, 395, 396, 397, 399, 400, 401, 404, 406, 407, 408, 411, 418
Czech, 144
Dalkeith, 198, 242, 259
Dark Mild, 49, 131, 210, 211, 212, 230, 234, 259, 281, 301
decoction, 144, 313
Deuchar, 242, 270
Dortmund, 19
Double Brown Stout, 200, 218
Double Stout, 198, 271
draught Stout, 190, 195
Dreher, 42
Dry Stout, 200, 271
Drybrough, 6, 7, 8, 9, 75, 76, 77, 78, 90, 91, 150, 151, 156, 157, 158, 159, 160, 161, 162, 163, 164, 165, 166, 167, 168, 170, 175, 177, 178, 179, 180, 188, 189, 191, 192, 200, 201, 203, 210, 213, 220, 221, 227, 228, 235, 237, 238, 242, 243, 249, 250, 251, 256, 257, 258, 259, 265, 272, 274, 275, 276, 286, 289, 290, 296, 298, 302, 310, 313, 413, 414, 415, 416, 417, 418, 419, 420, 421, 422, 423, 424, 425, 426, 427, 428, 429, 430, 431
Dublin, 19, 74
Duddingston, 77, 242, 245
Dunbar, 242, 270
Dundee, 13, 72, 242, 245, 253
Duty, 17, 148, 149
East Anglia, 16
East Indies, 31
Edinburgh, 8, 12, 13, 16, 17, 18, 19, 20, 23, 25, 28, 29, 30, 32, 38, 42, 44, 45, 46, 47, 48, 49, 50, 51, 52, 53, 54, 55, 56, 58, 59, 60, 61, 62, 63, 64, 65, 67, 68, 69, 70, 71, 74, 77, 87, 105, 107, 108, 109, 111, 112, 113, 114, 115, 116, 117, 118, 120, 121, 122, 124, 125, 126, 128, 130, 131, 132, 133, 135, 136, 138, 139, 141, 142, 143, 151, 156, 174, 175, 188, 207, 208, 209, 210, 211, 212, 213, 215, 217, 218, 219, 220, 221, 223, 224, 225, 226, 228, 229, 230, 231, 232, 233, 234, 236, 238, 242, 243,

245, 249, 250, 251, 253, 255, 263, 270, 271, 278, 282, 284, 285, 286, 287, 288, 289, 291, 292, 293, 294, 295, 296, 297, 298, 300, 301, 302, 303, 305, 306, 307, 308, 309, 310, 311, 312, 314, 315, 316, 317, 318, 319, 320, 321, 322, 323, 324, 325, 326, 327, 328, 329, 330, 331, 332, 333, 334, 335, 336, 337, 338, 339, 340, 341, 342, 343, 344, 345, 346, 347, 348, 349, 350, 351, 352, 353, 354, 355, 356, 357, 358, 359, 360, 361, 362, 363, 364, 365, 366, 367, 368, 369, 370, 371, 372, 373, 374, 375, 376, 377, 378, 379, 380, 381, 382, 383, 384, 385, 386, 387, 388, 389, 390, 391, 392, 393, 394, 395, 396, 397, 398, 399, 400, 401, 402, 403, 404, 405, 406, 407, 408, 409, 410, 411, 412, 413, 414, 415, 416, 417, 418, 419, 420, 421, 422, 423, 424, 425, 426, 427, 428, 429, 430, 431, 432, 433, 434, 435, 436, 437, 438, 439, 440, 441, 442, 443
Edinburgh Ale, 8, 44, 45, 46, 47, 48, 49, 50, 51, 52, 53, 54, 55, 56, 58, 59, 60, 61, 62, 63, 64, 65, 67, 68, 69, 70, 111, 112, 113, 114, 115, 116, 117, 118, 120, 122, 124, 125, 126, 128, 130, 131, 132, 133, 135, 136, 138, 139, 141, 142, 143, 151, 207, 208, 209, 210, 211, 212, 213, 215, 217, 218, 219, 220, 221, 223, 225, 226, 228, 229, 230, 231, 232, 233, 234, 236, 238, 282, 284, 285, 286, 287, 288, 289, 291, 292, 293, 294, 295, 296, 297, 298, 300, 301, 302, 303, 305, 306, 307, 308, 309, 310, 311, 312, 314, 315, 316, 317, 318, 319, 320, 321, 322, 323, 324, 325, 326, 327, 328, 329, 330, 331, 332, 333, 334, 335, 336, 337, 338, 339, 340, 341, 342, 343, 344, 345, 346, 347, 348, 349, 350, 351, 352, 353, 354, 355, 356, 357, 358, 359, 360, 361, 362, 363, 364, 365, 366, 367, 368, 369, 370, 371, 372, 373, 374, 375, 376, 377, 378, 379, 380, 381, 382, 383, 384, 385, 386, 387, 388, 389, 390, 391, 392, 393, 394, 395, 396, 397, 398, 399, 400, 401, 402, 403, 404, 405, 406, 407, 408, 409, 410, 411, 412, 413, 414, 415, 416, 417, 418, 419, 420, 421, 422, 423, 424, 425, 426, 427, 428, 429, 430, 431, 432, 433, 434, 435, 436, 437, 438, 439, 440, 441, 442, 443
England, 1, 2, 11, 12, 13, 14, 16, 17, 18, 21, 22, 25, 26, 27, 29, 34, 35, 41, 43, 47, 57, 59, 61, 65, 71, 74, 75, 76, 89, 93, 102, 103, 104, 107, 111, 112, 114, 119, 121, 133, 139, 140, 147, 148, 151, 156, 160, 174, 177, 181, 184, 187, 195, 197, 200, 212, 213, 224, 229, 242,

244, 245, 251, 258, 260, 261, 264, 273, 276, 279, 283, 286, 301, 303, 310, 312
English Mild, 38, 93, 103, 113, 178, 180, 207, 261
ES, 190, 193, 195, 197, 267, 268
Export, 4, 5, 8, 31, 32, 41, 60, 63, 65, 69, 70, 106, 123, 124, 127, 128, 131, 174, 186, 199, 212, 251, 255, 256, 257, 258, 259, 263, 271, 280, 292, 293, 298, 302, 307, 427, 431, 436, 438, 439
Extra Stout, 195, 199, 267, 270
Falkirk, 20, 107, 186, 242
flaked barley, 218, 223, 225, 226, 244, 257, 266, 274, 275, 276, 285, 287, 291, 295, 297, 299, 300, 301, 302, 308, 309, 310, 380, 381, 382, 424, 425, 436
flaked oats, 126, 128, 218, 244, 294
Fowler, 242, 298
France, 17, 65
Free Mash Tun Act, 75, 91, 112
Fuggles, 48, 111, 113, 114, 115, 116, 117, 118, 120, 128, 132, 133, 135, 136, 137, 138, 139, 141, 142, 207, 208, 209, 211, 212, 213, 214, 215, 217, 218, 219, 220, 221, 223, 225, 226, 227, 228, 229, 230, 231, 233, 234, 236, 238, 245, 282, 284, 285, 286, 287, 288, 289, 291, 292, 293, 294, 295, 296, 297, 298, 299, 300, 301, 302, 303, 305, 306, 307, 308, 309, 310, 311, 312, 313, 332, 335, 336, 337, 338, 339, 340, 341, 342, 343, 344, 345, 347, 348, 349, 350, 351, 352, 353, 354, 355, 356, 357, 358, 359, 360, 361, 362, 363, 364, 365, 366, 367, 368, 369, 370, 371, 372, 373, 374, 375, 376, 377, 378, 379, 380, 381, 382, 388, 389, 390, 391, 392, 393, 394, 395, 396, 397, 398, 399, 400, 401, 402, 403, 404, 405, 406, 407, 408, 411, 413, 414, 415, 416, 420, 421, 422, 423, 424, 425, 426, 427, 428, 429, 430, 431, 432, 433, 434, 435, 436, 437, 438, 439, 440, 441, 442, 443
Fuller, 85, 94, 96, 137, 158, 159, 169, 170, 171, 172, 175, 176, 248, 249, 250, 251, 259
George Younger, 197
Germany, 126
Glasgow, 13, 17, 20, 72, 74, 242, 253
glucose, 115, 125, 139, 150, 171, 176, 209, 276, 348, 349, 350, 351, 352, 353, 355, 358, 359, 360, 361, 362
Golden Pride, 259
Goldings, 43, 44, 46, 48, 49, 50, 51, 52, 53, 54, 55, 56, 58, 59, 60, 61, 62, 63, 64, 65, 67, 68, 70, 113, 117, 118, 126, 131, 132, 133, 136,

139, 141, 142, 143, 144, 209, 210, 211, 213, 217, 218, 220, 221, 223, 225, 226, 228, 229, 230, 232, 233, 234, 236, 238, 245, 282, 284, 286, 287, 288, 289, 291, 292, 293, 294, 295, 296, 297, 298, 300, 301, 302, 303, 305, 306, 307, 308, 309, 310, 311, 312, 313, 314, 315, 316, 317, 318, 319, 320, 321, 322, 324, 325, 326, 327, 328, 329, 330, 331, 332, 333, 334, 335, 337, 338, 339, 340, 341, 343, 344, 345, 346, 347, 348, 349, 350, 351, 352, 353, 354, 355, 356, 357, 359, 360, 361, 363, 364, 365, 366, 367, 368, 369, 370, 371, 372, 373, 374, 375, 376, 377, 378, 379, 380, 381, 382, 383, 386, 387, 388, 389, 390, 391, 392, 393, 394, 406, 408, 409, 410, 412, 413, 414, 415, 416, 417, 418, 419, 420, 421, 422, 423, 424, 425, 426, 427, 428, 429, 430, 431, 432, 433, 434, 435, 436, 437, 438, 439, 440, 441, 442, 443
Gordon & Blair, 242, 278
Gourvish, 12
Government Ale, 181, 209, 231
Greenock, 171, 191, 231
Guinness, 12, 74
Hallertau, 17, 47, 76, 91, 111, 115, 119, 120, 126, 131, 133, 143, 144, 245, 309, 313, 386, 387, 388, 430, 431, 432, 433
Hamburg, 15
Hammerton, 186, 264
Hertfordshire, 19
Hitler, 285
Hoare, 186, 227
Holland, 2
Holyrood, 18, 28, 63, 77, 87, 140, 144, 151, 229, 242, 243, 245
Holyrood Brewery, 63, 144, 229, 243
hops, 16, 17, 24, 27, 29, 30, 32, 33, 34, 35, 36, 38, 39, 40, 41, 42, 43, 45, 47, 48, 49, 50, 51, 52, 53, 54, 55, 56, 59, 60, 61, 62, 63, 65, 66, 67, 68, 69, 70, 76, 85, 86, 87, 89, 90, 91, 92, 93, 94, 95, 97, 98, 100, 102, 104, 106, 108, 109, 112, 114, 115, 116, 117, 118, 119, 121, 125, 126, 127, 129, 131, 132, 133, 135, 136, 137, 139, 140, 141, 142, 143, 144, 150, 151, 165, 166, 167, 169, 172, 173, 174, 175, 178, 179, 180, 181, 182, 183, 184, 185, 188, 189, 190, 191, 193, 194, 195, 201, 202, 207, 208, 209, 210, 211, 212, 214, 216, 217, 218, 219, 220, 222, 223, 224, 225, 226, 227, 228, 229, 230, 231, 233, 234, 235, 237, 238, 239, 243, 245, 255, 256, 259, 265, 266, 267, 272, 273, 274, 282, 283, 284, 286, 287, 288, 289, 291, 292, 293, 295, 296, 297, 298, 299, 300, 301,

302, 303, 304, 305, 306, 307, 308, 309, 310, 311, 312, 313, 315, 320, 321, 322, 323, 324, 325, 326, 327, 328, 329, 330, 331, 332, 333, 335, 337, 338, 339, 340, 341, 343, 344, 345, 346, 347, 349, 350, 351, 352, 353, 354, 355, 356, 357, 359, 360, 361, 363, 364, 365, 366, 367, 368, 369, 370, 371, 372, 373, 374, 375, 376, 377, 378, 379, 380, 381, 382, 383, 386, 387, 388, 389, 392, 393, 394, 408, 409, 410, 420, 421, 422, 423, 424, 425, 426, 427, 428, 429, 430, 431, 432, 434, 435, 436, 437, 438, 439, 440, 441, 442, 443
House of Commons, 12
Imperial Stout, 106, 127, 185, 198, 199, 200, 267, 270, 271
India, 14, 15, 29, 31, 32, 36, 37
Inverness, 74, 253
invert sugar, 17, 111, 113, 116, 117, 118, 119, 120, 126, 132, 133, 135, 138, 143, 144, 150, 176, 191, 192, 203, 207, 208, 209, 210, 212, 213, 214, 215, 219, 223, 224, 225, 226, 228, 230, 231, 232, 236, 238, 244, 282, 283, 284, 285, 286, 288, 289, 292, 293, 302, 303, 305, 307, 310, 311, 349, 350, 362, 363, 379, 389, 390, 391, 392, 393, 394, 395, 396, 397, 398, 399, 400, 401, 402, 403, 404, 405, 406, 407, 408, 409, 410, 411, 412, 420, 421, 422, 423, 424, 425, 426, 427, 428, 429, 430, 431, 432, 433, 434, 435, 436, 437, 438, 440, 441, 442, 443
IPA, 3, 5, 11, 16, 28, 29, 30, 31, 32, 60, 61, 62, 83, 85, 90, 92, 130, 132, 134, 135, 154, 172, 173, 174, 175, 222, 224, 234, 255, 256, 258, 301, 383, 412
Ireland, 12, 71, 74, 77, 86, 87, 88, 148, 149, 187
Irish Stout, 57
Jeffrey, 199, 205, 206, 242, 253, 269, 271
K Ales, 202
Keeping, 36, 106, 127
Keeping Porter, 36
keg, 229
KK, 24, 42, 97, 98, 99, 156, 165, 202, 204, 273, 276
KKK, 24, 42, 97, 98, 99, 156, 202, 204
KKKK, 202, 204, 273, 276
Lager, 3, 5, 6, 8, 9, 25, 26, 42, 89, 108, 109, 144, 205, 206, 279, 280, 313, 336
lager malt, 276, 277, 313
Leeds, 234
Leith, 77
Light Ale, 174, 181, 222, 261, 281

Light Bitter, 129
Light Mild, 224
Lloyd Hind, 19
London, 11, 12, 13, 19, 21, 22, 23, 24, 28, 29, 30, 32, 34, 35, 36, 37, 39, 40, 42, 43, 45, 46, 48, 49, 50, 54, 57, 59, 71, 73, 74, 77, 79, 82, 83, 87, 90, 91, 92, 93, 94, 95, 96, 97, 98, 99, 100, 102, 103, 104, 105, 106, 107, 108, 113, 119, 123, 126, 127, 128, 129, 132, 137, 152, 153, 154, 155, 156, 158, 159, 161, 162, 165, 167, 169, 174, 178, 179, 180, 181, 182, 183, 184, 185, 186, 187, 188, 190, 193, 195, 196, 197, 198, 199, 200, 202, 204, 205, 206, 207, 210, 213, 216, 222, 224, 227, 234, 239, 248, 249, 250, 255, 256, 258, 259, 261, 262, 263, 264, 267, 268, 269, 270, 271, 273, 274, 276, 277, 278, 279, 280, 281, 283, 294, 310, 327, 328
London Metropolitan Archive, 21, 22, 24, 34, 36, 37, 40, 42, 48, 59, 79, 82, 83, 87, 90, 91, 92, 94, 96, 98, 99, 100, 106, 108, 123, 127, 137, 153, 154, 156, 159, 161, 162, 165, 174, 179, 180, 181, 182, 185, 186, 187, 190, 193, 195, 197, 198, 199, 200, 202, 204, 205, 206, 222, 224, 227, 248, 249, 255, 256, 258, 261, 262, 263, 264, 267, 268, 269, 270, 271, 273, 274, 276, 277, 278, 279, 280
London Porter, 22, 28, 57, 59, 104, 106, 123, 127
London Stout, 37, 57, 104, 105, 127, 179, 188, 195, 196, 213, 267
Lorimer, 7, 156, 174, 177, 200, 201, 203, 222, 223, 224, 225, 226, 235, 236, 242
Lorimer & Clark, 7, 156, 174, 177, 200, 201, 203, 222, 223, 224, 225, 226, 235, 236, 242
MA, 6, 90, 95, 96, 103, 174, 178, 179, 180, 181, 183, 204, 207, 231, 262, 276, 400, 401, 405, 411
MA malt, 103, 204, 276
Mackay, 183, 242
Mackeson, 195, 197, 267, 268, 290
Maclay, 5, 6, 7, 8, 9, 78, 107, 111, 119, 120, 126, 127, 133, 143, 150, 200, 201, 203, 230, 235, 242, 244, 247, 249, 258, 259, 260, 266, 267, 268, 272, 274, 275, 294, 296, 306, 312, 432, 433, 434, 435, 436, 437, 438, 439
Maize, 299
malt, 74, 444
Malt, 3, 4, 6, 7, 8, 16, 17, 75, 105, 106, 107, 126, 128, 150, 151, 197, 244, 268, 276, 277, 294, 306, 362, 363, 394, 395
malt liquor, 30

maltings, 75, 86
Mann, 184, 227, 242, 264, 286, 289, 313
Mann Crossman, 264
Martyn Cornell, 109
Mauritius, 15
McEwan, 12, 71, 72, 186, 198, 199, 200, 205, 206, 241, 242, 252, 263, 269, 270, 271, 278, 279, 280
Meiklejohn, 16, 17
Mild, 3, 4, 5, 6, 8, 12, 16, 21, 24, 29, 38, 39, 40, 41, 46, 47, 48, 49, 50, 52, 53, 55, 66, 76, 77, 78, 85, 89, 90, 93, 94, 95, 96, 98, 99, 100, 102, 103, 111, 112, 113, 114, 118, 119, 120, 129, 131, 137, 139, 145, 150, 151, 152, 153, 165, 166, 170, 172, 177,178, 179, 180, 181, 182, 183, 184, 185, 186, 202, 207, 208, 210, 211, 212, 213, 224, 230, 231, 234, 237, 247, 248, 255, 256, 258, 259, 260, 261, 262, 264, 279, 281, 283, 285, 286, 288, 297, 301, 302, 303, 313, 318, 319, 324, 325, 433
Mild Ale, 3, 4, 5, 6, 8, 12, 16, 21, 29, 38, 39, 40, 41, 46, 47, 48, 49, 50, 52, 53, 55, 76, 77, 78, 85, 93, 94, 95, 96, 98, 99, 100, 102, 103, 112, 113, 114, 119, 129, 131, 137, 139, 145, 150, 151, 152, 153, 165, 170, 177, 178, 179, 180, 181, 182, 183, 185, 186, 202, 207, 208, 210, 212, 213, 256, 258, 260, 261, 262, 264, 279, 281, 283, 286, 288, 297, 302, 303, 313, 318, 319, 324, 325
mild malt, 43, 44, 197, 204, 258, 265, 266, 268, 269, 275, 281, 282, 284, 285, 287, 291, 295, 308, 378, 379, 382
Montrose, 242
Munich, 19, 25, 42, 121
Murray, 183, 198, 199, 242, 261, 263, 270, 271
New Zealand, 15
No.2 invert, 117, 295
No.3 invert, 117
oat malt, 107
Oatmeal Stout, 107, 126, 150, 191, 195, 199, 244, 268
oats, 107, 119, 126, 128, 193, 197, 218, 244, 266, 267, 268, 294, 297, 433, 436
Old Ale, 307
PA, 5, 7, 24, 28, 34, 61, 78, 80, 82, 83, 89, 90, 91, 92, 129, 131, 132, 152, 154, 155, 156, 159, 163, 164, 165, 166, 168, 169, 170, 171, 172, 173, 174, 175, 176, 177, 180, 193, 224, 227, 230, 231, 232, 247, 248, 251, 255, 256, 258, 259, 268, 269, 276, 296, 306, 383, 387, 389, 392, 393, 394, 402, 403, 405, 406, 409, 410, 417, 434, 436, 437, 439
PA malt, 92, 258, 269, 276
Pale Ale, 3, 4, 5, 6, 8, 14, 24, 27, 28, 29, 30, 32, 33, 34, 38, 49, 51, 57, 60, 61, 62, 63, 64, 76, 77, 78, 79, 82, 83, 85, 87, 89, 90, 91, 92, 100, 112, 114, 119, 123, 127, 129, 131, 132, 133, 136, 137, 140, 143, 144, 145, 151, 152, 154, 157, 158, 159, 160, 162,163, 165, 167, 169, 170, 171, 172, 173, 174, 175, 176, 177, 180, 182, 183, 185, 188, 201, 210, 211, 212, 219, 220, 222, 224, 226, 227, 228, 229, 230, 231, 232, 235, 237, 247, 248, 251, 252, 255, 256, 257, 258, 259, 260, 261, 263, 264, 265, 268, 272, 274, 279, 281, 283, 288, 290, 292, 295, 296, 297, 298, 301, 302, 303, 304, 306, 307, 310, 311, 312, 313
pale malt, 16, 30, 36, 37, 45, 46, 47, 48, 49, 50, 51, 52, 53, 54, 55, 56, 58, 59, 60, 61, 62, 63, 64, 65, 66, 67, 68, 69, 70, 75, 91, 92, 95, 96, 98, 99, 101, 103, 105, 106, 107, 111, 112, 113, 114, 115, 116, 117, 118, 120, 122, 123, 124, 125, 126, 128, 130, 131, 132, 133, 135, 136, 137, 138, 139, 141, 142, 143, 144, 170, 171, 172, 176, 177, 184, 185, 191, 192, 193, 196, 197, 203, 204, 207, 208, 209, 210, 211, 212, 213, 215, 217, 218, 219, 220, 221, 223, 224, 225, 226, 228, 229, 230, 231, 232, 233, 234, 236, 238, 257, 258, 259, 265, 266, 267, 268, 274, 275, 276, 277, 281, 282, 283, 284, 285, 286, 287, 288, 289, 291, 292, 293, 294, 295, 296, 297, 298, 299, 300, 301, 302, 303, 305, 306, 307, 308, 309, 310, 311, 312, 314, 315, 316, 317, 318, 319, 320, 321, 322, 323, 324, 325, 326, 327, 328, 329, 330, 331, 332, 333, 334, 335, 336, 337, 338, 339, 340, 341, 342, 343, 344, 345, 346, 347, 348, 349, 350, 351, 352, 353, 354, 355, 356, 357, 358, 359, 360, 361, 362, 363, 364, 365, 366, 367, 368, 369, 370, 371, 372, 373, 374, 375, 376, 377, 378, 379, 380, 381, 382, 383, 384, 385, 386, 387, 388, 389, 390, 391, 392, 393, 394, 395, 396, 397, 398, 399, 400, 401, 402, 403, 404, 405, 406, 407, 408, 409, 410, 411, 412, 413, 414, 415, 416, 417, 418, 419, 420, 421, 422, 423, 424, 425, 426, 427, 428, 429, 430, 431, 432, 433, 434, 435, 436, 437, 438, 439, 440, 441, 442, 443, 444
parti-gyle, 51, 64, 112, 128, 135, 143, 145, 150, 175, 185, 192, 196, 201, 210, 211, 212, 213, 226, 230, 231, 232, 235, 237, 252, 255, 259, 260, 272, 274, 281, 290, 292, 304, 306, 311, 312

parti-gyled, 128, 135, 143, 150, 185, 192, 201, 210, 211, 212, 213, 226, 230, 231, 232, 235, 237, 252, 255, 259, 260, 272, 274, 290, 292, 304, 306
parti-gyling, 64, 112, 192, 313
Pasteur, 77
Pils, 6, 144, 336
Pilsener, 206
pitching temperature, 29
Porter, 3, 4, 5, 16, 22, 28, 29, 35, 36, 37, 43, 57, 59, 77, 85, 104, 106, 123, 127, 137, 174, 187, 190, 191, 193, 195, 196, 197, 294, 319, 328
Prestonpans, 242
Queensland, 15
Reid, 32, 200
Reinheitsgebot, 16
rice, 76, 92, 96, 99, 100, 204, 220, 276, 304, 305, 437, 438
roast barley, 66, 196, 227, 266, 267, 268, 269, 288, 290, 291
roast malt, 193, 196, 197
Robert Younger, 8, 9, 247, 250, 251, 255, 256, 257, 258, 259, 266, 267, 290, 292, 303, 307, 311, 440, 441
Roberts, 18, 24, 25, 26, 28, 29, 31, 32, 38
Royal Mile, 18, 77, 245
Runner, 106, 127
Running, 57
S, 4, 20, 21, 22, 24, 25, 36, 37, 39, 41, 42, 59, 81, 100, 101, 106, 127, 151, 130, 193, 195, 197, 267, 268, 293, 315, 317, 319, 325, 329, 340
SA malt, 99, 100, 204, 269, 276
Saaz, 17, 33, 45, 47, 58, 65, 69, 70, 76, 115, 165, 216, 217, 218, 245, 299, 309, 320, 321, 322, 323, 324, 325, 326, 336, 343, 346, 347, 365, 366, 367, 368, 369, 370, 420, 421
Scotch Ale, 5, 6, 8, 23, 32, 38, 43, 52, 107, 140, 142, 143, 147, 151, 200, 201, 202, 203, 204, 205, 232, 233, 235, 271, 272, 277, 278, 279, 287
Scotland, 1, 3, 11, 12, 13, 14, 15, 16, 17, 21, 22, 25, 28, 29, 30, 31, 35, 36, 38, 42, 43, 45, 46, 49, 51, 52, 55, 57, 59, 66, 71, 72, 73, 75, 76, 77, 89, 104, 106, 107, 108, 109, 111, 113, 114, 119, 123, 129, 133, 137, 139, 140, 144, 146, 147, 148, 150, 151, 154, 156, 158, 167, 175, 177, 182, 185, 187, 194, 195, 197, 200, 204, 205, 208, 209, 210, 211, 212, 219, 227, 229, 231, 233, 239, 240, 241, 242, 243, 244, 245, 251, 255, 256, 260, 262, 268, 269, 276, 277, 279, 283, 286, 288, 293, 301, 304, 307, 312
Scottish, 28, 29
Scottish Ale, 24, 25, 26, 28, 29, 32, 38, 57, 62, 113, 227
Scottish Mild, 103, 137, 182, 183, 261, 281
Shilling Ales, 3, 5, 8, 12, 17, 23, 29, 38, 39, 41, 50, 51, 52, 53, 54, 55, 63, 66, 70, 75, 78, 80, 81, 84, 93, 100, 101, 102, 103, 107, 108, 110, 112, 115, 131, 137, 145, 183, 208, 264
Shore Brewery, 17
Singapore, 15
South Wales, 15
Southwark, 93
SS, 8, 36, 37, 57, 106, 127, 190, 191, 192, 247, 266, 267, 292
SSS, 36, 37, 106, 127, 190, 191, 192, 193, 195, 197
Steel Coulson, 263, 270, 271, 278, 280
Stirling, 20
Stock Ale, 3, 4, 5, 24, 29, 30, 41, 42, 50, 64, 65, 70, 76, 85, 97, 98, 99, 100, 139, 202, 268, 315, 317, 325, 326
Stout, 3, 4, 5, 6, 7, 8, 16, 21, 22, 29, 35, 36, 37, 38, 51, 56, 57, 59, 75, 77, 100, 104, 105, 106, 107, 112, 121, 122, 123, 124, 125, 126, 127, 128, 131, 145, 150, 151, 157, 159, 165, 174, 179, 185, 187, 188, 189, 190, 191, 192, 193, 194, 195, 196, 197, 198, 199, 200, 204, 212, 213, 214, 215, 216, 219, 227, 231, 233, 244, 247, 248, 251, 252, 258, 265, 266, 267, 268, 269, 270, 271, 275, 281, 287, 290, 292, 293, 294, 302, 306, 307, 311, 392, 394, 395, 411, 415, 418
strong Ale, 29
Strong Ale, 6, 9, 14, 57, 63, 66, 70, 78, 79, 80, 85, 107, 108, 112, 142, 143, 145, 147, 153, 165, 200, 201, 202, 203, 204, 224, 230, 231, 232, 235, 237, 240, 247, 248, 251, 252, 255, 271, 272, 273, 274, 275, 276, 277, 278, 283, 287, 298, 302, 306, 307, 311, 312, 435, 438, 443
sugar, 16, 17, 36, 37, 49, 74, 76, 91, 92, 95, 96, 98, 99, 100, 101, 103, 105, 106, 107, 111, 112, 113, 114, 116, 117, 118, 119, 120, 126, 128, 132, 133, 135, 136, 137, 138, 139, 140, 143, 144, 150, 170, 171, 172, 176, 177, 185, 191, 192, 193, 196, 197, 203, 204, 207, 208, 209, 210, 212, 213, 214, 215, 219, 220, 221, 223, 224, 225, 226, 227, 228, 230, 231, 232, 235, 236, 238, 243, 244, 257, 258, 259, 265, 266, 268, 269, 274, 276, 277, 282, 283, 284,

285, 286, 288, 289, 292, 293, 294, 295, 296, 302, 303, 305, 306, 307, 310, 311, 312, 314, 340, 343, 346, 347, 349, 350, 362, 363, 379, 384, 385, 386, 388, 389, 390, 391, 392, 393, 394, 395, 396, 397, 398, 399, 400, 401, 402, 403, 404, 405, 406, 407, 408, 409, 410, 411, 412, 413, 414, 415, 416, 417, 418, 419, 420, 421, 422, 423, 424, 425, 426, 427, 428, 429, 430, 431, 432, 433, 434, 435, 436, 437, 438, 440, 441, 442, 443

T & J Bernard, 9, 253, 263, 288, 442

Table Beer, 3, 4, 5, 21, 29, 30, 36, 43, 45, 50, 51, 54, 111, 310, 318, 328

Tennent, 42, 109, 198, 199, 200, 205, 206, 242, 269, 270, 271, 280

Tetley, 156, 227, 274, 277

Thomas Usher, 5, 6, 7, 9, 75, 76, 78, 79, 82, 89, 91, 95, 96, 97, 99, 102, 103, 105, 106, 112, 113, 116, 121, 122, 123, 124, 127, 128, 129, 130, 131, 132, 134, 135, 137, 138, 152, 154, 155, 157, 158, 168, 169, 170, 171, 173, 174, 177, 178, 179, 180, 183, 184, 185, 186, 187, 188, 191, 193, 196, 198, 199, 200, 201, 203, 205, 206, 207, 208, 209, 212, 214, 215, 219, 222, 227, 231, 232, 263, 270, 271, 280, 383, 384, 385, 386, 387, 388, 389, 390, 391, 392, 393, 394, 395, 396, 397, 398, 399, 400, 401, 402, 403, 404, 405, 406, 407, 408, 409, 410, 411, 412

top-fermenting, 42, 144

torrefied barley, 286, 289

Truman, 34, 52, 57, 94, 96, 106, 108, 127, 137, 162, 186, 209, 222, 227, 261, 264, 279

underlet, 79, 111, 133, 153, 154, 155, 156, 230, 303, 432, 434

underletting, 155

United Kingdom, 74, 148, 187

United States, 15

USA, 16, 17, 34, 47, 68, 76, 109, 115, 126, 244, 299

Usher, 75, 76, 78, 79, 80, 82, 83, 89, 90, 91, 92, 93, 94, 95, 96, 97, 98, 99, 102, 103, 105, 106, 112, 113, 116, 121, 122, 123, 124, 127, 128, 129, 130, 131, 132, 134, 135, 137, 138, 152, 153, 154, 155, 156, 157, 158, 168, 169, 170, 171, 172, 173, 174, 175, 176, 177, 178, 179, 180, 183, 184, 185, 186, 187, 188, 189, 191, 193, 196, 198, 199, 200, 201, 203, 205, 206, 207, 208, 209, 212, 214, 215, 219, 222, 227, 231, 232, 242, 263, 270, 271, 278, 280, 383, 384, 385, 386, 387, 388, 389, 390, 391, 392, 393, 394, 395, 396, 397, 398, 399, 400, 401, 402, 403, 404, 405, 406, 407, 408, 409, 410, 411, 412

Victoria, 15

Victorian, 129

Wales, 15, 148

Watney, 186, 227, 241, 242, 264, 286, 289, 313

Wee Heavy, 298

West Indies, 15, 107, 147

wheat, 276, 277, 286, 289

Whitbread, 24, 34, 35, 36, 37, 39, 40, 41, 42, 46, 48, 57, 59, 81, 82, 83, 90, 92, 93, 94, 96, 97, 98, 99, 100, 106, 107, 123, 127, 128, 129, 132, 137, 154, 158, 159, 174, 179, 180, 181, 182, 184, 185, 186, 187, 190, 191, 192, 193, 194, 195, 196, 197, 198, 199, 200, 205, 206, 222, 224, 227, 241, 242, 248, 249, 255, 256, 257, 258, 261, 262, 263, 264, 267, 268, 270, 271, 273, 274, 276, 277, 278, 279, 280, 281, 283, 288, 296, 297

Whitbread Gravity Book, 281

William Younger, 3, 4, 5, 6, 7, 8, 9, 12, 16, 17, 18, 19, 21, 22, 23, 24, 25, 26, 27, 28, 30, 32, 33, 34, 35, 36, 37, 38, 39, 40, 41, 43, 44, 45, 46, 47, 48, 49, 50, 51, 52, 53, 54, 55, 56, 57, 58, 59, 60, 61, 62, 63, 64, 65, 66, 67, 68, 69, 70, 75, 76, 77, 78, 79, 80, 81, 82, 83, 84, 85, 86, 89, 93, 94, 95, 97, 98, 100, 101, 103, 104, 105, 106, 108, 109, 111, 114, 115, 117, 118, 125, 131, 133, 136, 139, 140, 141, 142, 144, 145, 150, 151, 152, 153, 154, 155, 156, 160, 161, 162, 163, 164, 165, 172, 173, 177, 180, 181, 182, 183, 191, 192, 194, 195, 196, 200, 201, 202, 203, 204, 211, 216, 217, 218, 224, 229, 233, 234, 235, 241, 243, 245, 246, 247, 248, 249, 250, 251, 252, 255, 260, 261, 264, 265, 266, 267, 272, 273, 274, 275, 281, 282, 283, 284, 285, 287, 290, 291, 295, 296, 297, 298, 299, 300, 301, 308, 309, 314, 315, 316, 317, 318, 319, 320, 321, 322, 323, 324, 325, 326, 327, 328, 329, 330, 331, 332, 333, 334, 335, 336, 337, 338, 339, 340, 341, 342, 343, 344, 345, 346, 347, 348, 349, 350, 351, 352, 353, 354, 355, 356, 357, 358, 359, 360, 361, 362, 363, 364, 365, 366, 367, 368, 369, 370, 371, 372, 373, 374, 375, 376, 377, 378, 379, 380, 381, 382

WW I, 6, 29, 38, 48, 49, 68, 71, 73, 75, 76, 91, 94, 95, 96, 97, 100, 101, 102, 105, 108, 111, 112, 114, 117, 119, 126, 127, 128, 129, 133, 135, 136, 143, 145, 147, 148, 150, 151, 152, 157, 160, 162, 167, 168, 173, 177, 178, 180,

183, 187, 188, 193, 197, 205, 206, 207, 209, 210, 211, 213, 214, 216, 218, 221, 228, 229, 230, 231, 234, 240, 241, 244, 245, 246, 248, 251, 255, 257, 258, 260, 262, 264, 265, 267, 268, 278, 281, 285, 290, 292, 296, 299, 301, 302, 308, 309, 310, 311, 312

WW II, 29, 38, 49, 63, 108, 117, 133, 136, 157, 206, 207, 214, 213, 229, 230, 240, 241, 244, 245, 246, 248, 255, 262, 264, 265, 267, 268, 278, 285, 292, 295, 299, 302, 308, 309, 310, 311, 312

X, 4, 7, 21, 24, 39, 40, 46, 47, 48, 79, 80, 84, 85, 93, 94, 95, 96, 97, 99, 100, 102, 103, 107, 114, 119, 137, 139, 153, 154, 156, 161, 162, 164, 168, 174, 178, 179, 181, 182, 202, 207, 224, 231, 248, 250, 261, 262, 281, 283, 297, 324, 332, 336, 379, 384, 398, 402

X Ale, 21, 46, 48, 79, 84, 94, 96, 100, 107, 119, 137, 139, 153, 161, 162, 174, 178, 179, 182, 207, 281

XK, 170, 171, 172, 175, 176

XLK, 91, 92, 154, 156, 161, 162, 165

XP, 4, 32, 33, 34, 61, 63, 84, 85, 89, 163, 164, 172, 188, 191, 229, 260, 296, 323, 331, 345, 346, 353, 373, 375, 380

XX, 4, 5, 6, 7, 8, 24, 33, 40, 48, 84, 85, 93, 94, 95, 96, 97, 99, 102, 103, 107, 114, 118, 137, 138, 144, 156, 164, 181, 182, 183, 189, 192, 207, 211, 213, 224, 262, 281, 232, 283, 297, 318, 324, 337, 359, 367, 376, 336, 393, 415, 418

XXK, 93, 95

XXP, 7, 32, 33, 61, 63, 155, 156, 165, 172, 173, 174, 222, 223, 224, 225, 226, 229, 246, 249, 251, 252, 256, 257, 260, 261, 296, 301, 302, 316, 323, 372, 374, 379, 380, 381, 425, 426, 428, 430

XXX, 4, 7, 8, 39, 40, 47, 84, 85, 93, 95, 97, 99, 165, 174, 181, 188, 189, 191, 192, 199, 200, 213, 224, 247, 271, 274, 277, 281, 283, 284, 285, 290, 319, 332, 337, 349, 360, 368, 375, 388, 418

XXXX, 6, 41, 52, 85, 97, 98, 102, 103, 139, 273, 276, 325, 338, 350, 360

Yorkshire, 19, 156, 274, 277

Young, 242

Younger, 12, 16, 17, 18, 19, 21, 22, 23, 24, 25, 26, 27, 28, 30, 32, 33, 34, 35, 36, 37, 38, 39, 40, 41, 42, 43, 44, 45, 46, 47, 48, 49, 50, 51, 52, 53, 54, 55, 56, 57, 58, 59, 60, 61, 62, 63, 64, 65, 66, 67, 68, 69, 70, 75, 76, 77, 78, 79, 80, 81, 82, 83, 84, 85, 86, 87, 89, 93, 94, 95, 97, 98, 99, 100, 101, 103, 104, 105, 106, 108, 109, 111, 114, 115, 117, 118, 125, 131, 133, 136, 139, 140, 141, 142, 144, 145, 150, 151, 152, 153, 154, 155, 156, 160, 161, 162, 163, 164, 165, 172, 173, 177, 180, 181, 182, 183, 186, 191, 192, 194, 195, 196, 197, 198, 199, 200, 201, 202, 203, 204, 205, 206, 211, 216, 217, 218, 224, 229, 233, 234, 235, 241, 242, 243, 245, 246, 247, 248, 249, 250, 251, 252, 255, 256, 257, 258, 259, 260, 261, 263, 264, 265, 266, 267, 269, 270, 271, 272, 273, 274, 275, 276, 278, 279, 280, 281, 282, 283, 284, 285, 287, 290, 291, 292, 295, 296, 297, 298, 299, 300, 301, 303, 307, 308, 309, 311, 314, 315, 316, 317, 318, 319, 320, 321, 322, 323, 324, 325, 326, 327, 328, 329, 330, 331, 332, 333, 334, 335, 336, 337, 338, 339, 340, 341, 342, 343, 344, 345, 346, 347, 348, 349, 350, 351, 352, 353, 354, 355, 356, 357, 358, 359, 360, 361, 362, 363, 364, 365, 366, 367, 368, 369, 370, 371, 372, 373, 374, 375, 376, 377, 378, 379, 380, 381, 382, 440, 441

www.ingramcontent.com/pod-product-compliance
Lightning Source LLC
Chambersburg PA
CBHW050323230426
43663CB00010B/1727